MW01168977

Rethinking Creativity

This book presents a new perspective on creativity: that creative innovation depends on inside-of-the-box thinking. It shows that creativity
builds on what we know and how we use old ideas to produce new ones.
In a highly readable format, Robert W. Weisberg uses case studies of
seminal creative advances, such as Leonardo's 'Aerial Screw' and Frank
Lloyd Wright's award-winning house, 'Fallingwater.' These fascinating
examples are evaluated alongside cutting-edge research to present an
analysis of creativity that challenges us to think differently about this
intriguing cognitive ability.

ROBERT W. WEISBERG is a cognitive psychologist and Professor of
Psychology at Temple University, Philadelphia. His primary area of
interest is the cognitive mechanisms underlying creativity, on which
he has published numerous papers and books.

Rethinking Creativity

Inside-the-Box Thinking as the Basis for Innovation

ROBERT W. WEISBERG

Temple University

CAMBRIDGE
UNIVERSITY PRESS

CAMBRIDGE
UNIVERSITY PRESS

University Printing House, Cambridge CB2 8BS, United Kingdom

One Liberty Plaza, 20th Floor, New York, NY 10006, USA

477 Williamstown Road, Port Melbourne, VIC 3207, Australia

314–321, 3rd Floor, Plot 3, Splendor Forum, Jasola District Centre,
New Delhi – 110025, India

79 Anson Road, #06–04/06, Singapore 079906

Cambridge University Press is part of the University of Cambridge.

It furthers the University's mission by disseminating knowledge in the pursuit of
education, learning, and research at the highest international levels of excellence.

www.cambridge.org
Information on this title: www.cambridge.org/9781108479400
DOI: 10.1017/9781108785259

© Robert W. Weisberg 2020

First published 2020

A catalogue record for this publication is available from the British Library.

Library of Congress Cataloging-in-Publication Data
Names: Weisberg, Robert W., author.
Title: Rethinking creativity : inside-the-box thinking as the basis for innovation / Robert
W. Weisberg, Temple University, Philadelphia.
Description: United Kingdom ; New York : Cambridge University Press, 2020. | Includes
index.
Identifiers: LCCN 2019059906 (print) | LCCN 2019059907 (ebook) | ISBN 9781108479400
(hardback) | ISBN 9781108785259 (ebook)
Subjects: LCSH: Creative ability. | Creative thinking.
Classification: LCC BF408 .W388 2020 (print) | LCC BF408 (ebook) | DDC 153.3/5–dc23
LC record available at https://lccn.loc.gov/2019059906
LC ebook record available at https://lccn.loc.gov/2019059907

ISBN 978-1-108-47940-0 Hardback

ISBN 978-1-108-74290-0 Paperback

To the future:
Rebecca, Michael, Jillion
Alana and William

Contents

Figures

Tables

PART I

Introduction

1 | Setting the Stage

Introduction to the Study of Creativity

IDEO's Deep Dive: Creation of a New Shopping Cart

It is Saturday morning, and the shopping list on the refrigerator door is too long to ignore: you have to go to the supermarket. You get out of the house early, to beat the crowds, but everyone else had the same idea, so the store is crowded. You wrestle a shopping cart out of the line of carts at the entrance and push it into the store, heading to the meat aisle for your first purchase. Halfway down the aisle, your way is blocked by two carts, whose owners are chatting. You try to reverse your way out of the aisle, but you must drag the heavy cart to get it to turn around in the narrow space. On your roundabout trip to the meat aisle, you maneuver around a father trying to calm his upset child, who has almost succeeded in squirming his way out of the uncomfortable child seat in the cart – the flimsy strap could not hold the child in – but whose foot is wedged in the hinged seatback.

When you have gotten your meat, you head for the diary aisle, to get yogurt, milk, cheese, and eggs. As you reach that area, your path is again blocked by several carts. You could leave the cart and make your way through the maze of carts to the dairy case, but you don't think you can carry everything back to your cart in one trip. Rather than making multiple trips, you wait until you can push the cart to the case and load it up. After similar experiences with bread, cereal, juice, fruits and vegetables, paper towels, toilet paper, toothpaste, and coffee and tea, you check your list and find that one item, olive oil, remains. You head for the aisle that you think the olive oil is located in, based on your memory. However, the olive oil is not there: either you misremembered or the location has been changed. You need to talk to one of the store's staff members, but no one is in the immediate vicinity, and the customer-service counter is on the other side of the crowded store. You decide that you can live without olive oil for now and head for check-out.

There are long lines of carts at all the registers. You get on the shortest line and spend the time catching up on email and reading a magazine about

4   *Rethinking Creativity*

the latest scandal involving a young star's endless battle with her former spouse. When you finally get to the register, you strain to reach deep into the cart's large basket to retrieve some small items at the bottom. Finally, your items are bagged and paid for and loaded back into your cart. You push it to your car, unload your bags, and head for home, relieved to be finished with shopping – for the time being.

IDEO's Challenge: A New Shopping Cart

Such a frustrating experience of supermarket shopping is extremely common. That universality was what motivated the ABC show *Nightline* to invite IDEO (pronounced "eye-dee-oh"), the most well-known design-consulting firm in the world, to design a new shopping cart. IDEO is an *idea factory*: it sells its *creativity*, the process that it brings to the problems that its clients face. When IDEO began, over twenty-five years ago, its business was assisting in the development of new products for its clients, and it was very good at it. The company has received many design awards over the years, far more than any other design firm. More recently, IDEO has marketed its *process*. IDEO now offers to instill its creative process in the client's organization, changing the client, so that in the future the client can innovate on its own. IDEO has also developed a worldwide presence on the Internet, OpenIDEO (www.openideo.com), where their method is taught to anyone interested in participating and where large-scale problems are presented, with all members of the OpenIDEO community encouraged to participate in developing solutions.

Nightline asked IDEO to design a new shopping cart, while their cameras and reporter observed, and gave them a week to do it. The result is shown in Figure 1.1. IDEO's sleek creation makes the present-day shopping cart look like a dinosaur. It is built on a stainless-steel frame, in which are placed small, easily removable plastic baskets. Those baskets allow the shopper to leave the cart and make a series of trips to various locations to fill the baskets, which are then put back into the frame. The molded-plastic child seat, similar to a high chair – much more comfortable than the angular folding seat on the typical cart – has a safety bar that holds the child in place and also provides a play surface. The wheels, front and back, rotate 360 degrees, for ease of maneuvering. There is a microphone for direct communication with store personnel, as well as a scanner to permit self-checkout. When the baskets are removed at checkout, a series of hooks on the inside of the frame is exposed (they can be seen in Figure 1.1), from

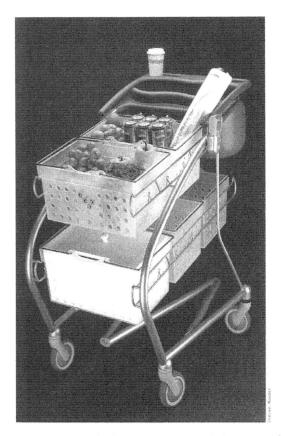

Figure 1.1 IDEO's shopping cart. © IDEO/Steven Moeder.

which one can hang filled bags, for transport to one's car. This cart, in an elegant manner, would alleviate many of the difficulties that we encounter when shopping. IDEO's creativity produced another winner.

The Mystery of Creativity

We have just examined a case study of creativity in action, but this example is not an isolated case: creativity is everywhere. Creativity, the capacity to produce new things – new ideas and new objects – fills our lives, often, but not always, for the better. Everything in the world that is not part of nature has been touched by creativity, and much of the natural world has also been changed by creativity. Babies are born healthier, and we all live longer and fuller lives, because of advances in science and medicine resulting from creativity. Our workdays are filled with products of creativity, ranging from the laptop on which I am writing this book to the word- and graphics-processing programs that I am using to put words and figures on pages. Our leisure time is filled with the results of creativity, many times over. The video-game platforms, televisions, music- and video-streaming devices, smartphones, tablets, and other systems that we use to acquire and display content have all been developed through creativity, as have the media themselves – social-media apps, music, games, books, art, and movies. Not every product of creativity has a positive effect, however: weapons of mass destruction also arise from creativity.

Humans, Gods, and Geniuses

The creative capacity has been taken as evidence of a god-like aspect in humans. As God created the heavens and the earth out of the void, so we humans can create something out of nothing. A songwriter sits down in front of a piano, and after a while there is a new song. An idea-factory is given the task of creating a new shopping cart, and five days later there is one.

The possibility of a human–god connection has, over the centuries, shaped much thinking about creativity (McMahon, 2013). In modern times, some of those god-like qualities were assumed to reside in the exceptionally creative person, the *creative genius*. Variations on this view, which I will refer to as the "genius view" of creativity, still are very much a part of the modern discussion of creativity, both in society in general and in the scientific community. I saw a *Smithsonian* magazine a few years ago with a cover story titled "Genius Happens: 17 People Changing Your Universe," which celebrated outstanding innovators. Soon after that, there was a long article in *National Geographic* entitled "What Makes a Genius?" And there was a TV series on the National Geographic Channel about Einstein, with the title *Genius*.

Concerning more formal analyses of thinking, the historian and cultural critic Jacques Barzun (e.g., 1960, 1989), as one example, has argued that there is something basically different in the thought processes underlying the creative advances of geniuses – Leonardo, Picasso, Mozart – and neither the geniuses nor we mere mortals can understand that process. The creative process of the genius results in outcomes that are completely new: the genius makes sudden leaps into the unknown. (See also Bloom (2002) and chapters in Murray (1989b) and in Simonton (2014).)

The general assumption of the genius view, that the creative individual is in some critical way different than ordinary – noncreative – people, is also pervasive in modern scientific analyses of creativity. Sometimes the emphasis is on differences in thinking and sometimes on differences in psychological characteristics – differences in personality structure. In this chapter, I focus on the thought processes assumed in the genius view to underlie creativity. The basic idea, familiar to and accepted by nearly all of us, is that creativity depends on *thinking outside the box*. Thinking creatively demands that we break away from the past, rejecting what we know, to make a leap into the unknown. The genius can do that, and thereby produce something truly new, while the rest of us remain mired in the quicksand of the past.

The general perspective of the genius view is seen also in the method that IDEO uses to deal with its clients' problems, a method designed to facilitate thinking outside the box. The domain of the problem does not matter: IDEO has produced innovations in a wide range of areas, from toothbrushes to electronic devices to ski goggles to an all-in-one fishing rod for children. IDEO's innovation process is called, for reasons that will become obvious, *The Deep Dive*.

IDEO's Deep Dive

The first step in IDEO's innovative process is the formation of a team, made up of individuals with a wide range of backgrounds, none of which is necessarily in the specific area of the client's problem. The shopping-cart team consisted of some twenty people, ranging from engineers to an MBA to a linguist. Since none of them was an expert on shopping carts, the team first broke into groups, each of which carried out a different type of research, which allowed them to delve into the area (the first component of the *Deep Dive*). They talked to supermarket employees, including the shopping-cart buyer for a supermarket chain, and observed and talked to shoppers using carts "in the wild." IDEO's team quickly became expert on difficulties faced by people who work with and use shopping carts daily.

Problems with Shopping Carts

Several problem areas immediately surfaced from the first round of research: user safety; difficulty of use during shopping; inefficiency at checkout; problems locating items in the store; and shopping cart loss due to pilferage. Concerning user safety, there are, among children aged five and under, thousands of injuries a year involving shopping carts, many of which are serious. Those accidents typically result from a child falling out of the child seat or out of the basket: as the parents and older siblings among us know, many young children will not sit in the uncomfortable fold-out seats in typical shopping carts, so some parents allow their children to sit – or stand – in the basket.

As a result of talking with the shopping-cart buyer, the IDEO staffers discovered that shopping-cart theft is a major problem for supermarkets. Shopping carts are used as mobile storage facilities, and the metal baskets are used as barbecues. Groups of IDEO team members also observed people using shopping carts. The team paid particular attention to professional shoppers, who buy items for online shopping-delivery services. Those professionals, working under heavy time pressure, provided extreme examples of the problems that shoppers face in using shopping carts. The professionals tended to leave the cart in one place, using it as a home base while making trips to the areas of the store that they needed to get to.

In this way, the team became a "super-expert" on the important issues concerning shopping carts, and it did so much more quickly than if the members had had to experience all the difficulties for themselves.

Brainstorming: Generating Ideas

On the next day, the team members began to *brainstorm* ideas to deal with the problems uncovered in their research. Brainstorming, the second step in the *Deep Dive*, is a technique for generating creative ideas in a group setting, developed in the 1960s by Alex Osborne, a well-known advertising executive (Osborne, 1963). Osborne's basic assumption was that creative thinking was fragile and could be stifled by negative judgment. Many ideas that we produce in response to a problem, especially those ideas that seem – to us as well as others – wild and crazy, might, if given a chance, turn out to be useful. Therefore, every idea, no matter how absurd, must be given consideration. Judgment comes later.

IDEO's rules for innovation are written around the walls in the rooms that the teams work in (ABC News, 1999, p. 9): (1) encourage wild ideas; (2) defer judgment; (3) build on the ideas of others. Rules (1) and (2) represent the core of Osborne's belief concerning the best way to find new ideas: *first* produce as many crazy ideas as you can, and *then* consider the potential usefulness of each. David Kelley, IDEO cofounder and CEO, described the process in an interview as follows:

> Yeah, see, you have to have some wild ideas. Then you build on those wild ideas and they end up being better ideas than if you said, if you, if everybody only came up with sane things, you know, kind of appropriate things you'd never, like, have any points to take off to build a really innovative idea. So you really encourage that kind of craziness 'cause sometimes it leads to the right things. (ABC News, 1999, p. 5)

IDEO's emphasis on wild ideas is based on the assumption that creativity depends on the free expression of the imagination. It is the job of the team leader to ensure that judgment does not get in the way of idea production. The leader even has a little bell, worn on the wrist.

> That's the hardest thing for people to do is to restrain themselves from criticizing an idea. So if anybody starts to nail an idea, they get the bell. (ABC News, 1999, p. 5)

The broader culture at IDEO is designed to play a role in the *Deep Dive* process. There is little in the way of hierarchical structure at the company, because, according to IDEO's philosophy, hierarchical structure gets in the way of the freedom needed for idea generation. As Kelley describes:

> I'll give you status. I'll give you a big red ball on a post and that says you're a big guy. If you've got a ball you're a senior vice president. You know, what do I care? ... In a very innovative culture you can't have a kind of hierarchy of here's the boss and the next person down and the next person down and the next person down because it's impossible that the boss is the one who's had the insightful experience with shopping carts. It's just not possible. (ABC News, 1999, p. 3)

To foster the lack of corporate hierarchy, Kelley specifically sets out to hire people who he hopes will not listen to his orders.

The IDEO team generated hundreds of ideas in response to the problems presented by the shopping cart. Many of those ideas were put on sticky notes and attached to the walls of the room, where they could be organized by area – shopping efficiency, safety, ease of checkout, and locating items – and considered and voted on by all the team members.

Prototyping

Once the ideas in each problem area had been voted on, the team moved to realize those ideas in a concrete product – a prototype. An important component of IDEO's creative process is to produce prototypes as early as possible. That way one can see if there are any deficiencies in the ideas that might not be obvious when one is considering them in the imagination or as written on a note stuck to the wall. This use of prototyping exemplified a motto at IDEO: "Fail often to succeed sooner." It is better to try to make things as concrete as possible as early as possible, so mistakes can be discovered before too much time and resources are invested in a project. For the shopping-cart project, four early prototypes were constructed, with the help of IDEO's machine shop, each dealing with one of the areas of concern. The prototype dealing with problems locating items had a transmitter and microphone that enabled the shopper to communicate directly with customer service in the store. To facilitate checking out, one prototype had a scanner that allowed the shopper to keep an electronic record of the items in the cart, which could be used for quick self-checkout. The best features of those prototypes were combined into the final product that so impressed the people at *Nightline* and, to judge from comments online, many others as well.

IDEO's Deep Dive: Conclusions

There is no doubt that IDEO's accomplishments are impressive, and they provide support for the claim that the company has harnessed the creative process. IDEO's teams work under an elaborated set of Osborne's rules, designed to ensure that the wildest possible set of ideas is generated in response to any problem. This type of idea generation maximizes the chances that out-of-the-box ideas will be produced. A first glance at IDEO's shopping cart seems to indicate that they succeeded in moving far outside the box, essentially breaking the mold. However, if we examine the shopping cart in a more analytic frame of mind, it is less groundbreaking than it seemed to be. We will see that, contrary to the claims made by IDEO, out-of-the-box thinking did *not* play a major role in its creation.

IDEO's Creative Process: Outside the Box – or Inside?

Logic and Creative Thinking

Table 1.1 presents an analysis of the novel components in IDEO's shopping cart (left-hand column). For each, I have indicated the difficulty or problem that was being addressed (middle column) and how the solution might have arisen (right-hand column). Consider first items 1 and 2, centering on the plastic baskets. Those baskets serve several purposes. *Plastic* baskets

Table 1.1 *Novel components of IDEO's shopping cart and where they might have come from*

I. NOVEL COMPONENT	II. DIFFICULTY	III. BASIS FOR INNOVATION
1) Plastic basket	Pilferage: metal baskets serve as barbecues	**Logic**
2) Small baskets can be removed and carried	Hard to navigate: easier to use cart as "home base" and bring items to cart	**Logic**
3) Casters allow sideways movement	Hard to navigate in aisles	**Near analogy:** wheels and casters
4) Safety bar on child's seat	Child safety: unattended child leaves safety seat	**Near analogy:** "safety seat" on roller coaster; high chair
5) Play surface on child's seat in cart	Child irritability	**Logic + near analogy:** play reduces child's irritability; high chair
6) Microphone in cart	Difficulty finding items ⇒ need to contact customer service	**Logic + near analogy** (cell phone?) + IDEO's "electronic gadgets" **expertise**
7) Scanner in cart	Checkout can be slow: avoid lines ⇒ self-checkout	**Logic** + IDEO's "cyberize" **expertise**
8) Hooks for bags on frame after baskets are removed checking out	Transporting heavy bags to car	**Logic**
9) Sleek design	Ugly shape	**Expertise:** designers' sensibilities

make the cart useless as a barbecue. *Small* and *removable* baskets allow the shopper to leave the cart in one spot and make quick trips to various locations in the store; they also result in the empty frame in the parking lot being useless as a storage device. The problems that the baskets were designed to solve were obtained from the experts, and IDEO's ideas can be understood as the result of logical analysis of each of those situations. If the cart is potentially valuable because it could be used as a barbecue, then you should construct it from material that cannot be used to build a fire in, such as plastic. Similarly, if the cart could serve for storage, eliminate the cart's storage capacity, by keeping the baskets in the supermarket. Finally, if shoppers want to use the cart as a home base while shopping, provide them with something – the small basket – to carry items in when they make their trips away from the cart. It should also be noted that small shopping baskets that can be carried are available in every supermarket, which might have played a role in IDEO's deciding to use small baskets in their cart. In sum, each of those creative advances depended on the application of logic – *inside-the-box* thinking – to the problem.

Analogical Transfer and Creativity

A different kind of inside-the-box thinking was involved in item 3 in Table 1.1: the use of casters – wheels that rotate – in place of fixed wheels at the back of the cart. Here we see *transfer of knowledge* from one situation to another. The use of casters on office chairs – something the IDEO team knew about – was transferred to the shopping cart, solving the problem of maneuverability. The office-chair and shopping-cart situations are *analogous*: they are similar in *structure*, although the specific objects involved are not the same. IDEO was faced with the problem of having to maneuver a large heavy object (a shopping cart) in a restricted space (a supermarket aisle), and the solution they devised was based on another situation in which there is difficulty in maneuvering a large heavy object (a desk chair) in a restricted space (the space behind a desk).

Psychologists have analyzed the relationship between the situations that play a role in *analogical transfer* – that is, transfer of knowledge from one situation to an analogous one (e.g., Chan & Schunn, 2015; Dunbar, 1995; Reeves & Weisberg, 1994; Weisberg, 2006). Let us say that we have a researcher in molecular biology who is investigating various aspects of the metabolism of HIV but runs into a problem with an experiment. If the researcher takes information from another HIV experiment that she knows about to fix that problem, that transfer would be *near* transfer, based on a *local* analogy: both situations involve HIV. If the researcher had used information from an experiment on a different virus, say HPV, to solve the problem, that would have been transfer based on a *regional* analogy. The needed information comes from the same "region" of the researcher's knowledge: experiments on viruses. I will refer to both local and regional analogies as "near" analogies. Finally, if the researcher used information from astrophysics, say, to overcome the problem with the HIV experiment, that would have been *far* or *remote* transfer, based on a *distant* analogy. Far transfer would represent a leap outside the box.

We can use that scale of similarity to examine how far IDEO's thinking ranged when they transferred information to the new shopping cart, and the conclusion is that they did not go very far. For example, IDEO's transfer of the desk-chair casters to the shopping cart represents a *regional* analogy, since the situations come from similar, though not identical, domains (i.e., both concern moving bulky objects in small spaces). Another use of a regional analogy can be seen in item 4, the use of a safety bar on the child's seat. The transferred solution – the safety seat from a ride at an amusement park – comes from another situation in which one is concerned with keeping a person in a seat in a potentially dangerous environment. Similarly, the shape of the child's seat comes from high chairs, and the play surface (item 5) does also. Those, too, are regional analogies. We see no examples of far transfer, based on distant analogies, in IDEO's creation of their shopping cart, as outlined in Table 1.1.

IDEO's Designers' Expertise

Several components of the shopping cart arose relatively directly out of the expertise of IDEO's designers (see items 6 through 9 in Table 1.1). The electronic-gadget culture in Silicon Valley played a role in the placement of the microphone in the cart for communication between the shopper and store personnel. The cell phone may have played a role here as well. If so, it was near transfer based on a local analogy; both situations involve person-to-person communication, which is cell-phone territory. Similar factors were at work behind the provision of a scanner for ease of checkout. Finally, the overall sleek look of the cart was greatly influenced by the "design" aesthetic that permeates IDEO and Silicon Valley, which makes "coolness" of appearance a critical aspect of any design. Similar analyses can be made for the other components of IDEO's shopping cart (see Table 1.1). It seems that we can understand this creative advance without assuming that outside-the-box thinking played an important role.

Incremental and "Green" Creativity: Continuity with the Past in Creative Thinking

A component of the outside-the-box perspective on creativity is the belief that thinking outside the box results in "creative leaps," or "leaps of insight," where a totally novel solution to a problem appears suddenly, in complete form (Barzun, 1989; Kounios & Beeman, 2015; Ohlsson, 2011; Perkins, 2000). Examining the development of IDEO's shopping cart contradicts the notion of a creative leap, in multiple ways. As we have seen, some of the new ideas in the shopping cart came about from the near transfer of knowledge, based on regional or local analogies. Other new ideas were based on logical analyses of the problems facing IDEO. The use of near analogies and logical thinking both contradict the idea of far-ranging creative leaps.

Tracing the cart's development also indicated that IDEO's creative process was *incremental*, which means that the creative process moved in steps – in increments – to something new, rather than in a creative leap, from nothing to a final product. IDEO's advance came about in several steps: acquiring information through research; using that research to break the larger problem – designing a new shopping cart – into smaller ones (safety, ease of use, maneuverability, etc.); working on the smaller problems; producing prototypes; combining the ideas from the prototypes into the finished product.

Finally, saying that the creative process is based on inside-the-box thinking means that we use *old* ideas in creating *new* ones. This is another way of saying that there is *never* a completely new idea. The creative process is *green: it recycles old ideas*. Many of the components of IDEO's shopping cart were adaptations of familiar ideas that were transferred to the cart. In addition, some of the creative advances evident in the cart were based on logical thinking, which begins with what you know and builds on it, in rule-governed ways, to produce new conclusions – that is, new ideas.

However, it must be strongly emphasized that recycling of old ideas in the production of new ones does not mean that there are no new ideas: those recycled ideas must be *modified* to fit the new problem. When someone on the IDEO team had the idea to use casters as the rear wheels on the shopping cart, the specific way that the casters were implemented had to be changed from the original use on a desk chair. Although the idea of using casters is an old one, using casters to make a *shopping cart* maneuverable was a new idea. Similarly, using a safety bar to hold a child in a seat was an old idea, but the way it was applied to the shopping cart resulted in something new. Using logic to deduce that the baskets in the cart should be made of a material that was not fire-resistant, to defeat would-be barbecue chefs, also resulted in something *new* – that is, a creative idea.

In sum, creative thinking is based on *continuity with the past*. It begins with old ideas and attempts to extend them to new situations. Creative thinking does not make a radical break with the past; we build on the old to get to the new.

Generation and Extension of Ideas: Two Stages in the Creative Process

When we come to an innovation from the outside, without knowing what the creator knew when he or she was working on it, we may be led – incorrectly – to the conclusion that the processes underlying that advance must be beyond our capacity. We ordinary folks simply could not have thought of the ideas underlying the innovation. ("She's just a genius!") It might also seem that we cannot even *understand* how someone else could have thought of it (Barzun, 1989).

Concerning whether we can make sense of creative advances after they occur, it seems that, in at least this one case, we can. Each of the components of IDEO's shopping cart came about in a manner comprehensible to an outsider. On taking a close look at the problem facing the creative thinker, as well as the information he or she had available, we could understand the basis for the advance. The creative thinker was working inside a box; we were just not aware of it at the beginning, because that box was different from our own. Numerous additional examples of creative advances will be discussed throughout the book, and they will provide further evidence for that proposed generalization.

Based on the discussion so far, several tentative conclusions concerning creative thinking can be offered. First, there are conclusions concerning IDEO's creative process. Contrary to IDEO's beliefs, their creative process does not seem to be based on thinking outside the box. The important components in IDEO's creative process are: (1) the immersion in the client's problem, resulting in the acquisition of expertise in the domain; (2) the use of logical thinking to draw novel conclusions that might be applicable to the problem; and (3) the use of analogical thinking to find ideas from other situations, typically *near* analogies, that might be recyclable – that is, applicable to the problem. This summary of the discussion of IDEO's creativity points to a more general conclusion: that creative thinking involves a two-stage process. Presentation of a problem first results in an individual *generating* an idea, as the result of a process of logical reasoning or through retrieval of an idea from a situation analogous to the problem one is faced with. When a possible solution comes to mind, the person then tries to *extend* that idea to the new situation. Any problem a person is facing is, by definition, new (if it were not new, then it would not be a problem). Therefore, an old idea will not directly solve it. The old idea must be shaped to meet the specific demands of the problem; as a result, the old idea can be extended to the new situation. As an example, in order to use casters on a shopping cart, the cart and/or the casters must be modified, because the common shopping cart is not made in a way that can accommodate casters. This distinction, between generating and extending ideas, has been discussed by many researchers in various forms (e.g., Campbell, 1960; Fleck & Weisberg, 2004, 2013; Fox & Beaty, 2019; Jung et al., 2013; Simonton, 2018; Weisberg & Suls, 1973), and it will be seen again and again throughout the book, as we work our way through other examples of creative thinking.

Ordinary or Analytic Thinking in Creativity

Let us assume that creative thinking depends on *inside-the-box* thinking. Another way of describing that view is to say that creativity is based on *ordinary thinking*, since those processes are ones that we all use all the time when we think about the situations that we face. The major role that logic plays in our day-to-day thinking needs little elaboration. Although perhaps not as obvious, analogies are also critical in thinking (Gentner & Maravilla, 2018; Weisberg, 2006). As an example, picked essentially at random, in planning a Christmas family gathering you may use ideas developed when you organized a similar get-together on Thanksgiving. Those two situations are analogous, another example of a regional analogy. Similarly, a college student trying to deal with a problem that has arisen with a professor may recall how she approached a problem with her boss at work. In those cases, and many more that will be presented later in the book, creative thinking progresses based on analogies. Thus, the thinking exemplified in the development of IDEO's shopping cart is based on ordinary thinking.

A Question of Definition

Some psychologists use the term *analytic thinking* to refer to thinking inside the box – to what I have just called ordinary thinking. Thinking outside the box is sometimes called thinking based on *insight* or *intuition*, which involves a sudden leap into the unknown (see Bowden & Grunwald, 2018; DeCaro, 2018; Gilhooly & Webb, 2018; Ohlsson, 2018; Weisberg, 2018b; all found in Vallée-Tourangeau, 2018). Another description that has been used to describe thought processes involved in creativity is *special process* thinking, which means just what it says: creative thinking is special (i.e., out-of-the-box). *Special process* thinking is contrasted with *business as*

Table 1.2 *Terms used to describe*
creative versus noncreative thinking

Creative Thinking	Noncreative Thinking
Outside-the-box	Inside-the-box
Insight	Analytic thinking
Intuition	
Special process	Business as usual
Creative thinking	Ordinary thinking

usual, which means the same as *ordinary thinking*: the same thought processes are involved in all cognitive activities, including creative thinking. These various terms are summarized in Table 1.2.

Given the various terms that have been used in the research literature to describe the same processes, it is best to choose one label and use it consistently. I will use the term *analytic thinking* as a substitute for inside-the-box, ordinary thinking, and business as usual. However, there will be some contexts where the term *ordinary thinking* will be used, to emphasize a specific point. No matter how it is labeled, the interpretation of creativity that I am presenting here is based on application of one's knowledge to the current situation, and using that knowledge as the basis for constructing something new.

Moving beyond IDEO

Questions can be raised about the generality of the conclusions that one might want to draw from the analysis of IDEO's invention of a new shopping cart. First, it is only a single example, so one cannot make broad claims from it. Second, one might raise the question of whether IDEO's shopping cart represents creative thinking of the highest order – that is, genius-level creativity. Third, there is the question of the domain involved: IDEO designed something new, a physical object that served a purpose. One might wonder if we could carry out a comparable analysis of creative thinking in the arts. It is possible that the thought processes underlying artistic creativity might be too "intuitive" or illogical, or too "subjective," to be captured by an analysis of the sort just carried out on IDEO's shopping cart. That conclusion is overly pessimistic: I have carried out a case

Figure 1.2 Picasso's *Guernica*. Pablo Picasso, Guernica (1937); © 2019 Estate of Pablo Picasso / Artists Rights Society (ARS), New York.

study of Picasso's creation of his great painting *Guernica* (see Figure 1.2; Weisberg, 2004, 2006), which is undoubtedly an artistic masterpiece (Chipp, 1988). The results of that case study, to which I now turn, demonstrated that it is indeed possible to analyze and "capture" the thought process of an artistic genius.

Genius-Level Artistic Creativity: Picasso's Creation of Guernica

Guernica and the Spanish Civil War

Guernica, a landmark of twentieth-century art, was painted in response to what was seen by many as a tragedy: the bombing, during the Spanish Civil War, of the Basque town of Guernica, in northern Spain (Chipp, 1988, ch. 3). The bombing was carried out on April 26, 1937, by the German air force, with some assistance from the Italian air force. Both Germany and Italy were allied with Generalissimo Francisco Franco, who became the Spanish dictator after his Fascist forces won the Civil War. When news of the bombing and its effects was reported over the next few days, the destruction of the town and killing of innocent people horrified the world. The final toll may have been more than 1,600 dead and almost 900 wounded.

Although he had been living in Paris for some thirty years, Picasso, a Spaniard, was still strongly connected to Spain and was strongly opposed to Franco. Early in 1937, Picasso had been asked by a group representing the Spanish government (i.e., the opposition to Franco, who were losing the Civil War) to create a painting for the government's pavilion at an international exhibition (a World's Fair) planned for Paris in June, 1937. Although the Spanish Civil War was raging, and Picasso had paid close attention to it through newspaper stories, the war had no obvious effect on the painting he was creating in response to the government's request: an artist and model in the studio, a subject that he had painted many times.

When reports of the bombing reached Paris, Picasso stopped working on the studio painting and over about six weeks produced *Guernica*, a painting that has been responded to universally as one of the great anti-war documents of modern times. The history of the painting also demonstrates its importance. In his will, Picasso stipulated that *Guernica* was to be loaned to the Museum of Modern Art, in New York City. However, it was to be sent to Spain when democracy was restored, that is, after Franco and his followers were gone. That occurred in 1981, soon after Franco's death, and the painting returned to Spain like a conquering hero and was put on permanent display in Madrid.

The Painting

When one examines *Guernica* as an anti-war statement, there seems to be something missing (Chipp, 1988). Created in response to a bombing, *Guernica* contains no planes dropping bombs. A war was going on, but there are no soldiers, no rifles or cannons, no tanks. In the left-hand portion of the painting, a bull stands over a mother, whose head is thrown back in an open-mouthed scream. She holds a dead baby whose head lolls backward. Below them, a broken statue of a man, the only human male presence, holds a broken sword – a hint of a military theme – and a flower. Next to the bull, a bird flies up toward a light. In the center of the painting, a horse, stabbed by a lance, raises its head in a scream of agony. In the upper center, a woman leans out of the window of a burning building, holding a light to illuminate the scene. Beneath the light-bearing woman, another woman hurriedly enters the scene from the right. At the far right, a woman on fire falls from a burning building. Picasso uses those characters to make us feel that something terrible is happening. Another striking aspect of the painting is that it has no color: it is monochromatic, painted in black, white, and shades of gray. This physical darkness produces a dark psychological mood, highlighted by a few bright objects, to which our gaze is drawn. The painting is also massive in size, measuring almost 12′ x 26′, which serves to increase the effect that it has on a viewer.

We can now examine the development of *Guernica*, comparable to what we did for IDEO's shopping cart. According to the genius view, the genius does not have to plan: new masterworks just erupt into existence. By examining the development of *Guernica*, which is undoubtedly a masterwork, we might be able to see if that claim is true.

Development of a Masterpiece

There are several sources of information that can help us understand how a work of art was created. Most importantly, creative thinkers, including painters, often carry out *planning*, in the form of preliminary work. Contrary to the genius view, artists, even artists of genius, think about what they might do before they make any large-scale commitment to doing anything. Painters often carry out preliminary work by producing *sketches* of various sorts, often small-scale pencil drawings on paper. Not everything an artist thinks about is put into sketches, because some ideas might be discarded immediately as unacceptable and others might be too fleeting to be put into a sketch. However, sketches can give us a global picture of the developmental sequence between the artist's early ideas and the final product.

Preliminary Work: Planning a Masterpiece

Picasso produced many preliminary sketches for all his major works, including forty-five sketches for *Guernica*. He also dated and numbered the sketches for *Guernica*, because he thought that others might be interested in how the painting progressed. The existence of sketches for *Guernica* immediately calls into question the claim of the genius view that works of genius spring into life fully formed. I will discuss that issue in more detail as we work through the analysis of the development of *Guernica*. In addition, photos were taken of the painting in progress by Dora Maar, Picasso's companion at the time, who was a photographer. Those photos also provide valuable information about Picasso's creative process.

What sort of evidence would support the idea that Picasso's creation of *Guernica* was based on analytic thinking? First, the development of the painting should be *incremental*: we should be able to see *Guernica* developing gradually over time. There should not be a sudden leap, or anything close to it, from nothing to the final work. Second, based on the hypothesis that analytic thinking is *green*, we should find that *Guernica* was built on old ideas, those of Picasso as well as of other artists.

The Sketches for Guernica: An Overview

Picasso produced his first preliminary sketches on May 1, 1937; the last sketch is dated June 4. He began work on the painting itself on approximately May 11, and the completed work was put on display early in June. Thus, there was some overlap between his sketching and the work of painting. That overlap of work is further evidence for incremental development of the painting to its final form – he was painting it while planning parts of it.

There are two types of sketches. Seven *composition studies* present overviews of the whole painting (see Figure 1.3A–B). The remaining sketches, *character studies*, examine characters individually or in small groups (see Figure 1.3C, D). The time that Picasso worked on the sketches can be reduced to three periods of work: the first two days (May 1–2); an additional six days, commencing about a week later (May 8–13); and a final two weeks of work, which began about a week later (May 20–June 4). During the first two days, Picasso produced only composition studies and studies of the horse, the central character, physically and psychologically, in the painting. (See Table 1.3A.) This pattern can be made clearer by combining categories of sketches. In the second period (see Table 1.3B), the composition studies are fewer, and other characters are examined. In the last period (see Table 1.3C), there are no composition studies, and peripheral characters (e.g., the falling person) are seen for the first time. These results indicate that Picasso spent time on the overall structure before he went on to sketches of the individual characters. Furthermore, Picasso seems to have followed the same procedure in all of his major works.

(a)

(b)

(c)

Figure 1.3 Examples of preliminary sketches for *Guernica*

A. Composition study (#1) Pablo Picasso, Study for Guernica (Sketch #1); © 2019 Estate of Pablo Picasso / Artists Rights Society (ARS), New York.

Table 1.3 A–C *Periods of work on* Guernica

A. *Preliminary works tabulated by periods of work*

Period	Comp.	Horse	Bull	Mother & child	Woman	Hand	Falling person	Man	Total
1 (May 1–2)	6	5	0	0	0	0	0	0	11
2 (May 8–13)	2	4	2	5	1	1	0	0	15
3 (May 20–June 4)	0	2	2	2	8	1	3	1	19

B. *Preliminary works summarized by periods and type of sketch: composition sketches versus all others*

Period	Composition	All others	Total
1	6	5	11
2	2	13	15
3	0	19	19
Total	8	37	45

C. *Preliminary works summarized by periods and type of sketch: composition sketches + horse + bull versus all others*

Period	Comp + horse + bull	All others	Total
1	11	0	11
2	8	7	15
3	4	15	19
Total	23	22	45

Deciding on an Idea: The Composition Studies

We can now investigate how Picasso decided on the overall structure for *Guernica*. First, did Picasso experiment with several radically different structures for the painting, or did he have one basic structure in mind when he

---

Caption for Figure 1.3   (cont.)

B. Pablo Picasso, Study for Guernica (Sketch #14). © 2019 Estate of Pablo Picasso / Artists Rights Society (ARS), New York.

C. Pablo Picasso, Study for Guernica (Sketch #15). © 2019 Estate of Pablo Picasso / Artists Rights Society (ARS), New York.

Table 1.4 *Summary of composition sketches for* Guernica

Sketch #	Date	Horse	Bull	Light-holding woman	Mother & child	Fleeing woman	Fallen person	Flying animal	Other
1	5/1	x	x	x				x	
2a			x	x					
2b		x	x					x	
3		x		x					
6		x	x	x			Soldier	x	
10	5/2	x	x	x			Soldier/ dead woman		
12	5/8	x	x			Mother & child	Soldier		
15	5/9	x	x	x	Woman/ dead adult	Mother & child			Wheel/ upraised arm

began to work? Second, once he had decided on the basic structure for the painting, how much did that structure change as Picasso worked further? When was the final structure arrived at: early or late in the overall process?

The structures of the eight composition studies are summarized in Table 1.4. The final structure of the painting is apparent in all the composition studies produced on the very first day of work, including the very first sketch. In six of the eight composition studies, the light-bearing woman is in the center, overlooking the horse. In addition, each of the central characters (the horse, the bull, the light-bearing woman) is present in almost all of the composition sketches, with other characters appearing less frequently. Picasso seems to have had what we can call the "skeleton" or "kernel" of *Guernica* in mind when he began to work.

A related question concerns how much Picasso had to work out that kernel of an idea: How much detail was present in Picasso's mind as he started to think about *Guernica*? There is evidence that the "kernel" was not in final form at the beginning of Picasso's work. First, as Picasso worked through the series of sketches, the number of discernible specific characters increased. In the first composition sketch (May 1; Figure 1.3A) there are four characters, while in the last composition sketch (May 9; the eighth such sketch; Figure 1.3B) there are nine. This change in the amount of detail indicates that Picasso was making specific a vague conception of the painting – evidence for the incremental nature of the development of his conception of *Guernica*.

A. Maar State I photo

B. Maar State V photo

Figure 1.4 States of *Guernica*: Dora Maar photos A. Dora Maar, Photo of Guernica – State I Photo; © 2019 Artists Rights Society (ARS), New York / ADAGP, Paris. B. Dora Maar, Photo of Guernica – State V Photo; © 2019 Artists Rights Society (ARS), New York / ADAGP, Paris.

Given that the conception's specifics changed over the series of composition *sketches*, we can now turn to the related question of whether that conception was complete when he began to *paint* or whether it changed even as Picasso was working on the painting. There is evidence that the structure was not final even as Picasso painted. As noted earlier, Dora Maar photographed *Guernica* several times as Picasso worked, and one of those photos was taken soon after he began to paint (Figure 1.4A – State 1; May 11). State 1 has features similar to the last composition sketch (#15; see Figure 1.3B) and which are not in the finished painting. In State 1, the bull's body is facing in the wrong direction, and his head was originally painted as it is in Sketch 15, although Picasso has already painted over it. Second, the horse's head is down rather than up and is upside down.

There are also numerous dead people at the bottom of the composition in Sketch #15, and in State 1, many more than are in the finished painting. Those elements from Sketch #15 were changed as Picasso painted. Furthermore, State 1 of the canvas contains elements *not* in Sketch #15, indicating that Picasso had already gone beyond that sketch. For example, the falling woman on fire on the right in State 1 is not in Sketch #15.

The similarities between Sketch #15 and State 1 demonstrate that Picasso used his sketches as the basis for the painting. However, the differences between Sketch #15 and State 1 indicate that Picasso had not yet completely decided on the final structure of the painting. Finally, the differences between State 1 and the final version of *Guernica* provide further evidence that the painting reached its final form incrementally. Maar's photos provide graphic evidence of the changes that occurred in the painting as Picasso worked. State V (Figure 1.4B) shows some of the large transformations in the canvas as Picasso painted. The bull's body has been turned around, and the components of his head have been altered, with both eyes on the same side of his face. The horse's head is now up in the center of the painting.

Generation-Extension in the Creation of Guernica

Consideration of the process whereby *Guernica* was created provided another example of the two-stage process – idea generation followed by extension – discussed earlier in the context of IDEO's creative process. Picasso produced a series of sketches, and, in many cases, one sketch is followed by another one of the same sort. For example, on the first two days, many of the sketches are composition studies. The horse was also drawn many times over the first few days. Later on, a series of sketches of women, or of a mother and child, were produced. In each of those series of sketches, one sees Picasso working out an idea. As one example, in the series of composition studies the same basic idea is present in all the sketches, but some of the details change from one sketch to another. That unchanging kernel indicates that Picasso had decided on the overall form very early. However, the changing details indicate that he still was evaluating aspects of those composition studies, trying to settle on a final – or at least acceptable – version, one that would allow him to start to paint.

Deciding on an Idea: Conclusion

Contrary to expectations from the genius view, *Guernica* did not come about in a creative leap. Picasso had in mind a kernel idea for the structure of the painting, but that kernel had to be developed in detail before he began to paint. In addition, the finished painting was very different from where he started in the first composition sketches and from where he started on the canvas. In conclusion, the final version of *Guernica* came about incrementally.

Picasso's Green Creative Process: Trying to Read Picasso's Mind

It was proposed earlier that one sort of evidence for analytic thinking in the creation of *Guernica* would involve the *green* nature of Picasso's process. We should be able to find evidence that the new ideas present in *Guernica* were based on old ideas, those of Picasso or of others. Furthermore, we should be able to determine the basis for Picasso's choice of the specific works that were recycled in creating *Guernica*. One could say that here we are trying to read Picasso's mind.

An Antecedent to the Kernel

The first place to look for green creativity in the creation of *Guernica* involves the kernel idea that we saw across the series of composition studies. Where did that kernel come from? When Picasso painted *Guernica*, he was in his mid-fifties and had been an artist since his childhood. He had available a deep personal history on which to draw, one that played a significant role in the creation of *Guernica*. One striking example of a Picasso work that may be an antecedent to *Guernica* is *Minotauromachy*, an etching made by Picasso in 1935 (see Figure 1.5). A dead woman in a matador's costume, holding a sword in one hand, is draped over the back of a rearing horse. A minotaur (the half-man/half-bull of mythology) raises a hand in front of his eyes to shield them from the light from a candle held by a young woman who is observing the scene. Two other women observe the scene from a window above, where two birds also stand. On the far left, a man is climbing a ladder. All those characters, or variations on them, are present in *Guernica* (see Table 1.5A).

Table 1.5 Minotauromachy/Guernica *correspondences*

A. *Characters*

Minotauromachy	Guernica
Bull (minotaur)	Bull
Horse (attitude)	Horse (attitude)
Dead person	Dead person (Statue)
Sword	Sword
Women observing	(a) Woman observing
Woman with light	(b) Holding light
Birds	Bird
Vertical man fleeing	Vertical woman falling

B. *Spatial correspondences of* Guernica *and reversed* Minotauromachy, *from left to right*

Minotauromachy (reversed)								
	Bull	Dead person + sword	Horse		Women above + birds	Woman + lantern		Vertical person
Mother and child	Bull	Dead person + sword	Horse	Bird	Light	Woman above + lantern	Fleeing woman	Vertical person
Guernica								

Furthermore, those strong correspondences between *Minotauromachy* and *Guernica* are an *underestimation* of the actual correspondences between the works. *Minotauromachy*, an etching, was printed from a drawing made by Picasso on a printing plate. When one makes a print from a drawing on a plate, the objects on the plate are *reversed* from left to right on the print. In other words, the scene Picasso drew on the plate was *reversed* from left to right in comparison with the print shown in Figure 1.5. Table 1.5B lays out the correspondences between *Guernica* and the reversed version of *Minotauromachy*. The "vertical person" was drawn on the right, and the bull was on the far left. The light-bearing female also faces in the same direction as the corresponding character in *Guernica*. The information presented in Table 1.5B supports the idea that *Minotauromachy* itself served to "guide" Picasso's hand as he drew the sketches and worked on the painting. Picasso's creative process, as expressed in the creation of the overall structure of *Guernica*, was indeed *green*.

Figure 1.5 Picasso's *Minotauromachy*. Pablo Picasso, Minotauromachy (1935); © 2019 Estate of Pablo Picasso / Artists Rights Society (ARS), New York.

Looking once again at the generation-extension analysis of the creative process, one can say that, when Picasso thought of the idea of using *Minotauromachy* as the skeleton on which to build *Guernica*, that idea, in general terms, at least struck him as acceptable – it could be extended to the new situation. We can see evidence for that decision in the fact that the basic structure of the painting did not change throughout the series of sketches.

Why Minotauromachy?

If we assume that Picasso recycled *Minotauromachy* in creating *Guernica*, we are led to ask why the bombing might have stimulated him to think of that work. Answers are not hard to find. The bombing occurred in Spain, and a central part of Spanish culture, especially when Picasso was growing up, was the bullfight. The bullfight had deep connections to Picasso throughout his life, and he painted bullfight scenes from his very earliest years (Chipp, 1988). *Minotauromachy* is a representation of a bullfight: it contains a bullfighter (the dead woman, draped over the horse's back, wears a matador's suit); a bull (the minotaur, a half-bull); a horse; a sword (which the bullfighter uses to kill the bull at the climax of the ritual); and "spectators" (the women overlooking the scene and the man on the ladder). Also, the name *Minotauromachy* is itself related to the bullfight. *Minotauromachy* is a play on words: it combines the word *minotaur* with *tauromachy*, Greek for *bullfight*. Thus, the link from the bombing to *Minotauromachy* can be seen as being based on Picasso's connection to his homeland, which was surely stimulated by the bombing. *Guernica*, too, can be looked at as a bullfight painting: it contains a bull and horse; a person with a sword (the statue); and "spectators" overlooking the scene. In addition, the emotionality of the bombing might have provided a further link to the bullfight, which is an event of great emotional significance for a Spaniard.

Antecedents to Characters in Guernica

Given that we can understand the origin of the kernel idea for *Guernica* – a recycling of *Minotauromachy* – we can consider the question of antecedents to specific characters in *Guernica*. We have already seen overlap between characters in *Minotauromachy* and those in *Guernica* (see Table 1.5A–B), so here I will concentrate on antecedents from other works. One example will serve to demonstrate that Picasso's thought process was structured by art with which he was familiar and which was relevant to the theme of *Guernica*.

Picasso's Sketch #14 (Figure 1.3C) contains a mother and child, with the woman distinctive in her sharply profiled head thrown back; her pose, with her outstretched left leg producing a distinctive overall triangular shape; and her skirt folding between her legs. This distinctive individual bears

Figure 1.6 Picasso/Goya correspondences: woman

striking resemblance to the woman shown in Figure 1.6. The latter figure is from an etching in a series by the Spanish artist Francisco de Goya (1746–1828) called *The Disasters of War* (1810–1820), created more than 100 years before *Guernica*, in response to events surrounding the invasion of Spain by Napoleon's forces. Goya was an artist with whom Picasso was very familiar, who was a fellow Spaniard, and whom Picasso respected deeply. In the specific example involving Figures 1.3C and 1.6, Goya's woman is similar to Picasso's, in facial profile and expression; in her posture, with her head thrown back and her outstretched left leg producing an overall triangular shape; and in her skirt being folded between her legs. Picasso adapted Goya's woman in his sketch: he added a dead baby, but the profile and overall shape of the woman is similar to that of Goya's woman.

In sum, in a parallel to the recycling we found in the development of the kernel idea in *Guernica*, we have also found evidence for Picasso's recycling of ideas in the creation of the individual characters. There are also additional works, from Goya and other artists, that were recycled in the creation of *Guernica*, but I have not discussed them here due to lack of space (for further discussion, see Weisberg, 2006, ch. 1). Let us now turn to the question of why the bombing of Guernica might have stimulated Picasso to think of Goya's *The Disasters of War*.

Guernica *and* The Disasters of War

There are several reasons why the bombing of Guernica might have led Picasso to think of Goya's *The Disasters of War*. First, as just noted, Goya, too, was a Spaniard, and he was an artist for whom Picasso had a great deal of respect. The bombing having occurred in Spain would have made it likely that Picasso would think of Goya in response. Goya also produced many works on the bullfight (*La Tauromaquia* is his most well-known), which provides a link to *Minotauromachy* and *Guernica*. In addition, the bombing was an example of outside aggression against Spain, and there were many innocent victims. The etchings in Goya's *The Disasters of War* were created to show the brutal effects on innocent victims of outside aggression against Spain. Goya's *The Disasters of War* was created in response to events analogous to those that stimulated Picasso's creative process: outside aggression against Spain, a regional analogy.

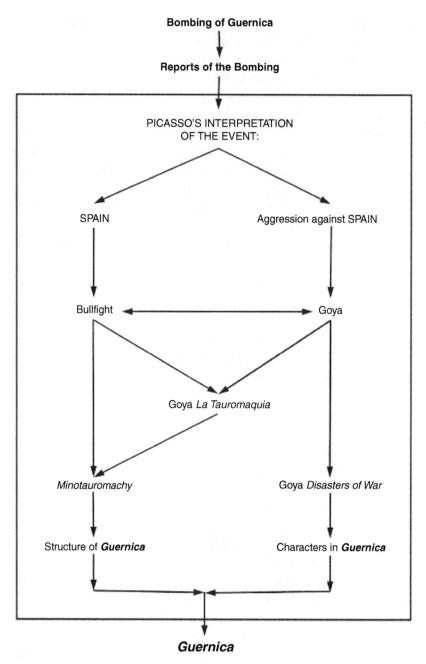

Figure 1.7 Picasso's idea connections

Reading Picasso's Mind: Conclusions

Based on this sort of reasoning, one can tentatively construct a web of links, outlined in Figure 1.7, connecting *Guernica*, *Minotauromachy*, and Goya's

The Disasters of War. It is not hard to understand why the bombing might have stimulated Picasso to think of *Minotauromachy* and of Goya, which resulted in the activation of ideas that played a role in directing his creative process. The links among the various elements that came together to produce *Guernica* are not particularly exotic; rather, they are connections among ideas and experiences that each of us might possess. It just happens that the links among ideas that we have been focusing on here are of particular interest, because they are based on the complex set of experiences unique to Picasso.

It has been possible to trace the origins of some microscopic aspects of *Guernica* – for example, the facial profiles and postures of some characters, as well as the overall appearances of some of the characters. However, questions remain concerning how often such links occur and how close the links will be psychologically. Such questions can be addressed through the analysis of the development of other creative works, presented later in the book. I hope to provide evidence that new ideas are always based on recycling – that is, new ideas always begin with old ideas.

Beyond Antecedents: Synthesizing the New with the Old

Let us assume for the sake of discussion that all those links in Figure 1.7 were indeed operative as Picasso created *Guernica*. However, *Guernica* was more than simply a recycling of old ideas: there are critical differences between the painting and the older works that played a role in its creation. As one example, *Guernica* depicts *a city on fire*: Picasso explicitly depicted flames in several places in the painting. The headline in a Parisian newspaper reporting the bombing mentioned that 1,000 incendiary bombs – "fire bombs" – had been dropped on Guernica. That information, or something like it, might have been the source of the flames in the sketches and the painting. Similarly, a dead baby is not part of a bullfight scene. Photos in newspaper reports showed dead victims of the bombing, which might have played a role here. Finally, a broken statue is also not part of a bullfight scene. However, one can discern a link between a broken statue and a city in ruins after a bombing. Thus, we can see instances where the specific event that stimulated the painting makes itself known in the final product. Picasso may have filtered the stimulus event through his knowledge of history and of art, but he did not ignore that stimulus. *Guernica* may be a bullfight painting, but it is a bullfight with military- and human-aggression overtones. The final work was a creative synthesis of the old and the new.

Generating versus Extending Ideas: Associative versus Executive Processes

The case studies discussed in this chapter indicate that one can analyze the creative process into stages: first, one *generates* a possible solution, perhaps based on analogy or on logical reasoning; then one tries to *extend* that idea to the specific new situation that one is facing. Thus, when one reads that a problem was solved as the result of analogical transfer, it is important to remember that that description is summarizing the operation of two general processes. First, there is the retrieval of a possible solution method, based on the analogical relationship between the new problem and some situation in memory. Second, there is the successful extension of that old idea to the new situation.

A similar distinction that a number of psychologists have made is between *associative* and *executive* processes in thinking. Generating an old idea in response to the current situation may be the result of an associative process: the current situation may be *associated*, or *linked* in memory, to that idea. For example, if I hear someone talking about preparing Thanksgiving dinner, I may recall the last Thanksgiving dinner at our house. The phrase "Thanksgiving dinner" is associated with the memory of our last dinner. The process is relatively passive on my part: I do not really *do anything*; I hear a person say something, and an idea comes to mind. Sometimes, that linkage can be less direct, as, for example, when the bombing of *Guernica* resulted in Picasso retrieving *Minotauromachy*. Possible links between the outside event and information in Picasso's database were outlined in Figure 1.7. A new idea can also be generated through logical reasoning, as we saw with several of IDEO's innovations for the shopping cart.

However, extending an old idea to a new problem involves going beyond the information that one has retrieved and modifying it so that it fits the new situation. So, once Picasso retrieved *Minotauromachy* in the context of creating a painting about the bombing of Guernica, he had to do extensive work on that old idea, to extend it, in order to make it fit the needs of the new problem. That adjustment involves *executive functioning* (Beaty et al., 2014) – that is, judgment, planning, directing one's attention to potentially relevant aspects of the situation, and decision-making, which goes beyond simply retrieving an old idea. Extending an old idea to a new situation is an *active* process, in which the individual's thought process plays a critical role.

Similarly, when someone on the IDEO team, while thinking about the problem of maneuvering a shopping cart in the narrow and crowded aisles of a supermarket, came up with the idea of casters on an office chair, it was the result of an associative process based on analogy. However, there still remained the task of extending that idea – that is, the casters had to be made to work with the shopping cart. Executive processes played a role there. The distinction between associative and executive processes will also play an important role in the discussion of creative thinking throughout the book.

Analytic Thinking in Creativity: Conclusions from the Two Case Studies

The most striking point to be drawn from these two case studies is that it seems possible to analyze the creative thought process – even at the highest levels – in a straightforward way. The creative process is highly structured and not different than the thought processes involved in more mundane activities. In developing the shopping cart, the IDEO team used information that came from domains closely related to the one in which they were working. No wide-ranging creative leaps occurred, in which ideas from totally unrelated areas were brought together, in some sort of magical synthesis. Similarly, Picasso did not leap far afield in creating *Guernica*: he built on his own work and incorporated related work by others. The products in both cases may have been extraordinary, but the processes by which they were brought about were not.

Ordinary Thinking in Creativity: Could Anyone Have Produced the Theory of Relativity?

If we can agree for now that all creative thinking is based on ordinary or analytic thinking, that raises an important question: could any one of us have produced any given creative advance? Could any one of us have created, say, Einstein's theory of relativity? Probably not. Some creative advances required expertise in a specialized and/or highly technical domain, which only a small number of people might be able to master in the first place. Let us put aside the question of highly advanced specialized knowledge and consider whether anyone could be creative in a situation where less highly specialized knowledge is needed. Could any one of us have created IDEO's shopping cart? Again, probably not. First, one would have to have carried out IDEO's research on shopping carts to acquire the information about problems facing supermarkets and their customers. Second, some aspects of the cart, such as the checkout scanner and the microphone for communication with customer service, were based on relatively specific expertise, which most of us might not possess.

Some features of the cart, however, such as its plastic baskets to eliminate its potential as a barbecue, and the casters instead of fixed rear wheels, were probably within the reach of most of us, if we had thought about the situation a bit. If you had talked to a supermarket manager, and she had mentioned that she had a problem with shopping carts being stolen because their metal baskets served as barbecues, you might have thought about making those baskets out of something that could not be used for cooking.

Similarly, concluding that ordinary or analytic thought processes underlie creative thinking does not mean that just anyone could have produced *Guernica* (see also Klahr & Simon, 1999). Picasso had been an artist for some forty years when he painted it, so one would have to have had his unique lifetime's worth of experiences and expertise. Furthermore, in Picasso's work, one sees references to classical mythology (the minotaur) and other bodies of knowledge. One would have to acquire that data base, ranging far beyond painting itself, before one could produce works with the broad range of connections that people find in the works of Picasso. Thus, even though creative work may not go beyond ordinary thinking processes, that does not mean that creative work is effortless and that anyone could do it.

Green Creativity? Antecedents for New Ideas and the Question of "Real" Creativity

We have seen in these two case studies several examples of green creativity: new ideas firmly planted on ones that came before. The reason that it sometimes looks like an idea comes out of nothing is because we observers are ignorant of the knowledge base of the individual producing the new idea. In response to these sorts of demonstrations, some people dismiss the examples as not being creative and propose that we must look elsewhere for "real" creativity. If IDEO's shopping cart was based on green creativity and thinking inside the box, then it did not involve *real* creativity, because real creativity depends on thinking *outside* the box. Likewise, if *Guernica* was based on recycled ideas, then, renowned or not, it was not a truly creative work.

That conclusion, however, is incorrect: *green creativity is **real** creativity*. Simply because a new work is related to – or based on, or developed out of – an earlier work does not mean that the new work is not novel. The difficulty with that reasoning arises because it assumes that a creative product must be *completely novel* (Barzun, 1989; Bloom, 2002). However, I believe that the case studies just presented, although few in number, are representative of all creative thinking: *no* creative product is completely novel. Although I cannot prove it, it is my belief that one will *never* find a creative product for which there are no antecedents. I will try to get as close as I can to proving that claim, by examining a wide range of products, from a wide range of domains, and showing the antecedents for each of them. This may help make people more willing to entertain the idea that perhaps there are no creative products without antecedents. The burden of proof then shifts to those who advocate the genius view and who postulate outside-the-box thinking as the basis for creativity. It is their task to *demonstrate* that creative advances come about through creative leaps; they cannot simply assume that that is true.

Outline of the Book

The book is structured in six parts. Part 1, Introduction, consists of this chapter and the next, which provide background to the discussion of creativity in the rest of the book. In Chapter 2 we will examine the critical concepts (which I have left undefined in this chapter), and we will trace the historical development of the notion of genius.

Part II, Analytic Thinking in Creativity, consists of Chapters 3 to 6 and presents in detail the analysis of creative thinking as based on analytic thinking. Chapter 3 reviews laboratory research on problem-solving, which will provide an introduction to how new ideas come about. Chapter 4 presents several case studies of creative thinking, to examine further the role of analytic thinking in creative advances of all sorts. Chapter 5 examines the role of talent – innate abilities – in creative thinking. It has recently been proposed that expertise, acquired through years of practice, is the critical component in world-class performance of all sorts, including creative accomplishments (Ericsson & Poole, 2016). In this view, innate abilities are given little or no place. We will examine whether one can explain all creative accomplishment solely on the basis of expertise acquired through years of practice. Chapter 6 examines the role of analogical thinking in problem-solving. Some researchers have proposed that analogical thinking is the core component of cognition, so it is of interest to examine in detail how analogies function in problem-solving and creative thinking.

Part III, The Question of Extraordinary Thought Processes in Creativity (Chapters 7 through 9), examines several phenomena that seem to raise problems for the idea that analytic thinking underlies creativity. Chapter 7 looks at the question of leaps of insight in problem-solving, the idea that creative advances come about in an *Aha!* experience, in which an individual suddenly becomes aware of a new way to approach a problem. We will examine whether it is possible to understand leaps of insight as coming about through analytic thinking. Chapter 8 discusses the notion that unconscious processes play a significant role in creative thinking. Chapter 9 considers the question of genius and madness, the idea that psychopathology can facilitate creative thinking.

Part IV, The Psychometrics of Creativity: Can We Identify Creative People?, consists of three chapters that examine one of the most important thrusts of the modern study of creativity, the attempt to measure people's creative potential and the characteristics of creative people. Chapter 10 reviews research that has tried to develop tests to measure people's creative potential. Chapter 11 discusses research that has tried to isolate the personality characteristics of creative people. Are there any psychological characteristics that are common in creative people, and what role might those characteristics play in creative accomplishment? Chapter 12 examines several *confluence theories of creativity*, which attempt to explain creativity by the coming together, or confluence, of many factors, including cognition and personality.

Part V, The Neuroscience of Creativity, consists of a single chapter. Chapter 13 examines a relatively new area, and one that is growing quickly, that attempts to determine the brain processes underlying creative advances of various sorts. We will examine how recent research on the neuroscience of creativity provides new insights concerning creative functioning.

Organizing Themes

Several overarching themes will appear throughout the book and will serve to structure the discussion as we cover a wide range of topics.

The first theme, which has already been extensively discussed, is the idea that creative thinking and ordinary thinking are the same. There is no special kind of thinking – no outside-the-box thinking – which serves in the creation of new ideas. More specifically, creative thinking is green and incremental. There is, as mentioned, a long history, centering on what can be called the genius view, that argues that creativity does not come about in that way. According to the genius view, creative advances come about through creative leaps, which are neither green nor incremental. There are many examples in modern psychology of variations on the genius view, although those views are not always presented in that way. As we work our way through the study of creativity, I will point out those examples of the genius view and discuss areas in which the genius view and the analytic view are in conflict. We will try to determine if the analytic perspective can explain all creative advances.

A second theme, discussed in the context of both creative advances presented in this chapter, is the idea that the creative process can be analyzed into two large stages: the *generation* of a possible idea (based on associative processes or on reasoning); and the attempt to *extend* it to the new situation (which relies on judgment and other components of executive functioning). On being faced with a problem, for example, the person thinks of a possible solution and then tries to see if the idea will work as a solution to the problem. That process can result in the idea being accepted as is, modified in some way, or rejected, with a new idea then being searched for. We will see the applicability of this general conception at many points in the discussion later in the book, and we will also flesh out the details as we discuss other examples of creative thinking.

A third theme, which has been present in this chapter but has not been discussed in detail, is that creative thinking, since it is analytic or ordinary thinking, is conscious thinking. Here, too, we will come across numerous situations in which it has been argued that creative thinking goes beyond ordinary conscious thinking. We will see if it is necessary to go beyond conscious analytic thinking in order to understand how creative advances come about. A question of interest in this book is how far conscious analytic thinking can go in explaining how creative advances come about.

A final theme, and one that will be very important throughout the book, is that, in order to understand the operations of the creative process, it is necessary to obtain enough information to allow us to dig deeply into the underlying psychological processes. It is not enough to *assume* that one understands the processes involved: one must go beyond assumptions and obtain *evidence* for any claims that one makes about how the creative processes works. As one example, if one looked at IDEO's shopping cart by itself, one might agree with the proposal, made by IDEO, that the cart was the result of thinking outside the box. However, more careful analysis of the information available indicated that the outside-the-box assumption was incorrect. We shall see many times, throughout the discussion in the book, that seemingly obvious assumptions about the creative process may turn out, on close inspection, to be incorrect. So, the final theme is that we shall take nothing for granted in attempting to explain how creative thinking operates.

2 | Creativity

What It Is

Do You Want to Come Up to My Place to See My Meissoniers?

My wife and I met in an interesting way. I was at a bar one night when a woman sat down next to me. We began to talk, and she inquired about what I did. I told her that I was a psychologist interested in creativity. She asked if I was interested in art, and I said yes. She then invited me to go to her place to see her art collection; she thought she had something I might like to see. My curiosity was piqued, and when we got to her place I was astounded to find that, on her wall, she had a painting by Vincent van Gogh (1853–90), one of the greatest painters of the nineteenth century. His works are on display in all the major museums and have been the subject of numerous exhibits around the world, which draw large and enthusiastic crowds. Van Gogh's paintings sell these days for millions of dollars. If you had a Van Gogh on your wall, you too would be eager to show it to other people.

It is informative to compare that story (all made-up, including, alas, the owning of a Van Gogh) with what might have happened if it had occurred around the end of the nineteenth century, not long after Van Gogh died. At that time, there almost certainly would have been *no* paintings by Van Gogh on my future wife's wall. Rather, an upwardly striving art collector, if she were rich and lucky, might have had on her wall a painting by Jean-Louis-Ernest Meissonier (1815–91). Who is Meissonier? Most of us have neither heard of him nor seen any of his works. Why would anyone have been proud to display his paintings? Why would there be no Van Goghs on the wall? Were none available? Were they too expensive?

Many of us know at least the outline of Van Gogh's sad life story: the classic tortured artist; cut off his ear, perhaps for a woman; spent time in insane asylums; died an early death, perhaps by his own hand. However, tortured or not, he did produce many works, some 900 in all. Sadly, however, even though there were Van Goghs available for the taking, almost no one bought them. Although details are sketchy, Van Gogh

41

probably sold only a few paintings in his lifetime. Works that are now worth tens of millions of dollars went without buyers. Van Gogh died unknown, unappreciated, and penniless. Our art collector would not have had any Van Goghs on her wall because she would not have heard of him. And what about Meissonier? He was at that time the exact opposite of Van Gogh: one of the most successful French painters of the second half of the nineteenth century, occupying a place of highest honor in the art world (King, 2006). Meissonier's works were displayed in museums and won awards at exhibitions. Collectors paid Meissonier large commissions for works created for them. Today, however, things are radically different: almost no one knows anything about Meissonier, and his paintings in all those museums draw no interest from viewers.

We have here two artists whose careers followed diametrically opposing trajectories, over about the same time. One died an unknown but post-humously achieved greatness; the other achieved greatness in his lifetime but faded into obscurity after he died. The radical changes in reputation and status seen in Van Gogh and Meissonier – and similar changes can be seen in the careers of many other individuals who engage in creative work, ranging from the visual arts to music to the sciences – raise important issues. Some researchers believe that those changes in *reputation* – that is, changes in the *value* placed on an artist's work – are a component of that individual's *creativity* (Csikszentmihalyi, 2014). From that perspective, the posthumous changes in the reputations of Van Gogh and Meissonier mean that Van Gogh became more creative after he died, and Meissonier became less creative.

I avoided defining creativity in Chapter 1, based on the assumption that we all were familiar enough with the important concepts for the discussion to be understood. However, to delve deeper into the issues surrounding the study of creativity, we need to specify what we are talking about, which we will do in this chapter.

Outline of the Chapter

This chapter will present two sorts of background information to support our examination of creativity. We will begin by reviewing how psychologists have defined the topics of interest. There has been some disagreement among researchers concerning the most useful definitions for *creative* and related topics, so I will present the various positions before settling on a definition for use in this book. I will then shift gears a bit and trace the historical development of the genius view of creativity. We will examine how the concept of *genius* has changed over the generations and how current views show the influences of ideas that have, in various forms, existed for centuries.

The Beginning: Guilford's Definition

The modern psychological study of creativity can be said to begin around seventy years ago, with J. P. Guilford's presidential address to the American Psychological Association, in which he urged psychologists to take up the study of creativity (Guilford, 1950). Guilford was one of the leaders of the mental testing movement, an expert in IQ testing. He had examined the recent literature in psychology and found what he considered an appalling lack of research on creativity. Guilford proposed methods whereby that lack of research could be remedied. He first presented a definition of creativity, and he then made suggestions concerning tests that psychologists could use to measure and study it. Gilford's suggestions concerning how creativity could be studied – in other words, *his creative ideas concerning how to carry out research on creativity* – were built on his experience with IQ testing. In another example of *green creativity*, Guilford recycled an old idea as the basis for development of a new one. At this point we are interested in Guilford's definition of *creative* and related concepts. The tests that he proposed will be examined in Chapter 10.

Guilford began with the idea that creativity is a configuration of *traits*: people's characteristics or abilities. Creativity consists in those specific traits that we find in creative persons. We can take creative people and measure their psychological characteristics, and those characteristics define creativity. That proposal leaves us with another question, however: How do we identify creative people? Guilford proposed that creative people exhibit *creative behavior*, "such activities as inventing, designing, contriving, composing, and planning. People who exhibit these types of behavior to a marked degree are recognized as being creative" (p. 444). Thus, Guilford relied ultimately on *achievement* as the basis for defining creativity. The people who have produced outstanding creative achievements are the ones we want to understand better.

The "Standard" Definition: Creative = Novelty + Value

In the years since Guilford's (1950) address, psychologists have made great strides in the study of creativity. There are now hundreds of papers published each year on creativity and related topics, multiple journals that publish that research, and several large-scale texts that cover the basic scientific findings. There has also developed a consensus on the definition of the phenomena of interest: almost all psychologists now define a *creative product* as something that is *novel* and *of value* (Runco & Jaeger, 2012). We can call this the two-criterion or two-factor definition, since the basis for calling something creative is that it must possess two qualities: *novelty* and *value*. The two-factor definition has been called the *standard* definition (Runco & Jaeger, 2012), since it has been adopted by almost everyone in the field.

Value and Creativity: The Systems View

The standard definition of creativity is one component of a broader approach to creativity, called the "systems view" (Csikszentmihalyi, 1988, 2014), that also has been adopted by most researchers. In the systems view, designating a product as creative is the result of a complex social process, one that goes far beyond the product and the person who created it (see Figure 2.1). The process is cyclical. Let us start with an *individual* who works in some creative profession, or *field* – say, a painter. That person produces something new. We might be tempted at that point to say that the person has produced something creative, but the systems view counts that as only the first step in the process. To become recognized as creative, a product must be positively evaluated by other members of the field.

Consider a work of art: What makes a painting valuable? Members of the field of painting – art critics, museum curators, other artists, gallery owners, and the art-appreciative public, among others – are those that endow a painting with value (Csikszentmihalyi, 1988, 2014). If no one is interested in the work – if no one positively values it – it will remain in the artist's studio, and no one will ever see it. On the other hand, if other members of the field find a new work to be of value, the work moves into the light and thereby becomes a part of what can be called the *domain of painting* (again, see Figure 2.1). The domain is the concrete record of work in the field; in the case of the field of art, the domain consists of those works found on display in museums and galleries; in art reference books; and on the walls of art collectors. The individuals who direct the museums and galleries, who write those reference books, and who serve as advisors to art collectors function as *gatekeepers*. They determine which works become part of the

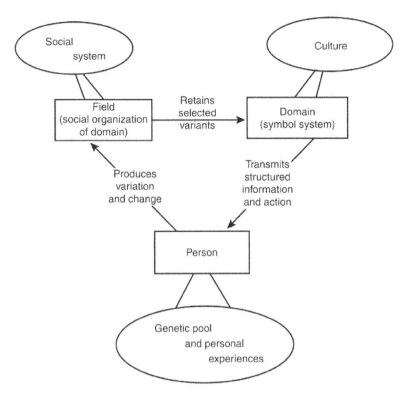

Figure 2.1 Systems view of creativity. Csikszentmihalyi, M. (1988). Society, culture, and person: A systems view of creativity. In R. J. Sternberg (ed.), The Nature of Creativity: Current Psychological Perspectives (pp. 325–339). Cambridge: Cambridge University Press.

domain. When a work becomes part of the domain, it can influence the next generation of members of the field, as part of a tradition.

A similar process occurs in science. When a neuroscientist, for example, produces a paper presenting new research findings, the value of that work is determined by other neuroscientists. Scientists of established reputation serve as editors and reviewers for the journals and books in the field, and every research paper or book published in the field must first undergo "peer review." The *peers* of the author – that is, other members of the field – determine whether the new research is worthy of becoming part of the domain (again, the concrete record of progress in the field). If, in the opinions of the gatekeepers, the work is not worthy of inclusion, the research goes into the researcher's file drawer or trash can. It will be as if the research was never carried out.

According to the systems view, art historians, art critics, and museum directors play a role in making a painting creative; other scientists determine whether new scientific research is creative; and musicians, scholars who study music, and music critics determine whether new music is creative. This conception of the creative process (see Figure 2.1 once more), incorporates within it the standard definition of *creative* – that is, a product that is novel and of value (Csikszentmihalyi, 2014; Sternberg & Bridges, 2014).

Meissonier versus Van Gogh: The Problem with Using Value in Determining What or Who Is Creative

On the standard definition, *creativity* is the production of outcomes that are *novel* and *valuable*. The requirement of novelty goes almost without saying: if what you are producing is not new, then it cannot be creative. The requirement of novelty does raise one further issue, however: for whom must the outcome be novel? Consider a student who is reading a research paper and who gets an idea for a new experiment, which she jots down in the margin. She turns the page and finds, much to her distress, that the researchers have already carried out "her study" as the next one in the research. Was the student creative in proposing an experiment that had already been carried out? Certainly: So long as she was not aware of her study's earlier incarnation, then she was creative when she proposed it (Boden, 1990; Weisberg, 1986). One must make a distinction between an idea that is creative for an individual versus creative for society. The student was creative on the individual level – the proposed experiment was novel *for her* – but not on the level of society.

If we agree that novelty is necessary for calling something creative, we can now turn to *value*, the second criterion. Value is included in the standard definition because researchers are concerned that using novelty alone might result in some things being called creative that should not be (Runco & Jaeger, 2012). Let's say you present a friend with a very difficult problem to solve. Your friend works for a while and then gets frustrated. He takes the paper that the problem is written on and eats it, saying, "Problem solved." That response is novel, but is it creative? No, it is merely *bizarre*. Your friend's response is not valuable because it did not solve the problem you presented to him. Similarly, let's say you presented a problem to someone suffering from mental illness. He or she might produce something novel, such as an incomprehensible string of words – a "word salad" – but that response would be totally unrelated to the problem. It too would be bizarre rather than creative. The criterion of value allows us to eliminate bizarre responses and concentrate on those that are truly creative. However, I believe that postulating value as a criterion brings with it several thorny problems, and I have concluded that we should remove value as a component of our definition (Weisberg, 2015, 2018c).

Problems with Using Value in the Definition of Creative

When Gatekeepers Disagree

When we include the value of a product in the definition, that means we are bringing people's judgments into the process, but whose judgments do we use? It seems reasonable to use the judgments of experts, but there are many examples, in the arts and in science, of experts sharply disagreeing as to whether some work was of value. Consider Andy Warhol's paintings of soup cans: not only did experts disagree on whether those works were *of value*, but they disagreed on whether they were even *art* (Ketner, 2013). If we rely on experts' judgments, we will have occasions when we cannot say whether a work, or the person who produced it, was creative, because the gatekeepers are undecided. That seems to be an unsatisfactory basis for the scientific study of creativity.

Conflicts with Ordinary Language

The standard definition and the systems view also conflict with the definition of creativity in our ordinary language. In the Merriam-Webster online dictionary, the verb *create* is defined in part as follows:

transitive verb
1 to bring into existence – God *created* the heaven and the earth – Genesis 1.1 (King James Version)

. . .

4a to produce through imaginative skill – *create* a painting

. . .

intransitive verb
1. to make or bring into existence something new – an artist who is good at imitating but not at *creating*

This authoritative source defines creativity in terms of *novelty* and says nothing about the value of what is produced. We have here, then, a conflict between the dictionary definition and the one used by researchers. The task of the psychologist studying creativity is to demonstrate that we can understand and explain it. To achieve that goal, it is important that we all – psychologists and nonpsychologists – begin and end at the same place. We see here another difficulty concerning the standard definition.

Becoming Creative after Death?

A further problem for the systems view, also stemming from the use of value in determining whether a work is creative, becomes apparent if we consider again the histories of Meissonier and Van Gogh. The systems view leads to the conclusion that Meissonier became uncreative after he died, because his work was no longer valued. Conversely, Van Gogh was not creative when he was producing his works, since they were of no value to anyone. After he died, however, evolving tastes in art resulted in his work becoming valued, and, therefore, Van Gogh became creative. This argument is stated clearly by Csikszentmihalyi (2014).

> The only reason we call Van Gogh creative is because, after his death, some of the most respected art historians and collectors discovered in his work qualities that were not visible to his contemporaries when he was still alive ... Van Gogh's paintings became creative only after the carnage of World War I made it impossible for lovers of art to hold on to the standards of pretty serenity prevalent in the canvases painted before the War. Instead, the hallucinating vibrancy of Van Gogh's canvases provided an alternative standard by which to appreciate a work of art: harmony and beauty were out, suffering and conflict were in ... In other words, the social environment is always a cocreator, without which the creation cannot happen, and the process of creation cannot be understood. (p. 537)

That conclusion strikes me as strange: Can someone become creative – or not creative – after death? The problem with saying that a person's creativity can change, positively or negatively, after death can be made clear if we examine in a little more detail the meaning of *creative* by considering how we use it in sentences. Try to paraphrase sentence (1).

(1) Van Gogh was creative when he was young, but then he became noncreative.

I take that sentence to mean that the young van Gogh produced original works, but then his works became less original, either because he began to produce works that looked like those of other artists or because he was repeating himself so that his later works looked much like his earlier ones. Looking at sentence (1), we see that becoming creative or not creative depends on the types of works one produces – that is, whether those works are original.

Now consider sentence (2).

(2) Van Gogh was creative when alive, but then he died and became not creative.

After thinking about sentence (1), one sees that sentence (2), although it looks like sentence (1), is not like it. Sentence (2) contains a term – *creative* – that can only be applied to a person based on what he or she *produces*, but in sentence (2) that term is applied to a dead person. There is a basic mistake there, because one *cannot produce anything* after one dies. Dead persons cannot become more creative, or less creative, because they cannot do the things that becoming more, or less, creative depends on. We all know that a dead person cannot become more or less funny (or grumpy, or happy, or loving, etc.). Those are characteristics of a living person, *and so is creativity*. In sum, including *value* in the definition of *creative* leads us to say things that other people will find confusing.

Whom Shall We Study?

Including *value* in the definition also raises problems for researchers. Let's say that an early researcher in psychology, who worked in France around 1900, was interested in studying the psychological characteristics of creative individuals – for instance, creative artists. As an example of a creative artist – based on the value of his works, as demonstrated by their presence in museums and on the receipt of prizes – the researcher chose Meissonier. What about a noncreative artist to use as a comparison? She chose Van Gogh as the noncreative comparison group. (Ignore, for the sake of discussion, that one creative person versus another noncreative person is too small a sample from which to draw any conclusions.) The researcher went to Meissonier and asked him to take psychological tests; she did the same with Van Gogh. She finds significant differences between their responses, and she publishes her conclusions about the psychological characteristics of creative versus noncreative people.

However, consider the situation in ten years. The researcher must retract her findings, because things have flipped: the characteristics of her *creative* individual – Meissonier – have now become characteristics of a *noncreative* individual, and vice versa for Van Gogh. Any conclusions that researchers draw about any creative individuals will always be *tentative*, because we do not know what the next generation of gatekeepers will say. We cannot get away from this problem by choosing to study those individuals whose work has stood the test of time, because there is no guarantee that there will not be very large changes in the evaluation even of those works. Large shifts in appreciation (and in value) have occurred relatively frequently over the last several centuries (Cuelemans, 2010; Ginsburgh & Weyers, 2014). An example of a significant shift in value can be seen in the career history of J. S. Bach (1685–1750), who is today considered one of the greatest composers of classical music. For about fifty years after he died, Bach's music was *ignored*, because tastes had changed and Bach was considered old-fashioned. Thus, people at the very highest level of a field can have their work change significantly in value over a few generations.

This conclusion is supported by several studies that have examined changes in "the canon" – that is, those members of any field whose works are considered of highest value. Cuelemans (2010) looked at changes in reputation of composers of the Baroque era (Bach's contemporaries) by looking at seven music reference books spanning the period 1750–2000. He was looking at changes in the canon of classical music over 250 years. When Cuelemans looked at the composers ranked in the top fifty by each of those authors, he found that approximately half of the "canon" changed over time. Furthermore, and not surprisingly, the further apart any two books were in time, the less agreement occurred in their rankings of the composers. Those results indicate that the reputations of a significant proportion of those "great" composers underwent relatively large-scale changes over time. Similar findings were reported by Ginsburgh and Weyers (2006, 2010; see discussion in Ginsburgh & Weyers, 2014), who examined the canon for painting, by determining which artists were discussed in art reference books from 1600 to 2000. Like that in classical music, the canon in painting is by no means constant or even close to constant. Changes of a similar sort also occur in the sciences, although I will not discuss them here due to space limitations.

Three-Factor Definitions

Some researchers (e.g., Boden, 1990; Simonton, 2014) have proposed a third factor that should be included in the definition of creative: to be creative, the outcome must be *novel*, *of value*, and also *surprising*. A creative product must impress us with its unusual nature: "run-of-the-mill" novelty, even if it is of value, is not enough. As far as the present discussion is concerned, this elaborated definition still includes value, so it is subject to the same problems just discussed for the standard definition and should also be rejected.

Creativity and Value: Conclusions

If we define creativity based on the positive value placed on a novel work, we will run into multiple problems. We will have difficulty communicating about the concepts we are studying, since researchers will say things about creativity that nonresearchers will not understand. Furthermore, we will be in a position in which we can draw no general conclusions about creative individuals. That will be because judgments of value turn out to be too unreliable to serve as the basis of a scientific investigation of creativity.

Creativity Is Goal-Directed Novelty

If, based on this discussion, we agree that value should not be used in determining whether something is creative, we are left with the criterion of novelty, as already discussed. We are also left with the question of how we can separate creative responses from bizarre ones (your friend eating the paper with the problem on it). In my work, I have come to define a creative work as one that is **novel** and is **produced intentionally** in response to the situation (Weisberg, 2015, 2018c). Including the person's *intention* in the definition allows us to make the distinction between creative and bizarre responses.

As an example of how this intentional-novelty definition works, imagine an artist who, while working on a canvas (say, a portrait of a friend), accidentally knocks over a can of paint, spilling paint on the canvas and ruining it as far as she is concerned. She puts the canvas on the throw-out pile. She is then visited by a museum director, who takes one look at the discarded canvas (not knowing that it is trash), loves the "new direction" in the artist's work, and on the spot purchases it for the museum. The painting is then included in several art reference books, thereby becoming part of the domain. Was the artist creative in producing that painting? No: because the work was produced by accident, she (and we) know that she was lucky, not creative. Let's say, in contrast, that the artist had decided, as the result of her analysis of her portrait-in-progress, that it might be more effective if she spilled some paint on the partially completed canvas. Doing that, she suspects, might increase the emotional level of the portrait. She tries it and is pleased with the effect, so this time the canvas is not on the throw-out pile. In this case, we can call the work and the artist creative, since the outcome was the result of her intention.

Excluding Merely Bizarre Responses from Consideration as Creative

Now consider again your friend who ate the paper your problem was written on, declaring that the problem was solved. Was that a creative solution to the problem? No: it did not solve the problem you gave him. His response might have been a creative solution to the problem of removing himself from an uncomfortable situation (i.e., not being able to solve a problem with you watching him), but it was not a creative solution to the original problem. Our new definition seems to work here as well. Finally, we have the word salad of the schizophrenic. Is that a creative solution to a problem? No, because someone in a schizophrenic state cannot deal with a problem in such a way as to intentionally produce a solution. We would therefore be able to exclude that response. So once again the new definition seems to meet our needs.

Creativity Is Permanent

Defining creative work as intentional novelty also allows us to specify, once and for all, whether something is creative. If a work is novel and produced intentionally, it is creative, and it will *never* lose that designation, except if we find that we made a factual error. That is, either the product was not novel, even though we thought it was, or it was not produced intentionally, again, even though we thought it was. Barring those sorts of mistakes, if some outcome is designated as creative at one point in time, it will stay that way forever. There are several sorts of information that can help in determining the creator's intentions. First, we can ask the individual if the outcome was intentional. If we do not want to rely on the person's uncorroborated report, there might be a witness, who could tell us, for example, that the artist was surprised and distressed when the paint spilled on the canvas that is now hanging in the museum. That testimony would be evidence for the accidental nature of the "creative advance." Similarly, if the canvas with the spilled paint is found in the trash, that too would support the idea that what seems like a creative advance was an accidental outcome. Conversely, if the artist had been heard talking about how she wanted to make some changes in her painting technique, so that she did not always use the brush to apply paint, that would be evidence that her spilling of paint was intentional. Thus, it is possible to gather evidence beyond the individual's report concerning his or her intentions.

Determining the Novelty of a Product

We have seen that it seems possible to determine if a product has been produced intentionally. There is an additional question that must be considered in discussing the proposed definition of creativity: how do we tell if a product is *novel*? Two methods are possible (Weisberg, 2015, 2018c). First, we can ask people who are familiar with the area if an individual's work is novel. We can ask scientists, for example, if another scientist's work is novel. We can ask poetry critics if a new poem is novel. We do not have to rely on the opinion of the person who produced the work, because that individual might be incorrect. For example, a person might forget, several years earlier, producing a work very similar to the one just produced. Going beyond the person can help us determine whether some product is novel.

In addition, developments in artificial intelligence have made it possible to obtain objective measures of the novelty of a product. Elgammal and Saleh (2015) carried out a computer analysis of the novelty of paintings, using two sets of digitized paintings, covering the years 1400–2000. One set contained 1,710 images, and the other contained more than 62,000. The researchers designed an algorithm to quantify the novelty of each painting, based on analysis of low-level visual features, such as the density of brushstrokes, independent of any input from the researchers. The algorithm analyzed the similarity between all pairs of paintings in each set, which is a measure of the originality of any work in the set. In a similar vein, Li, Yao, Hendriks, and Wang (2012) used a computer program to analyze two small sets of paintings, one containing paintings by van Gogh and the other consisting of paintings by his contemporaries. They found that the output of an algorithm, designed to analyze the pattern of brushstrokes in those paintings, reliably separated the paintings by van Gogh from those of the other painters. It is also notable that Li and colleagues found that their categorization of the paintings – those done by van Gogh versus those done by his contemporaries – corresponded to that produced by art historians. Thus, one might say that the judgments by the art historians were "objective," in the sense that they were supported by the output of an algorithm. In addition, the researchers used the algorithm's output to date three other van Gogh paintings that had been subject to some dispute among art historians concerning when they had been produced. Similar programs are available in other domains, for example, musical composition (e.g., Cope, 2014); literary works, such as novels, stories, and poems; and historical documents (see, for example, chapters in Erlin & Tatlock, 2014; Laramée, 2018; Llano, Colton, Hepworth & Gow, 2016; Underwood, Bamman & Lee 2018). In conclusion, assessing novelty in an objective manner seems possible. There are available algorithms that assesses the novelty of products of interest, independently of human input.

Creativity as Intentional Novelty: Conclusions

To sum up, we can return one more time to van Gogh and Meissonier. We can say that, if Meissonier was creative when he was alive, then he remained creative after he died. His work became less *valued* after he died but not less *creative*. Van Gogh's work was also creative when he produced it, and it became more valued after he died. Changes in the audience's sensitivity can change their appreciation for an artist's work. Those changes can sometimes be brought about by large-scale external events, in this case World War I (Csikszentmihalyi, 2014, p. 537). However, questions about changes in reputation and value are independent of the designation of the works as creative. The perspective on creativity that underlies my discussion here is presented in Figure 2.2. The individual's production of a novel product is designated as the creative process (Weisberg, 1993). The rest of the systems view is relevant to the value of a product, and therefore is not directly relevant to creativity.

There is one more background question that should be considered before we move forward. We must discuss the development of the concept of genius. Examination of the historical development of that idea will make explicit the origins of some assumptions that still shape how modern researchers approach the study of creativity and creative people.

The Concept of Genius

A genius is someone who can produce things that no one else can: the *Divine Comedy* of Dante; the *Jupiter Symphony* of Mozart; the bebop solos of Charlie Parker; *King Lear* by Shakespeare; *Hamilton* by Lin-Manuel Miranda; the *Mona Lisa* of Leonardo; the *David* of Michelangelo; *Beloved* by Toni Morrison; the scientific advances of Darwin, Einstein, and Watson and Crick. The number of individuals who can produce works of that quality is miniscule. Furthermore, no one, not even the geniuses themselves, is able

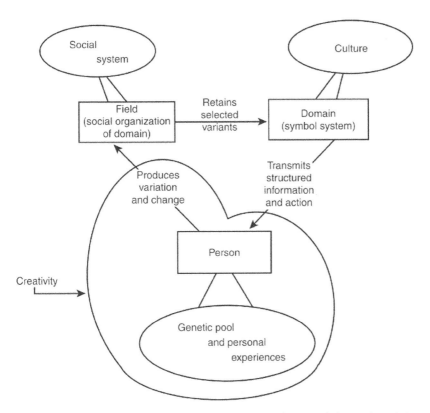

Figure 2.2 Intentional novelty definition of creativity. Csikszentmihalyi, M. (1988). Society, culture, and person: A systems view of creativity. In R. J. Sternberg (ed.), The Nature of Creativity: Current Psychological Perspectives (pp. 325–339). Cambridge: Cambridge University Press

to understand how they produce those wondrous things. Murray (1989a, p. 1) makes clear these aspects of genius:

> We attribute the extraordinary quality of, for example, Shakespeare's poetry, Mozart's music and Leonardo's paintings to the genius of their creators because we recognize that such works are not simply the product of learning, technique, or sheer hard work. Of course we can trace sources and influences, . . . but no amount of analysis has yet been able to explain the capacities of those rare and gifted individuals who can produce creative work of lasting quality and value. If we ask how Mozart was able to compose music of such purity and perfection, . . . we can only answer, "because he was a genius," which is tantamount to saying that we do not know. For in each age and in each art, genius is that which defies analysis.

Murray here nicely lays out the challenge for anyone, including the psychologist, who hopes to understand the creative process at all levels, including the highest, that is, genius-level creativity (see also Barzun,

1989; Bloom, 2002). We can try to understand genius-level creativity, but we are bound to fail.

However, before we decide that we can say nothing about creative works at the highest level, we should keep in mind that the case study of *Guernica* in Chapter 1 did provide us with some understanding of Picasso's creative process. Although it would be absurd to say that we fully understand how that work of genius was created, we were able to gain some insight into the processes involved. So, we might be able to understand some aspects of the creative process of the genius. Given this cautiously optimistic perspective, let us turn to a brief examination of the development of the modern conception of genius, which will enable us to see the origins of the ideas that have led Murray (1989a) and others (e.g., Barzun, 1989; Bloom, 2002) to conclude that any attempt to understand the creative process at the highest level is bound to fail. This discussion is of interest to us because those ideas have also affected how psychologists approach the study of creativity. A summary of the historical discussion is presented in Table 2.1.

Genius in Ancient Greece

The ancient Greeks had no words comparable to the English words *creativity* or *genius*, which might lead one to conclude that they did not think about the issues we are discussing here. However, the Greeks did attempt to understand the process that resulted in great poetry, considered to be the height of human accomplishment (McMahon, 2013). Plato, who lived in the fourth–third centuries BCE, extensively discussed the creative process, concentrating on how great poets were able to produce verse that moved others to intense emotion. He proposed that the poet in the midst of creation is *possessed* by the Muses – by the goddesses of poetry – and creates in a frenzy or furor. The Muses were the nine daughters of Zeus and Mnemosyne (pronounced "ni-mos-i-nee"), the goddess of memory. Each Muse had control over a different domain or domains. They brought about creative activity within those domains by bestowing their *graces* on an individual, which resulted in the person being able to produce outstanding results.

In Plato's view, the poet when creating great verse was mad: out of his mind (Becker, 1978). However, this madness was not ordinary insanity; rather, it was an irrational state – a creative frenzy, what Plato called a "poetic furor" – brought about because the muse was in possession of the poet's faculties. The muse created through the poet. It was a "divine

Table 2.1 *History of "genius"*

Period	Approximate time	Major beliefs concerning genius and creativity
Ancient Greece	Fifth–third century BCE	Possession by the Muses Poetic furor Creative ability as long-term gift from gods
Ancient Rome	First–fifth century CE	Genius = spirit watching over place or person Religious belief
Middle Ages	500–1500 CE	Artists tried to portray ideal world; no originality Artists seen as craftspeople
Renaissance	1500–1600 CE	Rebirth of interest in classical culture "Create" refers to human ability Human creation similar to God's creation Artists become important individuals Artists' works become valued
Enlightenment	1670–1770 CE	Rationality emphasized as core of creativity Judgment & "taste"
Romantic	1775–1850 CE	Deep emotional response to nature as first step in creativity Free – "unfettered" – imagination as basis for works of genius Rationality and taste discounted

madness," and, when the creative process was over, the poet's "madness" disappeared. We talk today of a creative individual "having an inspiration" or "being inspired." *Inspiration* means "a breathing in," and *inspiration* and *being inspired* come from the Muses: they provided the creative spark by *breathing into the individual*.

Plato seems to have been first in Western culture to argue that the creative process was *irrational* at its core (Becker, 1978); that is, poetry was not produced through the operation of the rational mind but was the result of a nonrational process – the Muse's possession of the poet – working through the poet. We see traces of this irrational component when modern theorists discuss various mechanisms that might enable creative individuals to think outside the box, such as unconscious processes (Weisberg,

2006). Unconscious processes are irrational, since they are – by definition – not under control of our conscious, rational selves. The most extreme modern view that builds on the idea of being out of one's mind in the throes of creation is the notion of genius and madness: the view that psychopathology might significantly facilitate the creative process (e.g., Jamison, 1993; Kyaga, 2018; Kinney & Richards, 2014; Taylor, 2017).

We have examined the situation where the Muse provided inspiration for a specific creative act. There were also discussions of longer-term relationships between the Muses and mortals (McMahon, 2013). Some individuals were believed to have received, as a gift from the gods, the long-term ability to create at the highest level. Similar ideas are seen in modern discussions of genius, such as the idea that creative achievement might run in families – that is, the ability to create at a high level might have a genetic basis.

The Genius in Ancient Rome

The ancient Romans, too, extensively discussed the concepts that we are interested in, and their Latin is the source of the English word *genius*. In ancient Roman religion, the *genius* was a *spirit* that watched over a person or a place. Each person had a genius, coming into existence when the person was born, that looked over them and guided them through life – usually, but not always, in a protective manner. That meaning of the term *genius* stayed dominant through the Middle Ages and into the eighteenth century (Murray, 1989a). The second meaning, referring to a person's natural ability to carry out some activity, sometimes at a very high level, was not seen until the seventeenth century. That term was then transferred to the person who possessed that ability, which brings us close to the modern view.

Genius in the Middle Ages

During the long period of the Middle Ages (500–1500 CE), there was no lack of creative achievements, produced under sponsorship of the Church, including cathedrals and other buildings; statues of saints; and paintings of biblical scenes. However, the people who produced those works, some of which are viewed today as undoubted masterworks, are unknown. Painters did not sign their works, and, during the Middle Ages, continuing a tradition going back to ancient Greece, painters, sculptors, and architects were afforded relatively low status. They were looked upon as craftspeople rather than a special class of people – that is, "artists." In addition, the purpose of the painter was to portray an ideal world, in which holiness and faith prevailed. There was little room for individual expression, beyond each individual's attempt to portray that ideal world as best he or she could. Creative activity was *imitative* at its base, as the artist imitated the world, and tried to paint it in idealized form, to faithfully capture God's creation (McMahon, 2013). See Table 2.1, earlier, for a summary.

The Renaissance and the Birth of the Genius

During the sixteenth century, there came together a series of wide-scale cultural changes that we have come to call the Renaissance. *Renaissance*, meaning "rebirth," referred to the renewal of interest in the "classical" culture of ancient Greece and Rome, including the arts. Here, one begins to see the use of the term "create" to refer to human activity; before, that word had been limited to God's creation of the heavens and the earth (McMahon, 2013). That change was significant, moving human creative activity to a higher level and distinguishing it from other less God-like human accomplishments.

The center of the Renaissance was Italy, where the arts were given increasing importance (McMahon, 2013). The role of the artist was to provide works for the nobility, including the nobility of the Church, but soon artists began to think of themselves less as workers carrying out the directions of others and more as independent thinkers, whose values and opinions played a significant role in the works they produced. It is said, for example, that when Michelangelo was called to Rome by Pope Julius II, to paint the ceiling of the Sistine Chapel, the artist bickered with the pope about aspects of the proposed design. Ultimately, Michelangelo was given the freedom to paint what he thought appropriate.

Such changes in attitudes were seen more broadly, in several interconnected ways. First, artists began to sign their works, taking credit for and placing value on what they produced. Also, the nobility competed to have certain individuals – for example, Leonardo and Michelangelo – produce works for them. The artists became celebrities in themselves. In 1550, Giorgio Vasari published the first edition of *The Lives of the Artists*, a large-scale book, recounting the history of what can be called Italian Renaissance art (Vasari, 1991 [1550]). Vasari's book can be said to have invented the field of art history. Vasari used the term "genius" to refer to many, but not all, of the artists whom he chronicled, most particularly Michelangelo.

Also, Vasari generally used the word Italian work *artifice* ("maker") to refer to the artists he discussed. That term had been used in theological writings to describe God, the maker of the creation. Thus, the artist in Vasari's view contained some of the characteristics of the Divine Creator (i.e., of God).

In sum, by the end of the Renaissance, some creative individuals, at least, had been elevated to positions of honor and were seen as being very different from the ordinary individual. This movement of the artist to a position far away from the average was carried further over the next two centuries, through what are called the *Age of Enlightenment* and the *Romantic* period.

The Genius in the Enlightenment

The Age of Enlightenment, from approximately the end of the seventeenth century through the beginning of the nineteenth, was a period of great economic development centered on the industrial revolution (McMahon, 2013). There was a feeling that human progress based on human rationality was inevitable, with no limit. The advances that contributed to the industrial revolution depended on human innovation, ranging from the development of steam engines that could be used to power machines in factories to the invention of the factory machines themselves. During the Enlightenment, creative production came to be increasingly valued, and a wider range of activities was recognized as creative, such as science and invention. Sir Isaac Newton, for example, was raised to God-like status.

During the Enlightenment, there was an influence of the rational philosophy on society's attitude toward creative individuals (Gerard, 1774). It was believed that, in additional to the "irrational" component of genius, dating back to Plato, there must also be a rational component – called "taste" – in the creative process. Without taste, creative works would not reach the highest level of perfection. An example of the emphasis on the rational component of the creative process can be seen in the following anecdote. The young Mozart's father, Leopold, reported that Joseph Haydn (1732–1809), at that time the greatest living composer, said the following to him about his son: "Before God and as an honest man I tell you that your son is the greatest composer known to me either in person or by name; he has taste, and, furthermore, the most profound knowledge of composition" (quoted in Wikipedia, https://en.wikipedia.org/wiki/Haydn_and_Mozart; accessed January 24, 2020).

In conclusion, we have, at the end of the eighteenth century, a two-part conception of the greatest creators – the geniuses. A creative imagination is the first component. The second component is the ability to subject the products of the imagination to a process of judgment, so that the possible excesses of the imagination can be brought within the bounds of "taste" – that is, of rationality (for discussion, see Gerard, 1774, p. 70). (See Table 2.1 for a summary.)

The Genius in the Romantic Era

The overall perspective of the Enlightenment toward genius changed radically during the Romantic era, which lasted from 1775 to 1850, and the changes brought by the Romantics play an important role in our modern conception of genius. The Romantic period can be looked upon as a time of strong negative response to some of the outcomes of the Age of Enlightenment, including political developments, and the consequences of the industrial revolution. One important political development was the American and French revolutions, particularly the latter, with its reign of terror. The reign of terror indicated to many, including the group of poets and other thinkers who would become known as the Romantics, that human rationality did not always have positive outcomes. That negative philosophy was seen in the conception of the creative process developed by the Romantics, one that deviated from the Enlightenment view that rationality and taste were critical components of creativity. The Romantics argued that creativity came about through the direct outpouring of emotion, without control of the will. The Romantics used such terms as *intuition* and *phantasy* to describe the creative process (Becker, 1978, p. 26), demonstrating their conception of the imagination as free and spontaneous. Here is a clear statement of the Romantic view of creativity by the Schlegel brothers, Romantic poets and literary critics:

> The beginning of all poetry is to suspend the course and the laws of rationally thinking reason, and to transport us again into the lovely vagaries of fancy and the primitive chaos of human nature . . . . The free-will of the poet submits to no law. (quoted in Nordau, 1900, p. 73)

The creative process of the genius is subject to no laws; it makes up the laws as it goes (Kant, 1951 [1892]). Throughout the Romantic period, one reads descriptions of the works of the genius that emphasize their mystical and mysterious qualities. Examples of the terms used are the "force of creation," a "natural endowment," an "instinct," and "intuition" (Becker, 1978, p. 27).

Wordsworth, one of the Romantic poets, wrote of the creation of poetry as follows:

> I have said that poetry is the spontaneous overflow of powerful feelings: it takes its origin from emotion recollected in tranquility: the emotion is contemplated till, by a species of reaction, the tranquility gradually disappears, and an emotion, kindred to that which was before the subject of contemplation, is gradually produced, and does itself actually exist in the mind. (Wordsworth, 1899, p. 26)

For the Romantics, the critical points in creation were, first, to be capable of having an intense emotional reaction to one's experiences – seeing a sunset, the face of a beautiful child, the graveyard by a country church – and, second, to be able to re-experience that emotion at a later time and channel it into a work of art. The strength of the poet's original emotion came about through the poet's being able to "commune" with nature – that is, to feel strong emotion in response to the natural world. The genius of the Romantic era is a person who has strong direct feelings about nature and whose imagination is "unfettered" – that is, not subject to constraints on the intensity of feeling.

Development of Genius: Summary

Tracing the development of the conception of genius through two millennia, we have seen large-scale changes in thinking about exceptional creative individuals. There has been a movement away from the idea that the creative process depends on the possession of the creative genius by the muses to the idea that the genius is the possessor of an imagination that is able to respond deeply to the world and is able to transmit those responses to us. We have also seen that there have been two general orientations toward genius in the recent past, that of the Enlightenment versus that of the Romantics. The Enlightenment view emphasized the rational aspect of the creative process, although there was also a place for imagination as the generator of new ideas. The Romantics, on the other hand, placed almost total emphasis on the free imagination as the engine for creativity and said nothing about rationality, except to emphasize that the creative process has to be free of the "laws of rationality." We now turn to a brief examination of modern views of genius, and we will see the strong influence of the Romantics on modern views.

We All Think Like Geniuses? Really? The Modern Genius View

Clear and forceful presentations of what one could call the "Neo-Romantic" genius view are seen in the writings of two distinguished cultural critics, Barzun (e.g., 1960, 1989) and Bloom (2002).

Barzun on Genius

Barzun raised strong objections to any proposal claiming that "creative thinking," as carried out by ordinary folks, could be anything like that carried out by geniuses. He dismissed most attempts to use the term *creativity* to describe everyday activities. As an example of what he considered the meaningless use of the term *creativity*, Barzun reported reading a "Study of Creativity in Everyday Life," which proposed to "illuminate the creative life" (1989, p. 340). The study provided an Index of Creativity, which readers could use to measure themselves as far as their level of creativity was concerned. The scale ranged from Minor Creativity (a secretary who sometimes edits books on the side) to Exceptional (an amateur biologist who limits his hours at work so that he can spend long hours working on botanical experiments). In Barzun's view, those examples did not involve creativity in any meaningful sense: the first involved a desire for autonomy, to do something independent of one's employment responsibilities; and the second was, at most, an "absorbing hobby."

Based on an analysis of the historical development of the term, Barzun (1989, p. 343) concluded that "in the blanket term *creativity* there are at least four layers of meaning." The lowest layer entails the moves toward autonomy, such as that of the secretary editing books. The second involves those people who show a knack for artistic endeavors, say, such as drawing, singing, or dancing; and the activities of the amateur botanist. Those activities are typically reserved for private use. At the next level is the trained artist, who produces novel things but whose work is within the styles set by the times. IDEO's shopping cart might fit here. Finally, we have the genius.

> The genius fashioned masterpieces that startled by their form and substance, thereby proving all rules wrong or futile ... Since the works of genius, being born of a unique imagination, do not resemble one another or those made earlier, each seemed a world complete in itself. The analogy with God's creation became obvious and inevitable. (Barzun, 1989, pp. 342–343)

The works of the genius are startlingly different, and each seems unrelated to anything that came before, even other works by the same person. Thus, each work of genius breaks any rules that might have been established within any discipline. Such results support the claim that some people are like God: they seem to be able to create something from nothing.

In conclusion, Barzun (1989) emphasized the idea that there is something basically different in the thought processes of those exceptionally creative individuals whom we refer to as geniuses. On reading Barzun's discussion of genius, one can see the residue of the religious origins of the genius, as the spirit of a person. That strain is seen also in the writings on genus of Bloom (2002).

Bloom on Genius

Bloom (2002) provided a discussion of 100 literary geniuses. Genius is seen by Bloom, similar to Barzun, in the production of works of complete originality, independent from what has come before. The emergence of the genius cannot be predicted from the environment in which the individual is raised.

> All genius, in my judgment, is idiosyncratic and grandly arbitrary, and ultimately stands alone. A contemporary of Dante could have had precisely his relation to tradition, his exact learning, and something like his love for quite another Beatrice, but only Dante wrote the *Commedia*. (p. xi)

There is something internal to the genius – call it imagination – that takes ordinary experiences, seemingly available to everyone, and turns them into extraordinary products. Bloom (2002) also believed, as we saw in Barzun (1989), that the works of the genius arise independently of the works of others: "Fierce originality is one crucial component of literary genius" (p. 11). Furthermore, Bloom proposed, the works of a genius are also independent from the genius's own earlier works.

> When did Shakespeare become Shakespeare? *The Comedy of Errors* is already a work of genius, yet who could have prophesied *Twelfth Night* on the basis of that early farce? (2002, p. 12)

What, then, is the basis of genius? Bloom places it in the level of consciousness that the person of genius is able to reach:

> Consciousness is what defines genius: Shakespeare, like his Hamlet, exceeds us in consciousness, goes beyond the highest order of consciousness that we are capable of knowing without him. (2002, p. 12)

One sees here the idea of a power of genius – asserting power over us – which also is reminiscent of the religious roots of the concept.

Bloom also made a distinction between talent and genius. Talent means a high level of skill in some domain, but genius brings out things in us that talent cannot.

> We all learn to distinguish, firmly and definitively, between genius and talent. A "talent" classically was a weight or sum of money, and as such, however large, was necessarily limited. But "genius," even in its linguistic origins, has no limits [p. 7] . . . The question we need to put to any writer must be: does she or he augment our consciousness, and how is it done? I find this a rough but effectual test: however I have been entertained, has my awareness been intensified, my consciousness widened and clarified? If not, then I have encountered talent, not genius. What is best and oldest in myself has not been activated. (Bloom, 2002, p. 12)

Modern Views on Genius: Conclusions

Barzun (1989) and Bloom (2002) provided similar descriptions of genius. There is a level of creative achievement, limited to a very small number of us, that defies analysis and understanding. Works of genius come about through the special individual's capacity to experience the world more deeply than the rest of us do: "genius . . . has no limits" (Bloom, 2002, p. 7). This is clearly the residue of the Romantics' emphasis on intensity of emotion as the basis for the creation of poetry of genius. Beyond the arts, the scientist of genius is able, through intellectual power, to understand things that are beyond the ken of the rest of us.

The quasi-religious and worshipful aspect of our feelings toward the genius can be seen far beyond the discussions in the academic literature. As one striking example of the veneration of the genius, a museum in Philadelphia advertises itself as the place where one can see "Einstein's pipe!" Here is a close parallel to the religious relics – the hair of a saint, or other body parts, for example – that are preserved in holy places. Like the saints, the genius can be taken to be our link to God (McMahon, 2013).

The Genius View in Modern Psychology

Although the religious connotations of genius have not been carried forth by modern psychologists, many psychological researchers adhere to aspects of the genius view. As one example, Dean Simonton, an influential researcher on creativity, has edited *The Wiley Handbook of Genius* (2014). In that volume, researchers from a broad range of disciplines discuss various aspects of extraordinarily creative individuals. In addition, Simonton (2011) presents the following quotations in an article.

> Genius does what it must, and Talent does what it can. (Owen Meredith)
>
> Mediocrity knows nothing higher than itself, but talent instantly recognizes genius. (Sir Arthur Conan Doyle)
>
> Talent hits a target no one else can hit; Genius hits a target no one else can see. (Arthur Schopenhauer)

The tone of those quotations points to an unknowable difference between geniuses and the rest of us, which parallels what we saw in Barzun (1989) and Bloom (2002). The message in those quotations typifies the general orientation of most modern discussions of genius.

Furthermore, many psychologists, who may never think about genius in exactly those terms, maintain beliefs about creativity that encapsulate the central assumptions of the genius perspective, although in slightly different clothes. We will, later in the book, examine much research aimed at illuminating the thinking patterns and personality characteristics of creative individuals in comparison with the noncreative. Although the term *genius* might never be used in the articles that present that research, the researchers' interest in that general topic comes out of the same set of beliefs as those that underlie the genius view: creative people are different in basic ways from the rest of us.

To set the stage for the later discussion, we can examine briefly a very influential analysis of creative thinking that can be seen as coming out of the genius perspective, that of Mednick (1962). Mednick's conception of creativity, presented in a single short paper, has shaped the way many modern psychologists think about creativity. Graphic evidence for his influence can be seen in the multiple citations his ideas receive in recent writings (see, for example, Kounios & Beeman, 2015; Vartanian et al., 2018; Volle, 2018; Zabelina, 2018). Although Mednick never mentioned *genius* in his paper, his view encapsulated the basic idea just outlined: that the thought processes of creative people are different than those of noncreative people. In addition, Mednick proposed a psychological mechanism to explain the creative imagination.

The Basis for Creative Genius: Mednick's Associative Hierarchies

In Mednick's (1962) analysis, any situation that demands creative thinking can be analyzed as a set of stimulus elements, each of which has many other elements or ideas associated to it. The thinker's analysis of the situation results in the elements of the situation evoking some subset of all those associated elements. These evoked elements, now "active" in consciousness, can combine to produce a new idea; thinking a new thought is the result of a new combination of elements. Mednick defined the creative thinking process as "the forming of associative elements into new combinations which either meet specified requirements or are in some way useful. The more mutually remote the elements of the new combination, the more creative the process of solution" (p. 221). In other words, to think creatively involves bringing together ideas that are originally far apart ("mutually remote"). The notion that creative thinking depends on bringing together ideas that are "remotely associated" – ideas that are not connected – has become central to many psychologists' thinking about creativity, and we will come across it many times throughout the book.

Mednick's (1962) analysis leads to a simple conception of how individuals may differ in the ability to produce creative ideas. Creative people are somehow able to bring together ideas that are far apart, ideas that noncreative people cannot bring together. The basic component in Mednick's analysis is the *associative hierarchy*, or the organization of an individual's associative responses to a given situation. Some people, those who will *not* think creatively, have restricted or *steep* hierarchies, in which there are one or two dominant responses (see Figure 2.3). Those responses would tend to occur often and quickly and would block production of other responses. Individuals with steep hierarchies would tend to produce stereotyped and familiar responses to a situation, and so would be at a disadvantage when novel responses (i.e., nonstereotyped and unfamiliar responses) are demanded.

Creative individuals, in contrast, possess *flat* associative hierarchies in which are available a relatively large number of responses, of more or less equal probability (Figure 2.3). The flat hierarchy allows the creative thinker to bring together ideas that cannot be connected by the noncreative individual. Individuals with flat hierarchies would have a much greater likelihood of coming up with a relatively unusual response to a situation,

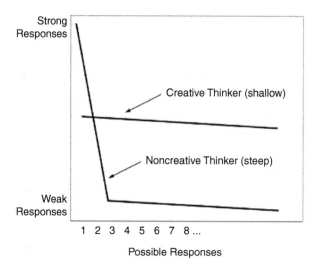

Figure 2.3 Mednick's creative (shallow) and noncreative (steep) associative hierarchies

which could result in a creative outcome. The flat hierarchy is the psychological mechanism underlying genius.

Analytic Thinking in Creativity: The Un-genius View

The view that motivates this book can be looked upon as the opposite of the genius view. The conclusions of Barzun (1989), Bloom (2002), and Mednick (1962) may strike one as right on the mark (see also Murray, 1989a). How can one assume that we ordinary folks carry out the same thought processes that are involved in one of Leonardo's advances or in Picasso creating a masterpiece? However, it must be emphasized that Barzun, Bloom, and Mednick were making empirical – that is, *testable* – claims. Barzun and Bloom seemed to assume that, once one contemplated the creative advances of geniuses, the conclusions they drew would be obvious. That is one way to gather support for one's claims about genius and creativity: present striking examples and assume that everyone will have no choice but to agree with you that those examples are inexplicable. Similarly, Mednick did not provide direct empirical support for his proposal that creative thinking depends on bringing together ideas that are far apart. He seems to have assumed that everyone would agree with his analysis of the creative process, and he then proposed his associative hierarchies as an explanation for the creative process. The flat associative hierarchy is a mechanism that can explain the "unfettered imagination" of the Romantics.

There are, however, other avenues open to someone who is interested in understanding creativity, including creativity at the genius level. One could, for example, examine the development of different sorts of creative products and attempt to determine, as accurately as possible, the thought processes that played a role in their coming into existence. Carrying out that exercise should provide evidence as to whether Barzun (1989) and Bloom (2002) are correct concerning the unanalyzable nature of the thought processes of the genius. Furthermore, if the thought processes of the genius can be analyzed, we should be able to determine if they are totally different than those underlying any other advances that we might want to label as "creative." Putting the discussion in Mednick's (1962) terms, we should be able to determine if seminal creative advances come about as the result of flat associative hierarchies. In other words, do seminal creative advances come about as the result of bringing together previously unrelated ideas? As discussed in Chapter 1, one of the themes underlying the analysis in this book is that we can never take anything for granted in discussing creative thinking. Thus, it is necessary to obtain information that will allow us to determine if creative thinking is indeed based on flat associative hierarchies.

We already have discussed evidence relevant to this question in Chapter 1, and it does not support the genius view. Analysis of Picasso's creation of *Guernica* indicated that it was based on older works by him, as well as those of other artists. When Picasso created *Guernica*, he used ideas that were *already linked* in his mind. Figure 1.7 presented the associative connections assumed to underlie the creation of *Guernica*. Although those connections are based on my speculations, the fact that we can even speculate on the basis for Picasso's thought process raises questions about the genius view. According to Barzun (1989) and Bloom (2002) – and Mednick (1962) – we should not even have been able to construct Figure 1.7. There should be no connections between *Guernica* and other works, and there should also be no connections among the specific ideas that were used in creating *Guernica*. However, the analysis in Chapter 1 indicates that there were such connections.

In conclusion, I propose to do in various places in this book what Barzun (1989) and Bloom (2002) would think is a waste of time. I will carry out additional examinations of genius-level advances, similar to the investigation of *Guernica* carried out in Chapter 1. According to the genius view, we cannot even begin to understand how genius-level advances are brought about. Contrary to that pessimistic view, examining other genius-level advances will provide further evidence that the creative process, even at the highest level, can be analyzed and, perhaps, understood. As we have already seen from consideration of Picasso's creation of *Guernica*, the thought processes of even the genius are not unknowable.

Those additional case studies of genius-level creative accomplishment will also serve to test another claim about genius: that the works of the genius are completely new – that is, each work is independent of what other people have done and even of what the genius has done in the past. We have already seen, from the examination of the development of *Guernica*, that, contrary to Barzun (1989), Bloom (2002), and their interpretation of the genius view, genius-level advances are not completely new. We will carry out additional studies of genius-level creative advances later in the book, and we will find the same pattern of antecedents and influences in each one.

I will then apply the same methods to new ideas and objects produced by nongeniuses. This is a further waste of time from the perspective of Barzun (1989) and Bloom (2002), because they would dismiss those examples as not creative. At this point I ask the reader's indulgence when I analyze those examples of creativity, because, contrary to the claims of Barzun and Bloom, there will be rewards coming from those analyses. Most importantly, we will see that the thought processes involved in nongenius advances are the same as those involved in the genius-level advances. Therefore, the claim that genius-level creativity is in a class all its own will be shown to be incorrect. Putting this conclusion in Mednick's (1962) terms, we shall see that the associative hierarchies of the genius and the nongenius are the same. All creative advances are built out of what we know.

The Question of the "Purity" and "Perfection" of the Works of Genius

There is one issue concerning genius that has been left out of the discussion so far. At the beginning of the section on genius, a quotation from Murray (1989a) was presented, in which she asked an important question:

> If we ask how Mozart was able to compose music of such purity and perfection, ... we can only answer, 'because he was a genius,' which is tantamount to saying that we do not know. For in each age and in each art, genius is that which defies analysis. (1989a, p. 1)

Murray's question seems impossible to answer: How could Mozart have known that what he was producing would be pure and perfect? The question of how Mozart was able to write "pure and perfect" music might not be a question for the cognitive psychologist to try to answer. We have seen that there are two aspects of creativity and, of particular importance here, two aspects of genius. Those two aspects are, first, *how* novel ideas come about and, second, the *value* that we as a society place on those ideas; and those should be separated in our analysis.

The question of how novel ideas come about is in the domain of psychological science and therefore is a question that we can examine, as we began to do in Chapter 1. The "purity" and "perfection" of Mozart's music are related to the *value* that we place on them. Value, as we have seen, depends on factors *outside of the creator* that determine the worth that *we* – the members of society – place on some creative product. We saw earlier, for example, that, according to Csikszentmihalyi (2014), one of the effects of World War I was to change society's attitudes in ways that changed the value of the work of van Gogh. Going back to Murray's (1989a) example, Mozart produces music, and then *we* say: "That music is pure and perfect." That is, we, in exercising our judgment, *make* Mozart's music pure and perfect. The question of how the "purity and perfection" of a creative work come about is one that we will address in several places, but it is not the primary focus of our discussion.

In sum, with all due respect to Barzun (1989), Bloom (2002), and Murray (1989a), I believe that the ideas that motivated the writing of this book will be supported: (1) the creative process, at all levels, is comprehensible; (2) the creative process, at all levels, depends on the cognitive operations that we all carry out all the time in our day-to-day activities; and, therefore (3) we are all capable of creative thinking. We now turn to a review of laboratory research on problem-solving, which will provide the next steps in the journey of trying to understand creative thinking.

PART II

Analytic Thinking in Creativity

3 | Problem-Solving

Problem-Solving that Changed the Course of History:
The Rescue at Dunkirk

World War II began on September 1, 1939, when the German army invaded Poland, its neighbor to the east. Great Britain, France, and their allies declared war on Germany on September 3 but could do little to stop the invasion of Poland. The Poles surrendered after about a month. Great Britain sent a large "expeditionary force" – the British army – to Europe in the fall of 1939. After what became known as the "phoney war" (in British English spelling) of the winter of 1939–1940, when, although war had been declared, no large-scale land battles were fought, the conflict began in earnest in the spring of 1940. The Germans turned westward in early May, invading the Low Countries: Belgium, Luxemburg, and the Netherlands. Those countries too fell relatively quickly, and the Germans continued into France. There also, although fighting was sometimes fierce, the Germans were victorious, driving back the British and French forces and their Belgian allies and, finally, on May 24, pinning them in the area around the city of Dunkirk on the northwest French coast (see Figure 3.1).

The Allied forces were surrounded on three sides by the Germans and had their backs to the sea, a seemingly impossible situation. It would only be a matter of time before the Germans attacked in force, destroying the Allied armies. There were approximately 350,000 troops on the beach at Dunkirk, mostly British and French, waiting for rescue to England. However, the gloomy estimate in London was that perhaps 30,000 could be rescued. That is, the British were resigned to losing 90 percent of the Allies' armies, a blow that would have had devastating effects on their ability to continue fighting the war. In a speech to the House of Commons, British Prime Minister Winston Churchill called the then-evolving situation at Dunkirk "a colossal military disaster" and said that "the whole root and core and brain of the British Army" seemed about to perish or be captured (Lord, 1983). Thus, the British government was faced with a problem of historic magnitude: How could those troops be rescued?

(a)

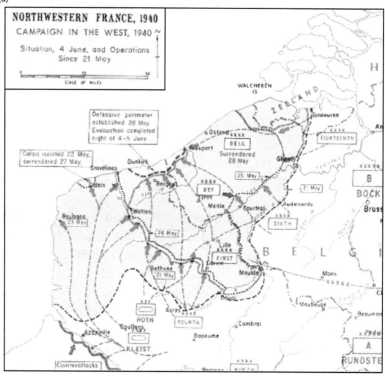

(b)

West Mole   East Mole

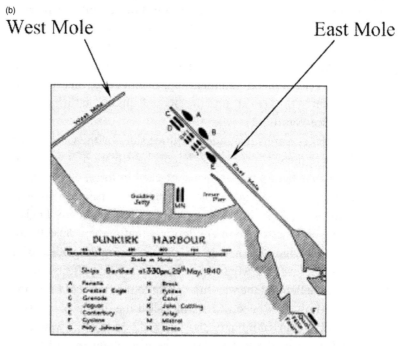

Figure 3.1 A. Map of Dunkirk (Map courtesy of the United States Military Academy Department of History).
B. Dunkirk harbor, 1940 / Crown Copyright 1954.

Dunkirk, a sea-harbor city, was only about twenty miles from England, across the English Channel, and England is a seafaring nation with a large navy, so it might seem that it would be easy to rescue the troops: send a few large ships to Dunkirk harbor, load soldiers aboard, take them to England, and repeat as many times as needed. However, that simple plan could not be carried out, because the main harbor facilities at Dunkirk had been destroyed by German bombings, so there were no docks for large ships. The lack of docking facilities meant that something had to be done from the beach, but evacuating large numbers of troops directly from the beach seemed impossible. The most pressing difficulty was that the water at the beach was shallow, so large ships could not approach close enough to shore to pick up soldiers. If a large ship ran aground, it would be stranded, ripe for destruction by German artillery or by the German air force, which was patrolling the area in force.

There were two seawalls or jetties – called "moles" – at the opening to the harbor (see Figure 3.1). One of them – the east mole – extended from the beach, reasonably close to where the troops were waiting for rescue. However, the moles were not docks: they had not been designed to serve as landings for large ships. There were posts on the moles, where boats could be tied, but they had been used for small harbor craft, not naval vessels. Furthermore, possible docking places alongside the moles were not deep enough to allow a large ship to dock and pick up large numbers of soldiers. In addition, there was, as just noted, the German air force patrolling in the area. Although the British Royal Air Force also had planes over the beach to try to protect the soldiers and ships, there was the possibility that a large ship, full of troops being evacuated, might be bombed by the Germans, resulting in high levels of casualties. How, then, to rescue the troops?

The British Royal Navy solved the evacuation problem by using two inter-coordinated plans. Captain William Tennant, the officer on site in charge of the evacuation, first ordered large ships to come as close to the beach as possible and then have their lifeboats rowed to the beach to pick up soldiers. However, the work was very slow (it took six to twelve hours to fully load a ship with troops), and rowing in the heavy surf was back-breaking, so Tennant searched for other ways. On surveying the scene, he noticed that the east mole had been left relatively undamaged by the German bombings. He therefore decided to try to use it as a dock for smaller naval vessels, such as destroyers. Those ships could navigate in the waters alongside the mole and, if they were able to dock, could load troops directly.

Since the mole had been used before only for small harbor vessels, it was not obvious that it could serve as a dock for naval ships. A relatively large naval vessel might be pushed against the mole by the waves, resulting in damage to the mole and/or the ship. Given the desperate circumstances, however, Tennant ordered a ship to attempt to dock. The docking was successful, and troops were able to walk down the mole to the ship and board relatively easily. Loading 600 men took twenty minutes, instead of over six hours. From then on, a regular cycle of ships was set up, which continued for the remainder of the evacuation. That cycle was disrupted several times, however, by raids by the German air force, which sank several ships near the mole, some loaded with troops. However, 200,000 troops were evacuated from the mole.

Using the mole still did not provide enough docking space to rescue all the troops from the beach quickly enough. In response to that problem, the British produced an additional plan, one that has become legendary. We have already seen that the officers directing the rescue operation knew that small vessels, that did not need deep water to sail in, could approach the beach without running aground. Therefore, a large number of small vessels might be able to serve in the rescue mission. Lifeboats had already been used for exactly that purpose, but, being rowed rather than motorized, they had great difficulties with the surf at the beaches. Also, there were not enough lifeboats available from the vessels at Dunkirk. How, then, to procure a large number of small motorized vessels that could approach close enough to the beaches to rescue the troops there?

The Royal Navy solved that problem by calling into service from England approximately 800 small private boats – called the "small ships": pleasure boats, fishing boats, small commercial boats – to serve as rescue vessels. Many of the small ships were sailed into the battle zone by their civilian-volunteer owners, in an amazing show of bravery. A flotilla of small ships sailed across the Channel toward Dunkirk. They were able to come in close to the beach, where each took on as many soldiers as it could hold. Some of the small ships then ferried their passengers to larger naval vessels farther out at sea, while others took their loads of troops directly to England.

The results of those two rescue operations – the eastern mole and the small ships – changed the course of history. Approximately 325,000 troops were evacuated between May 26 and June 4, ten times more than originally expected, and a catastrophic setback was averted. This event, of obviously major significance historically, is also interesting because it provides two examples of problem-solving under the most difficult of circumstances.

Problem-Solving and Creative Thinking

We are now familiar with three situations in which creative advances came about as the result of problem-solving. One is the Dunkirk rescue, just discussed, which involved multiple examples of problems. We also have the two case studies analyzed in Chapter 1: IDEO's creation of a new shopping cart; and Picasso's creation of *Guernica*. When those case studies were presented in Chapter 1, I did not explicitly discuss how problem-solving was related to creative thinking. It is now time to examine in more detail the thought processes underlying creative advances. That is the purpose of Chapters 3–6 of this book, which will provide the foundation for the analysis of many examples of creative thinking. This chapter begins the discussion, by considering in detail the processes underlying problem-solving.

Outline of the Chapter

The chapter begins with a consideration of the general question of the definition of "a problem." I then discuss how the problem-solving process unfolded in the three examples that we have available: Dunkirk, IDEO's shopping cart, and *Guernica*. Problem-solving is a core component of analytic thinking, so I then specify in detail what we mean when we talk about "analytic thinking," which will equip us with a set of concepts that we can use when we examine problem-solving and creative thinking throughout the rest of the book. I then turn to an examination of laboratory research on problem-solving to provide a more formal description of the processes involved. Finally, we will discuss the mechanisms underlying "green" creativity during problem-solving – the mechanisms underlying the recycling of ideas to deal with a problem. Those mechanisms, generating a possible solution and attempting to extend the old idea to the new situation, are of critical importance in understanding creative thinking. We have already discussed them in the analysis of IDEO's creation of the shopping cart and Picasso's creation of *Guernica*. In this chapter we will look at the relevance of those mechanisms to other situations.

What Is a Problem?

You have a problem when you are in a situation that you do not want to be in and cannot see immediately how to change that situation into one that is more satisfactory. If you cannot immediately carry out some *action* to turn the present situation into a better one, then you must resort to *thinking* (Duncker, 1945). The situation that you do not want to be in is called the *problem state* or the *initial state* of the problem. The situation that you would prefer to be in is the *goal state*. The behaviors that you can carry out to solve the problem are called *moves* or *operators*. Any sequence of moves that transforms the problem state into the goal state is a *solution* to the problem. It is important to note that a situation that is problematic for me may not be so for you: if you know how to bring about the goal, then there is no problem for you. Similarly, the same situation may be problematic for you at one time but not at another. Once you have solved a problem, the next time you encounter that situation it is no longer a problem. Thus, whether a situation is a problem is context-dependent (Novick & Bassock, 2012).

Examples of Problem-Solving

The Rescue of the Troops at Dunkirk

The rescue at Dunkirk provides two examples of problem-solving carried out "in the wild" – that is, in the world – and under the most trying conditions. The successful use of the east mole as a dock for ships was a case of near-analogical transfer, similar to those discussed in Chapter 1. It involved generation of a possible solution based on analogy and the successful extension of that idea to the situation. The use of the small ships to rescue the soldiers on the beach came about through two cycles of *logical analysis* of the situation and *deduction* of a possible solution, followed in each case by an extension of the idea to the new situation. That method is similar to that used by IDEO as part of the process of designing the new shopping cart.

The East Mole

The proposal by Captain Tennant that the east mole could serve as a makeshift dock for small naval vessels was a creative idea, since the mole had not been used that way before. The origin of that idea seems easy to understand, as an example of retrieval based on a near analogy. One way to solve the problem of evacuating a large number of troops from the beach would be to find a substitute for the destroyed docks in Dunkirk harbor.

The mole might be able to meet that need: it extended far into the sea, as a dock does, and the water near it was deep enough for some ships to dock. In addition, it had been used as a dock for small vessels. Thus, the mole possessed some of the characteristics of a dock. The critical questions were, first, whether the mole would be able to withstand the possible battering from a ship being driven against it by the sea and, second, whether a ship might be destroyed by crashing against the rocks. Those uncertainties existed because the mole was only *similar* to a dock for large ships: it was not *actually* such a dock. Captain Tennant took a risk, ordered a ship to try to dock, and had a positive outcome.

   Thus, we can understand the first component of the Dunkirk rescue – using the east mole as a dock – as coming about through analogical transfer, originating because of the overlap of physical characteristics between the mole and a harbor dock. That solution is an example of *green creativity*, since Captain Tennant's knowledge about docking structures served as the basis for the idea to try to use the east mole. Thus, in terms of generation of a new idea, retrieval based on analogical structure served that purpose. During the attempt to extend that idea, there was concern that the east mole could not serve as a dock for naval vessels. Under ordinary circumstances, the east mole might have been rejected, but, given the desperate situation, Captain Tennant decided to take a risk.

The Small Ships

The second component of the Dunkirk rescue problem, the use of the small ships as rescue vessels, came about in two cycles. The first cycle involved dealing with the problem of the too-shallow water at the beach. If the water at the beach is too shallow for large ships, then what else might be used? That question leads to the possibility of sending in small vessels that can maneuver in shallow water. That conclusion was based on logic: if large boats cannot be used because they are too large, try smaller boats. The use of small vessels was the first step in the solution, and it represented a new idea; that is, it was something not thought of before in the Dunkirk context. The idea of using small vessels to carry out the rescue raised a further problem, however, since the Royal Navy did not have available the large number of small boats needed to carry out a rescue plan of the magnitude demanded by the situation at Dunkirk. That second problem was solved by the presence of large numbers of small motor vessels along the English coast. Those vessels became the "small ships" that were called into service. That solution too was based on logic: if you need small boats and you know that there are a lot of small boats available, and you have authority to take over those boats (which the Royal Navy had in time of war), then do so.

A Heuristic Method

The use of logical analysis to deal with a problem is an example of a *heuristic* method, a general method or *rule of thumb* that can be applied to many different sorts of problems. Heuristic methods come into play when one does not possess specific knowledge to bring to bear on a problem. A heuristic method, being potentially applicable to a wide range of problems – think of all the situations that you can analyze, or have analyzed, using logic – is not guaranteed to work for any one of them. However, it is worth trying if nothing else is available, and at Dunkirk it worked. Thus, we have here an example of the production of a solution to a problem, which undoubtedly had a large-scale effect on history, through a small-scale heuristic method, logical thinking, which is something we all do all the time.

IDEO's Creation of a New Shopping Cart

When IDEO was asked to design a new shopping cart, that request set a problem for them. The solution involved a complex set of processes and, as we know, demanded creative thinking.

Gathering Information: Another Heuristic Method

The first thing the IDEO team did was to go into the field to do research. They observed and interviewed people who used shopping carts on a regular basis, looking for problems with the old cart that their new cart could solve. The reason they had to carry out research was that they did not know much about shopping carts beyond what we all know from our visits to supermarkets. That first step in IDEO's creative process is another heuristic method, also applicable to a wide variety of problems. Indeed, IDEO applies that *gathering-information heuristic* to many projects that they deal with, because they are not experts in everything.

Solving Shopping-Cart Problems

IDEO's research on shopping carts provided them with information about numerous problems, including difficulties maneuvering bulky carts; safety issues involving children; and problems getting close to the items one wanted to buy, due to crowded store aisles. Analytic thought processes that were utilized in solving those problems included using logical reasoning to deduce conclusions from information in the problem. That heuristic played a role in IDEO's decision to use plastic baskets in the cart to make it unusable as a barbecue. The IDEO team also demonstrated *green creativity*, using analogical reasoning to transfer knowledge from similar situations (use casters for all the wheels; use the seat design from amusement-park rides as the basis for the child's seat).

In conclusion, the IDEO team attacked the overall problem of designing a new shopping cart by first acquiring information about problems with shopping carts and then solving those problems using analytic thinking. They then combined the solutions to those problems into a new cart. Breaking down the problem into parts – into what can be called *subproblems* – is another heuristic method (Best, 1987).

Picasso Creating Guernica: Problem-Solving at the Genius Level

Picasso's creation of *Guernica*, which also entailed problem-solving, is perhaps more important for us than the Dunkirk and IDEO examples, because *Guernica* represents genius-level creativity. It might be argued that the rescue from Dunkirk, and the new shopping cart, while no doubt creative achievements (and, in the case of the Dunkirk rescue, an event of great historical importance), did not represent creative thinking at the highest level. That argument is harder to make against *Guernica*, because it has been acknowledged by many as being a work of genius (Chipp, 1988). Therefore, conclusions drawn from examination of Picasso's creative process have relevance for evaluating the genius view – that is, the broader question of the thought processes underlying creative thinking at the highest level.

Creation of *Guernica* involved Picasso's solution of several problems. The first was posed when he initially was asked to create a painting for the Spanish government's pavilion at the Paris Exposition. He had to decide on the subject of his painting. He began creating a painting of an artist and model in the studio, something he had done before. Thus, that first step in Picasso's creative process involved green creativity, recycling an idea. He was working out the details for *The Studio* – solving additional problems – when news of the bombing reached Paris. The news of the tragedy at Guernica set a new problem for Picasso, for which *Guernica* was the solution. It was an adaptation of his etching *Minotauromachy*, a bullfight scene, with the addition of some other features – the broken statue; the people and buildings on fire; the dead baby – presumably in response to the specific event that stimulated it. That is, Picasso again demonstrated green creativity. As we also know, Picasso did not conceive the new composition whole. He first thought of a general idea concerning the structure of the new work, and he then filled in the details of that idea – solving additional problems – and in so doing went beyond the bullfight. He extended the old idea to the new situation. He used his knowledge of other artists' works, as well as of his own, as the basis for creating something new.

We have now looked at several examples of real-world problem-solving and have found similarities among the processes involved. We can now carry out a more detailed analysis of problem-solving and its relationship to creative thinking based on laboratory research.

Weak versus Strong Methods for Solving Problems

Psychologists distinguish among several types of solution methods that people use when solving problems. One can conceive of a continuum of methods, based on the specificity of the match between the method and the problem. At one end of this continuum are the *heuristic methods*, the general rules of thumb. The decision to apply a heuristic method is based on very general characteristics of the problem. For example, no specific information from the problem plays a role in the application of a heuristic such as "logically analyze the situation you are facing." Researchers call heuristics *weak* methods of solving problems, because they are based on only a general match with the problem, which means that there is a chance that a heuristic might not work. That is why they are "weak." Heuristic methods were seen in the Dunkirk and IDEO problem-solving examples.

The second class of methods is based on the transfer of knowledge to a problem, which depends on a more precise match between the problem and the person's knowledge. These methods are called *strong* methods, because there is a higher chance that they will be useful. Strong methods were seen in all the case studies of creative thinking. Captain Tennant's use of the east mole as a dock was based on his expertise, as was the Royal Navy's calling the small ships into service. IDEO's use of casters as the wheels for their new cart, as well as the transfer of the safety seat from an amusement-park ride to the cart, were the result of strong methods. Similarly, Picasso's use of *Minotauromachy* as the basis for the structure of *Guernica*, as well as his using other artists' works as the basis for several of the specific characters in the painting were examples of strong methods. Strong methods underlie green creativity.

At the far end of the continuum, opposite to heuristics, are *algorithms*, a type of strong method that is based on formal rules for solving a class of problems. If an algorithm can be applied to a problem, and if that algorithm is carried out correctly, it guarantees that the correct solution will be produced. One set of algorithms that we all know is the rules for arithmetic. If you are given an addition problem, for example, and if you correctly carry out the rules of addition, you will produce the correct answer. Using an algorithm to solve a new problem involves little in the way of creativity, since the method used on the new problem, while not identical to what you have done in the past, is nonetheless very similar. From the perspective of trying to understand creative thinking, both weak methods (heuristics) and strong methods (transfer of knowledge to a new problem) may be more interesting. As we examine more examples of creative thinking, ranging from seminal innovations to smaller-scale achievements in a variety of contexts, we shall see the range of methods that people can bring to the task of producing new things. We will see more evidence that both weak and strong methods contribute to creative advances at the highest levels, with implications for the genius view of creativity.

Components of Analytic Thinking and Their Possible Role in Creativity

If we are to entertain seriously the possibility that analytic thinking under-lies creativity, it is necessary that we obtain a fuller understanding of the components of analytic thinking. I will first examine the general compo-nents of analytic thinking and then consider more specific components.

General Components of Analytic Thinking

General characteristics of analytic thinking, some of which are already familiar from the earlier discussion, are listed in Table 3.1. First, there is *structure* in analytic thinking, which means that thoughts typically follow one another in regular ways. Since at least Aristotle, it has been recognized that thoughts can be linked through *associations* – that is, connections between them (Mandler & Mandler, 1964). Associative connections come about because our thoughts often mirror our experiences. If two experi-ences have been linked in our past, then the thoughts referring to those

Table 3.1 *General characteristics of analytic thinking*

Analytic thinking has *structure*: our thoughts follow one from another, or are related to one another.

Analytic thinking *depends on the past*: analytic thinking exhibits *continuity* with the past.

Analytic thinking demonstrates *top-down processing*: knowledge and concepts direct analytic thinking.

Analytic thinking *can be influenced by environmental events*: analytic thinking is *sensitive to environmental events.*

experiences will also be linked. Meeting a friend brings to mind thoughts of experiences you have shared, as well as thoughts of other friends with whom you shared those experiences.

Thoughts can also be linked through logical connections. One thought can be associated with other thoughts because it follows from those thoughts as the conclusion of an act of reasoning. An example is IDEO's concluding that plastic baskets would be useful in their shopping cart because they could not serve as a barbecue. Finally, one thought can bring another to mind because the situations that the thoughts refer to are similar in various ways, including having analogous structures. At Dunkirk, the need to have a structure available at which ships could dock to take on soldiers might cause one to think about the east mole. That is, when Captain Tennant was thinking about the need for a dock, his attention might have switched to the east mole and, if he was on the beach, his eye might have been drawn there.

The second general component of analytic thinking is that it is dependent on the past. It uses the past, in the form of our knowledge, to deal with the present (and, also, as we shall see, to deal with the future). That mechanism underlies green creativity. Another way of saying this is that analytic thinking exhibits *continuity with the past*. We make no radical breaks with the past when we deal with the present. Green creativity shows continuity with the past in such examples as Picasso's building *Guernica* on the foundation of *Minotauromachy*, IDEO's using casters on a new shopping cart, and the Royal Navy's use of the east mole as a dock.

When we use the past as the basis for dealing with the present, one can say that the past – our knowledge – is *directing* our thinking, which is the third characteristic of analytic thought. Psychologists call such a situation *top-down processing*, because information "from the top" – that is, our knowledge – plays a directing role in our dealing with a problem in the

here-and-now (Weisberg & Reeves, 2013). *Bottom-up processing*, the opposite of top-down processing, occurs when the thinker's efforts are based
directly on the objects and events in the environment, with knowledge
playing a minimal role. An example of bottom-up processing would be if
one tried to open a combination lock by randomly turning the dial, hoping
to hit on the correct sequence of numbers. In contrast, the Royal Navy used
its collective knowledge to determine that large ships could not carry out
the Dunkirk rescue. Picasso's using the structure of *Minotauromachy* as the
basis for the structure of *Guernica* was also an example of top-down
direction. Still another example of top-down processing occurred when
the IDEO team used their knowledge to direct the design of the child's
safety seat in their shopping cart. Any time a person uses a strong method
to solve a problem, top-down processing is directing the solution process.
In other words, top-down processing plays an important role in extending
an old idea to a new situation.

Finally, although analytic thinking exhibits continuity with the *past*, it is
not completely disconnected from the *present*. An important feature of
analytic thinking is that it is sensitive to environmental events. Our attention can be "captured" by significant events in the world, and those events
can cause a change in the direction of our chain of thought (Weisberg &
Reeves, 2013). An obvious example of that sensitivity is the change in
direction in Picasso's creative process when he learned about the bombing
of Guernica. Similarly, on hearing from a team member about the numerous accidents suffered by children in their interactions with shopping carts,
IDEO's team decided that one component of their new shopping cart had
to be a safer seat for children.

We now understand the general characteristics of analytic thought
and how they contributed to the examples of creative thinking that we
have reviewed. We should also consider specific components of analytic thinking, because that will lead to a deeper understanding of the
role of analytic thinking in creativity. As we shall see, we have, all our
lives, been using analytic thinking in creative ways without giving it a
second thought.

Specific Components of Analytic Thinking

Table 3.2 presents some of the specific activities that a person might be
referring to when replying to the question "What are you doing?" by saying
"I'm thinking." Those specific activities are not independent; there are
overlaps among them, which is reflected in the structure of Table 3.2.

Table 3.2 *Specific components of analytic thinking*

Thought Activity		Processes Involved	Creativity?
Remembering		Retrieval of information from memory	No
	Remembering using imagination	Recalling experienced event	No
Imagining		Imagining (creating) new event	Yes
Planning		Familiar event: memory	No
		New event: creative imagination	Yes
	Anticipating the outcome of an action	Familiar circumstances: memory	No
		New circumstances: creative imagination	Yes
	Judging the acceptability of the outcome of an action	Familiar circumstances: memory	No
		New circumstances: creative imagination	Yes
	Deciding between plans of action	Familiar circumstances: memory	No
		New circumstances: creative imagination	Yes
Perceiving a pattern in a set of experiences		Inductive reasoning: new conclusion/generalization is formed	Yes
Interpretation of information		Language and perceptual processes	___
	Comprehension of verbal information	Verbal comprehension processes	Perhaps – new information acquired
	Recognizing that a conclusion follows from a set of statements or that statements are contradictory	Logical reasoning processes	Yes – results in a new thought
	Interpreting a picture or diagram	Visual comprehension processes	Perhaps – new information acquired
	Deriving implications from a picture or diagram	Reasoning based on visual information	Yes – results in new information

Remembering

Perhaps the simplest situation involving thinking is *remembering* an event that you experienced ("I'm thinking about that party we went to"). That activity would involve little or no creativity, since nothing new is produced. An act of recall could be based on one's *imagining* being at the party ("I can clearly see that ugly shirt that Joe was wearing"), but the creativity is, nonetheless, nil. As we have seen, remembering can also be triggered by analogical similarity between events. An event you are immersed in now can trigger recall of information from analogous events. That remembering can begin the creative process, although remembering itself is not a creative act.

Imagining

In addition to remembering some experience by imagining it, one can imagine something that one has never experienced, such as when you say to yourself, "It's a good thing that John was not at the party because, if he had seen his girlfriend Jane getting friendly with Joe, he might have started a fight." If you can imagine that interaction occurring, you are using imagery in a creative manner, since you are producing something new. If, before painting or drawing anything, Picasso imagined a character in *Guernica* based on a transformation of one of the characters in Goya's *Disasters of War*, that would be creative imagery.

Planning

A similar analysis applies to *planning*. You can plan to do something based directly on memory, with minimal creativity, as when you plan a holiday dinner based on previous holiday dinners. However, you can also plan an activity that you have never carried out before, which is a creative act. Imagination plays a role in such planning. Picasso's use of composition sketches in the creation of *Guernica* would be an example of planning. Although those sketches might have been based on *Minotauromachy*, they were nonetheless different from *Minotauromachy* and so were an example of planning as a creative act. Planning is an example of executive functioning.

  The general act of planning is built out of several specific components (see Table 3.2). An important part of planning entails *anticipating the outcome of an action*. You can anticipate the outcome of an action that you have never carried out before, in which case you would be using your imagination in support of creative thinking. That would be a critical component of attempting to extend an idea to a new situation after it had been generated. For example, as just mentioned, you might conclude that seating a certain pair of people next to each other at your holiday dinner might result in a negative outcome, because the two people's political beliefs are in opposition and both are outspoken. Those circumstances could lead to a disagreement. Anticipating such a disagreement, which is something that you have not experienced, would be a creative act. Similarly, Captain Tennant's concern about whether the east mole at Dunkirk could serve as a dock, which led him to experiment with one ship attempting to dock, was based on his anticipation of possible problems.

Related to that act of anticipation is using *judgment* to determine the acceptability of the outcome of that action. Using judgment in this way is also a component of the action of *deciding* between two alternative plans of action, which uses *imagination* to generate possible outcomes and *judgment* to choose among them. It also involves executive functioning. You might be thinking about rearranging the furniture in a room but then decide against one possible plan, because you can "see" that that arrangement would make it difficult to move around in the room. That is, you try to extend the idea to the situation, and you find that it will not work. The Royal Navy's decision not to send large ships directly to rescue the troops on the beach at Dunkirk was based on the realization that those ships would run aground, which was an anticipation of a negative outcome. That realization came about as the result of the attempt to extend the new idea to the current situation.

This complex form of activity was also seen in Picasso's creation of *Guernica*. In the last composition sketch, he drew an upraised arm in the center of the picture (see Figure 1.3C). When he began to paint on canvas, that arm was there, but he began to modify it and then removed it completely (see Figures 1.4A and 1.4B). One hypothesis as to why he did that is that he came to the decision the upraised arm was a too-obvious symbol of Communism, which would have made the painting more overtly political than he wanted it to be (Chipp, 1988). That would be an example of evaluation – of judging an outcome of an action as unacceptable – and modifying the situation to remove that unacceptable aspect.

Interpretation of Information

An additional set of analytic-thinking processes centers on interpretation of information obtained through language or through perception. The act of *comprehending* verbal or other information results in your acquiring new information. Acts of comprehension play a role in creative thinking. The Royal Navy's understanding of the conditions at the beach at Dunkirk led to the realization that use of large ships was impossible. IDEO's understanding of the information conveyed to them by the people they interviewed played a significant role in the team's formulation of the problems that their new cart would have to solve. Similarly, Picasso's understanding of the images printed in the Paris newspapers the day after Guernica was bombed played into his creative process.

A related thought process, based specifically on comprehension of language, involves the relationship between two or more verbal messages. Speakers of a language are capable of *recognizing* that one statement follows from another, or, in contrast, that two statements are contradictory. Those skills, which are part of our linguistic competence, result in our acquiring new information but in this case that information depends on the structure of an argument that someone is making. If the argument is one not encountered before, the person is carrying out creative thinking in drawing that positive or negative conclusion.

Components of Analytic Thinking: Conclusions

When we say that a person is thinking, we are referring to the skills just enumerated, plus others. One perhaps surprising conclusion that arises from this brief exposition is that many of our "ordinary" thought processes contain within them a grain of creativity, since carrying them out can result in a novel outcome. Producing a major creative advance like *Guernica*, for example, involves many of those processes working together in a complex manner in which each process may be called on multiple times.

Creative Thinking and Problem-Solving

The discussion of the components of analytic thinking provides support for the proposal that we can begin to understand creative thinking, even genius-level creative thinking, using the methods of psychological science. We now turn to perhaps the most important question facing the psychological study of creativity: How is creative thinking able to formulate new ideas? One way to begin to answer that question is to review laboratory research on problem-solving, which may be the simplest situation in which creative thinking is carried out.

Is All Creativity Based on Problem-Solving?

Studying problem-solving may also be important for understanding creativity for another reason: Newell and Simon, pioneers in the study of problem-solving, proposed that *all* creative thinking is problem-solving (Newell, Shaw & Simon, 1962; Newell & Simon, 1972). That proposal may be too strong, because one can question whether *every* painter when painting a picture is solving a problem; or whether *every* poet when writing a poem is solving a problem (Weisberg, 2006). Nonetheless, we have seen that problem-solving played a significant role in the Dunkirk rescue, IDEO's development of the new shopping cart, and Picasso's creation of *Guernica*. Even if problem-solving might not be relevant to all creative advances, there is no doubt that it is relevant to a wide range of them. Therefore, understanding the processes underlying problem-solving will provide us with insight concerning creative thinking.

Verbal Protocols as a Window into the Thinking Process

Psychologists hoping to obtain detailed information concerning thought processes sometimes ask people to think aloud – to provide a running verbal stream of thought or *verbal protocol* – as they deal with problems and other situations that demand thinking. Much useful information concerning mental processes has been obtained through the collection of verbal protocols since the method was introduced by the Gestalt psychologists almost 100 years ago (e.g., Duncker, 1945; Wertheimer, 1982). However, there are some precautions that must be taken when collecting verbal protocols. First, some thoughts may be difficult to put into words, and asking people to try to verbalize those thoughts might interfere with the thought processes that one hopes to study. Therefore, it is important to be confident that the collection of a protocol did not interfere with the thinking process. One must instruct the participants that it might not be possible for them to verbalize everything that comes across their mind as they carry out some task. They should do the best they can to verbalize everything, but they should not worry about things that they are unable to verbalize.

In addition, analyses by Ericsson and Simon (1996) have indicated that other aspects of the instructions given to the experimental participants can have a significant effect on whether collecting verbal protocols interferes with the thought processes. It must be emphasized to the people in the experiment that they should just let the words flow as they are working, as if they were talking to themselves, without providing reasons for anything that they do. When people provide reasons, that will interfere with and/or significantly change their performance. If they make no judgments and just provide an unedited stream of verbalization, accepting the fact that not everything can be verbalized, then the protocol can be used as evidence concerning the thought processes underlying the observed behavior.

It is also of critical importance that the researcher provide evidence that collecting protocols did not interfere with the thinking process. The best way to do that is to include a non-protocol control condition in every situation in which protocols are collected (Fleck & Weisberg, 2004, 2013; Weisberg & Suls, 1973). One can then make detailed comparisons of various measures of performance between the protocol and non-protocol conditions, to demonstrate that those measures are not affected by asking people to think aloud. Examples of such measures in an experiment on problem-solving might be the proportion of people solving the problem, how long it takes them to solve it, and the kinds of methods that they use. If there are no differences across any of those sorts of measures of behavior, then one can feel confident that collecting the protocols did not interfere with the thought processes being carried out by the participants. When I discuss studies that have collected verbal protocols, in this chapter and elsewhere, they will have followed the guidelines just presented.

Laboratory Investigations of Problem-Solving: Introduction

The next several sections of the chapter present results from laboratory investigations of problem-solving. The specific problems that were chosen for discussion provide evidence concerning several different sorts of methods – weak and strong – that play a role in problem-solving. The first problem, the Triangle of Coins (Fleck & Weisberg, 2013), is one for which people do not possess any detailed, or problem-specific, knowledge that they can transfer to the problem. This problem provides information concerning the ways in which heuristic methods contribute to creative thinking. The second problem, the Candle Problem (Fleck & Weisberg, 2004), is different, because it is one in which people can bring strong methods to bear in working out a solution. Examination of performance on that problem will provide information concerning the central question raised by the notion of *green creativity*: How are people able to recycle old ideas in new situations?

Before reading further, please try to solve the Triangle of Coins problem, presented in Figure 3.2. If possible, try to work by arranging ten objects as in the figure (coins, buttons, paper clips, whatever) and manipulating them in order to try to produce the solution.

Problem: The triangle (A) below points to the bottom of the page. How can you move only three coins and make the triangle point to the top of the page, as in B?

A   B

Solution: Coins to be moved are at the bottom, top left, and top right.

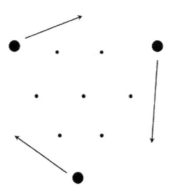

Figure 3.2 The Triangle of Coins problem

Heuristic Methods in Solution of the Triangle of Coins: Hill-Climbing plus Logic

Fleck and Weisberg (2013) observed people in the laboratory as they thought aloud while they tried to solve the Triangle of Coins problem, and found some sophisticated methods being developed in real time. One method that people used was a variant on what is called the *hill-climbing* heuristic: they carried out a reasoning process as they tried to transform the problem situation so that it became more similar to the goal. They were "climbing the hill" toward the goal. The description that follows is not taken from a specific protocol; rather, it distills the general characteristics of how hill-climbing was sometimes applied to the problem. For details, see Fleck & Weisberg (2013). In Figure 3.3A, the coins are replaced by numbers, which will make clear how people used hill-climbing to solve it.

- If one moves the single coin (#10) from the bottom to the top (Figure 3.3B), there is now one coin on top, "pointing up."
- Working down from that new top coin, some of the remaining rows need to be changed.
- The new second row, which contains four coins, must be changed to one with two coins, which can be accomplished by removing the two end coins (#1 and #4; Figure 3.3C).
- The new third row contains three coins, so it does not have to be changed.
- The new fourth row contains two coins, and it needs to have four; the two coins available from the second row fit there (Figure 3.3D), which solves the problem.

We see that, in solving the Triangle of Coins, people construct a solution by using spatial-reasoning skills to transform the initial display into the desired goal. The method combines the general heuristic strategy of hill-climbing with the more specific heuristics of logical and arithmetic analysis of the intermediate steps to determine exactly which move should be carried out next. In the example in Figure 3.3A–D, each of the moves results from the person's analysis of the then-current configuration of coins combined with the understanding of how the solution triangle must look, based on memory of the interpretation of the instructions. The specific configuration of the solution is not given in the instructions for the problem, which just say to "make it so that the triangle points up." That means the individual must have *created* a representation of the solution, detailed enough so that it can be used to monitor progress toward the goal. Construction of that representation in response to the instructions is itself a small-scale creative act. It should also be noted that each of those intermediate states, as the triangle is gradually being transformed, is also the result of a creative act. We see here several examples of how an individual can use heuristic methods as he or she tries to extend an old idea to a new situation.

A) Problem as presented (numbers replace coins):

B) Participant moves bottom coin (**10**) to the top center (Hill-Climbing – making the situation more like the goal); has moved one coin:

C) Participant counts coins in each row; sees that the second row has two coins too many; moves corner coins (**1** and **4**) off that row; has moved three coins:

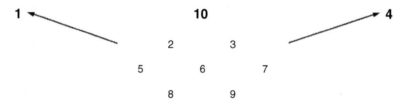

D) Bottom row is now missing two coins, one at each end; moves coins **1** and **4** to the ends of that row; has still moved only three coins; problem solved:

Figure 3.3 Diagrams to complement Triangle of Coins protocol presented in Heuristics

Heuristic Methods in Problem-Solving and Creative Thinking: Summary

The results we have reviewed so far come from a knowledge-lean labora-tory problem – a problem about which the person does not possess detailed knowledge – that was solved through heuristic methods. Even though a person might be faced with a problem for which they do not possess specific knowledge, that does not mean that they can do nothing about solving it. People can develop relatively sophisticated solution methods based solely on heuristics. Knowledge-lean problems are laboratory analogues of the situation that IDEO's team found itself in when it was asked to design a new shopping cart. There were two cycles of heuristic methods used in carrying out that project. First, the IDEO team carried out research in the problem domain, which is a heuristic method and which allowed them to discover several problems with shopping carts that their new cart could solve. Second, a number of those shopping-cart problems were solved through the use of heuristic methods, mainly logical reasoning. Similarly, the Royal Navy used reasoning to determine that the only way to rescue the large number of troops on the beach at Dunkirk was through the use of small vessels.

One can also find examples of heuristic methods in Picasso's creation of *Guernica*. We concluded that Picasso used the structure of *Minotauromachy* as the basis for the overall composition of *Guernica*. The first sketches that Picasso produced were composition sketches, meaning that he started with that overall structure and then worked on the individual characters. That could be taken as an example of planning. Thus, the use of heuristic methods is not limited to people participating in laboratory investigations of problem-solving. Similar examples of the use of heuristic methods will be noted when we examine other creative advances later in the book.

Beyond Heuristic Methods: Green Creativity in the Solution of Knowledge-Rich Problems

Although heuristic methods can play a significant role in creative thinking, many real-world creative advances involve knowledge-rich problems – that is, problems for which people possess knowledge about the objects and requirements. One can begin to solve such problems by attempting to transfer that knowledge using strong methods and green creativity. One then tries to extend any retrieved ideas to the new situation. I now turn to consideration of the Candle Problem (Fleck & Weisberg, 2004), which will provide us with a laboratory demonstration of green creativity and with more information concerning the mechanisms through which an old idea can be transferred to a problem.

Before reading further, please take a few minutes to try mentally to solve the Candle Problem, presented in Figure 3.4. Use a piece of paper to jot down notes, in as much detail as you can, concerning the specifics of your proposed solutions.

Let's say that there has been a power outage, so that your home is dark. You need to read some material in preparation for a quiz tomorrow. Given the materials below, how could you attach the candle to the wall so that it would provide light for you to read?

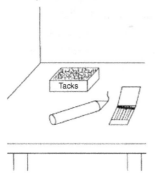

Figure 3.4 The Candle Problem

Green Creativity in the Solution of the Candle Problem

The Candle Problem was introduced to psychology many years ago, by Duncker (1945), and has been part of the domain ever since (e.g., Glucksberg & Weisberg, 1966; Weisberg & Suls, 1973; Fleck & Weisberg, 2004). The problem is simple, involving only a few items, but people are remarkably clever in devising solutions to the difficulty it poses. Some typical solutions to the Candle Problem are presented in Figure 3.5. Although the situation is highly "concentrated," we will see multiple examples of creation of new ideas and will gain insight concerning how new ideas develop out of attempts to extend old ideas to new situations – that is, how green creativity works.

Recycling Ideas: A Partial Match with Knowledge as the First Step in Green Creativity

People attempting to solve the candle problem exhibit a consistent pattern of behavior (Fleck & Weisberg, 2004; Weisberg & Suls, 1973). Almost everyone begins by at least contemplating attaching the candle to the

A1) Tack – Possible Solution

B1) Wax "Glue" – Possible Solution

A2) Tack – Candle Modified

B2) Wax "Glue" – Candle Modified

A3) Tack Wedge

A+B) Wax "Glue" + Tack – Candle Modified

A4) Tack + Tack "Hanger"

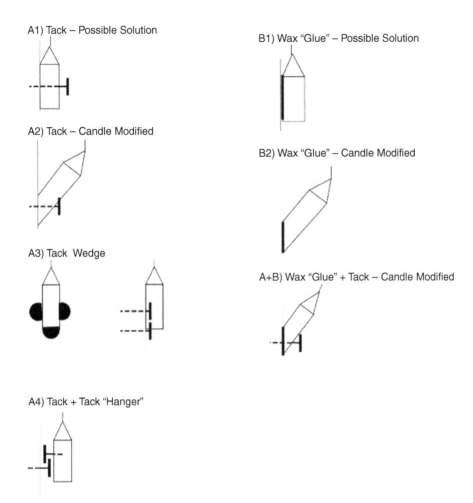

Figure 3.5 Solutions to the Candle Problem: tacks and wax

wall, by using the tacks, or using wax melted from the candle as an adhesive. (See Figure 3.5A1 and B1.) Since most people have never used tacks to attach a candle to the wall, or used melted wax to affix a candle to a vertical surface, just thinking of tacking a candle to the wall is a creative idea, as is thinking about "gluing" it to the wall.

We can now consider how those novel ideas arose. Everyone knows how to use tacks to fasten *things* to a wall, and they can apply that knowledge to the Candle Problem. A candle is a "thing," so using tacks in the Candle Problem is analogous to what people have done in the past. That is why that type of solution might come to mind. Concerning the possible use of wax as an adhesive, many people know that candle wax has weak adhesive properties (think of wax seals on letters); and some people have specifically used candle wax as an adhesive, to hold a candle in a candlestick or to help it to stand steady on a table top. Those experiences entailed using melted wax in attaching a candle to a *horizontal* surface, and the Candle Problem requires that a candle be attached to a *vertical* surface. Those two situations also are analogous: if one ignores "horizontal" versus "vertical," the situations are identical. Both "attaching" solutions – again, *creative ideas* – came about through transferring old ideas to the problem, because the old and new situations are *near* analogues.

We see here the basic mechanism underlying green creativity. Old ideas can be activated, based on a *partial match* between the new situation and the one in which those ideas were originally acquired. Contemplating the possibility of tacking the candle to the wall was based on the problem instructions – that the candle was to be attached to the wall – combined with the presence of tacks in the problem. Those features of the problem were sufficient to produce retrieval of knowledge about using tacks. Similarly, contemplating using melted wax as glue to attach the candle to the wall was based on a partial match between the information in the problem and people's experiences "attaching" candles using melted wax (Fleck & Weisberg, 2004; Weisberg & Suls, 1973). Thus, when facing a problem, one can retrieve an idea that was not in one's past directly associated with the problem. One can retrieve an idea from a related situation, an analogous situation that overlaps only partially with the problem.

Moving beyond Initial Ideas: Extending an Old Idea to a New Situation

Assume that the initial new ideas in the Candle Problem, as exemplified by the "attaching" approaches to the problem just discussed – tacks and wax-glue – come about as the result of retrieval of old ideas by the new situation, based on partial overlap. That is the first step in green creativity. However, the Candle Problem is more complex than it appears, because there are difficulties that arise as a person tries to extend those possible solutions to the problem. People's attempts to overcome those difficulties provide a window into further details of the green creative process, as additional new ideas emerge out of the ongoing interaction between the person and the situation.

Criteria for Tacking a Candle to the Wall

Consider the people who begin by contemplating using tacks to attach the candle to the wall (Figure 3.5A1). They then try to extend the tacking idea to tacking a candle. Some of those people, on examining the objects in the problem, conclude that the tacks are not long enough to go through the candle and into the wall (see Figure 3.4). That realization demonstrates the precision of the information that people use in trying to extend their knowledge to a new situation. Through using their imaginations to generate possible outcomes, people can determine whether a possible solution is worth pursuing. The fact that we can make precise judgments about what one can do with tacks provides a graphic example of the wide range of detailed information we have available that can be used in imagining the outcomes of actions.

Variations on Old Ideas

We now have a person who began by thinking about tacking the candle to the wall but then decided that that solution would not work because the tacks were too small. In response to the realization that the candle is too thick for a tack to pass through it and into the wall, there are two options that might come to mind, based on a logical analysis of the situation (a heuristic method): (1) make the tack longer (or find a longer tack); or (2) make the candle thinner. The former option is not possible: the tacks cannot be modified; and longer tacks are not available. Therefore, the person may concentrate on attempting to modify the candle, to make it thinner. That is another new idea, and it comes about because people's knowledge about candles includes the information that candle wax becomes soft and pliable when heated. That information opens several paths to overcoming the "too-fat-candle" difficulty. One way to do that, shown in Figure 3.5A2, is to warm the bottom of the candle to make it soft and pliable and then press and spread it to reduce its thickness. That might make it possible for the tack to pass through the candle and into the wall.

Another way to overcome the problem of the too-fat candle is to bypass entirely the thickness of the candle, by wedging tacks into its sides and bottom, so they hold it snugly enough so that it stays up, as shown in the front and side views in Figure 3.5A3. Still other people deal with the small-tacks difficulty in a very different way, by using two tacks, with their heads overlapping, to construct a "hanger" for the candle, as shown in Figure 3.5A4.

In sum, we have seen several different solutions to the Candle Problem, using the tacks in various ways (Figure 3.5A2–4). Those solutions are produced in response to difficulties arising from the individual's attempt to extend, to the new situation, the old idea retrieved by the problem. The individual's initial attempts to use the objects in the problem are not successful, which results in modifications to those initial attempts. Once again, it must be emphasized that those are creative responses to the situation: those solutions, although unsuccessful, are *novel*. A similar set of conclusions arises from examination of the actions of the people who initially think about trying to use the wax as glue to hold the candle to the wall (Figure 3.5B1), to which I briefly turn.

Problems Gluing a Candle to the Wall

Using melted wax to attach the candle to the wall is also difficult to implement. When one softens one side of the candle and then presses the softened wax to the wall, it is usually not strong enough to hold the candle. In response to that "too-weak-adhesive" difficulty, an individual may try to enlarge the surface area of the part of the candle that is softened and contacts the wall, to increase the probability that the softened wax will be able to work. That response would be based in part on a logical analysis of the situation, combined with imagination. We know that applying glue over a wider area increases the glue's holding power (see Figure 3.5B2). Here is further evidence of the detailed nature of our knowledge about everyday objects. Finally, in response to the possible continuing weakness of the wax-glue, the individual may use a tack, in combination with the softening and flattening of the candle, as shown in Figure 3.5A–B. These results with wax-glue support those just discussed concerning the subtleties in the thought processes underlying extending an old idea – in this case, the possible use of the tacks to attach the candle to the wall.

Beyond Attaching Solutions: Candle Holders and Shelves

What we have seen here is the role of failure in stimulating creative ideas. The feedback from a failed solution provides new information to the person, which serves as the basis for a reconsideration of the problem. That new analysis can result in significant "advances," beyond the ideas with which the people began. In attempting to deal with the obstacles that arise when trying to tack or glue the candle to the wall, some people conclude that neither of those attaching solutions will work. Those individuals may then consider the possibility of making some sort of *shelf* for the candle, which takes them further beyond the relatively simple initial solutions where everyone begins. This sort of solution – still another creative idea – arises from the same mechanisms already discussed. A shelf comes to mind because it is used to hold things up, and the person needs to hold up the candle. Thus, another partial match between the situation and the person's knowledge results in retrieval of an old idea, the attempt to extend that idea to the new situation, failure of that attempt, and a new idea coming to mind.

When a person thinks of the possibility of constructing a shelf, he or she will examine the objects in the problem to find something that might serve in that situation, based on an imagined solution. Here is still another example of the process involved in an attempt to extend an old idea. Some people use the tack-box, emptied of its contents and tacked to the wall, as a shelf for the candle (see Figure 3.6A); this result is called the "box solution" in the psychological literature. Others use the matchbook, tacked to the wall, as a holder for the candle (see Figure 3.6B). Evidence from protocols supports the hypothesis that shelf solutions come about in response to difficulties with attaching solutions (Fleck & Weisberg, 2004). One can sometimes hear people work their way through a series of problematic solutions before arriving at the idea to build a shelf.

Additional results from the laboratory also indicate that shelf solutions evolve out of failures of earlier tacks and wax-glue solutions. The frequency with which individuals produce the box solution is related to the *size of the*

A) Tack-Box Shelf or platform ("Box" Solution)

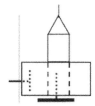

B) Matchbook Shelf or Platform

Figure 3.6 Solutions to the Candle Problem: shelves
A. Matchbook
B. Tack-box

tacks that are in the box (Weisberg & Suls, 1973). If the tacks are very small, as in Figure 3.4, then the box solution is relatively frequent; on the other hand, if the tacks are large, then box solutions are less frequent. The person, on imagining using the small tacks – trying to extend that idea to the new situation – will conclude that they will not work. That negative result raises the likelihood that people would go on to other possibilities, including building a shelf, which can lead to using the box. The large tacks, in contrast, are more likely to be seen as effective in attaching the candle to the wall. Therefore, there is a greater likelihood that people will solve the problem using the large tacks and will never get to the need for a shelf.

The results from the Candle Problem are summarized in Figure 3.7, which outlines the paths taken through the problem just discussed (for more details, see Fleck & Weisberg, 2004, 2013; and Weisberg & Suls, 1973). The important point to be taken away from this discussion is the complex set of links that are involved, even in this simple problem, as new solutions develop as people work through the problem.

Green Creativity and the Origins of New Ideas: Summary

Based on the discussion of the Candle Problem, we can draw some preliminary conclusions concerning the specifics of green creativity. We transfer knowledge to a new situation based on a partial match between that knowledge and the situation, often based on an analogical relation between the old and the new. When a person facing the Candle Problem contemplates tacking the candle to the wall, it is based on the partial match between the current "attach-a-candle" situation and previous "attach-things" situations that the person has experienced. The fact that the instructions ask the person to "attach the candle ... " – plus the presence of the tacks in the problem – leads to the person thinking about using the tacks. With the Candle Problem presented as in Figure 3.4, most people's attaching knowledge results in them rejecting the tacking solution as it comes to mind. That is, the attempt to extend the old idea to the new problem is almost immediately seen as failing. That rejection leads to further thinking and to the development of additional new ideas.

Creative Thinking as a Dynamic Process

An important insight arising from the discussion so far is that there is a dynamic interaction between the creative process and the evolving

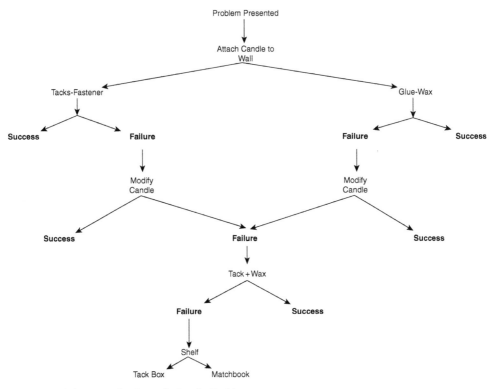

Figure 3.7 Solution paths through Candle Problem

environment. New information becomes available as the person operates on the situation, especially when a proposed solution does not work. A negative outcome, arising from the attempt to extend an old idea to the new situation, tells the person something new about that situation, which can result in transfer of a new solution type. That new transfer changes the way the person approaches the situation, and so forth, in an ongoing cycle. More specifically, if the person fails to solve the Candle Problem using the tacks or the wax-glue, that failure leads to a search for another way to hold things up on walls. That leads to the idea of a shelf, which in turn leads to a search of the environment to find a shelf or, if no shelf is available, an object that can serve as a shelf, for example the tack-box.

Problem Representations and Solutions

We have seen that the person's interaction with a problem can play a large role in whether he or she can solve it. Presentation of a problem typically involves verbal instructions, perhaps accompanied by a diagram or by objects to manipulate. The first step in dealing with a problem is therefore the same as what happens when any verbal message is presented: the person must interpret the problem (the message) to understand what it asks for. Psychologists call the person's interpretation of the problem the *representation* of the problem. It is the representation of the problem, *rather than the problem as presented by the researcher*, that determines how the person will approach it (Bassock & Novick, 2012). Sometimes a person will interpret a problem in such a way that he or she will produce an incorrect solution or no solution whatever. An example of a problem that can become impossible – or very difficult – to solve, depending on the representation that one develops, is the Trains and Bird Problem. Please try to solve it before reading further into the next section.

Trains and Bird Problem

> Two trains, each having a speed of 30 km/h, are headed at each other on the same straight track. A bird that can fly 60 km/h flies off the front of one train when they are 60 km apart and heads directly for the other train. On reaching the other train, the bird flies directly back to the first train, and so forth. What is the total distance the bird travels before the trains collide?

Many people find the Trains and Bird Problem impossible to solve. They begin by imagining the bird flying from one train – the first train – to the other, but then they realize that, as the bird is flying toward the second train, that train is also approaching the bird, which means that the distance that the bird flies before it meets the second train will not be the full distance between the stations. Furthermore, as the trains keep moving toward each other, the distances the bird flies between the trains keep decreasing, and most people have no idea how to determine what those ever-decreasing distances are. Thus, based on that representation of the problem, from the perspective of the bird's path, it becomes very difficult to solve (see Table 3.3A). It turns out that there is a way to solve the problem from the perspective of the bird's path using a mathematical method (summing an infinite series), but most people are not familiar with it.

However, there is another, much simpler, way to approach the problem. One can consider the situation from the perspective of the *trains* (see Table 3.3B). It will take the trains an hour before they meet. One can then determine how far the bird will fly in that hour, which is the solution to

Table 3.3 *Two representations of Trains and Bird Problem*

A. From the perspective of the **bird**.

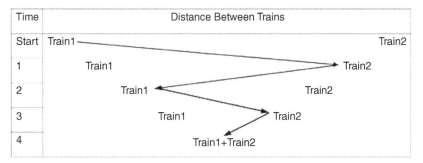

Time	Distance Between Trains
Start	Train1 ... Train2
1	Train1 ... Train2
2	Train1 ... Train2
3	Train1 ... Train2
4	Train1+Train2

B. From the perspective of the **trains**.

Train1 ———————————————▶ ◀——————————— Train2

the problem. In sum, a person's representation of a problem plays a critical role in whether he or she will be able to solve it.

Problem-Solving, Analytic Thinking, and Creative Thinking: Conclusions

This review of research on problem-solving has provided a foundation for the understanding of creative thinking. We first considered a knowledge-lean problem, the Triangle of Coins, which provided examples of the use of heuristic methods in solving problems. Those methods can be used in a complex manner and can produce relatively sophisticated solutions. We then turned the Candle Problem, a knowledge-rich problem, where people produce many different solutions based on the transfer of knowledge to the problem. Analysis of the Candle Problem provided insight into the basic mechanism behind green creativity: the transfer of knowledge to a new situation was the result of a *partial match* between the new situation and the situation in memory in which the knowledge was acquired. That partial match often depended on an analogical relation – typically, a *near analogy* – between the problem situation and one's knowledge. The person then attempts to extend that old idea to the new problem. However, possible solutions that arise as the result of transfer based on a partial match cannot always be extended to the problem. That failure may provide new information about the problem.

New ideas, leading to different solutions, can develop through attempts to overcome failures. Some of those later solutions can be relatively far removed from the ideas with which the person began working on the problem.

A Model of Problem-Solving

The discussion of problem-solving can be summarized in the form of a model of problem-solving that postulates a series of stages that people go through when solving problems (Fleck & Weisberg, 2013; Weisberg, 2018b; Weisberg & Suls, 1973; see Figure 3.8). The problem-solving process, like all cognition, begins with an attempt to match the external situation with information in memory (Stage 1A). This is the top-down processing that was discussed earlier as a component of analytic thinking (see Table 3.1). A partial match between a problem and memory can result in an old idea being generated and an attempt being made to extend it to the new situation. If there is information in memory that is relevant to this particular problem (Stage 1A – Positive match), then a possible solution will be brought to mind that the person will use in an attempt to solve the problem (Stage 1B). If that method is successful (Stage 1B – Success), the problem is solved (Stage 1C). If the proposed solution does not work (Stage 1B – Failure), then there may be new information that becomes available (Stage 1D – Yes), which sends the person back to the beginning, with what has become a new problem based on the newly discovered information arising from the failed solution. There can now be brought to mind a new possible solution to the problem based on that new information.

If there is no information in memory that is relevant to the problem (Stage 1A – No match), or if the failed solution in Stage 1D provides no new information (Stage 1D – No), the person goes to Stage 2 and tries to apply heuristic methods to the problem. If no heuristic method is found (Stage 2A – No), then the person has failed to solve the problem. If a heuristic method is found that is applicable to the problem (Stage 2A – Yes) and, after the person tries to extend it to the problem, it works (Stage 2B – Success), then the problem is solved (Stage 2C). If the heuristic method fails to work and that failure provides no new information (Stage 2D – No), then the person has failed to solve the problem. If there is a failed heuristic solution but the failure provides new information about the problem (Stage 2D – Yes), that new information serves as the basis for a new search of memory (Stage 2E; the same as Stage 1A), and the cycle begins again, with the possibility of

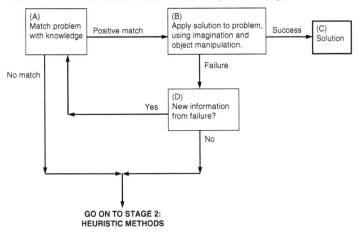

STAGE 1 – MATCHING A PROBLEM WITH KNOWLEDGE (Green Creativity)

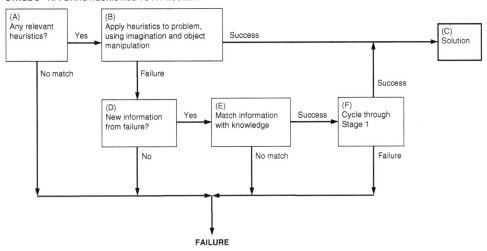

STAGE 2 – APPLYING HEURISTICS TO A PROBLEM

Figure 3.8 Outline of a model of problem-solving based on analytic thinking

solution (Stage 2F – Success) or failure (Stage 2f – Failure). It might be a valuable learning exercise to try to use the model in Figure 3.8 as the basis for analyzing the solution results for the Candle problem, as outlined in Figure 3.7.

Two Components of the Creative Process

The model in Figure 3.8 points to two substages in the creative process. The first substage (Stage 1A in Figure 3.8) involves the attempt to match the problem with information in memory, which can result in retrieval of a possible solution. That process is automatic and is a critical component of all cognition: our knowledge plays a central role in all our cognitive activities (Weisberg, 2006). We do not choose to interpret events based on what we know: we are designed to do so. This substage can be described as *bottom-up*, since it depends on events in the world driving the process. Those events "work their way up," into the system, until they match with information in memory or fail to do so. That first substage, if successful, results in information being retrieved from memory (one may say something like "Say, this reminds me of . . . "). An idea is generated that can serve as the solution to the problem. Examples of the output of this substage include IDEO's idea to use casters as wheels for its shopping cart and the use of a safety seat/high chair for the child. Similarly, Picasso's thinking of *Minotauromachy* when contemplating the bombing of Guernica was based on associative connections outlined in Figure 1.7. In Dunkirk, also, similar processes were at work in Captain Tennant's thinking about using the east mole as a possible dock. This is the idea-generation stage that we have discussed several times already.

The information retrieved in Stage 1A then serves as the basis for a possible solution (Stage 1B in Figure 3.8). In this substage, the person tries to extend the old idea to the problem, modifying it as necessary, and so forth, as already discussed. This substage is "top-down" in nature, since the person's knowledge – "at the top" – is driving, or controlling, or directing the process. As we have seen, another description for this substage is *executive* processing, since higher-order processes – *executive processes* – are controlling the operations that are being carried out. Examples of the operation of this substage were seen in the modifications that Picasso carried out as he worked through the sketches for *Guernica*. We will have occasion to see this distinction between associative/bottom-up processes and top-down/executive processes in many places in the rest of the book.

Going Forward

We now have the beginnings of an understanding of how green creativity works, based on the analysis in this chapter of people's performance on the Candle Problem. We turn in the next three chapters to a broader discussion of aspects of creativity, using the discussion in this chapter as the foundation. In Chapter 4, we will analyze a wide range of creative advances, ranging from genius-level acts to small-scale advances produced by ordinary folks in their day-to-day activities. We will examine the role analytic thinking played in those creative acts. One of the conclusions arising from the discussion so far has been the importance of analogical thinking in creativity, in the form of analogical transfer. This conclusion will be strengthened as a result of the discussion in Chapter 4. In Chapter 5, we will deepen the analysis of analytic thinking in creativity by discussing in detail the processes involved in analogical thinking and how they play a role in creativity. In Chapter 6, we will conclude the discussion of the role of analytic thinking in creativity by examining the role of practice versus talent in the development of world-class achievement, including creative achievement.

4 | Case Studies of Creativity

The Universality of Creativity

Under-the-Radar Innovation: Painting over Typing Mistakes

In what seems ages ago in technology terms (i.e., in the mid-twentieth century), formal written communication was produced using the typewriter, a mechanical device that had a keyboard – similar to the keyboards on today's electronic devices – connected to mechanical levers. Pressing a key resulted in the corresponding letter striking an inked ribbon, which printed the letter on the paper. A problem for anyone using a typewriter was typing errors and how to correct them. In early generations of typewriters, errors could be removed easily, by erasing; one could then type the correct letter in the space. After World War II, IBM introduced electric typewriters that were much more reliable than mechanical typewriters. IBM typewriters used carbon-film ribbons, rather than inked ribbons, to print the letters, which resulted in precise letters and much more attractive documents. However, the new machines had one major drawback: the new ribbons did not allow erasing to correct errors. Thus, even a professional typist might have to retype whole pages because of one or two errors.

That difficult situation was remedied by Bette Graham (1924–1980; Robinson & Stern, 1997). Graham was executive secretary for the chairman of a bank, which was, at that time, about the highest position that a woman could hold in a business organization. An excellent typist, she was still bothered by the problem of uncorrectable typing errors. In December 1951, she was watching painters applying Christmas decorations on the bank's glass windows. (In some versions of this story, Graham herself was painting the windows, working part-time as a commercial artist. In still other versions, Graham is described as an artist painting canvases in her studio. Those possibilities are irrelevant as far as the points being made here are concerned.) The painters occasionally made errors, and they corrected them by simply painting over them. That observation gave her an idea for correcting typing errors. Graham mixed a batch of white paint and, with a small brush, applied a dot of white over each of her errors, covering them.

After the paint dried, which did not take long, she could type the correct material. Over several years, she perfected the fluid and began to sell it, calling it *Mistake Out*. Her first customers were secretaries at the bank. Ultimately, she founded a company that was sold in 1979 for almost $50 million, comparable to over $150 million today.

Mistake Out was a creative idea, produced by someone who was "under the radar," someone not engaged in research and development (R&D) activities. Graham was an ordinary person who produced a creative idea. Her innovation came about through an already-familiar mechanism: near analogical transfer. She transferred information from a painter correcting errors to her problem, a typist correcting errors. A new idea was generated based on analogy and that idea was then extended to the situation Graham was facing.

Innovation by ordinary folks – under-the-radar-innovation – has important implications for our understanding of creativity. The perspective on creativity presented in this book proposes that all creative advances are based on analytic thinking – on ordinary thought processes or inside-the-box thinking. There are two related predictions that come from that assumption. First, those thought processes should be found in all examples of creativity. Second, since analytic thinking is "ordinary thinking," ordinary folks should be capable of creative thinking. The purpose of this chapter is to provide further support for those predictions.

Outline of the Chapter: Everyone Is Creative

Psychologists have made a distinction among what one could call different levels of creative achievement (Kaufman & Beghetto, 2009). At the top are the seminal advances that have shaped our lives and culture, the products of geniuses ("big-c" creativity). The first section of the chapter presents several case studies of genius-level creative advances, to provide further evidence that big-c advances depend on analytic thinking, involving heuristic methods and near analogical transfer. These new case studies will support the analysis of the genius-level advance already presented, the creation of *Guernica*.

The next level of creative achievement is "professional creativity" (or pro-c creativity), advances made by people in their professional activities. Pro-c products are significant advances, but they do not have the wide-ranging transformative effects on the world that big-c advances do. A scientist, for example, might design an experiment to test a prediction from an important new theory. Designing that experiment is an act of pro-c creativity. Creating the significant new theory was big-c creativity. The second section of the chapter presents several case studies of creative advances produced by people whose professional lives have centered around innovation. Those case studies will show that the processes underlying genius-level advances are seen in the creative thinking of nongenius innovators, a further demonstration of the universality analytic thinking in creativity. The discussion builds on the analyses of IDEO's shopping cart and the Dunkirk rescue.

On a still-lower level is what we can call day-to-day or "little-c" creativity, which refers to those bursts of innovation that we all exhibit in our daily lives. You might improvise while preparing a recipe, because you are missing an ingredient – you use something else that does a good-enough job. I will refer to little-c creativity as *under-the-radar creativity*, since it comes from people who might not be expected to produce creative advances. The final section of the chapter demonstrates that ordinary people frequently produce creative ideas in their everyday lives. We have just seen one example of under-the-radar creativity, Graham's *White Out*. The discussion of under-the-radar creativity will close the circle, showing that ordinary thinking underlies all creative advances and that creativity is universal among us.

Architectural Genius: The Most Famous Private Dwelling in the World

"Come along, E. J. We're ready for you." Those words, uttered early in the morning of Sunday, September 22, 1935, by the architect Frank Lloyd Wright, are said to have signaled the creation of one of the most famous and admired buildings in the world. Wright was responding to a telephone call from E. J. Kaufmann, a businessman and art connoisseur from Pittsburgh. Approximately nine months earlier, in December 1934, Kaufmann had commissioned Wright to build a summer house for the Kaufmann family, on Bear Run, a stream in a rugged area in western Pennsylvania. Wright had established his reputation early in the twentieth century, but by the mid-1930s, as he approached seventy years of age, his reputation was in decline; Wright was looked upon as someone whom modern architecture had passed by (Toker, 2003). By 1938, all that had changed: one of Wright's designs had been the subject of a major exhibit at the Museum of Modern Art, in New York; and it and Wright had been on the cover of *Time* magazine. The design was *Fallingwater*, the result of Kaufmann's commission (see Figure 4.1; and for a marvelous video on the

Figure 4.1 Frank Lloyd Wright's *Fallingwater*. Photo by © Richard A. Cooke, Corbis, Getty Images.

house, see www.curbed.com/2015/5/26/9957034/fly-through-frank-lloyd-wrights-fallingwater-with-this-incredible).

Creating Something from Nothing?

Wright's creation of *Fallingwater* seems to provide a classic example of a genius at work. On December 18, 1934, Wright and the Kaufmanns visited the site on Bear Run, and Wright was impressed with its rugged beauty. However, it is said that Wright did no work on plans for the house for months after that initial visit (Toker, 2003), although he corresponded with Kaufmann, telling him – perhaps misleadingly – that plans were underway. Then came the phone call from Kaufmann, on that Sunday morning in September 1935. Kaufmann was in Milwaukee on business, not far from *Taliesin*, Wright's home and studio in Wisconsin, and he wanted to come for lunch, to see the completed plans. Wright cheerily invited him

("Come along E. J. We're ready for you."), seemingly oblivious to the task that he had just set for himself.

Wright hung up the phone, went to his drafting table, and started to draw. Several of Wright's apprentices, who were studying with Wright and living at *Taliesin*, stood watching. Those apprentices, now in near panic, had not seen Wright doing any work on the plans since receiving the commission, and they were totally surprised by Kaufmann's call and his proposal to visit. As far as they could tell, nothing would be ready to show Kaufmann. However, the apprentices were astounded by what happened over the next couple of hours. As one reported: "The plans came pouring out of him" (Toker, 2003). In the short time between Kaufmann's call and his arrival, the plans were drawn and ready to show to him. This most-lauded architectural creation – surely, a work of genius – came into existence in a few hours. One is reminded again of God, creating something from nothing.

How Might Wright's Genius Have Expressed Itself?

There are two possible ways in which Wright's genius might have worked in creating *Fallingwater*. The design for the house might have sprung complete in Wright's mind during the December visit to the site, and he then just drew the plans when they were needed. On this interpretation, Kaufmann's surprise visit did not faze Wright, because, unknown to everyone else, he had been ready from the first day. On the other hand, it is also possible that Wright did *nothing* during the nine months before Kaufmann's phone call. The design then sprang complete in Wright's mind in response to the call. In either case, the design was created whole – the only question is when that creative leap occurred. Our first task is to determine if either of those variants on the genius view is to be believed. We will find that *Fallingwater* did *not* spring whole into Wright's mind, either during the December visit to Bear Run or in response to Kaufmann's phone call. We will then consider how analytic thinking served as the basis for this genius-level creation.

The December Visit to Bear Run

In a television interview in 1953, almost twenty years after he first visited Bear Run, Wright recalled the effects the visit had on him.

> There in a beautiful forest was a solid, high rock-ledge rising beside a waterfall and *the natural thing* seemed to be to cantilever the house

from that rock-bank over the falling water. (quoted in Toker, 2003, p. 137; emphasis added)

Wright's comment could be taken to indicate that he had formulated the design for the house on first seeing the falls. Toker (2003, p. 139) seems to have adopted that interpretation. "The instant he saw Bear Run, Frank Lloyd Wright seems to have grasped how to place by the falls a house that would flow as effortlessly as the waterfall itself." However, Wright did not say that a *complete* plan for the house was in his mind. He simply said that cantilevering the house over the falls – building the house over the falls on long beams – seemed like "the natural thing," which may mean no more than that he thought it was a good idea in general.

There are several reasons to believe that the design did not spring full-blown into Wright's imagination when he first saw the site. In a letter Wright wrote to Kaufmann, dated December 26, 1934, eight days after the visit to Bear Run, he described the effects of the visit very differently than he had many years later in the TV interview (Toker, 2003, pp. 139–140):

> The visit to the waterfall in the woods stays with me and a domicile has *taken vague shape in my mind* to the music of the stream. (emphasis added)

Here, Wright clearly indicated that he had not fully formulated the design for the house. Also, Wright visited the site at least three, and, possibly, four times between that first visit and the day that he drew the plans for Kaufmann (Toker, 2003). Those return visits indicate that there was further work to do on the design. Given this information, how are we to interpret Wright's recollection, in the 1953 interview, that he had thought cantilevering the house over the stream was a "natural thing"? Based on his December 26 letter, Wright may have meant only that he had had a general idea of what he was going to do, which, although vague, seemed "natural" to him. We now turn to the possibility that the design for *Fallingwater* arose complete in response to Kaufmann's phone call.

The Response to Kaufmann's Phone Call

The plans that Wright drew for Kaufmann on that Sunday morning have been preserved, and they do not support the idea that the design was complete in Wright's mind when he started drawing. There are erasures and modifications on the plans, and one of those changes, involving the soaring second-floor balcony, was important. In the initial drawing of the second floor, the balcony was drawn so that it came out only halfway over the first-floor balcony. Wright then erased and redrew the second-floor balcony, extending it far over the first floor. Thus, the most dramatic aspect of the house was not present in Wright's mind as he first drew the plans.

In conclusion, Wright did not make a creative leap to the complete design – either when he first visited Bear Run or when he received the call from Kaufmann. Wright was a genius, but his creative process does not support the genius view. It now becomes of interest to consider the development of *Fallingwater* from the analytic-thinking perspective. We can begin with Wright's comment arising from his first visit to the site that cantilevering a house over the waterfall was a "natural thing." Where did that idea come from? It turns out that cantilevering a structure over a waterfall was a natural thing for Wright because he had done it before: *Fallingwater* is another example of green creativity.

A Natural Thing: Analogical Transfer in the Creation *of* Fallingwater

Water had played an important role in many of Wright's projects. One prominent example is *Taliesen*, his multi-structured living/working compound in Wisconsin, which was begun in 1911, with construction extending through the 1920s. The buildings are on a hilltop overlooking a lake. Wright had a stream running out of that lake dammed, resulting in a waterfall. In the mid-1920s, to provide electricity for *Taliesin*, Wright had a power plant built. He used the power from the artificial waterfall as the basis for generating electricity by cantilevering the power-plant building over it. Thus, a building cantilevered over a waterfall was "natural" because Wright had had experience in an analogous situation and he transferred that experience to the new project. Wright's decision to cantilever the Kaufmanns' house over the falls was an idea generated on the basis of a near analogy. Let us now consider the next stage in Wright's creative process: extending the retrieved idea to the new problem. Once he had decided to cantilever the house over Bear Run, how did Wright decide on the specific design?

Specifics of the Design as Another Example of Green Creativity: Fallingwater *Is a* Prairie House

Early in the twentieth century, some thirty years before creating *Fallingwater*, Wright created the *Prairie Houses*, a series of private homes for families living around Chicago (see Figure 4.2). The Prairie Houses established Wright's reputation as a young architect. Those houses had several characteristics in common: low overhanging roofs, sometimes flat; two cantilevered balconies; walls of windows looking out on the balconies; and a central cross-shaped – "cruciform" – core, organized around a fireplace. *Fallingwater* contains all those characteristics; in other words, *Fallingwater* is a Prairie House cantilevered over the waterfall. Wright himself drew that conclusion.

> The ideas involved here are in no wise (*sic*) changed from those of earlier work. . . . The effects you see in this house are not superficial effects, and are entirely consistent with the Prairie Houses of 1901–10. (quoted in McCarter, 1997, p. 7)

Thus, the specific design for *Fallingwater* was also based on green creativity – near-analogical transfer of the *Prairie House* design to the site at Bear Run.

In conclusion, it has been possible to analyze and understand multiple aspects of Wright's creation of *Fallingwater*, one of the seminal creative advances of the twentieth century, based on analytic thinking. Both the design in general and many of its specific features were based on the transfer of knowledge from Wright's experiences designing houses. Those ideas were then modified to fit the specific problem Wright was facing – designing a house to sit over the falls at Bear Run. Let us now broaden our analysis and examine a creative insight of Leonardo da Vinci

Figure 4.2 A Frank Lloyd Wright *Prairie House* – the Gale House. Photo by Frank Lloyd Wright Preservation Trust, Getty Images.

(Richter, 1952), the quintessential "Renaissance Man," renowned for his creative achievements in art, science, and invention.

Creativity of a Renaissance Genius: Leonardo's Design for a Flying Machine

Leonardo da Vinci surely is one of the first people most of us would think of if asked to name a "genius." One of his most fascinating inventions is a proposal for a flying machine – an *aerial screw* – shown in Figure 4.3. The device is designed so that four people can stand on the platform and turn the screw-shaped sail by pushing the bars extending from the central shaft. Leonardo hypothesized that, if the screw could be turned quickly enough, it would bore into the air, and the machine would be drawn up into the air, like a twisting wood screw is drawn into a ceiling beam. That is, the aerial screw would fly.

Leonardo's Leap of Genius: Outside-the-Box Thinking?

The idea behind the aerial screw was based on a connection that Leonardo made between two domains, screws and the air. For most of us, those domains are completely unconnected. Creative leaps of that sort are what

Figure 4.3 Leonardo's aerial screw. Helicopter flying machine, Victor Habbick Visions, Science Photo Library, Getty Images.

motivated people such as Barzun (1989) and Bloom (2002) to propose that the genius created through processes that no one could understand. Perkins (2000) also discussed the surprising nature of the connection that Leonardo made.

> Leonardo's insight made a connection between two very different things. He saw a relationship between screws and the challenge of flight. A propeller amounts to an air screw, holding on to air much as a wood screw holds on to wood, albeit less firmly. (p. 3)

Perkins (2000, p. 6) described Leonardo's invention as being based on "the sort of creativity that makes a decisive break with the past." Leonardo's breakthrough came when he "reached for an analogy" (p. 5), a move outside the box. Perkins proposed that there is a special kind of thinking, *breakthrough thinking,* that allows one to think outside the box and take a new perspective on a problem. Perkins presented several suggestions for how one might deal with a problem demanding breakthrough thinking (2000, pp. 51–58). The method that is relevant here is *roving*: one should explore solution possibilities in as wide a manner as possible, so that one does not restrict one's search (see also Kounios & Beeman, 2015; Ohlsson, 2011, 2018). Perkins's discussion is similar to Mednick's (1962) notion of flat hierarchies serving as the basis for creation of new ideas (see Figure 2.3).

The analytic-thinking view, in contrast, predicts that we should find *links* in Leonardo's knowledge that allowed him to make the connection between screws and flight. The areas of screws and flight, which seemed to Perkins (2000), to be so far apart, should *not* be far apart for Leonardo.

Analytic Thinking and Leonardo's Analogy between Screws and Flight

If we examine Leonardo's history as a scientist, we can construct a plausible scenario through which he might have been able to use analytic thinking to make the connection between screws and flight. Among his many scientific activities, Leonardo had studied the properties of air, one of the basic elements in Renaissance science (fire, water, and earth were the others). Leonardo found that air was *compressible*: it could, through pressure, be forced into a small space. Water, which he also studied, was not compressible. Leonardo already knew that wood was compressible, so the new finding meant that air was like wood in that respect (see Table 4.1). There was thus an analogical link in Leonardo's

Table 4.1 *An outline of possible conceptual links leading to Leonardo's invention of the aerial screw through analytic thinking*

New Discovery: air is compressible

⇓

Leonardo's Knowledge:
Wood is compressible + a screw can be pulled through wood
(A screw moves up into a horizontal beam)
Birds soar in screw-shaped spiral paths through the air

⇓

A screw can be pulled through air
(Hypothesis/Inference/Based on Analogy)

⇓

Aerial Screw
Outcome (Conclusion)

mind between air and wood. Leonardo also knew that screws can be driven into wood because of its compressibility. A twisting screw bores into a wooden beam – that is, moves up into a horizontal beam – by compressing the beam's fibers and moving through them. Leonardo might then have used reasoning by analogy – a *near* analogy – to formulate the hypothesis that screws could also be driven into air. The idea for the aerial screw then follows.

In addition, Leonardo had observed birds in flight, soaring on rising currents of air without flapping their wings. He wrote in his notebook that the paths taken by those birds were sometimes spiral, "in the manner of a screw" (Richter, 1952, p. 97). That description provides another link between wood screws and the aerial screw. In sum, to understand how Leonardo was able to draw the analogy between screws and flight, we do not need to postulate a special kind of thinking. There was a link, or links, in his knowledge – again, based on a *near* analogy – between the two concepts, which provided a scaffold on which he could construct a process of analogical reasoning. Leonardo *generated* a new idea based on analogy, a mechanism we have already seen many times. He then had more work to do to *extend* the new idea to flight: he had to design a new kind of screw, one that could use people's muscle-power to rise up into the air.

The examples of genius-level creativity discussed so far – Picasso's *Guernica*, Wright's *Fallingwater*, and Leonardo's aerial screw – involved creation of a new physical object. To demonstrate the broad relevance of analytic thinking to the highest levels of creative achievement, we can examine the creation of a whole new style of painting by Jackson Pollock in the 1940s.

Changing the Structure of the Art World: Pollock's Dripped Paintings

Around the middle of the twentieth century, the center of the modern art world underwent two significant shifts. Its physical center moved from Paris to New York; and its conceptual center – the central focus of many artists – also changed, from *representational* works, which contained recognizable objects, such as people and flowers, to *nonrepresentational* or *abstract* works, in which no traces of objects could be found. A critical stimulus in both those shifts was the work of the Abstract Expressionists, a group of painters centered around New York City who radically changed what modern painting was about. One of the most important of the Abstract Expressionists was Jackson Pollock (1912–1956), who, beginning in the late 1940s, produced a series of paintings in a revolutionary new style.

Pollock's Radical New Style

Pollock did away with the brush and instead used a stick dipped in paint to "draw," on the canvas, lines of paint of different thicknesses, colors, and textures (see Figure 4.4). In traditional painting, a line can outline an object, such as a face, and can also serve to provide boundaries for different areas in a painting, for example between "ground" and "sky." Pollock's lines had no function beyond their part in the overall pattern in the painting. During this period, if Pollock saw that lines that he had drawn suggested an object, he would draw more lines over and around that "object," to make it impossible to see. Pollock also sometimes poured paint directly from a can onto the canvas or squeezed paint from a tube directly onto the canvas, and he sometimes incorporated objects, such as keys or sand, into his paintings, or put handprints on them. In order to produce his new paintings, Pollock

Figure 4.4 A Jackson Pollock painting: *Autumn Rhyth*, © 2019 The Pollock-Krasner Foundation / Artists Rights Society (ARS), New York.

laid the canvas on the floor and worked by walking around them, in another departure from tradition.

Those Pollock works, with their seemingly constantly moving rhythmic lines, became the center of discussion in the art world; they earned Pollock a cover photo and article in *Life* magazine, a popular weekly, asking the question: "Jackson Pollock: Is He the Greatest Living Painter in the United States?" Over the years, Pollock's paintings have been the subject of major exhibitions; and many books, monographs, and articles have been written on Pollock's work (e.g., Landau, 1989). Pollock is now considered to be one of the most important American painters of the twentieth century. Pollock's radical stylistic advance – so different from what we think of when we consider what "painting a picture" means – would seem to be an example of a genius-level advance, something that came out of nowhere. However, if we examine Pollock's life, we will be able to find evidence for green creativity underlying his achievement. From inside Pollock's career, things were not as radically new as they might appear to be from outside.

The Siqueiros "Experimental Workshop"

In the mid-1930s, Pollock was a young painter in New York trying to support himself and his art classes. He received funding from the Federal Art Project, part of Roosevelt's New Deal that supported the visual arts. Artists were paid to produce works for public buildings and spaces; and many artists' workshops were funded, where artists could collaborate on projects and learn new techniques. One artists' workshop was directed by David Alfaro Siqueiros (1896–1974). Siqueiros was a Mexican painter who – with two compatriots, Diego Rivera and José Clemente Orosco – had established a reputation in Mexico and the United States through politically oriented artworks and political activism. Siqueiros and the other Mexicans, who all were communists, hoped to establish a new art that broke with tradition in various ways and connected directly with the lives of working people. Siqueiros advocated using modern materials and techniques, such as industrial lacquer paints in place of oil paint; painting on plywood and metal, instead of on canvas; and applying paint using airbrushes, in place of the traditional brush.

The Siqueiros workshop was called the "Experimental Workshop," and Axel Horn, one of the attendees, summarized the attitude toward tradition that developed under Siqueiros's direction:

> We were going to put out to pasture the "stick with hairs on its end" as Siqueiros called the brush. ... [E]verything became material for our investigations. For instance; lacquer [paint] opened up enormous possibilities in the application of color. We sprayed through stencils ..., embedded wood, metal, sand and paper. We used it in thin glazes or built it up into thick globs. We poured it, dripped it, spattered it, hurled it at the picture surface. ... What emerged was an endless variety of accidental effects. Siqueiros soon constructed a theory and system of "controlled accidents." (Horn, 1966, pp. 85–86)

One Siqueiros work, *Collective Suicide* (1936), was created using many of those methods for applying paint to canvas.

Pollock and Siqueiros

The Siqueiros workshop was disbanded in 1939, when Siqueiros left to fight in the Spanish Civil War. However, the workshop had wide-ranging effects on many young artists in New York. Most important for our analysis of Pollock's innovations, Pollock was a member of the workshop, participating in all the activities that Horn described. Pollock either witnessed *Collective Suicide* being painted or saw it soon after. Pollock thus had experience using methods of applying paint – by spilling, pouring, and using a stick – that became the basis for his new paintings. He had also had experience embedding sand and objects in a painting. At about this time, many other artists in New York were experimenting with pouring and dripping paint on canvas (Landau, 1989), but there was one critical difference between most of them and Pollock. Pollock took those methods and made them the source of a new style of painting. At least two other artists in New York at about that time had developed "all-over" abstract styles, similar to Pollock's, and he was familiar with those artists' works, which may be another source of inspiration for his style. Thus, the idea for Pollock's new style was the result of transfer based on a near analogy.

Development of Pollock's Revolutionary Technique

As we have seen in other cases, there was additional work required, as the new idea had to be extended to fit Pollock's problem. The development of Pollock's mature style took several additional years after the Siqueiros workshop disbanded. He painted some works with lines dripped on them in the early 1940s, but the lines did not completely cover the canvas and were not the sole component of the paintings. Pollock still had some development to go through: he had to take the various bits and pieces of experimental technique, acquired from the Siqueiros workshop and elsewhere, and bring them together into a unified whole that he could use to produce large-scale works that could stand on their own without any other "meaning." Again, he had to extend those ideas to his situation. It took several years for him to learn how to do that.

In conclusion, Pollock's radical stylistic advance seems to have come about in a nonradical way – through analytic thinking and green creativity. Let us now examine a radical advance in medicine to demonstrate that the same conclusions hold there.

Overthrowing Established Medical Doctrine: Bacteria and Ulcers

Until around 1990, people who suffered from ulcers in the digestive system – peptic ulcers – were told that their condition was the result of stress (Thagard, 1999). Stress overstimulated the production of acid in the stomach, and the acid damaged the stomach lining, causing the ulcers. The cure for ulcers was to reduce stress in one's life and to consume a bland diet, which would help counteract the effects of acid in the stomach and would also facilitate the healing of the ulcers, which were open sores. The basic strategy for dealing with ulcers had been stated by Schwarz in 1910: "no acid, no ulcers" (Fatović-Ferenčić & Banić, 2011).

However, there were several problems with the "no acid, no ulcers" theory. As new drugs were developed to regulate the amount of acid in the stomach, it was found that reducing excess acid would indeed result in ulcers healing; however, on ceasing treatment, the ulcers would return. This result was summarized as another component of the dominant view: "once an ulcer, always an ulcer." It was proposed by some researchers that certain people had an innate tendency toward ulcers, based on psychological and physiological factors. A psychological factor might be a sensitivity to stress; physiological factors might be a tendency to overproduction of acid or the shape of one's stomach. In addition, some people developed ulcers in the absence of excessive acid. Even in the face of those problems, the "no-acid, no-ulcers" view remained the dominant strategy for treating ulcers of the stomach – *gastric* ulcers – and of the small intestine – *duodenal* ulcers.

In 1979, a discovery was made that initiated a research project resulting in the overthrow of the excess-acid theory of ulcers and development of a completely new explanation. This change was a creative advance of the first order, which ultimately was recognized by the awarding of a Nobel Prize (for more details, see Marshall, 2002; Thagard, 1999, chs. 3–7). The initial step was carried out by Dr J. R. Warren, a pathologist at the Royal Perth Hospital in Perth, Australia. As part of his duties, Warren examined *biopsies*, small samples of tissue removed from ill patients, to determine specific causes of the conditions that brought them to the hospital and whether there might be additional problems to be dealt with. Warren had over his career developed an interest in gastric – stomach – biopsies and had developed a classification system for categorizing classes of *gastritis*, an inflammation of the stomach often seen in those biopsies. He also had interests in drawing and he sometimes drew structures that he saw on the biopsies. Warren had also experimented with various sorts of *stains*, chemicals added to the biopsy samples when they were put on microscope slides, that helped make visible different sorts of structures and objects.

One biopsy, from a patient suffering from gastritis, produced a surprising result. On examining the tissue under the microscope, Warren saw evidence of gastritis but he also saw a thin blue line on the slide. Under higher magnification, he saw that that "line" was made up of many small spiral-shaped organisms that looked like bacteria. They were congregated near the epithelial cells that line the stomach and produce mucus, which protects the stomach lining from the acid produced by other cells. Warren showed his slides to his superiors and colleagues, who at first did not see the organisms that he saw. Warren sent a sample to the electron microscope department of the hospital, and the electron micrograph (the picture that came back) showed what was unmistakable evidence of those organisms.

With the better pictures, the other doctors agreed that there were what looked like bacteria in the biopsy, but no one besides Warren was excited about the seemingly new organisms that he had discovered. The dominant belief was that nothing could live in the acidic environment of the stomach – that is, the stomach was *sterile*. Therefore, Warren's findings were dismissed: there must have been some contamination that brought those bacteria into the stomach from the outside. Warren, confident that there was no contamination in his biopsies, concluded that the bacteria were playing a role in the development of gastritis and perhaps other conditions. If he was correct, the presence of those bacteria indicated that *some* organisms could live in the stomach. However, even if bacteria could live in the stomach, it was possible that they might have developed as a *result* of the disease suffered by the patient rather than causing it. The first challenge that Warren's superiors set for him was to find more samples that contained those alleged bacteria, and the samples had to be from patients without ulcers or other conditions that might have produced the bacteria.

Over the next two years, Warren examined the gastric biopsies that were assigned to him and he also looked for those spiral-shaped organisms. He found that they were relatively frequent. They were in 135 biopsies, approximately one-half of the biopsies that he examined and they seemed to be related to the presence of severe gastritis. When there was no gastritis, there typically were no bacteria. He was ready to publish his results when a young medical researcher, Dr Barry Marshall, came to his office to discuss Warren's research. Marshall was undergoing advanced training in gastroenterology and, as part of that training, had to carry out a research study. It was suggested that Marshall should talk with Warren about his ongoing project. Marshall found the research interesting and agreed to help carry out a new study in which a large number of biopsies – 100 in total – would be analyzed for the presence of the bacteria, and any other conditions present in the biopsies would be recorded. That analysis would help determine if the bacteria were associated with the presence of any specific conditions, which is the first step in establishing a causal role for them.

Warren and Marshall published their findings in two waves. Soon after Marshall joined Warren, they each published a short report (a "letter" to the British medical journal *The Lancet*) describing the results of Warren's initial observational study and possible implications. Those reports were published together (Warren & Marshall, 1983). Then, in a longer study, based on results coming out of their collaboration, they examined in more detail the relationship between the bacteria and several gastrointestinal diseases.

In Warren's initial letter (Warren & Marshall, 1983), in addition to describing the results just discussed, he noted that the bacteria were hard to see, except if one used a specific type of stain (one he had become expert in using). That might be why there had not been many reports of those bacteria. He also drew several potentially important conclusions. First, the idea that the stomach was a sterile environment, in which no organisms could grow, was not correct. The bacteria he had observed seemed to live under the mucus layer on the surface of the stomach tissue and so were protected from direct contact with stomach acid. Second, if the bacteria were related to the development of gastritis, they might also be related to other gastric problems.

In Marshall's letter (Warren & Marshall, 1983), he addressed several questions concerning the bacteria observed by Warren. First, why had they not been seen before? Marshall noted that there *had* been reports of spiral-shaped bacteria in the stomach, going back over 40 years. In a very influential paper, however, Palmer (1954) reported that he had tried to find the bacteria that others had seen but was unsuccessful. Palmer concluded that any bacteria found by others were living in biopsy samples but had not been present in the living organisms, and he strongly reemphasized that nothing could live in the stomach. According to Marshall, in an echo of Warren, Palmer's lack of success in finding bacteria was because he had used the wrong stain. Marshall also gave reasons why the bacteria discovered by Warren were a new species rather than being a new variant on an already-known type. The new bacteria were called *Helicobacter pylori* (*H pylori*): *Helico*, from their helical shape; *bacter*, for *bacteria*; and *pylori*, because they were found in the area of the *pylorus*, the region where the stomach opens into the small intestine. Finally, Marshall did not explicitly discuss the question of whether the new bacteria were a *pathogen* – that is, whether they caused disease – but he did say that, if they *were* pathogens, "they may have a part to play in other poorly understood, gastritis associated diseases (i.e., peptic ulcer and gastric cancer)" (Warren & Marshall, 1983, p. 1275). Marshall's bold claim turned out to be correct.

Table 4.2 *Marshall and Warren (1984) results;* H pylori *bacteria and illness*

A. Patients without Ulcers		
Presence of *H pylori*?	Presence of Gastritis? (number of patients in parentheses)	Total Number
	Yes	No	
Yes	.97 (30)	.03 (1)	31
No	.26 (10)	.74 (28)	38
			69

B. Patients with Ulcers		
Type of Ulcer	*H pylori* Present? (number of patients in parentheses)	Total Number
	Yes	No	
Gastric	.82 (18)	.18 (4)	22
Duodenal	1.00 (13)	.00 (0)	13
			35

Koch's Postulates and the Bacterial Cause of Ulcers

Since the late nineteenth century, a set of rules, called Koch's postulates, after the physician who first used them, have served as the basis for establishing that a microorganism is the cause of a disease. The first step is to demonstrate a *relationship* between the presence versus absence of that organism and the presence versus absence of disease. Warren's early data (Warren & Marshall, 1983) supported such a connection, since the bacteria were associated with the presence of gastritis, and their absence was associated with its absence. After Marshall joined Warren, as noted, they carried out a larger-scale study, based on new biopsies from 100 patients (Marshall & Warren, 1984; see Table 4.2). The patients were first divided into those without ulcers (sixty-nine patients) and those with ulcers (thirty-one patients). The patients without ulcers allowed Marshall and Warren to examine the relationship between *H pylori* and gastritis, without any other possible complications. As can be seen in Table 4.2A, there was an association between presence/absence of *H pylori* and gastritis: almost all the patients who tested positive for the bacteria had gastritis, while only about a quarter of those who tested negative for *H pylori* were diagnosed with gastritis. The results, while not perfect, showed a definite relationship between bacterial infection and gastritis.

The results for the patients diagnosed with ulcers are shown in Table 4.2B, and they resulted in a significant new finding. Of the patients with gastric ulcers, 82 percent had *H pylori* present, raising the possibility that the bacteria played a role in the development of the ulcers. The case was stronger for duodenal ulcers: all thirteen patients with duodenal ulcers tested positive for *H pylori*. Marshall and Warren (1984) concluded that *H pylori* was the *cause* of duodenal ulcers, which was a radical claim at that time. As Marshall and Warren noted, their study was not designed to demonstrate that *H pylori* was the cause of any disease. The study was a correlational study: patients were tested for the presence of *H pylori* and for gastritis and ulcers.

According to Koch's postulates, once a relationship has been established between a bacterium and the disease it is assumed to cause, it is then necessary to culture the bacterium – to grow it in the laboratory. *H pylori* was successfully cultured in the laboratory in the hospital.

The next step entails introducing the bacteria into a healthy organism to show that they will produce the disease. That resulted in an ethical dilemma, because there are questions about whether one can make a person sick. Researchers sometimes use animals as "models," to demonstrate that a microorganism is a pathogen, but *H pylori* did not cause gastritis in animals. In order to demonstrate that *H pylori* was a pathogen, Marshall experimented on himself: he drank liquid in which *H pylori* were living (Marshall, 2002). Over the next few days, he developed a severe case of gastritis, indicating that *H pylori* was a causative agent in gastritis. The disease cleared up on its own over several days, so there was no chance to examine a possible connection between *H pylori* and ulcers. That connection was established in a different way. Patients with ulcers, with *H pylori* in their digestive tracts, were given antibiotics. That treatment eliminated the bacteria and it also cleared up the ulcers. Furthermore, so long as the bacteria did not recur, there was no recurrence of the ulcers. Elimination of *H pylori* resulted in a *cure* for ulcer disease.

Ulcers and Bacteria: Analytic Thinking

The development of the theory that *H pylori* infection is the cause of ulcers is an example of genius-level creativity. It has had a widespread influence on medical practice, going beyond ulcers to the possibility that *H pylori* may play a role in cancer of the stomach; and it resulted in Marshall and Warren winning the Nobel Prize. When we consider the thought processes underlying that momentous advance, we see once again the mechanisms of analytic thinking. Warren's initial noticing of *H pylori* on that first biopsy was part of his routine activities as a pathologist and was facilitated by his deep knowledge concerning the appearance of gastric biopsies. In addition, his visual skills, honed by drawing, might have helped him concerning perception of detail on that slide. Thus, Warren's generation of his initial idea – bacteria in the stomach – came out of his observations. Marshall and Warren extended Warren's idea by following Koch's postulates and satisfying them, one step at a time, using logical thinking and experimentation. Finally, the aspect of their investigation that has been noted most often, Marshall's ingestion of *H pylori* and subsequent gastritis, was not without precedent, as many researchers had used themselves as subjects in medical experiments (Altman, 1987). Again, near analogical transfer was the mechanism: generation of a new idea, based on a near analogy; followed by the extension of that idea to the present situation.

The Creative Process of the Genius – Conclusions

We have now added to our knowledge of the creative process at the genius level. We have examined creativity in the arts (*Guernica*, Pollock), science (Leonardo, ulcers), and architecture (*Fallingwater*). We have found consistencies across those several additional examples of genius-level creativity, and those consistencies were comprehensible on the basis of analytic thinking, since they could be understood as coming about through the use of heuristics and green creativity. The results are summarized in Table 4.3. We now can extend this analysis to additional examples of pro-c creativity. We will go beyond IDEO and Dunkirk and examine other advances brought about by people whose professional activities included innovation in the job description, to demonstrate further that the methods used by the genius are also seen in nongenius advances.

Innovations by Innovators

Using a Weak Adhesive

Spencer Silver was a researcher in the 3M company's research laboratory, specializing in adhesives (Robinson & Stern, 1997). In 1968, he was involved in attempts to develop strong adhesives for various uses, but

Table 4.3 *Analytic thinking in genius-level creativity*

| | Analytic Thinking | |
Creative Achievement	Heuristic Methods	Green Creativity
Picasso's *Guernica*	Planning; working backward	Near transfer: *Minotauromachy* and Goya's *Disasters of War*
Wright's *Fallingwater*	Logic – build up and out	Near transfer: power plant cantilevered over waterfall; Prairie House
Leonardo's *Aerial Screw*	Logical reasoning	Near transfer: compressibility of air and wood
Marshall and Warren: bacteria and ulcers	Logical reasoning – Koch's postulates	Analogical transfer: Koch's postulates; Marshall's ingestion of *H pylori*

one of his results was a very weak, "low-tack" adhesive, for which he could find no use. Silver tried to interest others at 3M in his product, but no one carried it forward. The low-tack adhesive seemed to be a failure.

Not long after, Art Frey, a chemist at 3M, was trying to figure out how he could keep track of the hymns he had to sing as a member of his church choir. Frey organized the hymns by putting scrap-paper bookmarks in his hymnal, but, by each week's second service, some of the bookmarks would fall out, leaving him lost. He needed a bookmark that would stay in place. Taping a piece of paper to the hymnal would work but would result in the page being damaged when it was removed. Frey, who worked on new product development, had attended one of Silver's talks, although at that time he could not think of a use for Silver's low-tack adhesive. That situation changed one Sunday in church. During a boring sermon, Fry was thinking about his bookmark problem, and it occurred to him that Silver's adhesive might be the solution: tacky enough to keep his bookmarks in place but not enough to damage the pages of the hymnal when they were removed. He would apply the adhesive to only about half of the bookmark, so that the piece protruding from the top of the page would not be sticky. Frey obtained some of Silver's adhesive and applied it to paper to make his bookmarks. They served that purpose well, and he began to use them at work also, putting them on documents to mark sections of importance. When he needed to make a comment to someone about a marked section, he naturally wrote on the paper. That was when the idea for what became Post-It Notes took something like its final form. It took years to perfect, with adhesive that would stay on the Post-It and not transfer to the other surface; and then more time to develop an audience for it, but now

Post-It Notes are everywhere. IDEO uses them during group brainstorming sessions.

The mechanism involved in the invention of Post-It Notes is a familiar one – analogical transfer. Frey's bookmark problem involved the need for an adhesive that would not damage the pages of his hymnal. That problem retrieved Silver's weak adhesive from Fry's memory. Once the bookmark problem had been solved, use of several heuristics resulted in the bookmark's evolving into the Post-It Note. Two more examples of pro-c creativity will provide further evidence for the role of analytic thinking in creativity.

Two Innovations in Medicine

Innovation has become a driving force in modern medicine, with medical centers attempting to foster innovation among their employees, and some establishing special units – innovation centers – designed to stimulate idea production and implementation throughout the organization. Two colleagues and I examined innovation policies at several medical centers (Speck, Weisberg & Fleisher, 2015; Weisberg, Speck & Fleisher, 2014). As part of that study, we interviewed employees, to gain some insights into pro-c innovations that they had produced. At one medical center, a large pediatric hospital in the northeastern United States, we interviewed Dr N., a pediatric urologist. He directs a large laboratory and has produced several important innovations, one of which was an artificial implanted kidney, under development when we interviewed him.

An Implantable Kidney

Dr N's implantable kidney would enable people with advanced kidney disease to live their lives without the need for regular dialysis. The typical dialysis regimen, with the patient hooked up to the dialysis machine for several hours, several days a week, is, at best, very difficult. Dr N.'s implanted kidney will remove waste products during the day, as a natural kidney does; and, at night, excessive water is removed while the patient sleeps. There is thus much less disruption of the patient's life.

The development of the artificial kidney followed an indirect path. Dr N. had been working with an engineering firm in Germany on a surgical robot for minimally invasive surgery. He was in Germany at a meeting with engineers from the company. Walking through the building, he came upon a display of an artificial heart that the company was developing for patients awaiting heart transplants. The device caught Dr N.'s attention. (The quotations in this chapter from medical professionals are from unpublished interview transcripts, available from the author.)

> [T]his heart device ... was kind of novel in the sense that the guy who designed it was a flow-dynamic person. ... [H]e added some dyes to watch the swirling effect ... within the heart device .... So, as I was looking at this I said, "You know, this would help probably like 1,000 people at most, because the people that survive to await a heart transplant are not that many, but this would make an amazing dialysis unit." So, we went to dinner that night with him, and, on the napkin and the table cloth, we basically drew out what I would think of as the dialysis unit, about a year and a half ago.

We have here another case of analogical transfer. Dr N. was always carrying around – in the back of his mind, at least – issues concerning kidney difficulties, since he sees patients with those problems frequently. The artificial heart, and its efficient current flow, served to retrieve that problem. The artificial heart was then modified – the idea was extended – to meet the needs of kidney patients.

A Medical Avatar

A very different area in which Dr N. has innovated involves more efficient delivery of health care, especially to his pediatric surgical patients. Patients are often kept in the hospital longer than needed because they cannot carry out routine tasks that one might not need a hospital staff for, such as monitoring vital signs and taking medicine on schedule. One area of innovation concerning patient maintenance entails the use of robot technology. That idea arose from Dr N.'s watching children engaged in a video game. The children were interacting with the game, and responding to feedback from the game, almost as if it was human or an avatar. He thought a similar set-up would be a way to engage a child in their own care. When the child comes to the hospital, an avatar for the child is created, and the avatar goes home with them after surgery. The avatar is loaded with information concerning how often the child needs to take medicine and carry out other tasks. The avatar interacts with the child, saying, "Hey, it's time to take our medicine," and if the child does not take the medicine, the avatar gets sick and explains why. Here we have another case of analogical transfer: Dr N. saw the engagement of the children with video games, and he transferred that information – extended the new idea – to his problem, getting children engaged with their own medical care.

Table 4.4 *Analytic thinking in pro-c creativity*

Creative Achievement	Analytic Thinking	
	Heuristic Methods	Green Creativity
IDEO's Shopping Cart	Logical reasoning	Near transfer: casters; safety seat; high-chair
Dunkirk rescue: east mole	Logical reasoning: need to quickly evacuate many men	Near transfer: mole used as a dock for small boats
Dunkirk rescue: small ships	Need for more ships; problems with rowed lifeboats	Near transfer: motorized small ships
Post-It Notes	Logical analysis of problem: need weak adhesive	Near analogy: Silver's Weak adhesive
Implantable artificial kidney		Near analogy: implantable heart to kidney
Health monitoring avatar		Near analogy: interactive video-game avatar to medical avatar

Pro-c Creativity: Conclusions

The just-presented results examining pro-c creativity support those from the earlier pro-c case studies – IDEO's shopping cart, and the Dunkirk rescue – in providing further support for the role of analytic thinking in pro-c creativity (see Table 4.4). New ideas are generated based on analogy or logical thinking; and those new ideas are then extended to the present situation. Those case studies provide further evidence that the thought mechanisms found in genius-level creativity are also seen in nongenius thinking, which indicates that the same mechanisms may be involved in all creative advances. In order to examine that possibility further, we now turn to additional examples of *under-the-radar* creativity: innovations produced by people for whom creativity is not part of the job description. Here we build on the earlier discussion of Graham's invention of *Mistake Out*.

The Universality of Creativity: Under-the-Radar Innovation

Under-the-radar innovation is important for two reasons. Demonstrating that under-the-radar innovation is commonplace would provide support for the idea that all of us have the capacity to innovate. In addition, if we discover that under-the-radar creativity depends on analytic thinking, it will provide evidence that analytic thinking functions in all levels of creative advances.

Innovation by an Airline's Staff

American Airlines for a long while had in place a program, called *IdeAAs*, designed to stimulate the generation of new ideas (*AA* is the symbol for *A*merican *A*irlines). The program had some success, and some of the ideas came from people who were under the radar. One might think, for example, that flight attendants or pilots would not be sources of innovation, since creativity would not seem to be an aspect of their jobs. However, many new ideas came from flight attendants, pilots, and other staff members (Robinson & Stern, 1997, p. 2). One example involved what seemed to be a very small-scale observation but had significant economic consequences.

Saving on Coffee Lids

Flight attendants spend a lot of time dispensing coffee served from metal pots, each of which is covered with a disposable plastic lid to keep the coffee warm and prevent splashing in case of turbulence. The airline catering service routinely put ten lids on each flight to ensure that there were enough. One flight attendant noticed that, at the end of all her flights, at least half of those lids were being thrown away unused. That meant that there were too many lids being supplied. The flight attendant suggested that the number of lids per flight be reduced by five. Each lid cost 1.5 cents, so 7.5 cents per flight could be saved. That might seem to be a trivial saving, but the airline operated over 2,300 flights per day, 365 days a year, so that suggestion saved the airline more than $62,000 a year (Robinson & Stern, 1997, p. 2). But we are more interested in the process that brought about the flight attendant's creative idea. It was based first on an observation and then on a familiar heuristic: logical reasoning from that observation. The conclusion that the airline could save money, a creative idea, was the result of analytic thinking.

Saving Time and Fuel

Another creative idea developed out of a pilot's observations concerning flight paths (Robinson & Stern, 1997, pp. 111–112). Planes flying out of

Miami, Florida, were routed around the former Homestead Air Force Base, a long detour, because of security and safety concerns. But Homestead had been destroyed by a hurricane in 1992 and officially closed. After the base had been closed, a pilot raised the question of why American's flights still had to avoid the former Homestead airspace, since the base no longer existed. The pilot suggested that, if they could fly over the base, much time and, perhaps more importantly, fuel could be saved. The suggestion was adopted, and the savings for the airline in fuel costs were almost $1 million in the first year. Again, the savings were significant to the airline, but the thought processes are more important to us. The new idea was based on a logical analysis of the pre- and post-hurricane situations and the changes that the destruction of the base had brought about. There was a contradiction in the post-hurricane situation: American's flights had to detour to avoid Homestead, but Homestead no longer existed. The pilot saw that the basic premise on which the whole process had been built was no longer true, which resulted in a faulty conclusion. We have here another creative advance, built on reasoning as well as on understanding verbal and pictorial information (the flight-plan map) – core components of analytic thinking.

Medical Innovation: Heating Up a Baby

Under-the-radar creativity can also be seen in medicine. In our study of medical innovation, we also interviewed Nurse S., who developed a head wrap, used post-surgically, for infants who had undergone coronary bypass surgery. Infant patients are subjected to a significant lowering of the body temperature, or induced hypothermia, which results in slowing of bodily functioning, allowing the surgeon to work more easily. Induced hypothermia also facilitates the patients' recovery from the surgery. It is sometimes difficult to bring the infant patients' temperatures back up to optimal, however, due in part to their less-developed temperature-regulation capacity. In addition, moving infant patients post-operatively involves traveling through hospital corridors that are often cold, which also interferes with infants' temperature returning to optimal.

Infants' difficulties recovering from hypothermia comprised, according to Nurse S., an "age-old" problem, well-known to all workers in pediatric operating rooms, and it had been discussed in staff meetings at her hospital. As part of an initiative by the medical center, Nurse S. chose to work on that problem, because of its importance, even though she had never produced any innovations in her role as a nurse. In carrying out research on bodily regulation of temperature, she began to focus on the head as a possible target, because the head is where we lose much of our heat. The head is sometimes cooled when bringing the temperature *down* by putting ice around it. Nurse S. noted that there were many procedures used to facilitate temperature recovery but nothing involving the head. She decided to try to positively affect temperature by *covering* the head: perhaps patients would then warm up more quickly. She first thought about a hat for the patient, but that might interfere with anesthesia that required access to blood vessels in the head, and putting on a hat might require moving the patient, which could interfere with the surgical procedure. Nurse S. overcame those difficulties by designing a head wrap, using insulating material. There was minimal interference with the patient, and the wrap facilitated temperature recovery.

Nurse S. told us that she had become the "poster girl" for the innovation center, because she was an example of how innovation could come from anywhere, not just the research and teaching staff who might be expected to be the leaders in innovation. (That would be pro-c innovation.) Nurse S. herself was a bit surprised by what she had accomplished. She was asked to tell the story of her invention at meetings, so that the entire medical staff could be sensitized to the possibility that they might be able to innovate.

Looking at the thought processes involved in this creative act, we see a pattern similar to those already discussed. Nurse S. concentrated on the head because it is a significant source of heat loss and nothing was being done that utilized it. Her new idea was generated through logical analysis of the problem. She then considered how one might counteract heat loss from the head, which led her to the possibility of a hat, an example of near analogical transfer. She then had to extend that idea to her problem situation, which was not trivially easy. A hat was rejected because of difficulties it raised, which were overcome by an insulated head wrap – again, near analogical transfer and logical thinking. In conclusion, this example of under-the-radar creativity came about as the result of the familiar processes of analytic thinking.

Under-the-Radar Creativity: Questions

The examples of little-c creative advances discussed so far in this chapter – Graham's *Mistake Out*; the reduction in coffee-pot lids on American Airlines' flights; the rerouting of American Airlines' planes; and Nurse S.'s infant-patient head wrap – exemplify a wide range of under-the-radar creativity. However, most of those examples came from environments in which innovation had been at least a topic of interest. It would be important in demonstrating the universality of creativity that we find creative advances from people in environments in which there was no outside pressure toward innovation. One such environment is the home, and it turns out to be relatively easy to find impressive examples of creative thinking by ordinary folks at home.

Real Under-the-Radar Creativity: Little-C Creativity at Home

Controlling Cooking Spray

When I cook, I sometimes use cooking spray: you spray a pot or pan, coating it lightly with oil, so the food cooks without sticking to the pan. However, when I spray the pan, the misted spray goes beyond the limits of the pan, fogging the air and coating wherever I happen to be holding the pan. I need to use cooking spray, but using it was not without difficulties. I found out by accident that someone had solved my problem, in an elegant way. I was in my son and daughter-in-law's kitchen and saw a cooking magazine on the counter. I was glancing through it and noticed that it had a section on cooking tips, sent in by readers. One of those readers had solved my cooking-spray problem. She suggested that, if you have a dishwasher, you can apply cooking spray while holding the pan inside the dishwasher. (I know it was a woman because she signed her letter.) All the excess spray goes into the dishwasher, where it does no harm and is washed away when the dishwasher is used.

Several things impressed me on reading that solution to the cooking-spray problem. On a professional level, it would have been very interesting to have been in that person's kitchen when she got that idea. Second, that idea was produced by an ordinary person, at home, dealing with a small-scale problem that arose while cooking – not someone assigned by a company to deal with customers' problems or working in an organization that emphasized innovation. Thus, that letter also provided an example of the universality of creativity. Furthermore, examples such as this one turn out to be extremely easy to find. That cooking magazine prints, in every issue, numerous suggestions from readers. More than 800 have been collected in a book (America's Test Kitchen, 2006). Here are several more examples, chosen essentially at random while leafing through that book.

Greasy Bottles? No Sweat

When one pours oil from a bottle, there can be a trickle that runs down the side of the bottle. If one does not see it and wipe it quickly, the oil can get on your hands or run down onto the shelf in the pantry after the bottle is put away. The bottle and the shelf can get sticky from the oil. One reader had solved that problem by putting a sweatband, the kind that you might wear on your wrist while exercising, around the bottle. The sweatband goes above the point where you hold the bottle; it catches any trickling oil, leaving clean the rest of the bottle and the pantry shelf. When the sweatband gets dirty from the oil, wash it and use it again.

Freezing Bacon, a Slice at a Time

Many people use less than a full package of bacon at once, so one is left with unused slices. One reader was concerned that the left-over bacon slices in the refrigerator might spoil before being used. The obvious idea was to freeze the bacon, but if she put the bacon package into the freezer she would have a solid block of bacon, making it impossible to retrieve a small number of slices. Her idea was to separate the leftover slices *before* putting them into the freezer and to roll each slice into a cylinder. The slices then froze into separate rolls of bacon, and they could then be stored together in a bag in the freezer. When she wanted bacon, she could take out the exact number of slices that she needed.

Keeping Clean the Food-Processor Lid

A food processor is a very useful kitchen appliance, but keeping it clean is not easy. The most difficult part to clean is the lid, which covers the bowl, to keep the chopped food from spraying the kitchen and to protect the user from the spinning sharp blade. The processor lid is made up of several parts, which take up a lot of dishwasher space. If one could keep the lid clean during food-processing, it would make things much easier. One reader suggested stretching a sheet of plastic wrap across the top of the processor bowl, *before* the lid is put into place. You close the lid over the plastic wrap, so the wrap sits stretched tight across the bowl, under the lid. Any food sent flying by the blade hits the plastic wrap and never touches the bottom of the lid. When you are finished processing the food, you open the clean lid and put it aside, remove the plastic wrap, and access the food. Only the bowl and blade need to be cleaned, which saves a lot of work.

Real Under-the-Radar Creativity at Work

I recently encountered an under-the-radar innovation in another work environment in which innovation might not be expected. I was in my neighborhood coffee bar, waiting for my order to be filled. A barista had a large pitcher, which he needed to fill with cold water. In front of me was a faucet, which was designed so that, if one pushed one's container against a lever, water would flow into the container for as long as the lever was being pushed by the container. Many of us have seen one of those devices: you press your glass or bottle against it, and it is filled with water. However, the pitcher that this man needed to fill was large, so he was going to have to hold it against that lever for a long time, probably tiring his arm in the process. He solved that problem very simply: he put the pitcher under the faucet and then pulled a rubber band around the lever, so that it also went around the pipe that the faucet came out of. The rubber band held the lever back, as if his pitcher were being held against it, so the water kept flowing. He was able to do other things while the pitcher filled. I asked him about the origin of the idea, and he told me that he could not take credit; the idea was told to him by his manager at the last coffee bar he worked at. It would have been interesting to talk to that manager about the origin of the idea. Although that was not possible, this innovation is another example of under-the-radar creativity.

Real Under-the-Radar Creativity: Conclusions

These examples are, to me, impressive evidence for the creative capacities of ordinary folks. If we can assume that most of the people who sent in those suggestions to the cooking magazine are not involved in innovative activities in their professions, then those are examples of true under-the-radar creativity. The same would seem to be true concerning the rubber-band waterfountain opener. We are led to the conclusion that we are all capable of thinking creatively. Table 4.5 summarizes the cases of under-the-radar creativity discussed in this chapter.

Table 4.5 *Analytic thinking in under-the-radar creativity*

Creative Achievement	Analytic Thinking	
	Heuristic Methods	Green creativity
Betty Graham's *Mistake Out*		Near analogical transfer: painters correcting mistakes
Saving coffee-pot lids	Logical reasoning	
Rerouting AA's flights	Logical reasoning	
Infant-patient head-wrap	Logical reasoning: head as heat source	Near analogical transfer: hat and head-wrap
Controlling cooking spray*		
Solving greasy bottles*		
Keeping food-processor lid clean*		
Keeping water fountain running while you are away*		

* No information is available on the details of the processes involved.

Analytic Processes in Creative Achievement: Conclusions and Questions

This discussion in this chapter has achieved the three goals laid out at the beginning. First, several case studies of genius-level creative advances provided further evidence that creative advances at the highest level depend on analytic thinking (see Table 4.3). Second, studies of pro-c advances showed that the same processes are seen in the creative thinking of non-genius innovators. The final section of the chapter showed that ordinary people produce creative ideas in their everyday lives, again using the mechanisms of analytic thinking. We have thus closed the circle, showing that ordinary thinking underlies all creative advances and that creativity is universal among us. There may be differences in *influence* or importance for different works, but, for the psychologist studying creative thinking, there may not be differences in the *processes* through which those different works were brought about.

The discussion in this chapter has provided more evidence that green creativity, the recycling of old ideas, is a crucial component of creative advances at all levels, ranging from genius-level creativity to under-the-radar innovations. In many cases, old ideas are retrieved from memory by the person's encountering a situation analogous to something in memory. In other cases, new ideas can result from logical analysis of a new situation or application of other heuristics. Any new idea developed through those methods must then be modified, so that it can be extended to the present situation.

The role of green creativity in innovation emphasizes the importance of analogical thinking in many creative advances. Therefore, in order to complete our analysis of analytic thinking in creativity, in the next chapter we will examine the structure and functioning of analogical thinking. A number of researchers have emphasized the importance of analogical thinking in cognition (e.g., Forbus, Ferguson, Lovett & Gentner, 2017; Gentner & Maravilla, 2018; Hofstadter & Sander, 2013; Loewenstein, 2010), so the discussion in the next chapter will build on the foundation of recent research to analyze how analogical thinking functions in creativity.

Analogy in Scientific Creativity: The Discovery
of the Double Helix

The discovery in 1953 of the double helix of DNA by James Watson and Francis Crick was one of the seminal scientific advances of the twentieth century (Weisberg, 2006, ch. 1) and won them the Nobel Prize. Understanding the structure of DNA led to a wide range of advances, including the decoding of the genome and the development of personalized cancer therapies or "designer drugs." The distinctive shape of the DNA molecule resembles a spiral staircase (Figure 5.1). There are two helical, or spiral, *backbones* on the outside, twisting around each other (hence, the "double helix"). Those backbones consist of long strings of alternating sugar and phosphate molecules. The "rungs" of the staircase are made up of pairs of four compounds, called *bases*, abbreviated as A, C, G, and T. The bases pair up in two ways (A with T and C with G).

Watson and Crick met at the Cavendish Laboratory at Cambridge University in the fall of 1951. They worked as a team for a year and a half before they successfully cracked the secret of the structure of DNA. They were part of a small scientific community comprised of three groups of researchers, each working on the problem of trying to determine the structure of DNA. The other two teams were composed of scientists of the highest levels of accomplishment, including two who would also win the Nobel Prize. Why were Watson and Crick successful?

At the very beginning of their collaboration, Watson and Crick made two crucial decisions about how they would approach the problem of determining the structure of DNA. One could call those decisions their "creative intuition." First, they would assume that DNA was a helix; second, they would construct a molecular model – a stick-and-ball model – to determine the specifics of the structure. Based on those decisions, Watson and Crick were able to focus on several specific questions and to restrict the information that they had to sift through. That focus kept them from going down paths that would turn out to be a waste of time. Both of the other research teams did spend time going down wrong paths. Thus, our question of interest shifts to the following: Where did

145

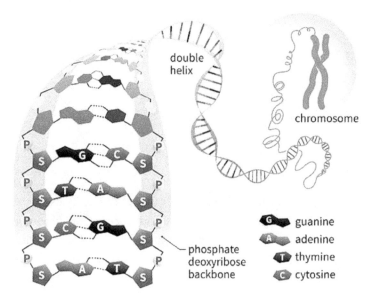

Figure 5.1 DNA, including breakdown of nucleotides.
DNA structure – From chromosome to deoxyribonucleic acid structure and base
pairing, jack0m, DigitalVision Vectors, Getty Images.

those two decisions come from? What was the source of Watson and Crick's
creative intuition?

Watson and Crick's "intuition" was another example of *green creativity*
based on a familiar mechanism: analogical transfer. They built their research
strategy on the work of Linus Pauling, a world-famous chemist, winner of
two Nobel prizes, and one of the other researchers attempting to determine
the structure of DNA. About a year earlier, Pauling had scored a scientific
triumph when he proposed a structure for the protein alpha-keratin. Alpha-
keratin is a strong molecule that forms fibers and is the principal component
of skin, hair, and fingernails, as well as the claws of predatory animals.
Pauling had proposed that the structure of alpha-keratin was a single-
stranded helix and had used molecular modeling to build that structure.

Of direct relevance to our analysis, proteins and DNA are *analogous molecules*. Both are *organic macromolecules* – that is, very large molecules involved
in biological processes, with carbon as an important component. In addition,
both DNA and proteins are constructed from *repeating units* or building-
blocks. In DNA, each unit, called a *nucleotide*, is made up of a sugar molecule,
a phosphate group, and a base (see Figure 5.1). Proteins, the basic components
of life, are made up of strings of amino acids. In a protein such as alpha-keratin,
the building-block is a *peptide*, made up of at least two amino acids.
Furthermore, in both DNA and alpha-keratin, those building-blocks are connected in a similar way. *Phosphate bonds* hold all the nucleotides together in

DNA, and *peptide bonds* serve to link the amino acids that make up alpha-keratin. Thus, DNA is a *polynucleotide*, and proteins are *polypeptides*. It is not hard to understand why thinking about DNA might bring to mind the alpha helix. The critical first steps in one of the most important discoveries of modern science were based on analogical thinking and green creativity (see Table 5.1).

Transferring a general strategy, based on Pauling's success with alpha-keratin, to the analysis of DNA went only so far, however, since the available research data indicated that the DNA molecule was thicker than a single-strand helix. Watson and Crick did not know, among other things, how many strands DNA contained or how those multiple strands were held together. The idea retrieved by the match between DNA and the alpha helix had to be modified – that is, extended to the new situation. Since they had no detailed information concerning the specifics of DNA, Watson and Crick used heuristic methods to move their research forward. As one example, they used information about the density of DNA, to *deduce*, through mathematics and logic, that the molecule was made up of *three* strands. As a rough analogy, let us say that someone asks us to determine, without looking, how many marbles are in a covered paper cup. All we have available is a scale, as well as the knowledge that marbles weigh 2 ounces each and the cup itself weighs .25 ounces. We weigh the cup and contents, and we see that they weigh 6.25 ounces. We can, from that information, deduce that there are three marbles in the cup. A similar process led Watson and Crick to build, as their first try at a model of DNA, a *triple helix*, a three-strand molecule.

The triple helix model was shown to one of the other research groups working on DNA, scientists at King's College, London, who strongly criticized several aspects of it. That negative feedback caused Watson and Crick, using their expertise as well as several heuristic methods, to rethink several of the model's components. It also turned out that the original information concerning the density of DNA, which Watson and Crick had used to determine that there were three strands, was incorrect. Because it was based on incorrect data, the triple helix was also incorrect. Watson and Crick obtained a number of additional pieces of information, from research on DNA carried out by other researchers, that pointed to two rather than three strands. Much of that information came from research carried out by Rosalind Franklin and

Table 5.1 *Correspondences between alpha-keratin and DNA*

Alpha-Keratin	Correspondence	DNA
Organic macromolecule	Type of molecule	Organic macromolecule
Peptide	Basic unit	Nucleotide
Peptide bonds	Connections between units	Phosphate bonds
Polypeptide	Chemical description	Polynucelotide

Maurice Wilkins, two King's College scientists. Therefore, Watson and Crick shifted to the belief that DNA was a two-stranded or double helix.

The final step in Watson and Crick's discovery involved determining how the two strands were held together. As mentioned, each of the nucleotide building-blocks of DNA is made up of a sugar, a phosphate, and one of four bases (A, C, G, and T; see Figure 5.1). It was thought that the bases might play a role in holding the strands together, but the details of how the bases were paired, and how they were linked, were unknown. Because there was no information available, Watson used another heuristic method, trial and error, to work out the combinations of the bases. He manipulated cardboard models of the bases on his desk until he discovered combinations that fit together in the required physical configurations (Watson, 1968; Weisberg, 2006, ch. 1).

In conclusion, the discovery of the double helix was based on familiar components of analytic thinking: analogical thinking and heuristic methods. In earlier chapters, we saw multiple examples of analogical thinking in the development of solutions to problems, ranging from laboratory problems, such as the Candle problem (Fleck & Weisberg, 2004), to problems "in the wild," such as IDEO's shopping cart, Frank Lloyd Wright's *Fallingwater*, and Dr N.'s development of an implantable kidney and a health-care avatar. A number of researchers (e.g., Forbus et al., 2017; Gentner & Maravilla, 2018; Hofstadter & Sander, 2013; Loewenstein, 2010) have argued that analogical thinking is a core process that underlies much of cognition, including creative thinking (Weisberg, 2006). The role of analogical thinking in creativity is the focus of this chapter.

Outline of the Chapter

We will first review general aspects of analogical thinking, which will lead to an examination of several mechanisms whereby analogical thinking plays a role in creativity. One such mechanism involves the now-familiar *analogical transfer*: the solution from a problem in memory is *transferred* to a new problem. A different use of analogical thinking in creativity may occur when a person has been working unsuccessfully on a problem and then puts it aside. The person then encounters an object in the world that is analogous to what is needed to solve the problem and provides an idea for the solution. This process has been called *opportunistic assimilation* of the new information (Seifert et al., 1995): *opportunistic*, because one is taking advantage of an opportunity; and *assimilation*, because the new information is taken in, or assimilated, and used as the basis for solving a problem. Opportunistic assimilation was seen in the

Dunkirk rescue. Captain Tennant was looking for a possible dock for naval rescue vessels, and his attention was drawn to the east mole. Similarly, Bette Graham had an unsolved problem with typing errors when she saw painters correcting their mistakes by painting over them. In this chapter, we will flesh out the details underlying use of analogies, including some situations in which analogical use is difficult.

Some Problems to Solve

In order to provide some information to serve as a foundation for the discussion in the chapter, it would be very helpful if you tried to solve several problems. The first problem is the General problem, presented in Table 5.2. Please try to solve it before reading further. Take notes, if you can, on thoughts that come to mind as you work on the problem.

Table 5.2 *The General problem*

A small country fell under the iron rule of a dictator. The dictator ruled the country from a strong fortress, situated in the middle of the country, surrounded by farms and villages. Many roads radiated outward from the fortress like spokes on a wheel.

A great general arose, who raised a large army at the border and vowed to capture the fortress and free the country from the dictator. The general knew that, if his entire army could attack the fortress at once, it could be captured. His troops were poised at the head of one of the roads leading to the fortress, ready to attack. However, a spy brought the general a disturbing report. The ruthless dictator had planted mines on each of the roads. The mines were set so that small bodies of men could pass over them safely, since the dictator needed to be able to move troops and workers to and from the fortress. However, any large force would detonate the mines. Not only would this blow up the road and render it impassable, but the dictator would then destroy many villages in retaliation. A full-scale direct attack on the fortress therefore appeared impossible. How could the General capture the fortress?

The General's Solution

The general divided the army into small groups, with each group at a different road. At a signal, each group moved down its road to the fortress. All of the small groups passed safely over the mines, and the army then came together and attacked the fortress at full strength. The general captured the fortress and overthrew the dictator. Now try to solve the Laser/Brain-Tumor problem (Figure 5.2), again, taking notes.

A neurosurgeon is treating a patient who has been diagnosed with a tumor deep in the brain. The person is very weak, so an operation is too dangerous. The neurosurgeon has available a type of laser that, at high intensity, will destroy the tumor. However, at that intensity, the laser will also destroy the healthy brain tissue that it passes through on the way to the tumor, which will also result in the patient's death. How can the neurosurgeon destroy the tumor with the laser, while keeping the patient alive?

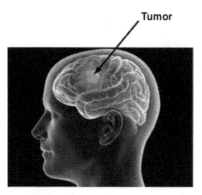

Figure 5.2 Laser/Brain-Tumor Problem Solution. Illustration of a brain, Sciepro, Science Photo Library, Getty Images.

Laser/Brain-Tumor Problem Solution

Rather than using the too-powerful laser, the neurosurgeon can use two weaker lasers, each set at, say, half the required intensity. Those weak lasers can be aimed at the tumor, so their beams will converge and combine at the tumor, as shown in Figure 5.3. The combined lasers will

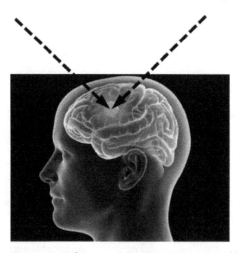

Figure 5.3 Solution to Laser/Brain-Tumor problem. Illustration of a brain, Sciepro, Science Photo Library, Getty Images.

be strong enough to destroy the tumor, but each alone will be too weak to harm the healthy brain tissue that it passes through on the way. This is called the *simultaneous-convergence solution* to the Laser/Brain-Tumor problem.

Now please try to solve the Radiation problem (Figure 5.4).

Imagine that you are a radiologist who specializes in treating cancerous tumors. A patient comes to you with a stomach tumor, shown in cross-section below. The patient is very weak from the effects of the cancer and cannot be operated on to remove the tumor. There is available a new kind of ray, which can be used to destroy the tumor. However, if you turn on the ray at the intensity needed to destroy the tumor, it will also damage the tissue that it passes through on the way to the tumor (see diagram). If the very weak patient suffers trauma of that sort, the patient will not survive the treatment. Is there any way that you can destroy the tumor while saving the patient? Take a few minutes to try to solve the problem, writing down solutions and making any notes as necessary.

Diagram of Radiation Problem

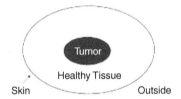

Figure 5.4 Radiation problem

Solution to the Radiation Problem

The doctor can take two bundles of weaker rays, each at, say, half the intensity needed to destroy the tumor, and aim them at the tumor so that they converge there (Duncker, 1945). The intensity of the rays will be low everywhere but at the tumor, so no healthy tissue will be affected, but the tumor will be destroyed. The solution here is also a *simultaneous-convergence solution*, very similar to that used to solve the Laser/Brain-Tumor problem.

Questions about the Problem-Solving Process

Here are several questions to think about that address issues that will be important in the discussion in this chapter.

1. Did you solve the General problem? It is not an easy problem, and was presented in the expectation that it might not be solved.
2. Did you solve the Laser/Brain-Tumor problem? It, too, is not an easy problem.

3. When you were reading the description of the Laser/Brain-Tumor problem, did you think of the solution from the General problem?
4. Did you solve the Radiation problem? The Radiation problem is also difficult for most people (e.g., Gick & Holyoak, 1980).
5. When you were reading the Radiation problem, did you think of the solution from either the Laser/Brain-Tumor or General problems?

Based on information provided by the examples of analogical thinking discussed already as well as information obtained from trying to solve the just-presented problems, we can now examine the mechanisms underlying the use of analogical thinking in creativity.

Analogical Thinking

Analogical thinking uses information from one situation, called the *base* or *source*, to deal with another situation, the *target*, that is analogous to the base. Two situations are analogous when they have the same *relational structure*; although the specific *objects* involved might be very different, the *relations* that those objects participate in are the same (Gentner & Maravilla, 2018; Holyoak, 2012). As we have seen, the problem of the structure of DNA (a poly-nucleotide) was analogous to the problem of the structure of alpha-keratin (a poly-peptide). Also, as discussed in Chapter 1, IDEO's problem of maneuvering a bulky shopping cart in a narrow supermarket aisle was analogous to the problem of maneuvering a bulky office chair in the small space behind a desk. Similarly, Goya's *The Disasters of War* was analogous to Picasso's *Guernica*.

Types of Analogies

As discussed in earlier chapters, cognitive psychologists classify analogies based on the similarity between the base and target information (Dunbar, 1995). In a *local* analogy, the base and target come from the same domain. As an example, a molecular geneticist trying to solve the problem of the structure of DNA might use information from other research on DNA to help to solve it. As discussed briefly, Watson and Crick used information from studies of DNA to help them analyze the structure of the molecule. In a local analogy, the two situations have many *surface elements* – the objects "on the surface" – in common. Here, both involve DNA.

We also know that Watson and Crick used information from Pauling's analysis of alpha-keratin, another organic macromolecule, to help them understand the structure of DNA. That was a *regional* analogy: both analyses involved organic macromolecules, but the surface elements were different. If the base and target contain *identical* elements, the analogy is *transparent* (Gentner & Maravilla, 2018). Transparency occurs in degrees. An analogy involving two DNA experiments is more transparent than one involving DNA and alpha-keratin. As noted in Chapter 1, I will refer to both local and regional analogies as "near" analogies. In contrast, consider the notion of a computer "virus" – a concept from the category of infectious organisms was transferred to a situation in which a computer is disabled by a program that makes it unable to function. That transfer was based on a *remote* analogy. The domains involved are "far apart," with no surface elements in common. I will refer to remote analogies as "far" analogies.

Components of Analogical Transfer

The components of analogical transfer are outlined in Figure 5.5. The first step occurs when presentation of some new situation – the *target* – reminds a person of a familiar situation that is of similar structure – the *base*. The target *retrieves* the base from memory (Figure 5.5A), and a new idea comes to mind. ("Hmm, *this* reminds me of *that*.") Watson and Crick's thinking about Pauling's work with alpha-keratin when they were working on the structure of DNA is an example of retrieval of a base (alpha-keratin) by a target (DNA). ("Hmm, DNA reminds me of alpha-keratin.")

Once a base has been retrieved by a target, there can then be a matching of other elements in the target and the base (Figure 5.5B). In the case of the Radiation and Laser/Brain-Tumor problems, the locations of the tumors can be matched (the stomach and the brain), as well as the mechanisms available to fight them (the rays and the lasers). There is also the concern about not harming healthy tissue as well as not being able to use the available "solution force" at full strength. Once those matchings or correspondences have been established, still further information from the base can be transferred to the target (Figure 5.5B). Most important for us, sometimes the information transferred can serve to solve a problem. In the case of the Radiation and Laser/Brain-Tumor problems, the simultaneous-convergence solution from the Laser/Brain-Tumor problem could be applied to the Radiation problem, using weak *rays* instead of weak *lasers*. However, since the two situations are not identical, the base information

A) RETRIEVAL OF BASE BY TARGET; BASED ON CORRESPONDENCE

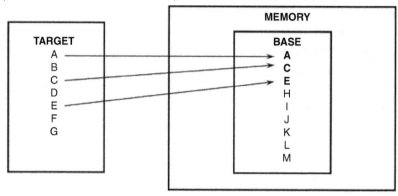

B) TRANSFER (POSSIBLE INFERENCES BASED ON I, K, M)

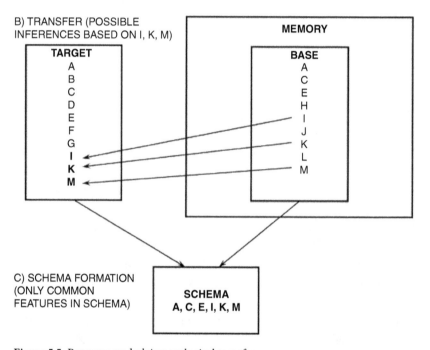

C) SCHEMA FORMATION (ONLY COMMON FEATURES IN SCHEMA)

Figure 5.5 Processes underlying analogical transfer
A Retrieval of base
B Transfer
C Construction of schema

cannot be directly applied to the target. The retrieved information must be modified to fit the specific demands of the target; in other words, the retrieved information from the base must be *extended* to the target.

After transferring a solution from one problem to an analogous one, the person may summarize the elements that the base and target have in common, which can result in the production of a *schema*, an abstract description of the situation (Figure 5.5C). After solving the Radiation problem by extending the convergence solution from the Laser/Brain-Tumor problem, you might think further about those two situations and summarize them in something like the following way.

- If you are faced with an obstacle that you want to eliminate;
- and you have available a force that will destroy that obstacle;
- but you cannot apply the force at the required intensity;
- try dividing the force into weaker parts, and combining those parts at the obstacle, to provide sufficient force to eliminate it.

That description would be the schema of the "simultaneous-convergence solution." It might be useful in solving other problems.

An important question addressed by researchers investigating analogical transfer centers on the basis for the retrieval of the base by the target. Is retrieval driven by the specific objects – the "surface elements" – in the target and base? That would be transfer based on a near analogy. Or can retrieval come about because the target and base contain the same *relations*, without specific objects in common? If so, that would be transfer based on a far analogy – what we could call a creative leap. All the examples of analogies in creative thinking that we have examined so far (see Chapters 1, 3, and 4) have been based on *near* analogical transfer. However, there are cases in which far analogies were important in creativity. As we work through several such examples, we will gain further insight into the mechanisms underlying creative thinking. We begin with an examination of laboratory studies of analogical transfer.

Analogical Transfer during Problem-Solving

The pioneering modern examination of analogical transfer in problem-solving was carried out by Gick and Holyoak (1980, Exp. 1; see also Gick & Holyoak, 1983), who used the Radiation problem as the target (Figure 5.4). There were three conditions in the Gick and Holyoak (1980, Exp. 1) study. First, a Control group simply tried to solve the Radiation problem and provided the "baseline" solution rate. The two other groups – *transfer* groups – were both given exposure to one base analogue, the General problem, and its solution (see Table 5.2) before trying to solve the Radiation problem. The General problem is a far analogue to the Radiation problem (see Table 5.3A), because the two situations overlap only in relations, not in specific objects. One of the transfer groups comprised a *Hint* condition: when the Radiation problem was presented, the participants were *told* that the General problem might help them solve it. If the Hint group did not solve the problem at a higher level than the control group, then the General problem was not useful, and the study was a waste of time. The real interest of the researchers, however, centered on the second transfer condition. Those people were given the Radiation problem, but they were *not* told that the General problem could help them solve it. That condition tested for the occurrence of "spontaneous" far transfer – that is, transfer without any external assistance.

The results of the Gick and Holyoak (1980) study are shown in Table 5.3B. The Control group did not perform well. The Hint group, on the other hand, performed very well, which indicated that the General problem *could* be very helpful in solving the Radiation problem. The question of interest was the performance of the Spontaneous Transfer group, and their performance was

Table 5.3 *Gick and Holyoak (1980) analogical transfer study*

A. Analogical relations between General and Radiation problems

General Problem	Radiation Problem
General	Doctor
Fortress	Tumor
Army	Rays
Using whole army ⇒ explode mines ⇒ kill soldiers	Using strong rays ⇒ kill healthy tissue ⇒ patient dies
Break up army into small groups, unite at fortress: "simultaneous convergence"	Use weak-intensity rays, unite at tumor: "simultaneous convergence"

B. Gick & Holyoak (1980) results – percentage of participants solving the Radiation problem after exposure to the General problem, with and without a hint

Condition	Solutions	Number of participants
Control	0%	10
Hint	92%	12
No hint ("spontaneous far transfer")	7%	15

Table 5.4 *Keane's (1987) analogical-transfer study*

Base Analogue	% Retrieving Base Analogue
Rays/Brain-Tumor (near)	88
General (far)	12

much closer to that of the Control condition than the Hint condition. Most participants did not, on their own, think of the General problem when the Radiation problem was presented. Spontaneous far analogical transfer did not occur. Those results are evidence that it is hard to produce a "creative leap" in the laboratory, which could be taken as negative evidence for the genius view.

That negative conclusion was supported by the results of a study by Keane (1987, Exp. 1) that directly compared transfer based on a near versus far analogy. Participants read one of two base analogues, and its solution, followed by presentation of the target Radiation problem. One base analogue was the already-familiar General problem (Table 5.2), with no surface elements in common with the Radiation problem. The second base problem involved a surgeon trying to remove a *brain tumor*, using *rays*, which was very similar to the Laser/Brain-Tumor problem (Figure 5.3), except that the doctor had "rays" available to destroy the tumor, rather than a laser. The Rays/Brain-Tumor problem and the Radiation problem formed a *near* analogy.

Keane's results are shown in Table 5.4. As Gick and Holyoak (1980) found, almost no one in Keane's (1987) study solved the Radiation problem after exposure to the General problem. In contrast, almost all the participants who first read the Rays/Brain-Tumor base analogue solved the Radiation problem. Thus, it is not necessary that the *identical* objects be present in the base and target problems: "similar" objects – rays and lasers; brain tumors and stomach tumors – are sufficient to produce spontaneous transfer. That conclusion fits with the examples of green creativity seen in the earlier chapters and also with Watson and Crick use of Pauling's alpha-helix as basis for their analysis of DNA.

Lack of Spontaneous Analogical Far Transfer: The Problem of Inert Knowledge in Creative Thinking

The pioneering research of Gick and Holyoak (1980) and Keane (1987) produced consistent results: near transfer, but no far transfer (for further discussion, see Gentner & Maravilla, 2018). The specific objects in the target problem – the surface elements – seemed to play a dominant role in memory search. When a potentially useful far analogue – the General problem – was available in memory, the retrieval outlined in Figure 5.5A did not occur. Psychologists have used the term *inert knowledge* (Whitehead, 1929) to describe that sort of situation. An individual possesses knowledge – the base – that could be very helpful in solving a target problem, but the individual does not make the connection between the base and the target. The person's knowledge is inert, or *inactive*.

The existence of inert knowledge has been of great interest to psychologists studying creative thinking, as well as to educators (Gentner & Maravilla, 2018; George & Wiley, 2018). Based on the outside-the-box perspective on creativity, if one hopes to increase people's ability to think creatively, then one should be concerned with how one could make inert knowledge active. The existence of inert knowledge also seems to indicate that our educational programs have fallen short of their goals, failing to prepare individuals to deal with some of the problems they will face in their lives. How can one change the ways that students are taught to think about what they are learning, so that a broader range of information is brought to bear when attempting to deal with problems?

The lack of far transfer reported by Gick and Holyoak (1980) and Keane (1987) stimulated two streams of research aimed finding ways to "activate" inert knowledge. One stream focused on changing the way the *base information* was stored originally in memory. It was hypothesized that storing relational information in memory – a *schema* of the base solution (see Figure 5.5C) – would make it more likely that a potentially useful base would be retrieved by presentation of a target. The second stream of investigations focused on changing the *information from the target* that was used *to search memory for relevant analogues*. Here, too, it was hypothesized that forming a schema – in this case a schema of the *target* – would make it more likely that a potentially useful base analogue would be retrieved.

Activating Inert Knowledge: I. Storing Base Schemas in Memory

In response to the lack of spontaneous far transfer in their first study, Gick and Holyoak carried out a second set of experiments (Gick & Holyoak, 1983), in which they presented *two* base analogues, rather than one, plus

Table 5.5 *Gick and Holyoak (1983) study*

A. *Red Adair problem*

An oil well in Saudi Arabia exploded and caught fire. The result was a blazing inferno
that consumed an enormous quantity of oil. Famed firefighter Red Adair was called
in. Adair knew that the fire could be put out if a huge amount of fire-retardant foam
could be dumped on the base of the well. There was enough foam available at the site
to do the job. However, there was no hose large enough to put all the foam on the fire
fast enough. The small hoses that were available could not shoot the foam quickly
enough to do any good. It looked like there would have to be a costly delay before
a serious attempt could be made.

However, Adair stationed men in a circle all around the fire, with all of the available
small hoses. When everyone was ready, all the hoses were opened up, and foam was
directed at the fire from all directions. In this way, a huge amount of foam quickly
struck the source of the fire, and the blaze was extinguished.

B. *Gick & Holyoak (1983) results*

Percentage of participants solving the Radiation problem after exposure to two analogous stories, the General story and the Red Adair story, without a hint, compared
with a control group who were exposed to one analogous and one non-analogous
story

Condition	% Complete Solutions	Number of Participants
Two analogues	39	28
Control	21	47

their solutions, to participants. The two analogues were the General problem
and a problem concerning oil-well firefighter Red Adair (see Table 5.5A) that
was also solved by simultaneous convergence. Gick and Holyoak reasoned
that presenting two base analogues and their solutions would make it more
likely that the participants would think about the relational elements that the
two solutions had in common. Those elements included the need to *divide
the force into parts* and then *bring those parts together* at the same place at the
same time – simultaneous convergence (see Figure 5.5C). Gick and Holyoak
tried to maximize the likelihood that the participants would think about the
schematic aspects of the solution by *instructing* them to do so. Participants
were asked to describe what the base analogues had in common as far as the
problems being faced and solutions that were produced. This "schematic"
processing of the base information was expected to make it more likely that
people would transfer the base solution to the Radiation problem.

However, as can be seen in Table 5.5B, there was not a large amount of transfer in this study. Transfer was greater after two analogues than one, but the two-analogue condition still showed much less transfer than that obtained by Gick and Holyoak (1980) from one analogue plus a hint. (See also Edwards et al. (2014); and Lowenstein, Thompson & Gentner (2003)). There was, however, one study, by Catrambone and Holyoak (1989), that did produce an impressive amount of spontaneous far transfer. The researchers had to work very hard, which has implications for understanding creativity.

Spontaneous Far Analogical Transfer

Catrambone and Holyoak (1989) presented *three* base analogues, rather than two, before the target: the General (Table 5.2); Red Adair (Table 5.5); and a third problem, another variation on the simultaneous-convergence principle. The researchers also changed the instructions designed to bring about construction of the simultaneous-convergence schema from the solutions to the three base problems. The new instructions provided details as to what aspects of the solutions the participants should concentrate on. The researchers also gave the participants questions to answer about the base solutions, designed to *direct them* to the important elements that the solutions had in common. Finally, the participants were provided with *ideal* answers, to ensure that they thought about the critical elements of the convergence solution (see Table 5.6).

Table 5.6 *Catrambone and Holyoak materials*

A. *Two questions and ideal answers*

---

1. How are the obstacles that made it difficult to capture the fortress and put out the fire similar? The obstacles are similar in the following ways:
    a. Only a small force can be aimed at the target from any given direction (only a small number of soldiers can go down a given path/only a single bucket of water can be thrown from any position).
    b. A small force by itself is not sufficient to do the job of a large force.
2. List all the important similarities you can think of in the *methods* used to capture the fortress and put out the fire. The methods are similar in the following ways:
    a. A large force (total number of soldiers/total amount of water available) was split up into many small forces.
    b. The small forces surrounded the target.
    c. The small forces simultaneously focused or converged on the target from all directions, thus adding up to a large force that focused on the target.

A week later, the participants returned to the laboratory, and the Radiation problem was presented. Compared to the weak results of the studies reviewed earlier (see Tables 5.2B and 5.4B), this study produced impressive amounts of spontaneous transfer, with more than 75 percent of the participants solving the target problem. To produce those positive results, however, Catrambone and Holyoak (1989) provided extensive "scaffolding" to support participants' analyses of the base analogues. Loewenstein (2010) reviewed other studies that have also facilitated far analogical transfer. Those studies, too, have emphasized the underlying structure of the base. For example, having the participants *explain* the base, which makes one think about the base in more relational terms, increases far transfer.

Encoding Base Schemas: Conclusion

It has been possible to demonstrate far analogical transfer in laboratory studies of problem-solving. However, the participants in those successful demonstrations were taught to analyze the base situations they encountered in ways that were of maximal potential usefulness. In order to facilitate far transfer, it seems necessary to analyze the relevant information at a relatively abstract level, so that it is possible to make a match between the target and base (see also George & Wiley (2018)). Now let us consider research that has tried to overcome inert knowledge from the other side, by changing the way people process the *target* information when they encounter it. If the target is processed at an abstract, or "schematic," level, that should change the cues that are used to search memory for potential base analogues.

Activating Inert Knowledge: II. Using Relations to Access Information in Memory

Gentner et al. (2009) demonstrated that relational information can be used to retrieve base information from memory. They examined the effect of *comparing* two current situations on the *retrieval* of analogous situations from memory. The procedure involved exposing individuals to two situations, in which people were negotiating a business agreement. Both the negotiations involved a *contingent contract*. Here is one example. Let us say that you and I are trying to reach an agreement on your factory producing sneakers for my company and delivering them to me. I am concerned that you will not be able to get them to me on time for the fall season, so I want you to deliver them to me by air-freight, which is fast but expensive; you want to deliver by container-ship, which is slower but much cheaper. We agree to the following: you will ship air-freight, and we will keep track of the progress of the ship you would have shipped the sneakers on. If the ship arrives in time for my selling season, then I will pay you the price for air-freight. However, if the ship is late, then I will only have to pay for the ship's costs, even though I got the goods air-freight. The payment is *contingent* on, or *depends on*, the outcome of the ship's travels.

In one condition of the study, the participants read the two business-agreement examples *separately*, and for each they described what was happening in that situation and how successful the solution was. The people in the *comparison* condition, in contrast, were asked to compare the two example situations as far as the similarities between them, describe the key parallels in the two situations, and describe the solution and how successful it was. All participants were then asked to *recall* a past event, preferably from their own experience, that embodied the same principle as the one that they had just described from the negotiating scenarios. The participants in the studies of interest here ranged from experienced managerial consultants to MBAs to students working toward an MA in accounting, so all had some experience with contract negotiation. Results indicated that participants in the *comparison* condition recalled contingent contracts more frequently than did participants in the *separate* condition. Also, a majority of the retrieved analogous situations were *not* similar to the examples in surface elements (Gentner et al., 2009, Exp. 1). Thus, the retrieval was based on the *relations* (see also Kurtz & Loewenstein, 2007).

In sum, people can use relations contained in the target information to retrieve base information from memory. However, as with the research that has demonstrated far analogical transfer based on storing the *base schema*, people may need to carry out complex processing on the *target* information, including comparing more than one target, before they will be able to retrieve a far analogy from memory.

Analogical Transfer in Problem-Solving: Conclusions

Surface elements in a problem seem to be of critical importance in analogical transfer: near transfer will almost always be the "default" option. However, far transfer can be brought about, if the relevant information is processed at an abstract, or schematic, level. That processing, which is a step beyond what we ordinarily carry out, can bring about a connection between a base and a target that are not related on the surface.

In the transfer situations discussed so far, a newly encountered target problem retrieves base information (a possible solution) from memory. Now let us look at the opposite situation, *opportunistic assimilation*, where an object or event in the environment provides the solution to a previously encountered, but unsolved, problem in memory (Seifert et al., 1995). In this case, the possible solution retrieves the problem. As noted earlier, Bette Graham's invention of *Mistake Out* came about through this mechanism.

Analogical Transfer and Opportunistic Assimilation: Repair of the Hubble Space Telescope

On April 24, 1990, the National Air and Space Administration of the United States (NASA) put into orbit the Hubble Space Telescope (see Figure 5.6). The Hubble was important for NASA in several ways.

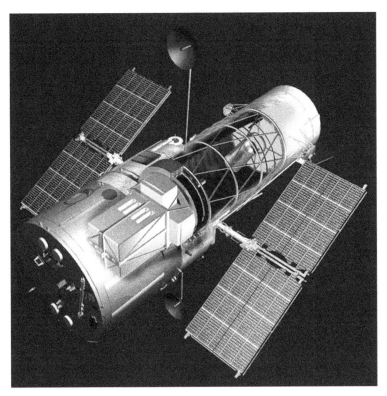

Figure 5.6 Hubble telescope. Hubble Space Telescope Views (Isolated), jamesbenet, E+, Getty Images.

The Wide Field Photo Camera (WFPC), the core of Hubble, would produce photographs of exceptional clarity of never-before-seen phenomena in the heavens, which would be very valuable for scientists and would also provide a public-relations bonanza for NASA. There were also several other pieces of equipment on board Hubble that were important to scientific investigations of several different sorts, although they did not have the intrinsic interest of the photos that the WFPC could produce. Therefore, the scientists directing the Hubble mission were excited when, about a month after Hubble was put into orbit, the first WFPC pictures were received.

WFPC Problems

However, although those pictures were better than those from an earth-based telescope, they looked much worse than expected, due to a lack of clarity. After a thorough analysis of the pictures, it was concluded that there was a problem involving the shape of the Hubble's primary mirror. That mirror captures the light from the object being examined and should focus it precisely, so that the telescope can produce images that otherwise could not be seen. The primary mirror, 94.5 inches (almost eight feet) in diameter, had been carefully ground and polished by an optical company under contract to NASA. Unfortunately, one of the machines used to calibrate the work – to determine that the shape of the mirror was correct – had been set wrong, so the mirror was flattened a bit at its outer part, by less than the width of a human hair. That error was enough to make the images blurred, because all the light was not focused precisely in one place. The problem with the Hubble mirror made national news headlines, and a magazine labeled the story "NASA's $1.5 billion mistake" (Zimmerman, 2010). The mirror problem also affected the other equipment on Hubble in much the same way, but most attention was paid to the poor WFPC pictures.

One possible solution to the problem of getting Hubble to focus light correctly was raised by Aden and Marjorie Meinel, astronomers and telescope designers, who were given a close look at the early Hubble images. NASA was building a back-up of the Hubble camera (WFPC-2), in case the one on Hubble needed to be replaced by astronauts. That new camera was fitted with a set of small mirrors, designed to reflect the light from Hubble's primary mirror – the primary mirror was too big to be changed – and focus it. Aden Meinel suggested that, if those small mirrors were *shaped* correctly, they could compensate for the defective shape of the primary mirror.

Meinel's solution, which was carried out in WFPC-2, was the result of analytic thinking: he reasoned it out. In December 1993, a space shuttle mission exchanged the WFPC with WFPC-2, which resulted in excellent pictures.

COSTAR

Adjusting the small mirrors on the WFPC-2 did not solve the problems with the other pieces of equipment. Many scientists were extremely upset at losing all opportunity to gather new information from the solar system. Adjusting the output from the primary mirror, so that the other pieces of equipment could function correctly, came about through near analogical transfer, based on opportunistic assimilation. A working group – the Space Telescope Strategy Panel, consisting of American and European scientists – met several times August–September 1990 (Zimmerman, 2010, pp. 148–151) to try to solve the problem of the defective mirror's making the other equipment unusable. During the first day of a meeting held September 3–4, 1990, in Germany, they considered launching a "correcting" mirror, but it would be too big to be launched. Another suggestion involved a "mosaic" of small mirrors above the primary mirror, but that would involve work too delicate to be carried out in space. One scientist noted that small correcting mirrors, placed in front of each of the various instruments, could solve the problem – in a near analogy to the WFPC-2 repair – but there was no way for an astronaut to install them at the precise positions that would compensate for the distortion in the primary mirror.

On the evening of September 3, after the Strategy Panel meeting ended, one member, Jim Crocker, an American engineer, kept thinking about the problem as he went to his hotel room. He was concerned that, if they could not fix the additional Hubble problems, it would be a blot on NASA's record and might stand in the way of future funding. Crocker went to shower and he had to deal with a European shower apparatus, which was different than a typical shower in the United States. The European shower had a showerhead that was attached to an arm clamped to a pipe. The arm moved up and down the pipe, for height adjustment. The arm also rotated around the pipe, to move the showerhead away from the wall, and the showerhead itself pivoted on the end of the arm to allow the user to change the angle of the spray (see Figure 5.7A).

That shower mechanism provided Crocker with a solution to the problem of installing mirrors in front of the remaining instruments. The

(a)

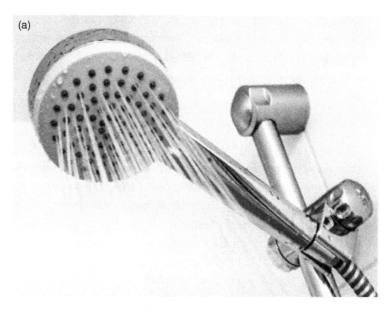

(b)

Figure 5.7 Hubble telescope repairs. A. European showerhead – analogical transfer for COSTAR. Low Angle View Of Shower In Bathroom, Martin Jahr, EyeEm, Getty Images. B. COSTAR. Photo by Eric Long, Smithsonian National Air and Space Museum (NASM 2013-02353).

required small mirrors could be placed on arms, like that holding the showerhead. The arms could be set to extend automatically to the position required by each instrument. When Crocker reported his insight to the Panel the next day, the other members accepted it immediately. Crocker's solution to the mirror problem was based on familiar mechanisms. First, the design of the small mirrors on WFPC-2 provided general aspects of the solution, through near analogical transfer. Second, the mechanism of the shower apparatus provided a near analogy to the mechanism needed to deploy the mirrors. The new idea then had to be extended to the Hubble situation. The device based on Crocker's idea, called COSTAR (Corrective Optics Space Telescope Axial Replacement), was installed on Hubble by astronauts in late December 1993, at the same time the WFPC-2 was installed (see Figure 5.7B). As can be seen, the arms holding the mirrors are similar to the design of the showerhead in Figure 5.7A. The mechanism of the showerhead provided an analogy to the needed apparatus.

Let us now examine another creative advance brought about through opportunistic assimilation. This one is much more down to earth.

Opportunistic Assimilation: Burrs, Dogs, and Zipperless Fasteners

One evening, as Swiss engineer Georges de Mestral and his wife were preparing to go out (Petroski, 1998), she asked for help with a stubborn zipper on her dress. De Mestral was an experienced inventor, and trying to get that zipper to work raised a problem in his mind: might it be possible to develop a fastener that could hold two pieces of cloth together as a zipper does, without a zipper's tendencies to jam and break? Not long afterward, de Mestral went for a walk with his dog in the Alpine woods. When they returned, his pants legs and the dog's fur were covered with burrs, from burdock plants that they had come into contact with. De Mestral spent much time removing the burrs, which held very strongly to his clothing and the dog's fur. Those burrs provided a possible solution to the problem of a zipperless fastener.

De Mestral examined one of the burrs under a microscope and found that its outer surface was made up of many thin hooks, which gripped tightly on the fibers of the cloth and fur (see Figure 5.8A). De Mestral spent more than a year, working in conjunction with a weaver, to develop a pair of materials: one with a surface layer of hooks, analogous to those on the burr; and a second, with a layer of fibrous material, analogous to his pants leg (see Figure 5.8B). Pressing the hooked surface against the fibrous one resulted in the two strongly sticking together. De Mestral derived a name for his new fastener from a combination of the French words *velour* (velvet) and *crochet* (hook); he called it *Velcro*.

From its beginnings as a design for a zipperless fastener on clothing, Velcro is now everywhere. People with problems with manual dexterity due to illness (e.g., arthritis) or lack of experience (the very young) can have securely closed shoes and jackets. During the first artificial-heart surgical procedure, Velcro was used to hold a human heart together (www.aps.org/publications/apsnews/

(a)

(b)

Figure 5.8 Velcro
A Burr picture (Getty image)
B Velcro parts (Getty image)

200402/history.cfm, accessed October 10, 2018). It was also adopted by NASA and used in various ways by astronauts in space, such as for attaching objects to surfaces in a zero-gravity environment – including the astronauts themselves, with Velcro on the soles of their shoes. Individuals without number had picked burrs off their clothing and the fur of their dogs before de Mestral's walk, but only he used it as the basis for an innovation.

Analytic Thinking in the Invention of Velcro

One important point in the invention of Velcro is how de Mestral used his encounter with the burrs. The burr itself was not the solution to the problem. Rather, as with Crocker's use of the shower apparatus, the *design* of the burr provided an *analogy* to the solution. The structure of the burr, as seen under the microscope, and its relation to the cloth provided information that de Mestral used to construct an artificial version of that situation. De Mestral had to extend the idea from the burr to the problem of the zipperless fastener. In addition, the invention of Velcro was based on a *far analogy*. The burr is far removed from the domain of zippers and other fasteners, but it served as the basis for a solution to a fastener problem. How might that linkage have come about? De Mestral might have formulated the problem with his wife's stubborn zipper as requiring something that would hold strongly to cloth, without a complex mechanism. The burr met those criteria. One could say that de Mestral had encoded his problem schematically, which allowed the far analogy – the burr holding strongly to his pants leg – to provide an idea for solution. That process would be parallel to the experimental studies we reviewed earlier that tried to activate inert knowledge by having participants store the base schema in memory (Gentner et al., 2009). On the other hand, De Mestral's difficulty removing the burrs from his pants and the dog's fur might have left him impressed with the strength of the burr's hold on fabric. That observation might have retrieved his problem with his wife's zipper. No matter how it came about, the invention of Velcro seems to be an example of the role of opportunistic assimilation in some creative advances.

Analogical Thinking in Creativity: Preliminary Conclusions

We have reviewed the role of analogical thinking in various aspects of creativity. In most of the situations we have examined, near analogies were the medium through which analogical thinking operated. Far analogy could also play a role in creative thinking, but, before far analogies were useful, the information had to be processed at a "schematic" level, so that a "far" connection could be made between the target and the base. Those results lead to the conclusion that near analogies are the mechanism through which human thinking typically works, including in creative thinking. That conclusion leads to an interesting problem. When one examines analogical thinking carried out by ordinary folks in the world, one finds numerous cases of people using far analogies without necessarily receiving extensive training or support (Dunbar, 1995; Dunbar & Blanchette, 2001). Dunbar called this situation the "analogical paradox"; the use of far analogies is difficult in the laboratory but frequent in real life. Analyzing this paradox will enable us to understand further how analogies are used in creative thinking.

The Analogical Paradox: Spontaneous Use of Far Analogies in the Real World Versus the Laboratory

Use of Far Analogies

Christensen and Schunn (2007) carried out a study of analogy use in an award-winning engineering company specializing in the design of plastic medical devices. The researchers followed the development of one project, which took two years and involved a total of nineteen expert engineering designers. The researchers studied one subgroup, with five members, that was assigned the task of developing novel features for the product, rather than improving existing features. The researchers hoped that the task of creating novel features would maximize the frequency of creative advances that they would be able to observe. Christensen and Schunn recorded weekly subgroup product-development meetings over the first five months of the project. Seven meetings, covering nine hours, were analyzed, and a total of 102 analogies were found, an average of more than eleven analogies per hour. The analogies were about evenly split between near and far analogies, with 55 percent near analogies and 45 percent far analogies. Some of the domains from which far analogies were drawn were: zippers, credit cards, children's slides, milk containers, Christmas decorations, Venetian blinds, and lingerie (Christensen & Schunn, 2007, p. 34). In sum, the designers used far analogies relatively frequently. Similar findings were reported by Kretz and Krawczyk (2014), who recorded meetings of a weekly reading group composed of economics professors and graduate students. Also, Richland, Holyoak, and Stigler (2004) examined analogy use by teachers in eighth-grade mathematics classes as part of an ongoing international research project focusing on teaching of mathematics. The teachers used analogies in their teaching, and many were far analogies. Because the far analogies were directed at eighth-graders, highly sophisticated conceptual skills may not be necessary to understand far analogies.

Similar results were reported by Dunbar and Blanchette (2001), who investigated the use of analogies in political discussion. They analyzed newspaper articles discussing a referendum in 1995 on the question of whether Quebec should remain part of Canada. More than 400 articles were analyzed, from all the issues of three Montreal newspapers published in the week before the referendum. There were over 200 analogies in those articles, more than 75 percent of which were far analogies, coming from domains including sports, religion, and agriculture. As one example, a politician trying to convince people to vote *against* independence for Quebec said that voting for independence "would be like leaving an ocean liner for a lifeboat, without paddles, on a stormy sea" (Dunbar, 2001, p. 313. Comparable to the eighth-grade mathematics teachers' use of far analogies, the politicians were attempting to communicate with ordinary folks, not experts on political issues.

At the very least, then, ordinary folks can *understand* far analogies. Could those ordinary folks also *produce* far analogies if they were taking part in a political discussion? Dunbar and Blanchette (2001, Exp. 2) asked a random selection of undergraduates to imagine that they were political consultants. Their task was to generate analogies that a client organization could use to convince people to take a position on the question of government debt. Half the students were asked to provide analogies to convince people that government debt was a bad thing and should be reduced and ultimately eliminated (see Table 5.7A). The other students were told that their client was in favor of maintaining some government debt, if the alternative resulted in large-scale elimination of social programs (see Table 5.7B). Approximately 80 percent of the analogies produced by the students were far analogies.

Generating Your Own Far Analogy versus Using Someone Else's

We have seen that people can understand far analogies in newspaper articles and political discussions; can use them to solve problems outside the laboratory; and can generate them when the circumstances might call for it. What is the difference between those situations and the typical laboratory transfer situation discussed earlier in the chapter, in which people are not able to use a far analogy that someone else has generated? (See the discussion of *inert knowledge*.) There are at least two possible explanations for the lack of far analogical transfer in most laboratory studies.

First, in all the laboratory transfer studies, the base situations – for example, the *General* and *Red Adair* problems – were not familiar to the participants. The base was simply presented to the participants, as part of the experiment. Perhaps, if the base had been a familiar situation, then there might be easier retrieval of a far analogy. Trench and Mervino (2015) tested that possibility in a transfer study, in which the base was a familiar film, such as *Jurassic Park*, *Spiderman*, or *Shrek*. An example experimental condition, based on *Jurassic Park*, is presented in Table 5.8. Participants

Table 5.7 *Dunbar and Blanchette (2001, Exp. 2) materials and results*

A. *Anti-Zero Deficit Condition*

You are a group of consultants and you have been hired by the National Association of
Community Groups (NACG). The NACG is currently organizing an important
nationwide campaign to sensitize both citizens and governments (federal and
provincial).

The NACG is aware that analogies, comparing one thing to another, are a powerful tool
for persuasion. Some analogies have already been used in a number of occasions in
politics. For example, in 1992 President Bush wanted to convince the American
population of the importance of the military intervention in the Persian Gulf. In his
efforts to do so, he made extensive use of the analogy to World War II, comparing
Saddam Hussein to Hitler.

The NACG has hired your group of consultants to come up with analogies that they
could use to persuade the public and the government leaders that the reduction of the
deficit is an important goal but that it should not be pursued at any cost. They do not
agree with reducing the deficit if it means less support for those who need it and
massive cuts to health, education, and social assistance; fewer jobs; and more poverty.
They want you to provide them with a list of analogies that support and illustrate this
position.

B. *Pro-Zero Deficit Condition*

You are a group of consultants and you have been hired by the National Association of
Community Groups (NACG). The NACG is currently organizing an important
nationwide campaign to sensitize both citizens and governments (federal and
provincial).

The NACG is aware that analogies, comparing one thing to another, are a powerful tool
for persuasion. Some analogies have already been used in a number of occasions in
politics. For example, in 1992 President Bush wanted to convince the American
population of the importance of the military intervention in the Persian Gulf. In his
efforts to do so, he made extensive use of the analogy to World War II, comparing
Saddam Hussein to Hitler.

The NARC has hired your group of consultants to come up with analogies that they
could use to persuade the public and the government leaders that the reduction of the
deficit should be our number one priority. They think that governments do not have
a choice and that citizens have to make some sacrifices. They want you to provide
them with a list of analogies that support and illustrate this position.

read one of two targets, one with overlap of surface elements with the base
(a near analogy to *Jurassic Park*) and one without (a far analogy). Nothing
was said about those relationships. The participants were asked to generate
analogies to convince the main character in the target story *not* to carry out
the plan that had been devised. After they had generated the analogies, they

Table 5.8 Jurassic Park *stimulus materials, adapted from Trench and Mervino (2014)*

Near Target	Far Target	*Jurassic Park* (Base)
A businessman had replicated mammoths from the Pleistocene Era out of a frozen embryo found in a glacier.	An astrophysicist was modeling Martian storms out of digital images captured by a space probe. He was able to produce those storms on earth, in a controlled environment.	A millionaire has cloned dinosaurs from the Jurassic Period out of fossil DNA taken from a mosquito.
		He has received experts' warnings about the impossibility of exerting total control over biological phenomena.
The businessman wants to open a zoo with mammoths on display.	The astrophysicist was planning to let researchers enter the experimental zone to study the storms first-hand.	The millionaire insisted on opening a park to exhibit the dinosaurs to the public.
		The dinosaurs break the security system of the park and attack human beings.
The participants' task was to produce analogies to dissuade the businessman from pursuing the project, warning him that, since animal behaviors are not completely manageable, mammoths could destroy the zoo cages, thus endangering people.	The participants' task was to produce analogies to dissuade the astrophysicist from pursuing his plan, on the grounds that, as extraterrestrial climatic phenomena are not well known, they could be dangerous for his colleagues.	

were asked if any films had been brought to mind as they worked on the task. Only the participants who were given the target with overlapping surface elements reported that *Jurassic Park* was brought to mind during the task. The fact that the base information was familiar to the participants did not affect retrieval in response to a target: participants still retrieved only near analogies.

The second possible explanation for the lack of far analogical transfer in most laboratory studies is that, in those studies there is no obvious analogical connection between the base and the target. Consider again the General and Radiation problems (see Table 5.2 and Figure 5.4). It is not clear, on just reading those stories, that there is an analogical relationship between them. One must *think about them* – that is, analyze them at a deep, "schematic" level – in order to find the connection. Therefore, why should we be surprised when research participants do not see that far analogy? A far analogy is, by definition, nontransparent, which means that such an analogy must be *constructed*: you must go beyond the objects in the base and target, to analyze the *relations* in each situation, in order to discover analogical connections between them.

Inert Knowledge or *Hidden* Knowledge: Resolving the Analogical Paradox?

The analogical paradox hinges on the question of why, given the ease of use of far analogies in many contexts, knowledge is sometimes inert in laboratory contexts. Based on the discussion in the last few sections, we should perhaps rephrase the question: Why should we be surprised when participants in a laboratory study do not make the connection between a base and target that form a far analogy? Since there are no obvious connections – surface connections – between the base and target, why should those participants *even think to try to link them* and thereby discover the hidden far analogy? The laboratory studies that have been described as studying "far analogical transfer" perhaps should be redescribed as studying "unaware participants' discovery of analogies *hidden by researchers*." The researcher presents two scenarios that, the researcher knows, comprise a far analogy, but the participants are not told of that. The researchers are then struck by the participants' lack of discovery of the analogy. However, without any information as to the existence of that potentially useful analogy, why should we expect the participants to think more deeply about the situation? Those laboratory transfer tasks are more complex than the researchers have realized. In this context, the need for hints in stimulating use of far analogies is exactly what one would expect: people can use far analogies when they have them available. When researchers *hide* a far analogy, by using base and target materials that have no surface elements in common, then participants will not, on their own, search for and uncover those analogies. However, when they are aware that far analogies are available, they use them with ease.

In conclusion, researchers' concentration on the analogical paradox might be based on mistaken assumptions concerning the processes underlying creative thinking. If one assumes that leaps of analogy are the normal mechanism of creative thinking, then the existence of inert knowledge is a puzzle to be explained. However, if one begins with the assumption that creative thinking works in small steps and moves incrementally to new ideas, then one would *expect* that people would not ordinarily think of a far analogy in response to presentation of a problem, except if they had previously thought about the materials schematically, so that links between the base and target had been created.

Are Far Analogies Useful in Creative Thinking?

As just discussed, there is a critical assumption – a residue of the genius view – that underlies much of the research on analogical thinking reviewed in this chapter: creative thinking works best when it uses far analogies, to make leaps beyond what is known. Any mechanism that allows you to move far away from what you are thinking about will facilitate production of new ideas. We can call this the conceptual-leap hypothesis (Chan, Dow & Schunn, 2015). That hypothesis is what makes inert knowledge a problem to be grappled with. Although it might sound reasonable, it is important to emphasize that the conceptual-leap hypothesis is just that, a *hypothesis*, and therefore it must be tested. Several recent studies have looked at the usefulness of far transfer in generating new ideas (Chan, Dow & Schunn, 2015; Chan & Schunn, 2015), and, perhaps surprisingly, the research does not support the conceptual-leap hypothesis.

Conceptual Distance and Creative Idea Generation

Chan, Dow, and Schunn (2015) examined the relation between "conceptual leaps" and the creativity of the ideas that arose from them. They examined ideas proposed on OpenIDEO, a web-based crowd-sourcing forum, briefly mentioned in Chapter 1, where large-scale social problems, called *challenges*, are outlined (see Table 5.9). Anyone, from anywhere in the world, can propose ideas to deal with a challenge. OpenIDEO's expert designers guide the contributors through a multistage process of producing new ideas to deal with a challenge. The first stage is *inspiration*, which typically

Table 5.9 *OpenIDEO Challenges from Chan, Dow, and Schunn (2014)*

Name/description	# of inspirations	# of concepts (# shortlisted)
How might we increase the number of registered bone marrow donors to help save more lives?	186	71 (7)
How might we inspire and enable communities to take more initiative in making their local environments better?	160	44 (11)
How can we manage e-waste and discarded electronics to safeguard human health and protect our environment?	60	26 (8)
How might we better connect food production and consumption?	266	147 (10)
How can technology help people working to uphold human rights in the face of unlawful detention?	248	62 (7)
How might we identify and celebrate businesses that innovate for world benefit and inspire other companies to do the same?	122	24 (13)

lasts about a month. During that time, individuals post descriptions of solutions to problems analogous to the challenge. The inspirations serve to help identify promising solution approaches.

In the second stage, *concepting*, which also lasts about a month, contributors post *concepts*, which are specific solutions to the challenge. The concepts were 150 words in length on average. A subset of the concepts, seen as promising by an expert panel composed of the OpenIDEO designers and a set of domain experts, is *shortlisted*. Shortlisted concepts are refined further. Contributors to OpenIDEO are encouraged to build on others' ideas, in the manner of brainstorming (see Chapter 1). Contributors also are encouraged to specify the ideas that inspired their contribution. That information allowed Chan and colleagues to determine the relationship – that is, the "conceptual distance" – between a challenge, an inspiration, and the concept that was produced. The question of interest was: Did concepts that were inspired by inspirations distantly related to a challenge have a higher probability of being shortlisted, as the conceptual-leap hypothesis would predict? In other words, if, based on a far analogy, the contributor had made a "mental leap" before producing a concept, was that concept more likely to be judged as creative?

The data set in the study comprised twelve challenges, for which a total of 2,341 concepts were posted. Of the total concepts posted, 707, or approximately 30 percent, cited at least one inspiration, and those were the ones that were studied by the researchers. Of those 707 concepts with inspirations, 110, or approximately 15 percent, were shortlisted. The researchers defined a concept as creative if it was shortlisted. To address the question of whether creative thinking was fostered by distant inspirations – far analogies – it was necessary to measure the "distance" between concepts. Chan and colleagues (2014) used a computer algorithm to determine the distance between pairs of concepts, by measuring the overlap of words that they have in common. Two concepts are "close" if many of the same words are used in talking about them. "Distant" concepts are talked about using different sets of words. Using this method, one can, for each inspiration, determine its distance from the topic of the challenge. One can then use that measure to determine if the far inspirations resulted in a greater proportion of shortlisted concepts.

The conceptual-leap hypothesis predicts that the larger the distance between the challenge and the inspiration, the greater the chances that the concept would be shortlisted. Figure 5.9 presents the results of the analyses by Chan and colleagues (2015). Contrary to the conceptual leap hypothesis, there was a strong *negative* relationship between the distance from an inspiration to the challenge and the probability that the concept

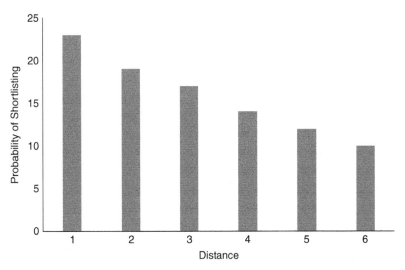

Figure 5.9 Chan, Dow, and Schunn (2014) OpenIDEO results: Shortlisting as a function of distance from source

arising from that inspiration was shortlisted. Concepts that were based on inspirations *far removed* from the challenge were clearly *less likely* to be shortlisted. Furthermore, that negative result held for all twelve of the challenges that Chan and colleagues studied. In this study, at least, it was better to rely on near analogies when trying to generate new ideas.

The research by Chan and colleagues (2015; see also Chan and Schunn, 2015) provides support for the idea that creative thinking is not facilitated by leaps to ideas far away from the problem that one has been thinking about. How can that be? It certainly does seem reasonable, on an intuitive basis and on the genius view, that creativity would be maximized if we were able to access ideas that are distantly or remotely related, or even unrelated, to the problem we are facing. What have we missed? Might the world be structured so that conceptual leaps would *not* be helpful? Might many problems be solvable by using information from situations that contain the same surface elements – that is, on the basis of *near* analogies?

The "Kind World" Hypothesis

Gentner proposed that searching memory based on near analogies – that is, based on surface elements – is often a useful strategy in solving problems. She called this the "kind world hypothesis" (Gentner & Maravilla, 2018). The world is not structured so that important information is hidden. Rather, the world is "kind": things often are what they *appear* to be. If one responds on the basis of *surface elements*, one will be on the right track. That does not mean that relying on surface elements will always be successful, because there might be situations in which far analogies might be critical. As one example, Ward (1995, 2018) has carried out research examining people's ability to imagine new things – say, creatures on a distant planet very different from earth. Most people, Ward noted, took the "path of least resistance"; they used familiar ideas as the basis for their creations, and the "new" creatures were very similar to those on earth. Ward found similar results when he examined creatures in science fiction. To produce something new, Ward concluded, the individual must consider unique aspects of the imagined environment in which the creature will function. This seems to be a situation in which the kind environment hypothesis is not useful, but it also may be an untypical situation, since the task is to produce something new and *different* from things already known. That is different than a situation in which, for example, one is trying to solve a problem and thinks of an analogous problem. In the latter situation, the kind world hypothesis may be worth following.

Analogical Thinking in Problem-Solving and Creativity: Conclusions

Transferring information to a new situation is often based on a near analogy between the new and the old. That finding supports the idea that green creativity – recycling of old ideas – is based on a partial match between the new situation and information in memory. That partial match can result in the retrieval of base information from memory; that is, in a new idea coming to mind. Furthermore, although both surface elements and relations can play important roles in analogical transfer, surface elements are particularly important, especially in the initial search of memory. Relations can also play a role in searching memory, but such a search depends on the individual having analyzed, in schematic terms, the situation that he or she faces. That sort of analysis, based on a deep understanding of the situation, will support thinking based on far analogies, as we saw with De Mestral's invention of Velcro.

Beyond Analytic Thinking?

This chapter completes the presentation of the details of analytic thinking as it plays out in creativity. In Part III of the book we turn to an examination of a number of analyses of creativity that seem to go against the analytic-thinking view. The main question of interest running through the next set of chapters will be how far we can extend the analytic-thinking explanation of creativity. Will there be a point at which we will have to incorporate aspects of the genius view into our understanding of the way the creative process works? We begin with an examination of the notion of *talent* in creativity. A critical component of the analytic view is that creative thinking depends on a person's knowledge. New ideas come about through green creativity, which entails building new ideas on the foundation of what we know. The notion of green creativity leads to the possibility that all creative achievements are based on what we know – that is, on our expertise. However, what about the role of *talent*, or innate abilities, in creative achievement? In recent years there has been extensive research focusing on the question of whether achievement at the highest levels is the result of accumulated experience – on expertise – or whether innate talents provide the basis for the highest achievements of which humans are capable. That question will be examined in Chapter 6.

PART III

The Question of Extraordinary Thought Processes in Creativity

6 | How Do You Get to Carnegie Hall? Practice, Talent, and Creativity

> A young man is walking in New York City, carrying a violin case and looking at a map on his phone, looking confused. He stops an older man. "Excuse me, sir, how do you get to Carnegie Hall?" The older man looks at the violin case and says: "Practice, practice, practice."

That little story, while centering on a play on words, encapsulates two very different views concerning how a person can reach the highest level of accomplishment. The play on words is based on a misunderstanding: the young man is asking for information about the physical path to Carnegie Hall, while the older man's answer provides directions concerning the "career path" that will result in the young man's becoming able to perform in Carnegie Hall. The older man's answer, in addition to surprising us by not answering the young man's question, may also be surprising in another way. He tells the young man to "practice, practice, practice." Is that all a person needs to do to become capable of performing at the highest level? Can anybody who practices enough get to Carnegie Hall? Don't you need *talent* to get to Carnegie Hall? This chapter will examine the factors that play a role in a person's reaching the highest level of achievement, including creative achievement. This question has been phrased historically as whether world-class achievement – in other words, *genius* – is the result of talent or practice. Is the genius *born* or *made*?

Outline of the Chapter

The chapter begins with a case study of creative development at the genius level. We will then review research examining whether genius is born or made. Some researchers have proposed that *all* accomplishment is based solely on practice and that genius and talent play no role. In response to that strong practice view, supporters of the notion of talent have presented evidence that high achievement requires more than practice. Recent advances have led several researchers to propose that the question of whether genius is born *or* made is not the correct question. One should study how people's inherited characteristics *and* their experiences work together to produce world-class achievement. We begin with a real-life story of how to get to Carnegie Hall.

A Skiffle Band Conquers the World

On the afternoon of July 6, 1967, The Quarrymen, a skiffle band formed by a group of English teenagers in Liverpool, played two sets of songs at a church carnival (this discussion is based on Lewisohn, 1992). Skiffle, a musical craze that had been sweeping England for more than a year, was formed out of American folk music and traditional American jazz. The development of skiffle stimulated many British teenagers to learn the guitar and form bands, several thousand of them. One such band was The Quarrymen, formed several months before by a seventeen-year-old named John. The name of the band came from a line in the school song from the Quarry Road School, which some of its members attended. The band had had some experience playing parties and informal dances, and they had entered a talent contest at a local theater but had not gotten very far.

That evening, the band was also scheduled to play at a dance at the church. As they were setting up, one of the band members introduced a friend, a sixteen-year-old named Paul, who had heard them play that afternoon. Paul possessed considerably more musical sophistication than the band members, including John. Paul's father was a musician, and Paul had some experience playing trumpet and piano. However, after attending a concert by the skiffle idol Lonnie Donegan, Paul took up the guitar. He showed off his skill by singing several current hits, favorites of John's, while accompanying himself on guitar. Not only could Paul play the songs, but he also remembered all the lyrics; remembering lyrics sometimes was a problem for John. After singing, Paul wrote out the lyrics for him. Even more impressive, Paul could tune a guitar, something none of The Quarrymen could do. They had to bring their guitars to a local musician, who tuned them, for a fee. A couple of weeks later, Paul was asked to join John's band and he agreed.

As John and Paul got to know each other, they began writing songs together; a musical partnership was formed. That partnership was similar to those in the thousands of bands playing the new music. Most of the bands, and the partnerships, quickly faded away. The partnership between John and Paul was different: it changed the world. Their songs altered the course of twentieth-century popular music, and their personalities, appearance, and behavior changed popular culture. John, the leader of The Quarrymen, was, of course, John Lennon, and Paul was Paul McCartney. One might therefore say that, on that day in July 1957, the Beatles were formed, although the two other members – George Harrison and Ringo Starr – were not yet in the band. The rest, as they say, is history.

Beginning in early 1963, the Beatles had an unprecedented run of success as songwriters and performers that lasted through the 1960s. In 1963, for example, they had four number one hits, all written by Lennon and McCartney. During the following years, they produced one number one hit after another, with one Beatles song often displacing another to become number one. Their concerts reached similar levels of success: they played to screaming crowds of adoring fans all around the world, including, on February 12, 1964, two concerts at Carnegie Hall. They also played in some of the world's biggest outdoor arenas, which marked the advent of stadium rock concerts. That frenzied reception, which became known as "Beatlemania," was so intense that, in 1966, the band stopped playing concerts. Neither they nor anyone else could hear anything they were playing, making the whole experience unsatisfying, at least for the band.

However, the Beatles kept producing music, and during the mid-1960s recorded three albums – *Rubber Soul* (1965), *Revolver* (1966), and *Sergeant Pepper's Lonely Hearts Club Band* (1967) – that are considered to be their best work and one of the high points of twentieth-century popular music (Everett, 2001). Those records changed the pop-musical landscape in several ways, ranging from the subject matter and structure of the songs to instruments and recording techniques that had not been used before in popular music. That trio of albums became the standard by which all subsequent popular music would be judged, for over 50 years and counting.

The Beatles and the Question of Talent

We have here a group of young men who made it big – who got to Carnegie Hall and more. What brought about the creative outburst known as The Beatles? The answer seems obvious: Lennon and McCartney were an exceptionally talented pair of musicians. I have, many times, seen Lennon and McCartney referred to as geniuses. That the Beatles were exceptionally talented is no doubt true: they produced one number one hit after another and their work has affected several generations of musicians around the world. However, when we say that the success of a team of songwriters is *explained* by their having exceptional talent, that 'explanation' leaves us with additional questions.

What Is Talent?

According to the *Oxford English Dictionary*, "talent" refers to a mental endowment or natural ability that someone brings to some activity, for example drawing, playing the guitar, mathematics, or poetry. If one says that a person has talent for mathematics, one means that she has shown exceptional skill at mathematics, and perhaps the skill was surprising in its *precociousness* – that is, in its early development, seemingly out of nowhere. Children who demonstrate high levels of talent are called *gifted* (Winner, 2014). A "natural ability" is one that is "built-in"; there is a genetic or inherited component to talent. A natural ability is also one that, obviously, comes naturally, with ease, rather than as the result of a long hard grind of practice. A person with a natural ability might be expected to reach a high level of performance more quickly than would non-talented individuals exposed to the same amount of instruction and practice. We have all heard stories about individuals who reach the highest levels of performance but who never practice. Talent also sets the limits on what anyone can achieve. If a person does not have talent, he can work as much as he wants, but he will never reach the very highest levels. (Gagné (2009, 2015) presents a different definition of talent.)

The Beatles: Learning to Write Great Music

The Beatles seem to present us with strong evidence for talent in song-writing. We see success after success rolling out of them, seemingly effort-lessly. If that is not talent (or genius), then nothing is. However, closer examination of the Beatles' career trajectory indicates that their success was *not* effortless, as the talent view would lead us to expect. The Beatles had to *learn* to write great music.

The Beatles' first record to make the charts was *Love Me Do*, which reached number seventeen in Britain, in October, 1962. Not bad for a first effort; and, as we have seen, it was quickly followed by an unprecedented string of blockbusters. But *Love Me Do* was *not* a first effort: it was recorded over five years after Lennon and McCartney met and began to write songs together. Most of their early songs – pre–*Love Me Do* – were not released until after the Beatles became stars, when anything they wrote became of great interest. Whoever was making the decisions concerning release of Beatles songs (and presumably the band members had a say in that) had decided that those early songs were not worth releasing, and so they were put aside. Furthermore, the three albums already mentioned, the high point of Beatles music, were not produced until four to five *more* years had elapsed, indicating that a considerable amount of time passed between the first Beatles songs and the fullest expression of their talent. *Sergeant Pepper* (1967), for example, was produced approximately ten years after Lennon and McCartney met. If one of the defining characteristics of talent is the *early* development of exceptional ability, then the Beatles seem to have fallen short: there is no doubt that exceptional ability was involved, but it took almost ten years to reach its peak.

A second component of talent is that the talented individual develops a high level of skill without expending time on the long-term practice that less-talented individuals must go through. Let us look at the Beatles' early career, to see what they were doing during those five-plus years before they began producing all those hits.

The Beatles as a Cover Band

Between 1957 and the end of 1962, from Lennon and McCartney's meeting to their first hit, the Beatles were an exceptionally hardworking cover band playing other people's songs. They performed approximately 900 times, with most of those performances coming after mid-1960. Thus, over a period of over two years, they performed more than once per day. In addition, some of those performances were marathons. The Beatles played several extended bookings, totaling some forty weeks, in Hamburg between mid-April 1960 and the end of December 1962 (Weisberg, 2006, ch. 5). Those performances required that they be on stage for more than four hours per night, seven days a week. During that intense time, the Beatles report that they really learned how to play. Furthermore, during that time, there were no Beatles songs on their playlists. Their repertoire consisted of the rock and roll hits of the day as well as some traditional songs played in rock style.

Even if we assume that the Beatles spent no time during this period learning and practicing new aspects of music – which is almost surely incorrect, as there are reports of the members of the group learning new techniques and sharing them with the others (Lewisohn, 2013) – there was an extended period of what one could call an apprenticeship before the Beatles were ready to begin to make their mark. Some of the characteristics of the music that they cut their teeth on can be heard in early Beatles songs (Everett, 2001). Thus, the Beatles' career involved three stages: (1) immersion in the music of others (years one through five); (2) production of new material within the existing styles (years five through eight); and (3) production of groundbreaking material (year eight and beyond).

In conclusion, the most innovative popular musicians in recent history needed time to learn their skills. In this case, the older man in the Carnegie Hall story was correct. It is not unreasonable to say that the Beatles' extraordinary creative accomplishments – including getting to Carnegie Hall – came about as the result of *practice*. That conclusion may strike one as absurd. The people who reach the highest level of creative accomplishment *must* be different in some basic ways from the rest of us, not just in the amount of practice that they engage in. What have we missed? To begin to answer that question, let us trace the development of research on outstanding achievement.

History of a Controversy: Are Geniuses Born or Made?

We saw in Chapter 2 that the ancients believed that certain individuals received gifts from the gods; those gifts are similar to the modern idea of innate talents or genius. The question of whether some of us might be "gifted" has been of interest to researchers for 150 years, going back to Sir Francis Galton (1979 [1869]), who formulated many of the issues that are being discussed today (Simonton, 2017).

Galton: Geniuses Are Born

Galton, a cousin of Charles Darwin, was influenced by Darwin's theory of evolution, which proposed that many of the physical characteristics of animals were inheritable – that is, passed down from one generation to the next. Galton explicitly extended Darwin's reasoning to humans. In Galton's (1979 [1869]) landmark book, *Hereditary Genius*, he proposed that achievement was based on "natural ability," a combination of intellectual capacity and the motivation to work hard. People with the highest level of this ability would reach the highest level of accomplishment. As a result, they would achieve the highest level of *eminence* – that is, the highest level of reputation. Galton proposed that natural ability was subject to the laws of biological inheritance, analogous to the physical characteristics of the animals discussed by Darwin. That reasoning leads to the hypothesis that eminence should run in families, so Galton examined the family trees of eminent individuals in many domains, including religion, politics, war, science, literature, music composition, and the visual arts. He found that eminence did run in families and concluded that there were strong inherited links in those characteristics that resulted in eminence. A person's experiences, what Galton called "social factors," played no role in achievement, he wrote. "[S]ocial hindrances cannot impede men of high ability, from becoming eminent [, and] social advantages are ... [unable] to give that status, to a man of moderate ability" (p. 41). Either one possessed the characteristics that led to eminence or one did not.

Geniuses Are Made

The genius-is-made view, the position opposite to Galton's, was advocated by researchers studying learning in the United States, the most important of whom was John B. Watson (e.g., 1930), the founder of American behaviorism. A core component of Watson's view was the idea that any differences from person to person in behaviors and abilities were the result of the particular learning experiences that each person went through. Any inherited factors, if they existed, were much less important. Watson proposed that he could take a random collection of infants and, by shaping their experiences, make them into anything he wished.

> Give me a dozen healthy infants, well-formed, and my own specified world to bring them up in and I'll guarantee to take any one at random and train him to become any type of specialist I might select – doctor, lawyer, artist, merchant-chief and, yes, even beggar-man and thief, regardless of his talents, penchants, tendencies, abilities, vocations, and race of his ancestors. I am going beyond my facts and I admit it, but so have the advocates of the contrary and they have been doing it for many thousands of years. (Watson, 1930, p. 82)

Although Watson acknowledged that he might have been going beyond the evidence, he was clear in expressing his beliefs.

The idea that the genius is made became the dominant view in psychology at the end of the twentieth century. A stream of research indicated that experience – in the form of "practice" – played a dominant role in a person's achieving the highest levels of accomplishment (see, e.g., chapters in Ericsson et al., 2018).

The Ten-Year Rule: Expertise and Problem-Solving in Chess

The pioneering modern study supporting the notion that genius is made was that of De Groot (1965), a psychologist and master chess player, who examined the question of how chess masters – people who play at world-class levels – choose the moves they make during a game. Chess is a game with many possible sequences of moves and countermoves, and one might think that chess grandmasters (the highest level of player) would search among those possible moves more extensively than would nonmasters. For example, let us say that it is my turn to move. I pick one possible move, and then I reason in something like the following way: "I could make this move, then she could do that, then I could do this, then she could do that . . . ." The more possible outcomes that I can imagine for a given move, the *deeper* is my search. Therefore, one basis for the grandmaster's skill might be deep search. Figure 6.1 presents a concrete representation of deep versus shallow searches.

In addition to searching deeply, the grandmaster might go through those imagined scenarios for many different possible moves. The more possible sequences of moves one considers, the more *broadly* one is searching (see Figure 6.1B). Based on this reasoning, the better a player one is, the more broadly and deeply he or she might be able to analyze possible moves. To test that possibility, De Groot (1965) gave high-level chess players, of

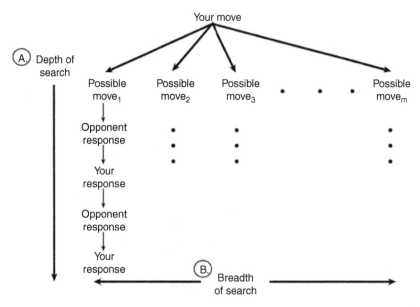

Figure 6.1 A. Depth and B. Breadth in searching for a chess move

different ability levels, the problem of choosing a move in the middle of a game. He set up the chess board as it was in the middle of a selected game (there are books recording the moves in games of chess played in tournaments), and he had the player choose the next move, while thinking aloud. There are agreed-upon "best moves" in those situations. Those verbal protocols were the data that De Groot analyzed.

Based on the protocols, De Groot discovered that grandmasters did not search more broadly, or more deeply, than did excellent players of lesser skill. Often, the grandmaster simply looked at the board and *saw* or *recognized* the one or two best moves, rather than having to think about or analyze which moves might be best. DeGroot concluded that, as a result of years of study and play, the grandmaster had in memory a large number of chess *positions* – configurations of pieces on the board – and the moves that work best from those positions. The grandmaster can recognize a new game position as at least somewhat familiar, which provides information to use in selecting a move. Once the one or two best moves had been recognized, the grandmaster then spent time analyzing them in depth to determine what was *the* best move in that position. This analysis involved search, such as that outlined earlier. Sometimes, during this analysis of a possible move, the grandmaster might discover a better move. To carry out such detailed in-depth analysis, the grandmaster must be able to form and maintain a detailed internal representation of the game (Ericsson & Pool, 2016; see also Chapter 3 in this volume). Evidence for the grandmaster's detailed memory representation of chess games comes from demonstrations that grandmasters can play – and win – numerous games simultaneously, while *blindfolded*.

De Groot (1965) used a memory test to obtain evidence for the importance of the chess master's knowledge in responding to game positions. Chess players of varying levels of skill were presented with chess positions from the middle of grandmaster-level games, containing approximately twenty-five pieces. The board was presented for two to ten seconds and then covered. The player was then given an empty board and a set of pieces and asked to reproduce the just-presented chess board. Grandmasters were essentially perfect in replacing the pieces after only a few seconds viewing the board. Players of lesser skill performed less well on the memory test. Those results might indicate nothing more than that having a great memory must be one of the requirements for becoming a chess grandmaster in the first place. However, Chase and Simon (1973a) replicated and extended De Groot's study and they included another condition, in which the chess pieces were placed *randomly* on the chess board, rather than in positions from chess games. Under those circumstances, performance declined greatly. Thus, chess masters have great memories only for master-level chess games.

The Origin of the Ten-Year Rule

Chase and Simon (1973b) also attempted to determine how the chess masters' knowledge was used in analyzing and recalling chess positions. They recorded the eye movements that players made when they were studying the board during the memory task; and they also recorded the order in which the pieces were put back on the board. The players analyzed the board as *clusters*, or *chunks* of pieces, that were meaningful in chess; and they tended to put those pieces back on the board together during the recall task. Thus, where a person ignorant of chess would see three or four separate pieces, the expert would see one *chunk*, made up of three or four *related* pieces, and would thereby be able to recall several times as much. Chase and Simon (1973b) estimated that the chess master was able to recognize 50,000 chunks from chess games and use them in playing and for recalling the board positions. That number of chunks might seem absurdly large until one realizes that a typical adult can recognize more than 20,000 words in their native language. Chess masters spend large amounts of time – many years – studying chess games, so they would have opportunity to learn that number of chunks.

Chase and Simon (1973b) reached the conclusion that genius – at least in chess – was *made* rather than born, in line with that of Watson (1930). They stated that although

> there clearly must be a set of specific aptitudes ... that together comprise a talent for chess, individual differences in such aptitudes are largely overshadowed by immense individual differences in chess experience. Hence, the overriding factor in chess skill is practice. (p. 279)

Chase and Simon concluded that, to reach world-class performance in chess, one needs to spend at least ten years deeply immersed in chess. That result, which has become known as the *Ten-Year Rule*, has been found to hold in many domains, including several which involve creative work, such as musical composition, painting, and the writing of poetry (Hayes, 1989; Weisberg, 2006). We already know that the Ten-Year Rule held for the Beatles.

Genius Is Made: Developing a World-Class Memory

Additional evidence that genius is made comes from a study by Ericsson, Chase, and Falloon (1980; see also Chase & Ericsson, 1982, examining outstanding memory performance). One very cooperative college student, identified as S. F., engaged in large amounts of practice on the *memory-span* or *digit-span* task (see Table 6.1). The average digit span for college students is about seven items, and S. F. began with an average digit span. The researchers presented S. F. with strings of random digits, starting with a very short string, and he tried to repeat the digits in order. If his recall was correct, the next random string was lengthened by one digit; if he was incorrect, it was shortened by one. The study involved a one-hour session per day, three to five days per week, for twenty months (a total of over 230 hours of practice). By the end of that time, S. F.'s digit span had reached eighty items, *more than ten times the average* and ten times his initial span. S. F.'s final performance was comparable to that of several "memory experts" who have been studied by cognitive scientists (e.g., Luria, 1968; see also Foer, 2011).

Ericsson and colleagues asked S. F. to think aloud as he tried to remember each string of digits. From that information, the researchers were able to track the development of S. F.'s extraordinary memory, which provided concrete evidence concerning how genius – in the sense of a world-class memory – was made. The researchers concluded that there were two critical processes underlying S. F.'s skill: (1) he used his knowledge to process or *code* groups of digits into *chunks*; and (2) he developed a method for *retrieving* the chunks from memory. Here I will concentrate on S. F.'s chunking strategy. S. F. at first tried to rehearse the items by

Table 6.1 *Digit-span test.*
Working from top to bottom, read each of the left-to-right strings of digits below once, and then try to repeat the numbers in order, without looking back at the string.

6	8	2	5						
5	7	2	1	4					
3	5	9	7	2	1				
9	2	5	4	6	3	8			
2	8	3	7	1	5	6	9		
7	3	2	4	9	6	8	5	1	
6	5	4	7	8	9	3	2	1	7

repeating them to himself as he heard them. This produced little success; his digit span did not improve. After about a week, he began to develop the skill that led to his increase in performance. S. F. was a distance runner, and some of the groups of digits reminded him of running times. For example, the group "3492" was coded as "3 minutes and 49.2 seconds, near world-record mile time" (Chase & Ericsson, 1982, p. 150). Running times were used to encode about 60 percent of the strings. The remainder were processed as ages (893 – "eighty-nine point three, very old man"), and dates (1944 – "near the end of World War II"). Thus, S. F.'s knowledge allowed him to detect patterns in the digit strings, and those patterns helped him increase his memory far beyond the ordinary person's level of performance.

To demonstrate the importance of S. F.'s reported strategy, the researchers constructed strings that could not easily be analyzed as running times, ages, or dates (Chase & Ericsson, 1982). On such strings, S. F.'s performance deteriorated. In contrast, when strings were constructed that fit his encoding scheme well, his performance improved. In addition, Chase and Ericsson (1982) taught S. F.'s scheme to another undergraduate runner, D. D., who also started with only an average digit span. D. D. was able to increase his digit span to 100 items, higher than S. F. Thus, the technique of encoding numbers into meaningful chunks was useful to people beyond S. F.

S. F.'s skill is no different than what we all can (and do) accomplish, although perhaps on a smaller scale, if the circumstances are right. Please read aloud the following string of letters *once*, and without looking at it again try to repeat it.

FL YDI GRU NPE NR OT

This string of letters is too long for most people to repeat without error after a single reading. Now, try to repeat the following string after reading it aloud once, while not looking at it.

FLY DIG RUN PEN ROT

Even though the letters are exactly the same in both strings, recall is usually much greater for the second, because there, the letters form words. We can encode the fifteen letters as five units or chunks, which greatly reduces the memory load, in the same way that strings of numbers became meaningful to S. F.

In sum, the Ericsson, Chase, and Falloon (1980) study demonstrated that – in one domain, at least – it was possible for an average individual to achieve world-class performance simply through extensive practice. The results, in conjunction with Chase and Simon's (1973b) analysis of the Ten-Year Rule in chess, provided support for the possibility that *any* world-class skill could be achieved by *anyone*, assuming they developed an efficient strategy and had sufficient practice using it.

The Ten-Year Rule in Creative Achievement

The genius-is-made view was also supported by a study by Hayes (1989) that demonstrated that no one produces creative work at the highest level without a long period of immersion in the domain. Hayes measured the time needed to produce outstanding creative work in the arts: composition of classical music, painting, and poetry. Hayes used a musical reference book as the basis for choosing classical composers to study; he assumed that the composers mentioned in that book were important in classical music. He examined the biographies of seventy-six composers, for whom he could determine the time between the individual's introduction to musical instruction and the production of the individual's first "notable" work or "masterwork." Hayes used a simple objective definition of a masterwork: a composition with at least five recordings available in a recording catalog. More than 500 masterworks were produced by his sample of seventy-six composers, and only *three* of those works were composed before year ten of the composer's career; those three "early" works were composed in career years eight and nine. Even Wolfgang Amadeus Mozart fit Hayes's pattern: Mozart's first masterwork was composed when he was twenty-one and had been studying music for more than ten years.

To study career development in painters, Hayes (1989) examined the biographies of 131 painters, to determine the time when the individual's painting career began. Masterworks were defined as paintings reproduced in at least one of several standard histories of painting. The career development of painters showed a pattern similar to that of the composers: there was an initial six-year period with no masterworks. This description fit the careers of even the most precocious and productive individuals, such as Picasso. Picasso began to paint under the tutelage of his father, also a painter, at about age eight or nine; his first notable works were produced at about age sixteen. Hayes also reported similar results from a study of poets: a significant time period between beginning one's career and production of significant works. Hayes's basic conclusions have been supported by similar findings reported by other investigators (e.g., Bloom, 1985; Gardner, 1993).

The Ten-Year Rule in Creativity: Conclusions

We have here support for the idea that some world-class creative contributions depend on a years-long process of development. These findings have been presented as supporting the "Ten-Year Rule," although that term is not quite accurate, since Hayes found that painters took, on average, less time than that. Thus, in this context, the "Ten-Year Rule" means only that everyone takes a long time – several years – before producing a significant creative accomplishment. The "Ten-Year Rule" should perhaps be the "Multiyear Rule."

Deliberate Practice and Expertise

The discovery of the Ten-Year Rule led to numerous studies of expertise in a broad range of areas (see chapters in Ericsson et al., 2018). One factor that has been implicated in the development of expertise is *deliberate practice*: the repetition, often under the supervision of a teacher or coach, of specific elements of skill that the individual wishes to improve. One does not become a great tennis player just by playing a lot of tennis. Rather, one must deliberately practice specific aspects of the skills that one wishes to acquire.

Ericsson, Krampe, and Tesch-Römer (1993) studied the relation between expertise and deliberate practice in four groups of musicians. One group was made up of elite professional violinists, members of world-class symphony orchestras; the other three groups were students at a prestigious music school. The best students were designated by their teachers as probably being headed for careers as soloists or members of elite orchestras; the lowest level of students were preparing for careers as teachers of music. All the musicians – professionals and students – were interviewed concerning their activities, musical and otherwise, and the groups of students were asked to keep diaries of their activities over a week, so that the amount of time spent on practice and other activities could be determined.

Results showed that the professionals spent more time practicing than the students did and also more time sleeping, which was taken to mean that practice was effortful (Ericsson et al., 1993). The best student-violinists had begun study

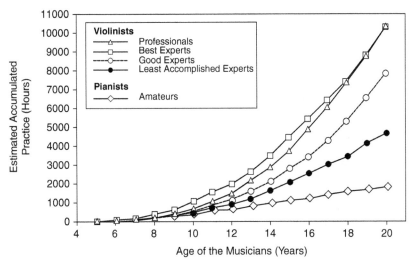

Figure 6.2 Ericsson et al. (1993) practice results

of the violin earlier in life than had the other students and had practiced more throughout their careers (see Figure 6.2). The highest-level student-violinists had accumulated more than 10,000 hours of practice by the age of twenty, compared with approximately 8,000 hours for the good violinists and 4,000 hours for those of lowest skill. A second study, of high-level pianists, produced similar results, as did a study by Bloom and coworkers (Bloom, 1985), who interviewed highly successful athletes, musicians, artists, and scientists.

Those sorts of findings led Ericsson (2006; Ericsson & Pool, 2016, ch. 8) to propose that practice was the critical factor in the development of *any* world-class performance and that innate factors – talent or genius – played no role.

> [I]t is possible to account for the development of elite performance among healthy children without recourse to unique talent (genetic endowment) – excepting the innate determinants of body size. (Ericsson, 2006, p. 4)

Deliberate Practice and World-Class Performance: No Place for Talent?

The claim that practice was the *sole* cause of performance differences among people stimulated strong responses by researchers who put emphasis on the importance of innate factors – talent, giftedness, or genius – in the development of world-class performance. First, questions were raised about the plausibility of the practice view. Second, objections were directed toward the reasoning underlying the deliberate-practice view. Finally, questions were raised concerning the empirical support for the idea that practice *alone* was the cause of differences in achievement that were discovered.

Rejecting Talent – Ignoring the Obvious?

In a wide-ranging critique of the deliberate-practice view, Sternberg (1996) began with a general objection: rejecting talent as a factor in the development of all world-class skills was absurd.

> We fail to see evidence all around us – scholarly and common-sensical – that people differ in their talents, and that no matter how hard some people try, they just cannot all become experts in the mathematical, scientific, literary, musical, or any other domains to which they may have aspired. (1996, p. 352)

In Sternberg's opinion, the practice view could not account for the "very early extraordinary creative expertise" (p. 351) of some individuals.

> Why was Mozart so damn good? ... What made Picasso so good so young? ... [W]hat Mozart did as a child most musical experts will never do nor be able to in their lifetimes, even after they have passed many times over the amount of time Mozart could possibly have had for deliberate practice as a child. ... The truth is that practice is only part of the picture. Most physicists will not become Einstein. And most composers will wonder why they can never be Mozart. (p. 350–3)

Sternberg proposed that Mozart's or Picasso's accomplishments as *children* could not be matched by most *adults*, even after unlimited practice.

Expertise and Practice: Questions about the Logic of the Argument

Much of the support for the deliberate practice view came from *retrospective* studies that measured the amounts of practice carried out by individuals who had already achieved different levels of accomplishment (Ericsson, Krampe & Tesch-Römer, 1993; see also chapters in Ericsson et al., 2018). In those studies, we have a *correlation* between two variables – reported practice and achievement – and we know that the practice came first. Researchers supporting the deliberate practice view then concluded that the different levels of practice were the *cause* of the different levels of achievement. However, it is equally possible that something else related to achievement – for example, *talent* – caused the differences in practice (Sternberg, 1996). High levels of talent might drive people to practice more – that is, to work through activities that most of us find deadly dull (Winner, 2014). To determine if differences in practice *cause* varying levels of achievement, one should carry out a controlled experiment, with a large sample of people randomly assigned to different levels of practice. Random assignment would ensure that the groups would be equivalent in talent before the study began. Any differences in achievement would then be the result of practice, assuming that the groups were equally motivated. That sort of experiment has not been carried out.

Another problem arises from the design of studies, such as that of Ericsson, Krampe, and Tesch-Römer (1993), that looked at the relationship between practice and the development of musical skill. All the musicians – professionals and students – in the high-practice groups, for example, were ones who *succeeded*. What about *failures*? We have no idea of the number of people who began to study music, and practiced diligently, but dropped out early because they were not advancing in spite of practicing (Sternberg, 1996). Those people could be called *high-practice failures*. Thus, one may be drawing conclusions from a biased sample of participants. Based on those sorts of objections, one cannot assume that practice *caused* high levels of performance.

How Strong Is the Relationship between Practice and Achievement?

If practice were the sole factor determining level of achievement in any domain, then the correlation between hours of practice and achievement should be positive and strong. Macnamara, Hambrick, and Oswald (2014) examined studies from a wide variety of domains, including music, chess, sports, education, and various professions, and reported that the typical correlations were approximately +.50 to +.60. That level of correlation, while significant and important, indicated that other factors played roles in determining the level of achievement. Those factors are what psychologists call *individual differences* – that is, differences between individuals on psychological characteristics that might affect achievement.

Individual Differences in Achievement

Intellectual-Cognitive Factors

Studies have examined whether individual differences among chess players play a role in the development of chess expertise (Ullén, Hambrick & Mosing, 2016). As one example, people who start to play at earlier ages tend to reach higher levels of accomplishment, on average, and they take less time – they need less practice – to do so. Those results indicate that there may be a *critical period* for learning chess: a maturational stage during which people might be especially ready to acquire and make use of information related to chess skill.

There is also evidence that differences in cognitive capacities – intelligence and working memory – may contribute to achievement (Ullén, Hambrick & Mosing, 2016). Working-memory capacity – that is, the ability to direct one's attention, among other things – is related to achievement in several domains. Thus, people may differ in their ability to process information and, therefore, to make use of practice. Thus, in explaining the effects of practice on achievement, one must take into account the processing capacities of the person carrying out that practice, which means that not all practice is equivalent.

Individual Differences in Memory Skills

One of the seminal findings in support of the deliberate-practice view was S. F.'s development of a world-class digit span, discussed earlier in this chapter (Chase & Ericsson, 1982; see also Foer, 2011). That result supported the hypothesis that anyone could achieve the highest level of memory performance and, by extension, perhaps in any skill. However, there is evidence that there might be built-in differences in people's memory capacities. LePort et al. (2012) reported on individuals who possessed what the researchers called "highly superior autobiographical memory," outstanding memory for life events. Based on extensive screening, the researchers identified eleven people who possessed exceptional memories for events in their lives. They were asked to recall details about such events as their first day at college; their first day of elementary school; and their last final exam in college. Those individuals were able to recall many details of those events. Importantly, the people had not practiced memorizing autobiographical information. They reported that, at one point in their lives, typically around eleven or twelve years of age, they realized that they possessed what might be an extraordinary skill. Interestingly, the participants were not superior on all measures of memory.

They were no better than controls on digit-span or on remembering random pairs of words. There seems to be a specific memory skill involved in remembering biographical information, which may develop without training.

Giftedness and Achievement

Winner (1996, 2014) has presented evidence for the existence of innate talent from studies of extraordinary young people – *gifted* children – who show high levels of ability in some domain seemingly without extensive amounts of practice. Gifted children exhibit three characteristics. First, they are precocious: they exhibit high-level abilities much earlier than average, and they learn very rapidly. Second, they "march to a different drummer": they learn, and solve problems, by themselves, without support from teachers or parents. Third, they have a "rage to master": they are highly intrinsically motivated, concentrate deeply, and become totally involved in attaining mastery. A prodigy is, in Winner's view, an extremely gifted child. Winner believes that, for example, the compulsion to draw often seen in precocious artists, and the great advances in skill that those children quickly achieve, indicate that they have an innate talent that is pushing them and allowing them to develop extraordinarily quickly.

An individual whose career trajectory provides support for the talent view is world chess champion Magnus Carlsen. In 2014, Carlsen reached the highest chess rating in history. Gobet and Ekru (2014) compared Carlsen's history with other top-ranked players in 2014, when Carlsen was twenty-three and world champion. At that time, eighteen years had intervened between his being introduced to chess and his becoming a grandmaster. The next ten ranked players (numbers two through eleven) had taken on average about twenty-five years to become a grandmaster, which was significantly higher than Carlsen's eighteen years. In other words, Carlsen had had significantly *fewer* years of practice, overall, than the next ten players. Carlsen seemed to have gotten more out of each year of practice. Gobet and Ekru considered the question of whether Carlsen has a particular talent for chess and concluded that "[t]he answer to this question is so obvious in the chess world that it is not even posed – Carlsen is known as the 'Mozart of chess'" (2014, p. 2). It is noteworthy that an explicit connection was made between Carlsen and Mozart, who was mentioned by Sternberg (1996) as a case of development that the deliberate-practice view could not explain.

Savants: Autistic and Acquired

Evidence for the existence of innate talents can be seen in the performance of *autistic savants* (or *savants*; Treffert, 2011). Those individuals may be severely disabled psychologically (i.e., fully autistic savants are severely withdrawn and unable and unwilling to communicate with others) and yet are able to perform at an extraordinarily high level in some restricted domain, and they almost always possess extraordinary memories for information in that domain. Most interesting for the present discussion are savants who show exceptional ability in some artistic domain – that is, savants who play music beautifully, without formal instruction, or who can draw with remarkable skill. The fact that talents can flourish in savants, who can be lacking in other aspects of intellectual and social development, is taken as evidence that talent is an isolated capacity, one that can be inherited but is independent of general "intelligence" and practice (Treffert, 2011).

Talent and Achievement: Summary and Conclusions

Several sorts of arguments have been made in support of the talent view. First, criticisms have been directed at the reasoning underlying the deliberate-practice view. Second, studies of individual differences in achievement have indicated that factors other than practice influence the level of achievement that a person may reach.

Effects of Practice: Group Means versus Individual Differences

The deliberate-practice versus talent views of achievement come out of different traditions in psychology: experimental versus psychometric (mental testing), respectively. Those traditions use different strategies for analyzing data. Researchers who support the practice view, for example, tend to analyze group means in accumulated practice time when testing hypotheses. Researchers supporting the talent view, in contrast, focus on individual differences in accumulated practice time needed to reach a given level of performance. Those differences in focus can result in conflicting interpretations of the same set of results. As an example, we can consider a study by Sloboda et al. (1996; see also Howe, Davison & Sloboda, 1998), which examined the development of musical skill in more than 250 schoolchildren in the United Kingdom, where children are given musical instruction and are given regular tests to determine levels of accomplishment. The students had attained five levels of achievement. The highest level was made up of those at a specialized music school, where graduates go on to professional careers. The second level consisted of students who had failed that school's entrance examination and who were therefore presumably very good, although not excellent, musicians. There were two other intermediate levels; then, at the bottom, came students who had tried an instrument but given it up after six months.

Sloboda et al. (1996) had the students provide estimates of the amount of practice time for each year of playing. By grade eight, the high-ability group was practicing 800 percent more than the group that would ultimately drop out (fifteen minutes versus two hours). Furthermore, *every child* in the sample who practiced over two hours per day achieved high levels of skill. There were *no* children in the lower skill levels – including those who had dropped out – who practiced more than two hours per day. Those "high-practice failures," emphasized by Sternberg (1996), were not found. If talent were needed for practice to have effects, then surely there would be some children at the lower levels of accomplishment for whom over two hours of practice was relatively ineffective.

Finally, Sloboda et al. (1996) calculated the amount of practice time needed as the students of various levels of achievement worked through the exam sequence. A talent hypothesis would predict that the more advanced groups would have required less practice to move from any given level to the next. That prediction was not supported: the most accomplished students required *just as many hours of practice*, on average, to advance from one level to the next as did the least accomplished ones. The "talented" group advanced more quickly because their practice was more *concentrated*, not because they needed *less* of it.

The results just presented provide support for the practice view. However, one also finds large amounts of variability in performance within each group in the study. A few students in each group passed the examinations after practicing for only 20 percent of the average for their group. Those people benefited more from practice. Sloboda et al. (1996, p. 301) suggested that there might be differences in efficiency of practicing within each group, or some students might have spent more practice time on material that was to be on the examination. Sloboda et al., supporters of the practice view, did not discuss other individual differences that might be related to talent, such as the possibility that some people might be better than others at remembering musical information or at integrating the movements involved in playing new material. Hambrick et al. (2016), who support the talent view, took those large differences in practice and achievement reported by Sloboda et al. as evidence for the role of talent in development of musical skill. We have here different conclusions, drawn from the same set of results.

Talent and Achievement: Preliminary Conclusions

Based on the research just discussed, it seems that, in order to explain achievement, one must go beyond practice. While there is no doubt that practice plays a significant role in all achievements, other factors also play a role. Some of those factors fit what we mean when we talk of *talent* – that is, an innate ability to deal with some domain. Evidence to support that view comes from studies of individual differences in achievement, including the relation of intelligence and working-memory capacity to achievement; from studies of gifted children; and from studies of savants. It should be noted, however, that the research supporting the talent view has so far been presented without critique. Several questions can be raised about that research, which should be considered before any firm conclusions are drawn.

Innate Talents and Creativity: Some Questions

Giftedness and Creativity Are Different

Winner (2014), who, as we have seen, has carried out research on gifted children, concluded that giftedness and creativity are different. Very few gifted individuals will become adults who leave their mark in a creative domain.

> [T]he skill of being a prodigy is not the same as the skill of being a big-c creator. A prodigy is someone who can easily and rapidly master an already-established domain with expertise. A creator is someone who changes a domain. (p. 314)

Similarly, very few savants have reached the level of creating new works (Treffert, 2011). Here, too, possession of exceptional skills does not mean that the individual will produce novel works. Furthermore, it took much time for savants' creativity to develop, as Hayes (1989) found in his analysis of creative development and as we saw in examining the development of the Beatles. Savant skills and creativity might be independent.

Precocity without Practice?

One characteristic of gifted children noted by Winner (2014) is their precocity – they exhibit high levels of skill early in life, seemingly without much in the way of practice or assistance from others. However, sometimes, the "data" concerning precocious development come from anecdotes in the popular media, and one must be very cautious about accepting anecdotes. Ericsson and Pool (2016, pp. 214–215) discussed the case of Mario Lemieux, one of the best hockey players of all time. Lemieux's prodigious accomplishments have been reported, such as his being able to skate from an early age and his ability to do things on the ice that much older boys could not do. Ericsson and Pool noted, however, that Lemieux had exceptional support for his hockey activities, and there were specific learning experiences underlying his precocious skills. Lemieux was the third of three boys in a "hockey-mad" family, and his older brothers spent much time playing hockey with him. The boys' father built an ice rink in the front yard, so the boys could play as much as they wanted. The family even set up an "indoor ice rink" for hockey at night, by bringing snow into the house, packing it down on the floor so it could be skated on, and leaving the doors and windows open so that the house was cold enough for the snow not to melt.

    Thus, by the time that young Mario was able to dazzle others with his skills, he had had years of practice. Ericsson has concluded, based on thirty years of studying prodigies, that there is never prodigious development without relevant learning experiences (Ericsson & Pool, 2016, p. 211). Given Ericsson's strong belief in practice, that conclusion is not surprising. However, there is other evidence that supports the conclusion that many prodigies may not be quite what we think them to be. Let us look again at Mozart and Picasso, whom Sternberg (1996) mentioned as two cases of development that the practice view could not explain.

Were the Young Mozart and Picasso Really So Good?

Mozart's Development as a Composer

Sternberg said the following about Mozart:

> [W]hat Mozart did as a child most musical experts will never do nor be able to in their lifetimes, even after they have passed many times over the amount of time Mozart could possibly have had for deliberate practice as

a child ... [M]ost composers will wonder why they can never be Mozart. (pp. 351–353)

Sternberg may have overstated the case for Mozart: much of what Mozart accomplished as a child *can* be matched by most musical experts.

Mozart's interest in music was stimulated by his sister's learning to play the harpsichord. Mozart's sister, Maria Anna, was four years older than Wolfgang, and she began to study the harpsichord under their father Leopold's tutelage when Wolfgang was around three. The young boy was so strongly attracted by his sister's lessons that he demanded lessons also, and he so quickly developed skill as a player that, by the age of six, he was performing for the royalty of Europe. Mozart's first "compositions" were produced at around that time. They are simple pieces for harpsichord, and, not surprisingly, they contain errors of various sorts. For example, one piece changes meter (changes "time"), from $\frac{3}{4}$ to $\frac{2}{4}$, in the middle, in a way which would not have been acceptable to a knowledgeable composer at that time. Since the boy did not yet know how to write music, the pieces are in Leopold's handwriting, which has resulted in some scholars wondering if Leopold might have played a role in the composition process, especially when one remembers that he, too, was a composer. Mozart's very earliest compositions, therefore, seem not to be real compositions. Perhaps one should just be in awe at what that child accomplished and leave it at that.

If we put aside those earliest pieces, we find that much time passed before Mozart produced anything substantial in the way of music. Mozart's piano concertos – pieces for piano and orchestra – can serve as a case study of his development as a composer, and they provide evidence that he was learning his trade. The first four piano concertos were written when Mozart was eleven. However, although those works were at one time thought to be compositions by Mozart, it turns out that they contain no music by him. Mozart's father took music from other composers, written for solo keyboard instruments. Mozart wrote orchestral parts, turning them into "concertos." Mozart's father might have been trying to teach the boy how to write in the concerto form without having to compose the music. Also, the original musical scores contain handwriting by both Wolfgang and Leopold, indicating that they might have involved joint activity (Weisberg, 2006). We now have an eleven-year-old composer still working out basic issues in composing.

Next was a set of three works, produced in 1771 or so, when Mozart was sixteen. These "Mozart concertos" also use music written by another composer, J. C. Bach, a son of J. S. Bach. The J. C. Bach works were also written for solo keyboard, and again Mozart mainly wrote orchestral parts. Here, too, sometimes the music is in Leopold's handwriting, indicating that the fifteen-year-old Mozart still might not have been completely independent of his father's teaching.

The next work, the Concerto No. 5 in D major, K. 175, is, finally, entirely made up of music by Mozart. It was composed in 1773, when he was seventeen. Thus, it took Mozart approximately six years to move from arranging the music of others, under the close watch of his father, to producing a large-scale original work on his own. We are also more than ten years from the very first "compositions." Also, according to most Mozart experts, the Piano Concerto No. 5 is not what one could call a "masterwork" in the sense of being notable for its musical value. That honor falls to the Piano Concerto No. 9, written in 1777, when Mozart was twenty-one (Weisberg, 2006, pp. 214–216). That piece was also the first "masterwork" found by Hayes (1989). We are now more than fifteen years beyond those very first "compositions." The young Mozart's performing skills might have been astounding, but his composing skills developed differently. Mozart, one of the most prolific, "talented," and precocious composers to ever live – surely a genius – needed significant time before his genius as a composer flowered. There is little doubt that most musicians learning to compose can match Mozart's childhood accomplishments, even without much more in terms of practice. Sternberg (1996) overstated the case for Mozart's precocity.

Was Picasso So Good So Young?

Sternberg (1996) also pointed to the childhood accomplishments of Picasso as another accelerated pattern of development that could not be explained without including the notion of talent. Picasso himself proclaimed that, early in life, he painted like the great painter Raphael (1483–1520), meaning that he did not need much time to develop as a painter.

> I have never done children's drawings. Never. Even when I was very small. I remember one of my first drawings. I was perhaps six, or even less. In my father's house there was a statue of Hercules with his club in the corridor, and I drew Hercules. But it wasn't a child's drawing. It was a real drawing, representing Hercules with his club. (Reprinted in Richardson, 1991, p. 29)

However, the historical record may not support Picasso's report about his development (Richardson, 1991). First of all, Picasso misremembered when he drew Hercules. The drawing has been preserved, and it is dated 1890, so Picasso was about nine when he drew it, not "six, or even less," as he recalled.

In Richardson's view, the drawing, while perhaps impressive for a nine-year-old, supports the rule that "no great painter has ever produced work of any serious interest before puberty. However, . . . [Picasso's] legend obliged him to have been a genius from his earliest days" (p. 29). Richardson is saying that, to maintain his legend, Picasso embellished his report. The Hercules statue and Picasso's drawing are presented in Figure 6.3, and readers can make their own judgments concerning the level of skill involved.

Additional evidence to support the claim that Picasso was less than a genius when he was a child comes from a study by Pariser (1987), who examined the childhood drawings of three famous painters: Picasso, Paul Klee (1879–1940), and Henri Toulouse-Lautrec (1864–1901). All three went through the same developmental sequence in which they learned to draw and paint. Contrary to what Picasso claimed, he too had to grapple with the problems that all children go through before they can accurately represent objects through drawing. One can see examples of Picasso trying to deal with those problems in the Hercules drawing. He seems to have had difficulty with the representation of objects in depth: he had to correct the

Figure 6.3 A. Hercules statue. Giambologna, Hercules with a Club. Bargello Museum, Florence; photo courtesy Ben Abel.
B. Picasso drawing. Pablo Picasso, Drawing of Hercules (1890); © 2019 Estate of Pablo Picasso / Artists Rights Society (ARS), New York.

arm-plus-club at least once; and the rotated head, left shoulder, arm and hand, right foot, and left leg of Hercules were not very well captured. The left foot may have been too difficult entirely, as it seems that Picasso gave up on it. It is true that here we are examining the drawing of a nine-year-old, and one might say that we are being hypercritical, as with Mozart. However, those individuals have been presented as having accomplished things as children that most people cannot come close to as adults (Sternberg, 1996). Furthermore, those claims are used as the basis for scientific conclusions concerning the development of creative capacities. Therefore, the evidence supporting those claims should be looked at carefully.

Questions about Talent: Conclusions

There seem to be a number of factors, beyond practice, that affect levels of achievement, including creative achievement. However, in some cases, the "data" presented to support claims about talent may not stand up to scrutiny. We must be careful about making broad claims about talent based on anecdotal case studies lacking "hard" data.

What Is Being Learned over Those Years?

Creative individuals, including those at the highest level, take years to develop the skills to produce masterworks. What is happening over those years? What skills are being developed? First, it turns out that the Ten-Year Rule may be a conservative estimate of the duration of the process of developing as a creator. As we just saw, Mozart's first truly notable composition, the Piano Concerto No. 9, came more than 15 years after the beginning of his career as a composer. Furthermore, there is evidence that Mozart's development as a composer was not near its end at that time. Kozbelt (2005) found that the quality of Mozart's compositions increased throughout his maturity. The proportion of masterworks increased over those years, indicating that the "creative learning process" is very long-term in its duration (see also Hass & Weisberg, 2009; Hass, Weisberg & Choi, 2010).

The continuing development of Mozart supports at least two conclusions. First, creative achievement may involve an ongoing learning process. That conclusion seems reasonable when one contemplates all the complex activities involved in composing large-scale musical compositions, such as operas and symphonies, which were central in Mozart's work. There are many "problems" involved in the composition of such pieces, which may take many attempts to solve. Second, the continually developing composer may be using feedback from the responses to compositions – audience responses and perhaps the composer's own responses – as the basis for composing later compositions. If composers respond to reactions to their works and take them into account when composing new ones, then we should be able to find evidence that composers can critically analyze their own works. Support for that hypothesis comes from another study by Kozbelt (2008), in which he examined the accuracy of Beethoven's criticisms of his own compositions.

Kozbelt (2008) examined every available critical comment that Beethoven made about his works, from the composer's letters as well as from reports by others of conversations with Beethoven. Kozbelt found criticisms of seventy of Beethoven's works, about one-third of his output, from throughout his career. Beethoven's assessments of those works were compared with several current evaluative measures, such as modern critics' assessments of the works, as well as how often various works were recorded. Beethoven's judgments of his own compositions were positively correlated with the current measures, meaning that Beethoven was successful in predicting the quality of his works. Also, the accuracy of Beethoven's predictions increased as he got older. If there is a learning process involved in assessing quality, then it seems that one can still learn in one's maturity.

If we can assume that the results just discussed – based on two composers of classical music – can be generalized to other creative individuals, there may be two different sorts of things being learned as a creative individual develops. First, to the degree that creative activity entails problem-solving, people become better at solving those problems. Second, if the creative process includes predicting how others will respond to one's work, creative individuals may get better at such predictions, as they acquire more experience with others' responses to their works.

Knowledge versus Creativity: The Tension View

The discussion throughout the book so far, including in this chapter, has centered on the core component of analytic thinking, the idea that one's knowledge – or experience, or expertise – serves as the foundation on which all creative advances are built. That is the *inside-the-box* aspect of analytic thinking and the central component of *green creativity*. However, as we have discussed, there is a long-lived tradition in psychology, which is very much alive today, in which creative thinking is assumed to require breaking away from experience. There is a *tension* between experience and creativity (e.g., Bilalić, McLoed & Gobet, 2008; Frensch & Sternberg, 1989; Simonton, 1999). The genius view and the related notion of thinking outside the box are examples of that tradition. The tension applies also to expertise: creativity should come about as the result of breaking away from expertise. Here is a presentation of the tension view by Sternberg (2018).

> [K]nowledge can lead to entrenchment, thus sometimes hurting creativity rather than facilitating it. ... [S]cholars become less creative in part because they are unable to combat their own entrenchment – their being used to, and comfortable, seeing things in a certain way. (pp. 52–54)

Research Support for the Tension View

In support of the tension view, Frensch and Sternberg (e.g., 1989), showed that experts in bridge, the card game, were limited in adjusting to changes in the game. The researchers had bridge experts and novices try to play changed versions of the game. *Surface* changes involved changes in the names and order of suits; such changes were not central to the game. In contrast, *deep* or *conceptual* changes resulted in a basic reorganization in how the game was played. As an example, the player who *lost* the last trick, rather than the *winner*, would lead the next one. The experts had a harder time adjusting to the deep changes than did bridge novices. Thus, expertise made for less flexible thinking in adjusting to changes in the world.

Additional evidence in support of the tension view was adduced by Simonton (1984, ch. 4). Based on the tension view, one might expect to find that people with very low or very high levels of education might not be the most creative. Too-low levels of education might limit creativity because the person does not know the domain well enough; while too-high levels of education might result in rigid thinking. Those who produce the most innovative advances might be at middle levels of education. Simonton examined the education levels of more than 300 highly creative individuals born between 1450 and 1850, including Beethoven, Mozart, Leonardo, Galileo, and Rembrandt. He found that the peak creators in this outstanding group had education equivalent to about half-way through modern undergraduate training. Most critically, more education than that was related to lower levels of creative accomplishment. Those results indicate that more training is a bad thing.

Another stream of research supporting the tension between knowledge and creativity has been carried out by Ward (1995, 2018), examining what he calls *structured imagination*. This research was briefly discussed in Chapter 5. Ward has looked at ordinary people's ability to imagine new things: for example, creatures on a distant planet very different from earth. Most of the imagined creatures contained the same features as those on earth, such as symmetry and pairs of sense organs. Most people, Ward noted, took the "path of least resistance." That is, they used familiar ideas as the basis for their creations. Ward also examined creatures in science fiction, and found that most of them also were closely related to earth creatures, even though most science fiction authors were trying to get away from earth. To produce something new, Ward concluded, the individual must consider, in detail, unique aspects of the imagined environment in which the creature will function. To the degree that the new environment is different than earth, the individual will be able to imagine new aspects of the creature. Otherwise, the deeply ingrained knowledge about earth creatures inhibits people's imaginations. Wiley (1998) also demonstrated that knowledge can interfere with problem-solving.

Questions about the Tension View

The results we have just discussed support the tension view, but other results indicate that true experts are not trapped by inflexible knowledge. Bilalić, McLoed, and Gobet (2008) examined the flexibility of chess experts' knowledge. They tested individuals who were at very high levels of expertise in chess (*super*-experts) and they tested players of lower skill, still experts but not at the very highest level. The test involved a chess puzzle: the player was presented with a position from a game and was asked to try to find the most direct way to win. To a person familiar with chess, the pattern of pieces on the board suggested one obvious way to win. However, a subtle change in the way the pieces were set up opened the way for an even easier, but much less familiar, strategy. The "ordinary" experts were not able to discover the novel solution: they could only find the familiar one. They seemed to be trapped by their knowledge. However, the super-experts found the less familiar method. They were not trapped by expertise: they could think flexibly and went beyond what they knew. As Bilalić and colleagues (2008, p. 97) concluded: "Inflexibility of experts is both reality and myth. But the greater the level of expertise, the more of a myth it becomes."

A similar conclusion comes from the case studies of seminal creative advances discussed so far in this book and elsewhere (see Weisberg, 2006). According to the tension view, if we examined the development of creative products, especially those of the first rank, we should see thinkers rejecting the past. Contrary to that prediction, we have seen much evidence for *green creativity*: creative thinking building on the past, with new ideas arising as the result of an individual's recycling, and elaborating on, old ideas (Picasso's *Guernica*; Wright's *Fallingwater*; Leonardo's *Aerial Screw*; Pollock's new painting style; and the bacterial theory of ulcers; see Chapters 1 and 4). In addition, we have seen that the Ten-Year Rule – including deliberate practice – applies to many creative thinkers, including the Beatles and Mozart, which also goes against the tension view.

The Tension View – Conclusions

In some circumstances, possessing knowledge can interfere with creative thinking. Knowledgeable individuals who are trying to produce new ideas may rely too much on what they know, which can restrict the breadth of ideas that they produce. When the environment is structured in such a way that one's knowledge is no longer applicable, people with more knowledge may find it difficult to adapt to the new situation. On the other hand, truly high levels of expertise may result in increased flexibility of thought. Furthermore, as we saw in Chapter 5, the world may typically be *kind* (Gentner & Maravilla, 2018), meaning that applying one's expertise may work more often than not. Therefore, the idea that expertise is in opposition to creative thinking may not be broadly correct.

How to Get to Carnegie Hall: Conclusions

Some Cautionary Thoughts

The cases of Mozart and Picasso, as well as those of the Beatles and Beethoven, support the conclusion that creative accomplishment takes a long time to develop. Furthermore, as discussed earlier, the development of creative skills may involve several complex facets. These conclusions raise questions concerning some of the phenomena that have been brought forth as supporting the critical role of talent in creative achievement. There may be examples of individuals who produce artworks of great skill, seemingly without training: gifted children, who draw with great detail and realism or who flawlessly play music of great complexity (Winner, 2014). Before we conclude from such examples that high levels of achievement, including creative achievement, can spring from nothing, those accomplishments must be examined critically. As we saw with the case of Mario Lemieux (Ericsson & Pool, 2016), prodigious accomplishments are sometimes exaggerations of what actually happened. Furthermore, most children who performed exceptionally in some domain do not go on to creative accomplishment (Winner, 2014), and those who do, such as Mozart and Picasso, need time to become creative achievers.

Similar cautions must be raised in the case of savants, who sometimes seem to have developed a skill out of the blue (Treffert, 2011). One must have available sufficient information to be able to critically analyze each case in detail. Did the exceptional skill really develop without learning or practice? Also, most savants, like prodigious children, do not produce creative works. Concerning those few "creative savants," how did that accomplishment play out over time? Was there something extraordinary about the savant's path to creativity, or was it the same years-long path taken by Mozart, Picasso, and the Beatles? The latter seems to be true.

The Genius Is Born and Made

Given those cautionary thoughts, based on the review in this chapter, some general conclusions can be drawn concerning the question of whether genius is born or made. There is no doubt that experience, broadly speaking, plays a critical role in high levels of achievement, including creative achievement. At the same time, characteristics that seem to have an inheritable component (IQ, working-memory capacity) also play a significant role. The critical question is not whether creative accomplishment depends on nature *or* nurture but, rather, how one's inherited characteristics interact with one's experiences to result in the production of novel works. That is, geniuses are born *and* made. Multiple factors help you to get to Carnegie Hall.

7 | Insight in Problem-Solving and Creative Thinking

A Leap of Insight in Creative Thinking: Wag Dodge's Invention of the Escape Fire

On August 4, 1949, a forest ranger reported a wildfire in Mann Gulch, Montana, a rugged backcountry area. A crew of fifteen young "smoke-jumpers" – firefighters who parachute in to fight fires in remote areas – was sent to the location, led by R. Wagner Dodge ("Wag" Dodge), an experienced smokejumper. The crew met the ranger, and they all headed down the gulch toward the fire. As the men approached the fire, the winds increased sharply, fanning the flames, and the fire quickly grew in size. It "crowned," moving along the tops of the trees, toward the men. Then it "blew up," increasing greatly in size, intensity, and speed, moving up the gulch fueled by thick growths of dry grass, the result of a recent hot period without rain. As the fire roared up the gulch, Dodge, realizing that it was now too big for them to fight, ordered the men to drop their heavy equipment and retreat up the gulch, away from the fire. However, the fire was moving faster than the men could run, and kept gaining ground. At that point, Dodge thought they all would die.

Dodge then had a sudden insight, one that has become legendary in the US Forest Service as well as in the study of creative thinking (Kounios & Beeman, 2015; Maclean, 1972). He stopped running, lit a match, and burned out a portion of grassy ground in front of him, in the direction in which he had been running and the fire was moving. The fire that Dodge lit quickly produced a burnt-out patch of ground, which meant that the oncoming fire could not burn there. Dodge stepped into that burnt and smoldering area and called to his men to join him. None of them responded – they did not understand what he was trying to do. Dodge took a cloth, wet it with water from his canteen, put it over his face, and lay down on the still-smoldering ground. The fire with its strong winds passed around him. The gusts of wind were so strong, that, several times they almost lifted Dodge off the ground. In his safe burnt-out area, Dodge was not harmed by the fire. Two members of the team, who ran up the walls of

215

the gulch to a rocky area, also survived. The other twelve smokejumpers perished, as did the ranger who discovered the fire. It took 450 firefighters four days to bring the fire under control.

Mann Gulch was one of the worst fire disasters in the history of the US Forest Service. There was an investigation into the tragedy by a Forest Service Review Board. Dodge was asked why he did what he did and he could not supply much information. He said that it had just seemed "logical" to him. Dodge's insight, setting an escape fire, became part of the training for smokejumpers.

A Leap of Insight

In discussing Dodge's response to the Mann Gulch fire, Kounios and Beeman (2015) argued that Dodge's creative advance depended on his breaking away from what he knew. In other words, Dodge's advance was not based on analytic thinking.

> Dodge's insight was a sudden flip of his understanding. IIis radical reinterpretation was utterly nonobvious: Fire wasn't just the problem – it was also the *solution*. He fought fire with fire. (p. 23, emphasis in original)

Terms like "a sudden flip of his understanding," "radical reinterpretation," and "utterly nonobvious" show that Kounios and Beeman believe that Dodge went into totally new territory. They emphasized that, for Dodge, setting an escape fire, "using a fire as a tool for creating a protective buffer zone, ... [was] weakly associated with elements of the problem" (2015, p. 89).

Describing Dodge's using fire to create a buffer zone as being "weakly associated with the elements of the problem," means that there was no precedent in Dodge's past that could have served as the basis for his making that connection. Kounios and Beeman (2015, p. 36) also emphasized Dodge's "openness to alternative, nonobvious interpretations. This is how he broke out of his box." Dodge's innovation was possible only because of his rejection of everything he knew about fighting fires, which came about through a radically new interpretation of the situation (through thinking outside the box). Kounios and Beeman's analysis of Dodge's insight builds on Mednick's (1962) notion of the flat associative hierarchy and remote associations as being the basis of creativity (see Chapter 2). We will see several variations on this view in this chapter and in the next several chapters.

Insight versus Analytic Thinking in Creativity

We have analyzed numerous creative advances, ranging from works produced by individuals of acknowledged genius (big-c creativity) to under-the-radar advances produced by people whom one might not expect to be innovative (little-c creativity). We found a common set of thought processes – analytic or ordinary thinking – underlying those examples. In this chapter, we will consider the phenomenon of *insight* in problem-solving, another challenge to the analytic-thinking view concerning creativity. "Insight" refers to the idea that creative solutions to problems come about suddenly, as the result of far-ranging creative leaps, in which thinking breaks away from what we know and moves far into the unknown. We are all familiar with the notion of leaps of insight. They are sometimes called *Aha!* or *Eureka!* experiences, because a person solving a problem in a burst of insight may make such an exclamation. If creative thinking is based on leaps of insight, then analytic thinking is irrelevant to creativity. This chapter examines the idea that creative thinking comes about through "leaps of insight."

Outline of the Chapter

We first examine several additional examples of creative advances that have been presented as being brought about by leaps of insight. The chapter then reviews the history of research and theory concerning insight, which was introduced more than 100 years ago into psychology by the Gestalt psychologists. In the early 1980s several research reports were published that raised questions about the role of insight in creative thinking. In response there was an upsurge of research and theorizing in support of the insight view (see chapters in Sternberg & Davidson, 1995), which has continued to today (see chapters in Vallée-Tourangeau, 2018). That upsurge in research has brought deeper understanding into the processes underlying insight. The chapter concludes with an analysis of insight in terms of analytic thinking.

Leaps of Insight in Creative Thinking

The Invention of Radar

In 1935, Arnold Wilkins, a British physicist working at the Radio Research Station, part of the Radio Department of the National

Physical Laboratory, was asked by his superior if it was possible to use radio waves to heat 8 pints of water from 98°F to 105°F, at a distance of 5 km and a height of 1 km. That request, made during a time of developing concern about war in Europe, was directed toward the possible development of a "death ray." Radio waves would be used to heat the blood of pilots of attacking planes, thereby killing them. That is why 8 pints of liquid were involved (human blood capacity), and 98°F to 105°F. Wilkins reported that the available technology could not carry out that task. Wilkins's disappointed superior then asked if there was anything they could do to assist in the war effort. "In a momentous act of inspiration" (Ohlsson, 2011, p. 53), Wilkins proposed that one could use radio waves to determine the locations of airplanes, which would provide critical information to the forces defending England. In that "momentous act of inspiration," Wilkins had conceived radar.

Edison's Light Bulb

Edison's invention of the light bulb has been presented as another example of a leap of insight (Ohlsson, 2011, p. 134). Edison and his laboratory staff spent much time attempting to design the "burner" for the light bulb (what we call the filament: a thin piece of material that could conduct electricity and would glow when electric current was passed through it). According to Ohlsson, Edison's team spent a year working with platinum wire, in various configurations, as a possible burner. They could not find a combination of length, thickness, and shape that would glow sufficiently brightly and for a long-enough time to serve in a usable light bulb. Then Edison changed to a new set of possibilities, and relatively easily found what he needed. "After a year with only partial progress Edison changed the direction of the search to focus on carbon compounds instead of platinum ones, a space in which success came rapidly" (Ohlsson, 2011, p. 134). Edison also broke out of the box and had success.

Ohlsson (2011, ch. 5) listed a wide range of seminal creative advances as examples of leaps of insight, including the Wright brothers' invention of the airplane; the invention of the telephone separately by Edison and by Bell; Mendeleyev's formulation of the periodic table of the chemical elements; the development of Impressionist painting; and Watson and Crick's discovery of the structure of DNA. There seems to be not much in the way of creative advances that were not created through a leap of insight.

Leaps of Insight: Summary

The examples just discussed have in common the idea that a solution to a problem occurred as the result of a link being forged between unconnected ideas through a leap outside the box: using fire to create a safe zone; using radio waves to locate aircraft; and using carbon as a possible burner for the electric light. Examining the history of the concept of insight will demonstrate the kinds of mechanisms that have been proposed to explain those leaps.

Impasse, Restructuring, and Insight in Problem-Solving

The Gestalt psychologists, who brought the notion of insight into psychology (e.g., Köhler, 1925; Wertheimer, 1982), had begun by investigating perception. They used concepts from the study of perception to understand problem-solving. In analyzing problem-solving, the Gestalt psychologists made a distinction between *reproductive* and *productive* thinking. Reproductive thinking is analytic thinking, using the past to deal with the present. One reproduces – repeats – what one has done before. That is an idea similar to *green creativity*. According to the Gestalt view, reproductive thinking cannot produce true innovation: to think creatively, one must think *productively*. Productive thinking goes beyond the past, dealing with each new situation on its own and not simply reproducing something that was done before.

In the Gestalt view, a problem is a situation in which there is more than one possible interpretation, or *structure*. The reason that a person has a problem is that he or she has structured the situation incorrectly, because analytic thinking can result in the person applying *inappropriate constraints* to a problem (Wiley & Jarosz, 2012). Those constraints are not stated in the problem: they are introduced – unnecessarily – by the individual. An incorrect structure will result in the person attempting solutions that will be unsuccessful. The person will therefore reach an *impasse*: he or she will have no further ideas concerning how to proceed. In order to make progress, the person must *restructure* the situation – that is, find a new way to look at the problem. According to the Gestalt psychologists, reaching an impasse can trigger a restructuring of a problem situation.

Mechanisms Underlying Restructuring in Problem-Solving

The Gestalt psychologists discussed the reversible cube as an analogy to a problem situation (Scheerer, 1963; see also Figure 7.1A). When one looks at that figure, one sees it in one orientation, facing in one of the two ways shown in Figure 7.1B. In other words, the perceiver "structures" the situation in one way. If one continues looking at the cube in Figure 7.1A, it will change its orientation, switching suddenly to the other possibility, in a *restructuring*. That change, from one orientation to the other, is *spontaneous* – that is, not under the perceiver's conscious control.

The basic reason that the reversible cube can be seen in two orientations is because its features – the set of lines used to draw it – can be interpreted in two meaningful ways by the visual system (see Column A of Table 7.1). When one

Table 7.1 *Spontaneous restructuring in perception and problem-solving*

A. Perception of Reversible Cube	B. Restructuring in Problem-Solving
1) Presentation of reversible cube	1) Presentation of problem
⇓	⇓
2) $Representation_1$ and $Representation_2$ are activated	2) $Structure_1$ and $Structure_2$ are activated
⇓	⇓
3) $Representation_1$ dominates	3) $Structure_1$ dominates (analytic thinking)
⇓	⇓
4) $Perceptual Experience_1$	4) Possible solutions produced and fail
⇓	⇓
5) Gradual decrease in strength of $Representation_1$	5) Gradual decrease in strength of $Structure_1$ (Impasse)
⇓	⇓
6) $Representation_2$ becomes dominant (spontaneous restructuring of perception; processes outside of conscious control)	6) $Structure_2$ becomes dominant (spontaneous restructuring of problem in response to impasse; processes outside of conscious control)
⇓	⇓
7) $Perceptual Experience_2$	7) New Solution path (Possible immediate solution and *Aha!*)

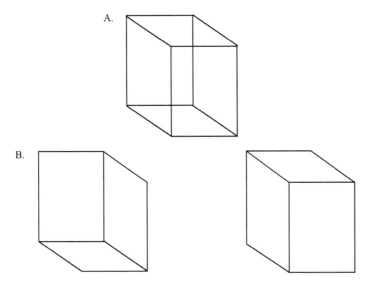

Figure 7.1 A. Reversible cube B. Two orientations of cube

first looks at the cube, those two interpretations compete for dominance in the visual system. One representation, which is momentarily stronger, "takes over," which results in that specific orientation of the cube being perceived (Table 7.1A3–A4). Interpreting the cube in that way gradually becomes weaker, which allows the other interpretation to take over (Table 7.1A5–A7), resulting in the person perceiving the cube in the other orientation.

Similar reasoning was applied to problem-solving (see Column B in Table 7.1). A problem is a situation with two possible structures. Problem presentation results in Structure$_1$ dominating, based on analytic thinking (Table 7.1B2–B3). Any solutions produced as a result of that representation will fail (Table 7.1B4), and the individual will then reach an impasse. Also, each of those failed solutions will result in a gradual decrease in strength of Structure$_1$ (Table 7.1B5). At some point, Structure$_1$ will become weak enough that structure$_2$ will become dominant, meaning that the person will experience a sudden *restructuring of the problem in response to impasse* (Table 7.1B6). That event, the result of processes not under conscious control, opens up a new solution path, which can bring with it a possible immediate solution and an *Aha!* reaction (Table 7.1B7). Kounios and Beeman's (2015, p. 25) description of Wag Dodge's "sudden flip of understanding" in inventing the escape fire is an example of the application of the Gestalt view to explain a creative advance.

The series of events that occurs when solving a problem through insight can be called the *insight sequence*:

problem $\Rightarrow$ impasse $\Rightarrow$ restructuring $\Rightarrow$ insight.

It is a critical component of modern versions of Gestalt theory (Danek & Salvi, 2018; DeCaro, 2018; Ohlsson, 2011; Wiley & Jarosz, 2012).

Insight Problems

In order to bring the study of insight into the laboratory, researchers developed numerous "insight problems" designed to provide small-scale situations in which the insight sequence is necessary for a creative advance. Please work through the problems in Figure 7.2 before reading further.

An insight problem is structured so that a person who approaches it through analytic thinking will be *misdirected* and led down an incorrect solution path. That misdirection will lead to impasse, which may result in a spontaneous restructuring of the problem, leading to a solution or, at the very least, a new way to approach the problem and, perhaps, an *Aha!* experience. The way each of the problems in Figure 7.2 serves as a miniaturization of the insight experience is easily seen. (See Figure 7.3 for solutions to the problems in Figure 7.2.) Presentation of the Lilies problem (Figure 7.2A) leads the person to think about arithmetic: if you have to find half of some period of time, divide it by two. That constraint makes the problem impossible to solve. Solution requires that the person first realize that the problem describes a *geometric* increase in the area of the lilies from one day to the next (2 lilies $\Rightarrow$ 4 lilies $\Rightarrow$ 8 $\Rightarrow$ 16, etc.), which means that simple division does not work. That reinterpretation, that new way of looking at the problem, may lead to the solution.

Compound Remote Associates problems (CRA; Figure 7.2F) have been used extensively in recent studies of insight. When people solve CRA problems, they sometimes report that the solution comes suddenly, in an insight or *Aha!* moment. Other times, they have to work through possible combinations of words, until they find the solution word. Researchers have used those reports to group solutions into those occurring through insight versus analysis. They have then looked at factors related to those different sorts of solutions, including the brain processes that have been active when someone reports insight versus analysis as the basis for solution (Danek & Salvi, 2018; Kounios & Beeman, 2015). (The neuroscience of insight will be discussed in Chapter 13.)

INSIGHT PROBLEMS

A. Lilies: Water lilies double in area every twenty-four hours. At the beginning of the summer there is one water lily on the lake. It takes sixty days for the lake to become completely covered with water lilies. On what day is the lake half-covered?

B. Triangle of Coins: The triangle below, made of coins, points to the bottom of the page. How can you move only three coins and make the triangle point to the top of the page? (Already discussed in Chapter 3.)

C. Candle: With the objects provided, attach the candle to the wall so that it can burn properly. (Already discussed in Chapter 3).

D. Antique Coin: A stranger approached a museum curator and offered him an ancient bronze coin. The coin had an authentic appearance and was marked with the date 544 BC. The curator had happily made acquisitions from suspicious sources before, but this time he promptly called the police and had the stranger arrested. Why?

E. Nine-Dot Problem: Connect all nine dots by drawing four straight lines, without lifting your pencil from the paper.

F. Compound Remote Associates (CRA): Generate a single solution word that can be combined with each of the problem words to yield a compound word or familiar phrase.
　　A. *Problem words:* CRAB, PINE, SAUCE
　　B. *Problem words:* BLUE, COTTAGE, MOUSE

AN ANALYTIC PROBLEM

G. The Cards: Three cards from an ordinary deck are lying on a table face down. The following information (for some peculiar reason) is known about those three cards (all the information refers to the same three cards):
　　To the left of a queen there is a jack. To the left of a spade there is a diamond. To the right of a heart there is a king. To the right of a king there is a spade.
　　Can you assign the proper suit to each face card?

Figure 7.2 Insight and analytic problems

INSIGHT PROBLEM SOLUTIONS

A. Lilies: If the lilies double in area each day, then the lake is half covered on the day before it is fully covered, or on day fifty-nine, the next-to-last day.

B. Triangle: Move the three coins from the points of the triangle around the central "rosette":

C. Candle: Use the tack box as a holder or shelf for the candle.

D. Antique Coin: How could the person who made the coin know that Christ would be born 544 years *later*? The coin must have been fake.

E. Nine-Dot: Draw lines outside the square.

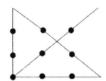

F. Compound Remote Associates (CRA)

    A. Solution: APPLE

    B. Solution: CHEESE

ANALYTIC PROBLEM SOLUTIONS

G. The Cards: You can work out the solution, using logic.

Figure 7.3 Insight problem solutions

Gestalt Theory: Summary

The Gestalt psychologists made a distinction between reproductive and productive thinking and they emphasized the role of insight in problem-solving. In the Gestalt view, analytic thinking, which deals with the present on the basis of the past, is doomed to fail in situations that demand creativity. This review has provided a summary of where things stood at about the middle of the twentieth century (see Bourne, Ekstrand & Dominowski, 1971). However, in the early 1980s, criticisms were raised concerning Gestalt theory (Perkins, 1981; Weisberg & Alba, 1981) that resulted in a surge of interest in insight, which continues today (e.g., Kounios & Beeman, 2015; Ohlsson, 2011, 2018; see also chapters in Vallée-Tourangeau, 2018). I will first examine the criticisms of the Gestalt view and then review the responses to those critiques.

Challenges to Gestalt Theory

Analytic Thinking in Insight

One question raised about insight came from research demonstrating that solution of insight problems could come about through analytic thought processes. This view has been called the "business as usual" or "nothing special" perspective on insight (Seifert et al., 1995, p. 68). It is "business as usual" because the thought processes are those used in analytic thinking – that is, in ordinary thinking. The opposite to the "business as usual" view of insight is the "special process" view, which proposes that insight is the result of a process different than ordinary thinking – a special process.

In an examination of the processes underlying insight, Perkins (1981) presented the Antique Coin problem to people (Figure 7.2D). When a participant solved the problem, he or she was asked to report immediately on the thoughts that had led up to solution. Two of those reports are presented in Table 7.2. One person (Abbott) reported that the solution "just snapped" together in an *Aha!* moment; the other (Binet) worked out the solution through analysis. Perkins analyzed those reports and concluded that the thought processes carried out by Abbott and Binet were very similar and that Abbott's leap of insight was not particularly special.

First, Abbott never reached impasse, meaning that impasse was not necessary for an *Aha!*, which goes against the importance of the insight sequence. Second, both Abbott and Binet focused on, or *recognized*, the date as the crucial piece of information – that is, Abbott's insight built on information available in the problem. There was no restructuring of the problem on Abbott's part. Again, this raised problems for Gestalt theory. Finally, Abbott's "leap" turned out to have required only a couple of steps of reasoning on Binet's part; that is, the insight process did not do much in the way of creative thinking. Abbott simply *realized* the impossibility of the coin maker's knowing that Christ would be born at some later date, while Binet reached that same conclusion through *reasoning*. Perkins (1981) proposed that we could understand *Aha!* experiences as being the result of processes such as *recognizing* or *realizing* that something is true or false – that is, processes involved in analytic thinking (see Chapter 3, Table 3.2). Perkins's analysis provided support for what became known as the business-as-usual view.

Table 7.2 *Perkins's two reports from the Antique Coin problem*
Abbott (Solution Through Insight)

1. Couldn't figure out what was wrong after reading through once.
2. Decided to read problem over again.
3. Asked himself, do archeologists dig up coins? Decided yes.
4. Asked himself, could the problem have something to do with bronze? Decided no.
5. Saw the word "marked." This was suspicious. Marked could mean many different things.
6. Decided to see what followed in the text.
7. Saw 544 BC (Imagined grungy coin in the dirt; had an impression of ancient times.)
8. Immediately realized–"it snapped"–that "BC" was the flaw.

Binet (Solution Through Analysis)

1. Thought perhaps they didn't mark coins with the date then.
2. Thought they didn't date at all – too early for calendar. (Image of backwards man hammering 544 on each little bronze coin.)
3. Focused on 544 BC.
4. Looked at BC.
5. Realized "BC – that means Before Christ."
6. Rationalized that it couldn't be before Christ since Christ hadn't been born yet.
7. Saw no possible way to anticipate when Christ was going to be born.
8. Concluded "Fake!"

Questions about Insight in the Nine-Dot Problem

A second challenge to the Gestalt view came from a study by Weisberg and Alba (1981), that examined performance on the Nine-Dot problem (Figure 7.2E). The Nine-Dot problem is extremely difficult to solve (see, for example, Weisberg & Alba, 1981; Kershaw & Ohlsson, 2004; Chein & Weisberg, 2014). According to the Gestalt analysis (Bourne, Ekstrand & Dominowski, 1971, p. 42; Scheerer, 1963), solution of the problem is interfered with by inappropriate constraints brought to it by the individual. Based on the perceptual structure of the problem – the square shape formed by the dots – and people's experiences in similar situations – solving connect-the-dots puzzles – people constrain their solution attempts, keeping their lines within the square. They are *fixated* on the square shape formed by the dots. That constraint makes the problem unsolvable. If one could remove that focus on the square, solution should be easy.

Based on the Gestalt interpretation of the Nine-Dot problem, Weisberg and Alba (1981) presented it to college students with a critical hint: in order to solve it, they had to draw lines outside the square. Based on the Gestalt analysis, that "outside" hint should make the problem easy to solve. The hint did eliminate the fixation on the shape of the square, since almost everyone given the hint drew lines that went beyond the square's boundaries (see Figure 7.4A). However, the hint was not very effective in producing solutions. Also, those few people who did solve the problem after the "outside" hint needed multiple solution attempts and made only incremental progress before they were able to solve the problem. There was nothing like an *Aha!* moment with its sudden snapping into place of a solution.

In a second experiment, Weisberg and Alba (1981) gave undergraduates training in solving simple connect-the-dots problems, in which they had to draw lines outside the shape defined by the dots (see Figure 7.4B for examples). Training facilitated performance on the Nine-Dot problem, although not nearly all the participants solved it (see also Chein et al., 2010). Weisberg and Alba interpreted their results to mean that, contrary to the Gestalt view, the Nine-Dot problem was difficult because it required knowledge that most people do not possess. Similar results were reported by Lung and Dominowski (1985). Weisberg and Alba also raised questions about whether insight – as defined by the insight sequence – played a critical role when people attempted to solve the Nine-Dot problem.

A number of studies were stimulated by Weisberg and Alba's (1981) analysis of the Nine-Dot problem. MacGregor, Ormerod, and Chronicle (2001) proposed that heuristic methods played a major role in its solution. MacGregor, Ormerod, and Chronicle proposed that people faced with the Nine-Dot problem used a variant of the *hill-climbing* heuristic: they tried to draw lines that covered the maximum number of dots. So, for example, the first line drawn would be one that covered three dots, since that is the maximum that any line could cover. From then on, the individual would choose to draw the line that would cover the maximum number of remaining dots. A second factor that played an important role in people's performance was their ability to predict the outcome of drawing a specific pattern of lines, which MacGregor and colleagues called *lookahead*. A person with a larger lookahead would be able to predict whether a specific pattern of lines would solve the problem. Therefore, some people can monitor better their progress toward solution and can see that no pattern of lines that stays within the square will solve the problem. The theory of problem-solving

A. Responses to "Outside-the-box" hint: Lines outside the box versus solutions.

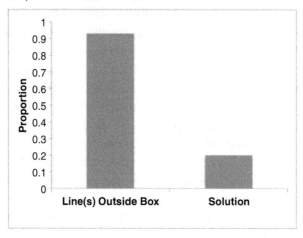

B. "Outside-Training" problems that facilitated solution of Nine-Dot problem.

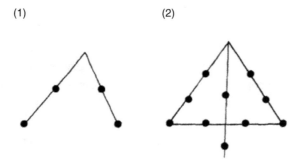

Figure 7.4 Results of Weisberg and Alba (1981) study of effectiveness of hints on solution of Nine-Dot problem
A. Results
B. Training problems

proposed by MacGregor, Ormerod, and Chronicle (2001) is called *progress monitoring* theory.

　　Chein et al. (2010) measured lookahead directly through working memory (WM) tests. High WM scores were taken as evidence for larger capacity for lookahead. Chein and colleagues found that people with larger WM capacity were more likely to solve the Nine-Dot problem in response to the "outside" hint (Weisberg & Alba, 1981; see also Figure 7.4). That result provided support for the proposal of MacGregor, Ormerod, and Chronicle that switching to drawing lines outside the square shape of the dots may depend on the person's ability to predict that no patterns of lines drawn within the square will produce the solution.

Critiques of Gestalt Theory: Summary

The studies of Perkins (1981) and Weisberg and Alba (1981) as well as subsequent research by MacGregor, Ormerod, and Chronicle (2001) and Chein et al. (2010), among others, supported the business-as-usual view: the idea that insight was not a special process in problem-solving. All problem-solving could be understood as the result of the operation of one set of mechanisms, those of analytic thinking (see also Kaplan & Simon, 1990). Supporters of Gestalt theory responded in several ways to that critique. First, researchers proposed elaborations of Gestalt theory – *neo*-Gestalt theory (*new*-Gestalt theory) – specifying the mechanisms underlying insight. Modern versions of Gestalt theory have been called "special process" views on insight (Davidson, 1995, p. 126). Second, research was carried out to demonstrate the importance of insight and related concepts in understanding how people solved problems.

Neo-Gestalt Theory

Ohlsson's Deep Learning

Ohlsson (1992, 2011, 2018) has developed an updated version of the Gestalt view, emphasizing the importance of restructuring and insight in our survival as a species (2011, p. 21). Ohlsson described the world as being in a state of constant, large-scale, and unpredictable change. Analytic thinking is of no help in dealing with such a world, because "experience is guaranteed to be misleading most of the time" (Ohlsson, 2011, p. 21). Ohlsson's view can be looked upon as the direct opposite of the "kind world" view, introduced in Chapter 5 (Gentner & Maravilla, 2018; see also Chapter 6), that proposed that the environment is typically receptive to the application of knowledge.

Ohlsson proposed that the mechanisms of *deep learning* have evolved to deal with an environment that resists our knowledge. Deep learning allows us to

> abandon, override, reject, retract or suppress knowledge that we had previously accepted as valid in order to track a *constantly shifting and fundamentally unpredictable environment* and thereby indirectly create mental space for alternative or even contradictory concepts, beliefs, ideas and strategies. (p. 21, emphasis added)

The mechanism of deep learning of interest here is problem-solving through insight. Ohlsson proposed that insights arise through the already-familiar *insight sequence*:

problem ⇒ impasse ⇒ restructuring ⇒ insight.

Ohlsson's theory is called *Representational Change Theory* (RCT), since the critical component in our adaptation is restructuring the situation – that is, changing our representation of the external environment.

Heuristics of Restructuring

In the early version of RCT, Ohlsson (1992) proposed a set of three heuristics called, collectively, "switch when stuck" heuristics. You are trying to *switch* the problem representation when you are *stuck* (see also Kaplan & Simon, 1990). Those restructuring heuristics were the following:

(1) *Elaboration.* The individual examines the situation to determine if there is overlooked information or object(s) that could be used in a new type of solution. In trying to solve the Candle problem (see Figure 7.2C), a new solution method might be stimulated by the realization that the previously ignored tack box could serve in a solution.

(2) *Re-encoding.* The individual analyses the situation in order to determine if there is a new way of thinking about any object. Again, focusing on the Candle problem, the tack box, which initially might have been looked upon as a container, could be seen as being flat and sturdy and so could serve as a shelf for the candle.

(3) *Constraint relaxation.* The individual attempts to change the representation of the goal. In the Candle problem, instead of trying to attach the candle to the wall, using the tacks or melted wax as glue, the person might change the goal into trying to build a shelf or holder for the candle. That change might lead to the use of the tack box.

Redistribution Theory

In a more recent version of RCT, Ohlsson (2011, chs. 4, 11; 2018) proposed that representational change, or restructuring, came about as the result of *redistribution of activation* in semantic memory. Ohlsson's analysis of the mechanisms of representational change follows closely the outline presented in Table 7.1B. Presentation of a problem results in activation of one of several possible representations in memory, comparable to the multiple representations of the reversible cube. Ohlsson assumed that any problem will activate representations of differing strengths based on experiences in similar situations. The strongest of those representations will dominate and will control the behaviors that are produced.

However, in situations that demand creative thinking, that initial representation based on the past will result in failed solutions (see the quotations from Ohlsson a few paragraphs earlier). Each time a solution arising out of some representation results in failure, that produces negative feedback for the representation. As outlined in Table 7.1B5, that representation is weakened each time it is unsuccessful. If those failures continue, in what amounts to an impasse, the dominant representation will become weak enough that one of the other possible representations will arise (Table 7.1B6). The person will then look at the problem in a different way, in a restructuring of the situation which may stimulate a new class of solutions. As Ohlsson (2011, ch. 4) noted, that analysis of restructuring in problem-solving is similar to the Gestalt psychologists' analysis of the spontaneous reversal of the reversible cube (see Table 7.1A). Restructuring comes about as the result of processes not under the conscious control of the person.

There is, however, a question that can be raised about the *redistribution of activation* explanation of restructuring and insight (Weisberg, 2018b). As can be seen in Table 7.1A, the two representations of the reversible cube exist in the visual system; nothing new is *created* in response to the presentation of the cube. Similarly, examining Table 7.1B, we see that the two – or more – structures available to analyze a problem exist in the system when the problem is presented. That means, perhaps surprisingly, that Ohlsson's redistribution view does not help us to understand how a person can produce a *novel* restructuring of a problem. All the possible structures that can be applied to a problem are available in memory and are simply activated by the problem rather than constructed by the individual as he or she tries to deal with the problem. Given that seeming difficulty for the redistribution theory, it seems more reasonable to stay with the earlier version of RCT, and its heuristics, which seem to fit better what happens as people solve problems with insight (Fleck & Weisberg, 2013).

In the most recent version of his view, Ohlsson (2018) has proposed that representational change can come about without failure and impasse. If information from the environment provides a mismatch with our expectations, which are based on previous input from the environment, then we may be forced to change our analysis of the situation. We change our analysis of the meaning of the environment – that is, we carry out a new semantic analysis of the situation. That change can result in a new approach to solving a problem. Since experience cannot be helpful at such a point, Ohlsson (2018, pp. 22–23) proposed that semantic analysis of the problem can result in a new structure.

Other Neo-Gestalt Views

A number of other researchers have developed neo-Gestalt views that share core components with classic Gestalt theory as well as with Ohlsson's representational change theory. Perkins (2000) proposed the need for *breakthrough thinking* in problem-solving. We are already familiar with Perkins's analysis of Leonardo's invention of the aerial screw as an example of a leap of insight (see Chapter 4). Perkins proposed that many problems do not yield to analytic thinking, which is based on *reason*; those stubborn problems are *unreasonable*. To deal with unreasonable situations, one must break away from analytic – "reasonable" – thinking and search in other ways for new ideas. Perkins's view is very similar to Ohlsson's (2011) idea of the constantly changing world that makes analytic thinking useless most of the time.

Wiley and her colleagues (e.g., Ash, Cushen & Wiley, 2009; Danek, Williams & Wiley, 2018; Wiley & Jarosz, 2012) have presented a similar view, proposing a sharp distinction between analysis and insight – that is, restructuring in response to impasse. The critical shortcoming of analytic thinking is that there are problem situations in which it is not useful.

> In these cases, prior experience elicits a problem representation that inappropriately constrains the search space or inappropriately combines problem elements. (Ash, Cushen & Wiley, 2009, p. 7)

In order to make progress, the thinker must reject analytic thinking and restructure the situation, through processes different than those involved in analytic thinking.

> [R]estructuring is a mechanism that cannot be accommodated by classic heuristic search accounts of problem solving, and requires an additional theoretical framework. (Ash, Cushen & Wiley, 2009, p. 8)

Thus, theories of problem-solving must incorporate a mechanism – spontaneous restructuring – that goes beyond analytic thinking. That spontaneous restructuring is often assumed to come about through processes occurring outside of consciousness (Danek & Salvi, 2018) (see Table 7.1B).

A similar viewpoint has been proposed by Kounios and Beeman and their colleagues (e.g., 2015), who have also emphasized the close relationship between creative thinking, restructuring, and insight. We are already familiar with their analysis of Wag Dodge's invention of the escape fire. Kounios and Beeman defined creative thinking as

> [T]he ability to reinterpret something by breaking it down into its elements and recombining those elements in a surprising way to achieve some goal. . . . [T]he less obvious the recombination, the more creative it is. . . . When this kind of creative recombination takes place in an instant, it's an insight. (pp. 9–10)

We see here also an emphasis on restructuring ("reinterpreting something"), as well as on the need to reject the past ("recombining those elements in a surprising way"). The break from the past is also clear in Kounios and Beeman's equating "more creative" combinations with those that are "less obvious" (see also Mednick (1962)).

Insight and Creativity

In the neo-Gestalt views, insight and creativity are closely linked. Both Ohlsson (2011) and Perkins (2000) use insight as the criterion for *defining* creative thinking. If a creative advance does not come about through insight – through restructuring of a problem – it is not creative. Similarly, Wiley and Jarosz (2012) distinguished between analytical problems (exemplified by verbally based mathematics problems) and "creative" problems, such as the insight problems in Figure 7.2. Wiley and Jarosz make no mention of the possibility that solutions to insight ("creative") problems could come about through analytic thinking. Other researchers have recently proposed that "insight" in problem-solving should be defined only by the occurrence of an *Aha!* reaction (Bowden & Grunewald, 2018; Danek & Salvi, 2018).

Laboratory Research in Support of Insight

Modern researchers supporting the insight view have tried to demonstrate that insight and analysis are different ways of solving problems.

Sudden Solution of Insight Problems

In a classic series of studies, Metcalfe (1986; Metcalfe & Weibe, 1987) attempted to demonstrate the suddenness of insight in the laboratory. She asked individuals to solve insight or analytic problems while providing ratings of how "warm" they felt they were – that is, how close they were to solution. For analytic problems, warmth increased gradually, presumably because people worked in step-wise fashion toward solution. For insight problems, in contrast, warmth ratings stayed low ("I'm very cold") until just before the solution, when they jumped to the maximum, as the notions of spontaneous restructuring and sudden insight would predict. More recently, researchers have investigated the suddenness of insight by having people try to analyze how magicians carry out their tricks (Danek, 2018; Hedne, Norman & Metcalfe, 2016). Those studies supported the idea that sudden insight into magic tricks came about through processes different from those underlying incremental understanding. Research by Gilhooly and Murphy (2005) also provided support for the insight–analysis distinction.

The Question of Executive Functioning in Insight

A related issue concerns the role of executive functioning in solving problems through insight versus analysis. Executive functioning serves in the direction and control of cognitive processes, including attention (see Chapters 1 and 3; De Caro, 2018; Engle, 2018; Gilhooly & Fioratou, 2009). Analytic thinking should depend on the component of executive functioning that controls planning (Chuderski & Jastrzębski, 2018). Insight, in contrast, would seem to be less reliant on planning and, therefore, less reliant on executive functioning, since it comes about through processes that occur outside of conscious control (see Table 7.1B).

Wiley and Jarosz (2012, p. 214) proposed that creative thinking may actually be *impaired* by strong executive functioning, especially attentional control (see also De Caro, 2018). Participants in a study by Jarosz, Colflesh, and Wiley (2012) were made intoxicated through ingestion of alcohol. Intoxication presumably interfered with cognitive control of attention. Performance of those individuals on CRA problems (Figure 7.4F) *improved* compared to a sober group. The conclusion was that intoxication, by making it harder to control attention, facilitated finding the solutions to those insight problems. (See also Benedek et al., 2014; Reverberi et al., 2005.) That analysis brings to mind the emphasis by the Romantics on the unfettered imagination of the genius as being crucial for true creativity (Becker, 1978; see Chapter 2).

Neo-Gestalt Views on Insight: Summary

Neo-Gestalt theory is built on the assumption that analytic thinking results in an individual putting inappropriate constraints on the thinking process, resulting in *fixation*. The only way to think creatively is to move away from analytic thinking and its reliance on one's knowledge (see Table 7.1B; see also Kershaw, Flynn & Gordon, 2013; Knöblich et al., 1999; Knöblich, Ohlsson & Raney, 2001; and Öllinger, Jones & Knöblich, 2014). Solutions to problems will be relatively easy if the constraints brought about by reliance on analytic thought can be eliminated (Scheerer, 1963). Here is a summary of that view:

> We hypothesize that insight problems are difficult because the key behavior needed for solution tends to be suppressed by multiple, accidentally converging factors related to perceptual factors . . ., prior knowledge and experience, and processing demands (e.g., amount of lookahead). (Kershaw and Ohlsson, 2004, p. 12)

Thus, the solution to an insight problem is waiting to "come out," but it is interfered with – "suppressed" – by "accidental" factors, including knowledge and experience, that get in the way. However, questions have been raised in response to the neo-Gestalt view and its conclusion that analytic thinking is irrelevant to creativity. I now turn to evidence that demonstrates that analytic thinking plays a significant role in creative thinking.

Analytic Thinking in Solving "Insight" Problems

The neo-Gestalt view proposes that insight comes about through the insight sequence (problem ⇒ impasse ⇒ restructuring ⇒ insight; see Figure 7.2 and Table 7.1). However, there is evidence that analytic thinking can bring about solutions to "insight" problems, including solutions based on restructuring, which raises questions about whether insight and analysis are different processes. Fleck and Weisberg (2004, 2013) examined people's performance on several insight problems, asking participants to think aloud while working (see Figure 7.2A–E). That procedure allowed Fleck and Weisberg to examine the processes involved in problem solution.

Fewer than 10 percent of the total solutions they obtained were the result of the full insight sequence. Many people experienced impasse, and many restructured the problems, but in most cases the impasse ⇒ restructuring link was not what led to a solution (see also Weisberg & Suls, 1973). Similar results were reported by Cranford and Moss (2012), who obtained verbal protocols while people solved CRA problems (see Figure 7.4F). Reports of *Aha!* experiences have been taken as evidence for the occurrence of the insight sequence during solution of CRA problems (e.g., Kounios & Beeman, 2015). Contrary to that conclusion, Cranford and Moss found that participants sometimes reported an *Aha!* experience when the solution came quickly, even though there was no evidence of impasse or restructuring.

The finding that the insight sequence does not play a role in a large majority of solutions to insight problems has two important implications. First, it raises questions about the relevance of the "insight sequence" in solving "insight problems." Second, it indicates that other solution mechanisms are involved. I will examine several of those mechanisms, which already are familiar to us, to further demonstrate the relevance of analytic thinking in "insight."

Analytic Thinking as a Dynamic Process: Restructuring from Failure

As discussed earlier, most insight problems are purposely designed so that attempting to transfer a solution from one's experience will be unsuccessful, resulting in impasse (see Table 7.1). However, there were several problems studied by Fleck and Weisberg where transfer was possible. One example is the Candle problem (Figure 7.2C; Fleck & Weisberg, 2004). This problem was discussed in Chapter 3 while examining the mechanisms underlying green creativity. Many of Fleck and Weisberg's participants tried to solve this problem – and some succeeded – by attaching the candle to the wall, using the tacks or using melted wax from the candle as "glue" (see Figure 3.8). Those sorts of solutions came about because, as we know, people can apply their knowledge to a new situation based on a *partial match* between it and the past (Weisberg & Suls, 1973). Often, however, those solutions failed. In some of those failures, restructuring occurred in response to new information that arose from the failure. A participant might try to tack the candle to the wall, only to find that it was too large and heavy. That information might lead to the possibility of making a shelf to hold the candle up, which would result in the box solution (see Figure 3.9). Those participants never reached impasse: they kept working, changing their approach in response to new information arising from the evolving situation.

Heuristic Methods

Most of the solutions in Fleck and Weisberg's (2004, 2013) study, including solutions arising from restructuring, were based on heuristic methods of several sorts. That finding is important because, as discussed earlier, it has been proposed by neo-Gestalt theorists that the occurrence of restructuring in problem-solving *cannot* come about through heuristic methods (Ash, Cushen & Wiley, 2009, p. 8; Ohlsson, 2018). Consider the Lilies problem – several individuals not familiar with geometric progressions nonetheless solved it by reasoning out the solution. The Lilies double in area each day; it therefore *follows logically* – if you think about it – that the day the lake is half covered is the day before the lake is fully covered – that is, day 59. This is evidence for restructuring of a problem based on logical reasoning – a heuristic method.

As we saw in Chapter 3, people sometimes use a *hill-climbing* heuristic to transform the problem situation so that it becomes more similar to the goal (they are "climbing the hill" toward the goal). That method was seen in the Triangle of Coins problem (Figure 7.2B), discussed in detail in Chapter 3 (see Figure 3.6). One can move the single coin from the bottom to the top, which changes the problem state into one more similar to the goal. The new second row contains four coins. It must be changed to a row containing two, which can be done by removing the end coins. The new third row contains three coins, so it can stay as is. The new fourth row needs to have four coins; the two removed from the second row fit there, solving the problem.

Conclusions and Implications

The Fleck and Weisberg (2004, 2013) results indicated that analytic methods can result in solution of insight problems. That conclusion has implications for the interpretation of the studies discussed earlier presented in support of the insight view. Examples are Metcalfe's (1986; Metcalfe & Weibe, 1987) studies of sudden solutions to insight problems; studies demonstrating sudden understanding of magic tricks (Danek, 2018; Hedne, Norman & Metcalfe, 2016); and studies demonstrating a lack of executive functioning in insight (e.g., Wiley & Jarosz, 2012). In all of those studies, the researchers simply assumed that, since an insight problem had been solved, the insight sequence must have occurred. However, as we have just seen, such an assumption is subject to question, because insight problems are often solved through analysis, much more often than through the insight sequence. Thus, the support for the insight view from laboratory studies may be weaker than it seems. We do not know, for example, how many of the participants in Metcalfe's studies were reporting *Aha!*

reactions based on solutions arising from analytic methods. Therefore, we should look more closely at the possible role of analytic thinking in "insight."

Analysis in Insight: Elaborated Model of Analytic Problem-Solving

In order to examine in more detail the role of analytic thinking in "insight," it will be helpful to look again at the problem-solving model discussed in Chapter 3, which is presented in Figure 7.5, with a third stage added to deal with insight. To review, Stage 1 involves the filtering of the problem through memory, which may result in an attempted solution through transfer of an old method (Stages 1A and 1B). If transfer fails, but new information arises out of that failure (Stage 1D), then the person searches memory again, with the possibility that a new method will come to mind (recycling through Stage 1A). Restructuring of the problem may occur as the result of this recycling – the new information may bring to mind a new way of analyzing the problem – but there is no impasse. This restructuring can be called "top-down" or "conceptually driven" restructuring: it uses the person's knowledge to correct the deficiencies in the failed solution. If the Stage 1 approach fails and no additional new information becomes available, then the person goes on to Stage 2 and attempts to apply heuristic methods to the problem. If a heuristic method fails at Stage 2B, but new information arises out of that failure (Stage 2D), there is another search of memory (Stage 2E). That search can result in a new solution method being retrieved, which can produce restructuring and a new solution type (Stage 2F). This would be another example of "top-down" restructuring, based on new information, arising from a failed solution attempt.

If there is no solution, and no new information from Stage 2, then the person is at an impasse and goes on to Stage 3, which is where the restructuring that is the focus of the neo-Gestalt theorists may come about. The expanded problem-solving model in Figure 7.5 incorporates Ohlsson's (1992) three restructuring heuristics, discussed earlier: *elaboration*, *re-encoding*, and *constraint relaxation* (see also Kaplan & Simon, 1990). Fleck and Weisberg (2013) reported that several of their participants went through something like those heuristics upon reaching impasse, so there is some empirical support for them. Those restructuring heuristics can produce what we can call "bottom-up" restructuring: it comes about though an examination of the objects in the problem without any

STAGE 1 – MATCHING A PROBLEM WITH KNOWLEDGE (Green Creativity)

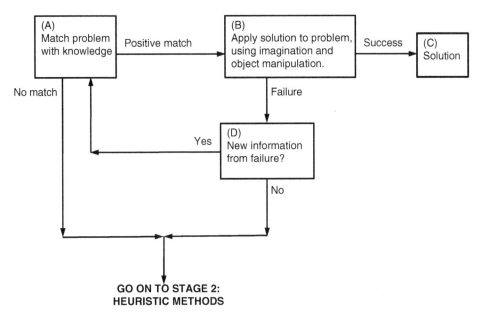

STAGE 2 – APPLYING HEURISTICS TO A PROBLEM

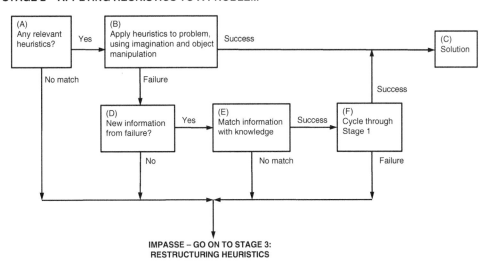

Figure 7.5 Model of problem-solving based on analytic thinking, elaborated to deal with "insight"

STAGE 3 – RESTRUCTURING HEURISTICS IN RESPONSE TO IMPASSE (BOTTOM-UP RESTRUCTURING)

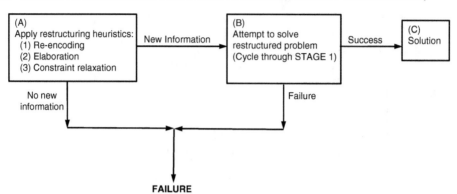

Figure 7.5 (Cont.)

overarching plan as to how the problem might be restructured, as would be expected if a person is at impasse.

Analytic Thinking as the Basis for Insight: Implications

The model outlined in Figure 7.5 can deal with the results concerning insight that we have discussed. Contrary to claims of neo-Gestalt researchers (Kounios & Beeman, 2015; Ohlsson, 2011, 2018; Wiley & Jarosz, 2012), analytic thinking is capable of producing solutions to laboratory insight problems, including solutions based on restructuring. It seems that Ash and colleagues (2009, p. 8) were mistaken when they proposed that "restructuring is a mechanism that cannot be accommodated by classic heuristic search accounts of problem solving, and requires an additional theoretical framework." The conclusion that analytic thinking can explain insight leaves us with the question of the possible role of analytic thinking in the real-world creative advances presented earlier in support of the insight view: Wilkins's invention of radar; Edison's carbon-filament light bulb; and Wag Dodge's escape fire. I will now demonstrate that analytic thinking played an important role in each of those advances (see also Weisberg, 2015, 2018a, 2018b).

Analytic Thinking in Creative Advances

From the analytic-thinking perspective, there should *always* be links between concepts brought together in any creative advance. In other words, the concepts were *not* remotely associated for the person proposing the new idea. For the advances presented earlier, as well as many others (Weisberg, 2006, chs. 1 & 5; 2015, 2018a, 2018b), it is possible to demonstrate such links.

Wilkins's Invention of Radar

Ohlsson (2011, p. 53) proposed that radar came about as the result of "a momentous act of inspiration" on the part of Wilkins, in which he realized that one could use radio waves to determine the locations of airplanes. How might Wilkins have brought those seemingly unrelated ideas together? That act of inspiration might have been firmly built on Wilkins's knowledge (Weisberg, 2018b). Wilkins was aware of a recent report by engineers in the British postal service discussing problems raised by aircraft interfering with transmission of radio waves. The idea that planes interfere with radio waves underlies radar and might have provided the basis for Wilkins's "momentous act of inspiration" (see Table 7.3).

Edison's Carbon Filament

Questions can also be raised about Ohlsson's (2011, p. 134) discussion of Edison's "insight" concerning the carbon burner for his light bulb. Again, the question of interest is where Edison got the idea of working with carbon. Was there, as Ohlsson proposed, no connection between carbon and a possible filament for the light bulb? There was such a connection. Edison was not the first to work on the light bulb: there had been

Table 7.3 *Outline of analytic processes in Wilkins's invention of radar*

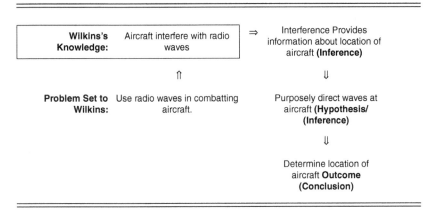

approximately a dozen previous unsuccessful attempts, and most had used either carbon or platinum, or both, as possible burners (Friedel, Israel & Finn, 1986). Edison concentrated on platinum and carbon as possible burners because of the precedents supporting their use, in an example of green creativity. Also, Ohlsson (2011, p. 134) described Edison's switching from platinum to carbon as if it had been the result of a restructuring of the situation and a move in a totally different direction. However, when Edison had *started* his research on the light bulb, over a year earlier, carbon was one of several materials that he tried to use for a burner. In order for carbon to be useful as a burner, it had to be in a vacuum, which meant that all the air had to be removed from the light bulb. At that time, the available vacuum pumps could not produce the vacuum that carbon required, so the light failed. Edison then turned to the other burner option, platinum, again based on his knowledge of earlier research. Thus, Edison's later switch to carbon was a switch *back* to carbon, an option with which he was already familiar.

In addition, that switch was not the result of a spontaneous restructuring triggered by impasse and independent of any new information: there was a reason for it. Edison's staff, based on a suggestion in a published article, had meanwhile developed a very efficient vacuum pump (Freidel et al., 1986), that was able to produce the vacuum needed for carbon to be used as the burner. Thus, Edison's return to carbon was motivated by the fact that the critical problem with carbon had been solved. Edison's advance, too, was based on analytic thinking.

Wag Dodge's Escape Fire

Wag Dodge's invention of the escape fire can be analyzed in a similar way. Kounios and Beeman (2015, p. 23) described Dodge's insight as being "utterly nonobvious: Fire wasn't just the problem – it was also the *solution*. He fought fire with fire" (emphasis in original). They also emphasized the novelty of "using fire as a tool for creating a protective buffer zone" (Kounios & Beeman, 2015, p. 89). However, again, we can trace the origins of Dodge's innovation; for Dodge, the escape fire was *not* "utterly nonobvious." First, from his training as a smokejumper, *Dodge knew how to fight fire with fire and about using fire to create a protective buffer zone* (Weisberg, 2015). Smokejumpers' training included building a *backfire* – a fire that moves toward the main fire, consuming the fuel that the main fire needs. A backfire *fights fire with fire*, and creates a buffer zone. Smokejumpers were also taught that they might be able to turn into the fire to find burnt-out safe spots – that is, an existing buffer zone. Dodge's invention can be seen as a combination of those methods. Instead of finding burnt-out space by walking into the advancing fire or by setting a backfire (producing burnt-out space between him and the fire), he produced it by setting his escape fire. The novelty in Dodge's action was the *direction* in which the fire was set, which might have been brought about by his looking up the gulch and seeing dry grass in front of him. Thus, contrary to Kounios and Beeman's (2015) conclusion, we can explain Dodge's insight on the basis of analytic thinking (see Table 7.4).

Analytic Thinking and Insight: Summary

Several creative advances presented in support of the insight view – radar, Edison's carbon burner, and Dodge's escape fire – can be explained as being the result of analytic thinking. In each of those cases, there were links

Table 7.4 *An outline of possible conceptual links leading to Wag Dodge's invention of the escape fire through analytic thinking*

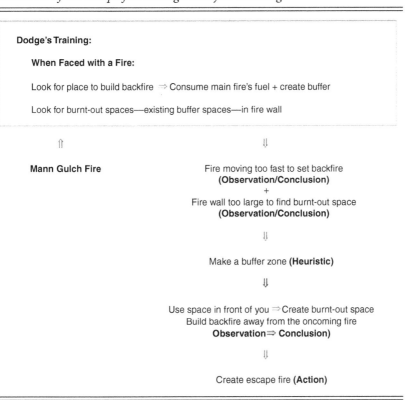

Dodge's Training:

When Faced with a Fire:

Look for place to build backfire ⇒ Consume main fire's fuel + create buffer

Look for burnt-out spaces—existing buffer spaces—in fire wall

⇑   ⇓

Mann Gulch Fire   Fire moving too fast to set backfire
                             (Observation/Conclusion)
                                          +
                             Fire wall too large to find burnt-out space
                             (Observation/Conclusion)

                                          ⇓

                             Make a buffer zone **(Heuristic)**

                                          ⇓

                             Use space in front of you ⇒ Create burnt-out space
                             Build backfire away from the oncoming fire
                             Observation ⇒ Conclusion)

                                          ⇓

                             Create escape fire **(Action)**

between the ideas that were brought together. A similar analysis was made in Chapter 4 regarding Leonardo's aerial screw. We can add to those results Fleck and Weisberg's (2004, 2013) findings showing the critical role of analytic thinking in the solution of insight problems. Many of the phenomena brought forth to support the neo-Gestalt view are, in fact, understandable as examples of analytic thinking. From this analysis, one can suggest that researchers' emphasis on insight as *the* critical component of creativity should change. Insight, in the sense of the insight sequence, is only one of several processes – and perhaps not a very frequent one – through which creative advances – even creative advances of great significance – take place.

Insight: Some Remaining Questions

How Important Is Insight in Creative Thinking?

Researchers have for 100 years studied insight based on the assumption that it is central in our creative dealings with the world. In Ohlsson's (2011, chs. 1, 3) view, for example, insight is nothing less than critical to our survival as a species. Beaty, Nusbaum, and Silvia (2014) recently examined the relationship between insight and creativity. They compared people's performance on laboratory insight problems with their real-world creative achievements. If insight is a skill that is of general importance in creative thinking, then there should be a positive relationship between those two measures. In two studies with large samples of undergraduates as participants there was no significant relationship between solving insight problems and creative achievement. Although one might raise questions about whether undergraduates are the best population in which to study creative achievement – undergraduates are perhaps too young to have accomplished very much – the negative results still raise questions about the contribution of insight to creativity.

On Executive Functioning in Insight: A Second Look

As we saw earlier, Wiley and Jarosz (2012) and their colleagues have proposed that a high level of executive functioning has negative effects on insight (see also DeCaro, 2018; Gilhooly & Webb, 2018). That view can be seen as a throwback to the "unfettered imagination" of the Romantics. In contrast, the analytic view (see Figure 7.5) would lead to the expectation that executive functioning should be important in insight. A study by

Chuderski and Jastrzębski (2018) provided strong support for the analytic view. A large number of participants were given a set of insight problems to solve, as well as tasks measuring logical reasoning and aspects of working memory, which were used as measures of executive functioning. Insight performance was closely related to the measures of executive functioning. That is, people who scored higher on executive functioning also produced more solutions overall for the insight problems, as well as more solutions accompanied by *Aha!* reactions, which supports the analytic view. A study by Cinan, Özen, and Hampshire (2013) presented evidence that planning processes are important in the solution of both analytic and insight problems, which supports Chuderski and Jastrzębski's conclusion.

Chuderski and Jastrzębski (2018) also raised methodological questions about studies that have found that executive functioning is not important in insight. As one example, several studies have concluded that there was no relationship between working memory and insight. However, that conclusion depends on acceptance of the null hypothesis, which, in turn, depends on the number of participants tested in the study. In the studies reporting no relationship between working memory and insight, the numbers of participants tested were not very large, which means that the studies might not have been sensitive enough to find a difference. Therefore, those negative conclusions can be brought into question. The studies conducted by Chuderski and Jastrzębski included large numbers of participants. In all, Chuderski and Jastrzębski concluded that their research provided strong support for the analytic view.

Executive Functioning in Insight: It Depends

Research reviewed in this chapter, concerning the possible role of executive functioning in insight, seems to produce conflicting sets of results. Some studies have shown that executive functioning has a positive relationship with problem-solving through insight (e.g., Chuderski & Jastrzębski, 2018). Other research supports the opposite view, that executive functioning is negatively related to insight or not related at all (Wiley & Jarosz, 2012). So, what sort of role does executive functioning play in problem-solving through insight? Perhaps the answer is "all of the above." DeCaro and her colleagues (e.g., DeCaro, 2018) have proposed that the role of executive functioning in problem-solving depends on various aspects of the structure of the problem being worked on. If a problem is complex, so that it is difficult for the individual to understand the problem instructions and, therefore, to create the problem representation, then high levels of executive functioning should be helpful. However, if a problem is not complex, then all individuals – high or low in executive functioning – should be able to set up the initial representation. DeCaro and others have assumed that, once an impasse has been reached while trying to solve a problem, restructuring and insight come about through processes that are independent of executive functioning. The model of problem-solving in Figure 7.5 leads one to expect that executive functioning would be important in insight, since the heuristic processes in stage 3 of the model would seem to require executive processes, first to develop heuristic methods for a given problem and then to carry them out. In sum, it seems that there are still some issues to be resolved concerning the role of executive functioning in insight.

On "Inappropriate" or "Unwarranted" Representations

A further point arising from the present analysis centers on the terms *"inappropriate"* and *"unwarranted"* as descriptions of the interpretations that people bring to insight problems (Ash, Cushen & Wiley, 2009; Wiley & Jarosz, 2012). Calling some behavior "inappropriate" indicates that someone has done something that they should not have done, such as making jokes at a funeral; the person should have known better. But could a person who constructed an "inappropriate" representation for an insight problem have known better? Consider an individual who approaches the Lilies problem (Figure 7.4A) as a simple arithmetic problem and proposes 60 days ÷ 2 = 30 days as the answer. From the perspective of that individual, that answer was totally appropriate. If the person was ignorant about geometric progressions, then interpreting the problem as involving arithmetic is completely reasonable. Therefore, it would be better if we used the term *incorrect* to describe a representation that does not lead to solution of a problem.

The *Aha!* Experience as the Defining Characteristic of Insight

The Gestalt psychologists built their theorizing on the concept of *restructuring* of the problem representation (e.g., Scheerer, 1963; Wertheimer, 1982). The *Aha!* reaction, while of interest, was not a crucial component of insight – what was crucial was that the person restructured the situation so that a new understanding came about, which could open up new ways of thinking about the problem. We have seen restructuring emphasized in several neo-Gestalt theories (e.g., Ash, Cushen & Wiley, 2009; Ohlsson, 2011, ch. 11; see also DeCaro, 2018). Recently, however, there has been a movement away from relying on restructuring as the defining aspect of insight and toward an emphasis on the *Aha!* experience itself (Bowden & Grunewald, 2018; Danek, 2018; Danek & Salvi, 2018). This new slant has arisen in response to findings such as those reported by Fleck and Weisberg (2013) indicating that "insight" problems can be solved by analytic methods without the *Aha!* experience. That result can be taken to indicate that some solutions to insight problems are irrelevant to the study of insight. Bowden and Grunewald, for example, have proposed that, if we want to study insight, we need to concentrate on situations in which an *Aha!* occurs. Bowden and Grunewald, and Danek, proposed measures that could be used to assess people's experiences while solving problems, which would allow us to determine if solution had been accompanied by a true *Aha!* experience.

This proposal is a significant change in the way insight is defined, and it might not be an improvement. The Gestalt psychologists' original emphasis on restructuring as the basis for insight, whether one agrees with it or not, made psychologists deal with an important question: What brings about what seem to be radically new approaches to solving a problem? I have emphasized that understanding restructuring does not require the postulation of mechanisms beyond those of analytic thinking. However, that does not mean that understanding restructuring is not important. In addition, using the *Aha!* experience in defining insight might lead to problems for researchers, because one can have what seems to be an *Aha!* experience in situations having nothing to do with creative thinking. One example of such a situation is when one is trying to recall a forgotten piece of information, say a person's name. One tries to recall, with no success, and then puts the matter aside. At a later point, the desired information unexpectedly comes to mind, and one may experience an *Aha!* moment. Researchers then will not be able to separate two very different types of events – solving a problem with insight and recalling a forgotten name – because both involve the *Aha!* experience. Therefore, to study insight in problem-solving we may need more than the occurrence of the subjective insight experience. More research will be needed to determine if the usefulness of the proposal to define insight by the occurrence of an *Aha!* experience.

Insight versus Analysis: Different Philosophies Concerning Creativity

Neo-Gestalt theory takes a two-pronged perspective on creativity. On the one hand, it is assumed that we are capable of productive thinking, of making leaps into the unknown. On the other hand, we often fail to think productively, because there are many factors that conspire against us. Those factors include the "inappropriate" constraints that people place on themselves (Ash, Cushen & Wiley, 2009); the large-scale changes in the world that make it resistant to transfer of knowledge (Ohlsson, 2011); the fact that the world is "unreasonable" (Perkins, 2000); and other factors that come together to interfere with productive thinking (Kershaw & Ohlsson, 2004).

In contrast, the analytic viewpoint is more positive, since it assumes that the world is often receptive to the transfer of knowledge. The present is similar-enough to the past that using the past to deal with the present is usually an effective strategy. Indeed, if that were not the case, it would be hard to understand why humans and animals developed the capacity to remember the past. This, once again, is the "kind world" hypothesis (Gentner & Maravilla, 2018). Using the past as the first step in dealing with the present, combined with the active nature of analytic thinking (see Figure 7.5), can be the basis of creative advances, including those at the highest level.

Based on the discussion in this chapter, it seems that we can account for "leaps of insight" through the mechanisms of analytic thinking. In the next chapter we will examine the idea that unconscious processes underlie creative thinking, which is another viewpoint that assumes that creative thinking goes beyond analytic thinking. We have already seen in this chapter that nonconscious processes have been brought forth to explain the occurrence of restructuring and insight in problem-solving (see Table 7.1B). Therefore, the discussion in Chapter 8 can be looked upon as an extension of that in Chapter 7.

| The Question of Unconscious Processes
in Creative Thinking

Scrambled Eggs

One morning in 1965 Beatle Paul McCartney awoke with a tune in his head. He liked it, so he quickly went to the piano and worked it out before he forgot it. Concerned that he might have plagiarized from another song, he asked everyone he talked to if they recognized the tune. Everyone said no. After about a month, he grew confident that the melody was his and he began to work on lyrics. There was little progress, so, as a placeholder, McCartney and John Lennon, his songwriting partner, used "Scrambled Eggs" as a title and as the basis for some "lyrics": "Scrambled eggs/Oh my baby how I love your legs/Not as much as I love scrambled eggs" (Coleman, 1995; Miles, 1997). After the melody had been around for a while and the rest of the Beatles were getting annoyed with the time McCartney was spending on it, he wrote lyrics and titled the song "Yesterday." That song became one of the most beloved in popular music and a high point of McCartney's songwriting career. According to McCartney's report, it arose out of the unconscious, in a dream. Many others have reported similar experiences.

Poincaré's Illuminations

Henri Poincaré (1854–1912), a world-renowned mathematician and scientist, was interested in the creative process and he reported how several of his important mathematical discoveries came about (Poincaré, 1913). Although we nonmathematicians will not be able to follow the details of Poincaré's discussion, that is not critically important. It has been assumed, by Poincaré and by others (e.g., Campbell, 1960; Csikszentmihalyi & Sawyer, 1995; Gilhooly, 2016; Koestler, 1964; Kounios & Beeman, 2015; Miller, 1996; Ritter & Dijksterhuis, 2014; Simonton, 1995), that similar processes are at work in all creative thinking. Much modern theorizing in psychology concerning creative thinking is built directly on Poincaré's reports.

The first segment of Poincaré's work involved an attempt to prove that a certain sort of mathematical function could not exist (Miller, 1996). His routine was to work on mathematics from 10 a.m. to 12 p.m. and from 7 p.m. to 9 p.m. At first, he made no progress. One night he drank black coffee and could not sleep. He then had an extraordinary experience.

> Ideas rose in crowds; I felt them collide until pairs interlocked, so to speak, making a stable combination. By the next morning I had established the existence of a class of fuchsian functions. . . . I had only to write out the results, which took but a few hours. (Poincaré, 1913, p. 387)

During that sleepless night, Poincaré established that one example of those presumed-impossible functions did exist. He called them *fuchsian* functions in honor of Lazarus Fuchs, a mathematician whose work had influenced his own research (Miller, 1996). Although Poincaré was conscious when those ideas arose, he felt that he played no role directing the thought process. He therefore concluded that he was observing the workings of his own unconscious, which, as he reported, involved ideas being combined, essentially at random, until "stable" combinations were found – that is, new ideas that "hung together."

After discovering fuchsian functions, Poincaré went to Coutances, a city not far from his home at Caen, to attend a geological conference (Miller, 1996). While away, he made another discovery, which was totally unexpected. Poincaré's report about that discovery has become one of the most important in the literature on creative thinking.

> The incidents of travel made me forget my mathematical work. Having reached Coutances, we entered an omnibus to go some place or other. At the moment when I put my foot on the step, . . . [the] idea came to me [that the fuchsian functions were identical to the transformations of non-Euclidean geometry], without anything in my former thoughts seeming to have paved the way for it. . . . I did not verify the idea; I should not have had time, as, upon taking my seat in the omnibus, I went on with a conversation already commenced, but I felt a perfect certainty. On my return to Caen, for conscience' sake, I verified the result at my leisure. (Poincaré, 1913, p. 388)

In the midst of a conversation having nothing to do with mathematics, Poincaré had a realization: the fuchsian functions were identical to a familiar set of mathematical functions. As far as he could determine, none of his previous thoughts had led up to that realization. Poincaré called that sudden discovery an *illumination* – it was like a light going on. He concluded that he must have been thinking about the fuchsian functions all along, on an unconscious level. It is also noteworthy that Poincaré felt certain the idea was correct. When he returned from his trip, conscious work demonstrated that his intuition had indeed been correct.

A similar phenomenon occurred soon after: Poincaré worked unsuccessfully on a problem, went away for a few days from home and work, and had an illumination; and again the connection seemed to occur outside of his conscious thought. Poincaré believed that those examples demonstrated the importance of unconscious processes in creative thinking. A sudden illumination was a "sign of long, unconscious prior work" (1913, p. 389).

Atoms, Serpents, and Benzene

Another very well-known report, also presented as evidence for unconscious processes in creativity, was produced by August Kekuké (1829–1896), one of the most renowned chemists of the nineteenth century. In an address at a celebration honoring his career accomplishments, he reported how several came about (http://web.mit.edu/redingtn/www/neta dv/SP20151130.html; Rocke, 2010). Kekulé started his story with a description of how the basic ideas for what he called his "structural theory" arose.

> One beautiful summer evening I was riding on the last omnibus through the deserted streets usually so filled with life. I rode as usual on the outside of the omnibus. I fell into a reverie. Atoms flitted before my eyes. I had always seen them in movement, these little beings, but I had never before succeeded in perceiving their manner of moving. That evening, however, I saw that frequently two smaller atoms were coupled together, that larger ones seized the two smaller ones, that still larger ones held fast three and even four of the smaller ones and that all whirled around in a bewildering dance. I saw how the larger atoms formed a row and one dragged along still smaller ones at the ends of the chain. ... The cry of the guard, "Clapham Road," waked me from my reverie; but I spent a part of the night writing down sketches of these dream pictures. Thus arose the structural theory. (Rocke, 2010)

In a "reverie," Kekulé had made a theoretical advance, gaining understanding of how complex molecules were structured out of atoms. However, *benzene* was one chemical compound which had proven very difficult for chemists to understand. Benzene, a component of oil, is what gives gasoline its distinctive odor. It was known that benzene contained six carbon atoms, plus other atoms, but the organization of those atoms was unclear. In another dream, Kekulé discovered a radically new structure for benzene.

> It was very much the same with the Benzene Theory. ... I was ... engaged in writing my text-book; but it wasn't going very well; my mind was on other things. I turned my chair toward the fireplace and sank into a doze. Again the atoms were flitting before my eyes. Smaller groups now kept modestly in the background. My mind's eye, sharpened by repeated visions of a similar sort, now distinguished larger structures of varying forms. Long rows frequently close together, all, in movement, winding and turning like serpents. And see! What was that? One of the serpents seized its own tail and the form whirled mockingly before my eyes. I came awake like a flash of lightning. This time also I spent the remainder of the night working out the consequences of the hypothesis. (Rocke, 2010)

In a "doze" in which a dancing serpent bit its own tail, Kekulé conceived a new structure for benzene: the six carbon atoms formed a circle. It was another important breakthrough, brought about through processes not under conscious control.

Outline of the Chapter

This chapter will examine from a historical perspective the role that the unconscious might play in creativity. The discussion can be looked upon as an extension of the analysis of insight in Chapter 7. As noted in that chapter, many researchers believe that *Aha!* experiences are the result of unconscious processes (e.g., see Danek & Salvi, 2018). Kekulé's "And see! What was that?" quoted earlier is an explicit example of an *Aha!* experience. Poincaré may have had similar experiences. We now have familiarity with several creative advances that have been interpreted as being the result of unconscious processes, so we can turn to the question of how the unconscious might work. We will begin with Poincaré's (1913) theory of how unconscious thinking functions in creativity, and will trace the development of modern views, many of which have built on Poincaré's ideas. This will lead us to recent research concerning the possible role of the unconscious in creative thinking. In this chapter, we are dealing with a very difficult question: how can one gather evidence concerning the unconscious, which is, by definition, not observable?

Poincaré's Theory of Unconscious Creative Thinking

Based on his observations during his sleepless night of ideas colliding until pairs interlocked, Poincaré concluded that the unconscious operated by building valuable combinations of ideas. Which combinations of ideas are most valuable?

> They are those which reveal to us unsuspected kinship between other facts, long known, but wrongly believed to be strangers to one another. Among chosen combinations the most fertile will often be those formed of elements drawn from domains which are far apart. (Poincaré, 1913, p. 386)

The notion that creative ideas depend on forging links between ideas from areas that are "far apart" – "remote" areas – has as we already know had great influence on the thinking of many psychologists. Perhaps the most important theorizing based on Poicaré's ideas is that of Mednick (1962), introduced in Chapter 2, which will be discussed in more detail shortly. Similar ideas, some of which have already been discussed in earlier chapters, have been presented by Csikszentmihalyi (1996), Simonton (1995), and Cushin and Wiley (2018). Kounios and Beeman's (2015) analysis of Wag Dodge's insight in Mann Gulch concerning the creation of the escape fire is built directly on Poincaré's ideas. In short, Poincaré's conception of the creative process is still very much with us.

Mechanisms of Combination of Ideas

The next question considered by Poincaré involved how those useful combinations of ideas "from domains which are far apart" might be brought about. There are in Poincaré's view at least two ways in which valuable combinations of ideas might be produced. First, the thinker might produce *only* potentially valuable ideas. The *conscious experience* of the thinker matches this alternative. "Never in the field of his consciousness do combinations appear that are not really useful" (Poincaré, 1913, p. 386). However, in Poincaré's view the possibility that the unconscious was able to produce only useful idea-combinations gave too much credit to the unconscious, which would have to possess some sort of complex intelligence. The second possibility, which Poincaré supported, is that many combinations of ideas, useful and worthless alike, are produced by unconscious processing but that only potentially useful ideas become conscious.

We are now left with two questions. How are combinations of ideas formed in the unconscious? And how are the valuable combinations determined, so they can be admitted into consciousness? Let us first consider how combinations of ideas come about. Poincaré writes:

> Figure the future elements of our combinations as something like the hooked atoms of Epicurus. During the complete repose of the mind, these atoms are motionless, they are, so to speak, hooked to the wall ... On the other hand, during a period of apparent rest and unconscious work, certain of them are detached from the wall and put in motion. ... Their mutual impacts may produce new combinations. (1913, p. 393)

Thus, when one is not consciously thinking about a problem, ideas – the "hooked atoms" discussed by the Greek philosopher Epicurus (341–270 BCE) – can still be "in motion" and can "hook together" to form new combinations. However, there must be some limitation on the number of ideas entering into those unconscious combinations or else there would be so many that the thinker would never be able to find potentially useful ones. The earlier *conscious* work on the problem, which seemed to produce no progress, actually served to restrict processing to those ideas that have some chance of producing useful combinations.

> We think we have done no good, because we have moved these elements a thousand different ways in seeking to assemble them, and have found no satisfactory aggregate. But, after this shaking up imposed upon them by our will [that is, by our conscious work on a problem], these atoms do not return to their primitive rest. They freely continue their dance. ... Then the mobilized atoms undergo impacts which make them enter into combinations among themselves or with other atoms at rest which they struck against in their course. ... [T]he only combinations that have a chance of forming are those where at least one of the elements is one of those atoms freely chosen by our will. Now, it is evidently among these that is found what I call the *good combination*. (Poincaré, 1913, p. 389)

The unconscious combinatorial process begins with ideas that were "set into motion" during preliminary conscious work on the problem. Some idea combinations can arise when an idea activated originally in conscious thought comes into contact with one "at rest" – that is, with an idea that had not in the current context been contemplated before. That new combination, if it became conscious, would surprise the thinker.

How a Combination Becomes Conscious

Sometimes the unconscious process of combination of ideas is successful: a potentially useful combination is hit upon and bursts suddenly into consciousness, where it is experienced as an illumination. An idea becomes conscious when it strikes the (unconscious) sensibility of the thinker as being "beautiful" or "harmonious." We now understand why Poincaré felt certain about the correctness of his illumination, concerning fuchsian functions and non-Euclidian geometry, formulated on boarding the omnibus. The idea had already been evaluated by the unconscious sensibility. That sensibility is also why we are never aware of the many useless combinations: they will not get past that "gatekeeper." Table 8.1A presents a summary of

Table 8.1 *Summary of theories of unconscious processing*

Theorist	Postulated Mechanism of Unconscious Thinking
A) Poincaré	Random combinations of ideas activated by conscious work; "good ideas" are those which combine distant domains, previously thought unrelated. Unconscious, aesthetically based judgmental process determines which combinations – those judged "beautiful" or "harmonious" – become conscious. Self-reports as evidence for illuminations and unconscious thinking.
B) Wallas	Formalized Poincaré's ideas into four stages: preparation; incubation; illumination; verification. Incubation involves unconscious processing. Evidence for unconscious processes: self-reports.
C) Campbell	Poincaré's sleepless night as evidence for random combination of ideas; unconscious processes.
D) Mednick	Adopted Poincaré's idea that most valuable new ideas depend on connections between ideas that previously were only distantly related; flat associative hierarchies as the basis for creation of new ideas.
E) Simonton	Unconscious combinations, based on Poincaré and Campbell. Creative thinker's associations organized into Mednick's flat associative hierarchies.
F) Csikszentmihalyi	Parallel processing, based on associations among ideas in unconscious, versus logical and constrained order of ideas in conscious thinking. Reports by creative individuals provide evidence for unconscious processes in incubation and illuminations.

Poincaré's view alongside those of several other theorists. Next we turn to Wallas (1926) and his stage theory of creative thinking, which was based directly on Poincaré's ideas.

Wallas's Stages of the Creative Process

Wallas (1926) formalized Poincaré's ideas on the creative process into a series of four stages that form the basis for many modern discussions of creativity (Sadler-Smith, 2015; see also Hadamard, 1945). The first stage, *preparation*, entails conscious work on the problem: the thinker becomes familiar with it and attempts solutions. If this work is unsuccessful, at some point the person will break off work. The unconscious, however, keeps working. This second stage is called *incubation* in an analogy to what happens inside an egg when it is warmed by a hen. The discovery of a new and potentially useful idea by the unconscious leads to the third stage, a conscious experience of *illumination*. The egg hatches. Finally, the illumination requires *verification*: its truth must be determined, which requires conscious thought (see Table 8.1B).

Wallas (1926) offered advice to thinkers based on his stage theory. One should sometimes completely stop thinking about a problem and give the unconscious processes time to do their work. The worst activity to carry out during incubation was "industrious passive reading" (p. 44). The thinking stimulated by reading will interfere with incubation. Similar advice is given by modern researchers (e.g., Kounios & Beeman, 2015).

Bringing Poincaré into the Mainstream

We have now examined Poincaré's theory of unconscious processing in creativity and its elaboration in Wallas's four-stage theory. Poincaré and Wallas were not psychologists, so that work was not immediately available to psychologists. Around 1960, Poincaré's ideas were highlighted in papers by Campbell (1960) and Mednick (1962). Those discussions greatly increased the spread of Poincaré's ideas.

Campbell's Evolutionary Theory of Creativity

Campbell (1960) proposed that creative ideas came about through a process of evolution analogous to the natural-selection process operating in Darwin's theory of organic evolution. In Darwin's theory, *blind variation* and *selective retention* determine how species evolve. There is first a *random variation* in the genetic material, caused, for example, by mutation brought about by some disturbance from outside, such as radiation. This variation is *blind*, since mutations occur randomly, without purpose; some are useful and some not. Those that are useful are *retained*, since the organisms that possess them will survive and pass their genes on to the next generation.

Similar processes operate in creative thinking. Campbell (1960) proposed that the creative process involved three stages. The first stage is a blind idea-generation process which produces random variations on ideas. Once those ideas are produced, there must be a set of criteria that determine which of them is worth preserving. Those criteria are provided by the problem situation that the person is facing: the ideas that will be preserved are those that solve the problem. Finally, there must be a mechanism – a memory of some sort – whereby any selected ideas can be retained for future use. The variations that have been selected will be preserved, so they are available to succeeding generations. Campbell presented Poincaré's (1913) description of his sleepless night as evidence for the random way in which new ideas are formed. Once new ideas are produced, they are subjected to a *selection process* that retains only those ideas that are successful. Campbell presented long quotations from Poincaré, including the discussion of the role of the unconscious in creating and selecting new ideas. Campbell's theory is summarized in Table 8.1C.

Mednick: Associative Hierarchies and Creativity

A second discussion that helped move Poincaré into the mainstream of psychology was Mednick's (1962) analysis of the mechanisms underlying creative thinking. We are already familiar with Mednick's theorizing from the brief discussion in Chapter 2 and elsewhere. One example of Poincarè's (1913) influence on Mednick can be seen in Mednick's definition of creativity. Mednick defined creativity as:

> the forming of associative elements into new combinations which either meet specified requirements or are in some way useful. The more mutually remote the elements of the new combination, the more creative the process of solution. (1962, p. 221)

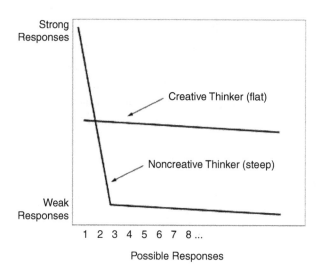

Figure 8.1 Mednick's theory of creativity, based on steep versus flat associative hierarchies

That definition echoes Poincaré (1913, p. 386): "Among chosen combinations the most fertile will often be those formed of elements drawn from domains which are far apart."

Mednick's (1962) analysis led him to a simple conception of how individuals might differ in factors that lead to creative ideas. The basic theoretical mechanism in Mednick's theory is the *associative hierarchy*, or the organization of an individual's associative responses to a situation. Some people, those who will *not* think creatively, have *restricted* or *steep* hierarchies, in which there are one or two strong responses (see Figure 8.1). Such individuals would tend to produce stereotyped and familiar responses to a situation, and so would be at a disadvantage when novel responses (i.e., relatively infrequent responses) are demanded. Creative individuals, in contrast, possess associative hierarchies in which are available a relatively large number of responses of more or less equal strength. That situation makes it more likely that the individual will produce a response that goes beyond the ordinary.

Mednick's (1962) conception of the mechanism underlying creativity, built on the foundation of Poincaré's theorizing, has strongly affected the way most psychologists think about creativity. For example, in Chapter 7, we reviewed Kounios and Beeman's (2015) discussion of Wag Dodge's inventing the escape fire. Kounios and Beeman emphasized that, for Dodge, setting an escape fire was "weakly associated with elements of the problem" (p. 89).

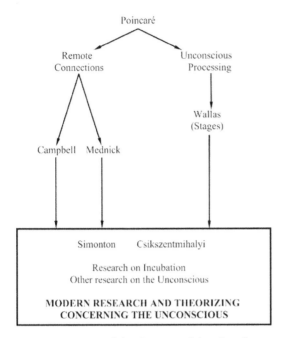

Figure 8.2 Historical development of theories of unconscious processing

That description is another version of Poincaré's elements "drawn from domains which are far apart" and Mednick's "flat hierarchies." Similar ideas have been proposed by Carson (2014, 2018) and Cushen and Wiley (2018). Mednick's theory is summarized in Table 8.1D.

We have now traced the main streams in psychology through the first half of the twentieth century focusing on the analysis of unconscious processes in creative thinking (see Figure 8.2). We can now follow the influence of those streams of thought on more modern theorizing. As specific examples, I will discuss the analyses of creative thinking proposed by Simonton (1995, 2016) and Csikszentmihalyi (1996), two influential researchers.

Simonton's Analysis of Creative Thinking

In his theorizing concerning the mechanisms underlying the creation of new ideas, Simonton (e.g., 1988, 1995, 1999, 2016) carried forth Poincaré's (1913) ideas, as elaborated by Campbell and Mednick. In Simonton's view (1995, p. 475), the generation of new ideas is brought about in the unconscious, as postulated by Poincaré. As we have seen, Campbell argued that ideational variation, to be truly effective, must be fully "blind." Use of that term resulted in criticisms of the theory (e.g., Sternberg, 1998), so Simonton (2016, 2018) changed his focus to the opposite perspective: he proposed that ideas generated in response to a problem can vary in their *sightedness*. The sightedness of a potential solution is a function of three components: the *probability* of the solution's being produced by the person in that situation; the person's prior knowledge of the *usefulness* or *utility* of that solution in situations like the one being faced now; and the *actual utility* or usefulness of the solution when it is applied to the problem. If a response has a high probability of being produced when a problem is presented, *and* if the person knows from experience that the solution will probably work, *and* if the solution does work, then the solution is high in sightedness. An idea high in sightedness is not creative. As an example, if one is given a simple addition problem, the high-probability solution is to carry out addition, which the person is confident will work, and which does work. In contrast, an idea is creative if it is novel (low probability); of value (high in utility); and *surprising* (i.e., the person has little expectation that the solution will work).

Simonton used those criteria to classify responses to problems as to their creativity or lack thereof. Parts of Simonton's classification system are presented in Table 8.2; the complete system involves eight different classes of responses to a problem, some of which are not of major interest here (for the complete system, see table 1 in Simonton (2016) or table 1.1 in Simonton (2018)). The least interesting situation is when all the values are high, as was just discussed concerning an addition problem. That situation is described as "reproductive" and based on expertise. The second situation, the "lucky guess," occurs when a person gives a high-

Table 8.2 *A simplified version of Simonton's (2018) classification system of responses to a problem*

Outcome	Initial Probability of Production	Prior Knowledge of Utility	Actual Utility
Routine, reproductive, or habitual responses; expertise	High	High	High
Fortuitous responses; the "lucky guess"	High	Low	High
Creative or productive responses	Low	Low	High

probability response, about which he or she has no idea concerning its usefulness (usefulness is low), that turns out to solve the problem (*actual utility* is high). The person is as surprised as everyone else at the turn of events. Simonton (2016) used the terms *creative* and *productive* to describe the responses of most interest – that is, novel solutions to problems. A creative response occurs when the probability of the person producing the response is close to zero; he or she has no knowledge that the possible solution will actually work; but the solution does work. Creativity in Simonton's analysis depends on a high-utility response (high value), about which you know little before producing it (low knowledge), and that is very unlikely to be produced in the situation (it is novel for you in that situation).

Simonton (1995) proposed that the creative process operates on what he referred to as *mental elements*, fundamental psychological units that can be manipulated in some manner, comparable to Poincaré's "hooked atoms" and Mednick's "associative elements." Simonton theorized that those elements must be free to enter into combinations, through a random process carried out in the unconscious. The combinations that are formed differ in *stability*, the chances that the combination will stay together. The greater the stability of a combination, the greater the chance that it will reach consciousness. Simonton's notion of "stability" is analogous to Poincaré's idea of selection based on the thinker's unconscious esthetic sensitivity.

In Simonton's (1995) view, individuals can vary along two dimensions in their ability to produce novel ideas. First, people differ in the total number of mental elements. The "genius" possesses more elements than the nongenius. In addition, those elements must be organized in a manner optimum for creative-idea production. Here, Simonton built on Mednick's (1962) theorizing. Creative thinkers possess "flatter" associative hierarchies; this allows them to be more free in responding. According to Simonton, there is a continuum underlying problem-solving. At one end is routine problem-solving, such as working out a problem in long division, using a straightforward procedure known to everyone. At the other end are the problems important in scientific research, where there are no well-known procedures. In those latter situations, the seemingly random "free-associative" process is crucial. Here, Simonton (1995) made an explicit connection to the ideas of Poincaré.

> As Poincaré (1913, p. 386) remarked: "[The most useful combinations of ideas] are those which reveal to us unsuggested kinship between other facts, long known, but wrongly believed to be strangers to one another. . . . [Therefore,] among chosen combinations the most fertile will often be

> those formed of elements drawn from domains which are far apart." . . .
> Probably the only way two irrelevant realms can be brought together is by
> the crazy confluence of rather haphazard and whimsical trains of associa-
> tion. (Simonton, 1995, p. 473; brackets Simonton's)

In explaining how those unusual combinations of ideas can be brought
about, Simonton relied on Poincaré: the combinations occur in the unconscious. Simonton's theorizing is summarized in Table 8.1E.

Csikszentmihalyi's Theory of the Unconscious in Creative Thinking

The influence of the streams of research in Figure 8.2 can also be seen in the
work of Csikszentmihalyi (1996; Csikszentmihalyi & Sawyer, 1995).
Csikszentmihalyi presented an analysis of the role of unconscious thought
in creativity based on interviews with almost 100 individuals who made
significant creative contributions in the arts, sciences, technology, and
business. In providing the theoretical background to his study,
Csikszentmihalyi relied on Wallas's (1926) stages.

> The second phase of the creative process is a period of incubation, during
> which ideas churn around below the threshold of consciousness. It is
> during this time that unusual connections are likely to be made. When we
> intend to solve a problem consciously, we process information in a linear,
> logical fashion. But when ideas call to each other on their own, without
> our leading them down a straight and narrow path, unexpected combina-
> tions may come into being. (1996, p. 79)

Csikszentmihalyi (1996, pp. 100–102) assumed that unconscious
thinking involves making connections among ideas based on laws
of simple association. Associative connections, which go beyond
strict logic, result in parallel processing, which produces what may
seem to be random combinations of ideas rather than the logical and
constrained serial processing of conscious analytical thought.
Csikszentmihalyi also echoed Poincaré's – and Simonton's – notion
concerning how ideas produced in the unconscious become conscious as illuminations:

> The insight presumably occurs when a subconscious connection
> between ideas fits so well that it is forced to pop out into conscious
> awareness, like a cork held underwater breaking out into the air after
> it is released. (p. 104)

As a specific example of how creative discovery came about, Csikszentmihalyi (1996) presented Kekulé's discovery of the circular structure of benzene, discussed earlier. (Csikszentmihalyi's description of the situation is different than Kekulé's own description, also presented earlier. That difference does not affect the conclusion.)

> Kekulé had the insight that the benzene molecule might be shaped like a ring after he fell asleep while watching sparks in the fireplace make circles in the air. If he had stayed awake, Kekulé would have presumably rejected as ridiculous the thought that there might be a connection between sparks and the shape of the molecule. But in the subconscious, rationality could not censor the connection, and so when he woke up he was no longer able to ignore its possibility. (p. 101)

This is an example of the unconscious bringing together ideas that conscious thought could not entertain. Csikszentmihalyi's theory is summarized in Table 8.1F.

Poincaré's Legacy: Unconscious Thinking in Creativity

This review has pointed to the importance of Poincaré's theorizing in the development of ideas in psychology through the twentieth century. There is large-scale agreement among psychologists that the stages postulated by Wallas (1926) – on the basis of Poincaré's reports, among others – are a useful description of the process of creative thinking. As summarized in Table 8.1 and Figure 8.2, many theorists agree that during incubation unconscious processing is taking place, which may result in an illumination.

In carrying out that historical analysis, we combined two separable ideas: (1) incubation – breaking away from a problem – is an important stage in creative thinking; (2) the solutions that arise after incubation are the result of unconscious processes. Those ideas were discussed together because researchers have usually discussed them together. However, going forward, we should separate those two issues. We will first consider the question of the "reality" of incubation – that is, whether breaking away from a problem plays a positive role in creative thinking. The evidence presented so far has come from subjective reports, such as those of Poincaré and Kekulé. As we shall see later, questions can be raised about the usefulness of self-reports as "data" for theorizing concerning unconscious processes in incubation. Stronger evidence in support of incubation comes from laboratory studies, which we will examine.

Once we have established the reality of incubation, we will examine the possible mechanisms whereby it might come about. In spite of the strong agreement concerning the importance of unconscious thinking in incubation, several other hypotheses, which do not rely on the unconscious have been brought forth to explain the occurrence of illuminations. We will review those various proposals and examine research support for each.

Demonstrating Incubation in the Laboratory

The basic experimental design to demonstrate incubation is shown in Table 8.3A. There typically are two conditions, a *Control* condition and an *Incubation* condition. People in both conditions are presented with a challenging target problem to solve (the *Preparation* period, time A in Table 8.3A). The kinds of tasks used in studies of incubation are summarized in Table 8.3B. If the preparation period ends with the target problem unsolved, then the control group continues to work, as designated by time B in row (1) in Table 8.3A. The *incubation* group is given time away from the problem (the *Incubation Period*, time X in Table 8.3A). During the incubation period, one of several events may occur. Most frequently, the incubation period is *filled* (see row (2a) in Table 8.3A). Another task is presented, a distractor task, that is unrelated to the unsolved target problem, and the participants work on it for the incubation period. The distractor is designed to distract the person from thinking about the target problem. Another condition that is sometimes used is to give the incubation group an unfilled break, during which they can do whatever they wish (the Empty Incubation Period; row (2b) in Table 8.3).

After the incubation period, the target problem is again presented (the *Final Work* period, time B in Table 8.2A). Thus, the total time spent trying to solve the target problem is the same for the control and incubation conditions (A+B; see final column in Table 8.2A). Performance of the Incubation group is compared with that of the Control group which has worked continuously on the target problem. If taking a break results in better performance, it means that, for some reason, the incubation period facilitated problem-solving.

Over the past sixty years many studies have been carried out using the design in Table 8.3A. Those studies have varied in many ways, including the type of target problem used, the length of the preparation period, the length of the incubation period, and the type of distractor task. Sio and Ormerod (2009) carried out a meta-analysis – a large-scale quantitative

Table 8.3 *Laboratory study to test for incubation*
A. *Delayed incubation design*

Condition	Periods of Work			Total Time on Target Problem
(1) Control	Preparation (Target Problem) ◄──TimeA──►	Final Work (Target Problem) ◄──TimeB──►		A+B
(2) Incubation a) Filled	Preparation (Target Problem) ◄──TimeA──►	Incubation Period (Distractor) ◄──TimeX──►	Final Work (Target Problem) ◄──TimeB──►	A+B
b) Empty	Preparation (Target Problem) ◄──TimeA──►	Incubation Period (No Distractor) ◄──TimeX──►	Final Work (Target Problem) ◄──TimeB──►	A+B

B. *Examples of problems used in incubation studies*

Type of Problem	Example
Open-ended creative thinking (more than one possible solution)	**Consequences:** What would happen if everyone suddenly lost the ability to read and write? List all the consequences that you can. Can be scored for number of responses, and creativity can be rated by judges.
	Unusual uses: Think of all the new unusual uses that you can for a brick. Example – as a weapon; as a paperweight. Test can be scored for number of uses produced; uses can also be rated by judges for creativity.
Insight problems (one solution)	**Linguistic: Compound Remote Associates Task (CRA)** (see Figure 7.2F and 7.3F). Three words are presented, and the person must think of a fourth word that is associated to all three. Example: **blue, cottage, mouse**; answer: **cheese**
	Spatial: Candle Problem (see Chapter 3; Figures 3.4–3.6). Person must attach a candle to the wall; available objects are a book of matches and a box of tacks.

review – of research on incubation, and their overall conclusion was that there was support for the occurrence of incubation. (See also Dodd, Ward & Smith, 2012.) Taking a break can facilitate solution. In addition, several factors play a role in the strength of the incubation effect. First, longer preparation times resulted in larger incubation effects. If two groups were given five minutes and ten minutes respectively to work on a problem before the break, the ten-minute group would show larger effects of incubation on returning to the problem. Several studies also showed that having a break filled with a distractor produced better performance than did an empty break (rows (2a) versus (2b) in Table 8.3A).

In summary, it has been demonstrated in the laboratory that taking a break facilitates problem-solving. That conclusion leads to a question. What might be happening during the incubation period that produces the improved performance of the incubation group when they return to the target: unconscious processes, conscious processes, or something else entirely?

Theories to Explain Illuminations

Several different types of theories have been brought forth to explain the occurrence of illuminations (Gilhooly, 2016; Weisberg, 2006). The first type of theory, already familiar, is unconscious processing. The other theories explain illuminations without assuming that unconscious processing plays a role. One possibility is that the individual never stops working consciously on the problem, even during the incubation period. This theory is called *conscious work*. Second, after time away from a problem, the person might simply return with a fresh perspective. That *fresh look* might result in a new solution method and success. Finally, during the time away from the problem, the person might come across an event that provides information relevant to solution. This hypothesis – *opportunistic assimilation* – is familiar to us from the discussion in Chapter 4 of analogical thinking in creativity. De Mestral's invention of Velcro came about through the opportunistic assimilation of the Burdock burr, which provided a method of solution to the problem of a zipper-less fastener. A similar process occurred during Crocker's using the mechanism from a European shower as the basis for the COSTAR repair of the Hubble telescope. We can now examine the evidence in support of each of those theories concerning what might be happening to produce an illumination. We begin with unconscious processing, since it has the longest history.

Unconscious Processing

The earliest evidence presented in support of unconscious processing in incubation was the already-discussed subjective reports of Poincaré and

Kekulé. Wallas (1926) did not go very far beyond Poincaré concerning evidence for his four-stage theory: he too relied on people's reports about their creative process. (See also Hadamard (1945); Ghiselin (1996 [1952].) More recently, subjective reports have been presented by Csikszentmihalyi and Sawyer (1995) in support of unconscious processing. We begin our examination of evidence in support of unconscious processing with a consideration of the usefulness of subjective reports as evidence.

Subjective Reports as Evidence for Unconscious Processing

One might argue that people's reports on their own psychological processes are the strongest sorts of evidence (see Ghiselin, 1996 [1952]). Who knows, better than the thinker, about what goes on in her mind? However, questions can be raised about how much confidence we should have in subjective reports (Gilhooly, 2016; Weisberg, 2006). As one example, Poincaré's public discussion of his discoveries was presented some thirty years after they occurred. Furthermore, several of those reports – for example, the discovery while stepping on the omnibus – dealt with events of extremely brief duration. It is difficult to believe that, after so long a period of time, Poincaré's recounting of the details of those experiences could be accurate. Also, one report, concerning the sleepless night when Poincaré observed ideas colliding and combining, says nothing about the unconscious, since he was *conscious* during that episode. Poincaré concluded that he must have been observing his unconscious at work but there is no evidence for that conclusion.

A question can also be raised about Kekulé's report about his discovery of the structure of benzene in a dream about a serpent biting its tail (Rocke, 2010; Weisberg, 2006). It is not clear that Kekulé was actually thinking about serpents. In his speech, Kekulé described his imagery as follows: "Long rows frequently close together, all, in movement, winding and turning like serpents." If Kekulé had been imagining *serpents*, would he have described them as moving "*like* serpents"? If one is imagining a serpent, then it does not wind and turn *like* a serpent; it simply winds and turns. Kekulé might have been imagining strings of atoms *as strings of atoms*, which he then *described as moving like serpents*, to assist his audience's understanding. Perhaps we should not take Kekulé's report literally, which raises questions about its value as evidence for unconscious processes during incubation. As we saw earlier, the details of Kekulé's "dream" were used by Csikszentmihalyi and Sawyer (1995) to draw conclusions about how the unconscious worked. Those conclusions may be based on a misinterpretation of what Kekulé was doing.

Additional evidence in support of unconscious thinking during incubation comes from the study of Csikszentmihalyi and Sawyer (1995), who analyzed the reports of their many interviewees. Let us see if those reports provide useful evidence concerning unconscious processes during incubation. Csikszentmihalyi and Sawyer's respondents described moments of insight as part of a four-stage process, corresponding to the stages of Wallas (1926). Many of the individuals claimed that they had developed the ability to direct their unconscious processes. They "structured their days to include a period of solitary idle time that follows a period of hard work. ... [W]ithout this solitary, quiet time, they would never have their most important ideas. This daily idle time seems to be a period during which a problem-solving incubation stage may be at work" (Csikszentmihalyi and Sawyer, 1995, p. 347). Keeping the mind idle sometimes involves simple repetitive physical activity. "Generally, the really high ideas come to me when I'm gardening" (p. 348).

All the respondents reported that insights came during that set-aside time. Some respondents carried notebooks with them, to take advantages of the ideas when they came. A banker reported the following:

> It often happens [that illuminations occur] when I'm sitting around a hotel room; I'm on a trip and nothing's going on and I sit and think. Or I'm sitting on a beach ... and I find myself writing myself notes. (p. 348)

One of the banker's insights is called the "memo from the beach"; in it he outlined the structure of the first consumer banking enterprise, in 1974.

> I was on a vacation, and I started out saying, "I'm sitting on the beach thinking about the business," and it went on for 30 pages. And it turned out to be the blueprint. I didn't sit down and say, "I'm gonna write a blueprint"; I said, "I'm sitting on the beach thinking," and I sort of thought through the business in a systematic way ... and I shared it with my colleagues. (p. 354)

The respondents were thus paving the way for the operation of their unconscious.

A similar process was described concerning an insight on a larger scale, by Freeman Dyson, a physicist-mathematician who was attempting to bring together two seemingly incompatible theoretical approaches to quantum mechanics, which had been proposed by two physicists, Feynman and

Schwinger. Here is what Dyson told Csikszentmihalyi and Sawyer (1995) when they interviewed him:

> I spent 6 months working very hard, to understand both of them clearly, ... and at the end of 6 months, I went off on a vacation, took the Greyhound bus to California ... [A]fter two weeks in California, where I wasn't doing any work, just sightseeing, I got on the Greyhound bus to come back to Princeton and suddenly, in the middle of the night, when we were going through Kansas, the whole thing sort of suddenly became crystal clear, so that was sort of the big revelation for me, the eureka experience (p. 359)

Based on such reports, Csikszentmihalyi and Sawyer (1995, p. 358) concluded that the occurrence of an illumination was the result of information being processed in parallel at an unconscious level.

Once again, however, questions can be raised concerning how we should interpret those reports. Consider the banker's "memo from the beach." He reported: "I didn't sit down and say, 'I'm gonna write a blueprint'; I said, 'I'm sitting on the beach thinking'" (Csikszentmihalyi & Sawyer, 1995, p. 354). This report seems to have nothing to do with unconscious processing: the banker was *thinking* about the business, and he *wrote* a memo, both of which are conscious acts. Consider also the report that "high ideas" come during gardening. That report has nothing to do with unconscious processing: she is gardening, but that does not preclude her thinking consciously about her work at the same time. Gardening is exactly the kind of nondemanding physical activity that allows one to do one thing while thinking about something else.

Finally, Dyson, the physicist-mathematician, described how, on the bus during the night in Kansas, he was able to unify two seemingly incompatible approaches to quantum mechanics. However, close examination indicates that there are several critical problems with Dyson's report that make it questionable as evidence concerning *Aha!* experiences and unconscious processes in creative thinking. Dyson's insight occurred in the summer of 1948, which means that he spoke to Csikszentmihalyi and Sawyer (1995) between forty and fifty years later. In a letter he wrote to his family in late summer 1948, however, he described his summer activities in detail, and the letter tells a different story than Dyson recounted to the researchers. The vacation trip was the second trip he took that summer. Before that trip, Dyson had embarked on what one can call a working trip, during which he drove across the country with Feynman, who was his colleague at Cornell University. They spent the time discussing physics before parting company at Albuquerque, New Mexico. Dyson went north to the University of Michigan and attended a summer school where Schwinger gave a series of lectures. Thus Dyson's "working very hard" entailed detailed interaction with the researchers whose perspectives he hoped to integrate. A few weeks later, he went on the trip he reported to Csikszentmihalyi and Sawyer (1995). He was on a bus heading east toward home when he had his realization. Dyson described that realization in his letter to his parents in a way that differs significantly from the report of his insight that he gave to Csikszentmihalyi and Sawyer:

> [G]oing into a sort of semi-stupor as one does after 48 hours of bus-riding, I began to think very hard about physics, and particularly about the rival radiation theories of Schwinger and Feynman. Gradually my thoughts grew more coherent, and before I knew where I was I had solved the problem that had been in the back of my mind all this year, which was to prove the equivalence of the two theories. Moreover, since each of the two theories is superior in certain features, the proof of the equivalence furnished incidentally a new form of the Schwinger theory which combines the advantages of both. (quoted in Kaiser, 2005, p. 74)

From Dyson's letter – again, written shortly after his insight – it seems that he did not have an *Aha!* experience of the sort that he described to Csikszentmihalyi and Sawyer (1995) so many years later. Dyson seems to have experienced an incremental coming-together of ideas rather than a sudden restructuring of a whole "gestalt." So here is another case where a subjective report must be interpreted with caution.

There is a second aspect of Dyson's report to Csikszentmihalyi and Sawyer (1995) that can be questioned: the idea that it provides evidence for the role of unconscious processes in creativity. Here is the crucial part of the passage quoted earlier by Csikszentmihalyi and Sawyer: "[S]uddenly, in the middle of the night, when we were going through Kansas, the whole thing sort of suddenly became crystal clear" (1995, p. 359). Even if we ignore the discrepancy between what Dyson wrote in his letter and the report he gave fifty years later to the researchers, on looking carefully at Dyson's later report it seems that it is not evidence for unconscious processes in creativity. Dyson was *conscious* the whole time, *thinking about the problem.* This fifty-year-old report, distorted as it may be, has nothing to do with the unconscious, and the much earlier letter supports the same conclusion.

In sum, there are weaknesses with subjective reports as evidence for unconscious processes in creative thinking. If those reports are not useful, it becomes necessary to provide other evidence for the occurrence of unconscious processes in creative thinking. We therefore turn to recent laboratory research.

Laboratory Studies of Unconscious Processing

The study of creativity is not the only area in which unconscious processes have been of interest to researchers. There has been interest in unconscious processing in the area of complex decision-making (for review, see Dijksterhuis & Strick, 2016). In one study, people were asked to decide which of a group of cars was most attractive for purchase. Participants were given much information about each of four cars – a total of twelve features for each car, including comfort, ride quality, gas mileage, price, models available, quality of dealer service, and so forth. One of the cars had more positive attributes (nine out of twelve) than the others did, so it was the best choice. In one condition, the participants decided which car they would like to buy immediately after all the information was presented. Other participants were given a few minutes to think consciously about the information before making the decision. A third group was given a distractor task for the same amount of time, so they were not able to think about the cars. The group given the distractor task performed best; they most often picked the car with the most positive features, even more often than the group who had time to consciously think about their decision before making it. The researchers concluded that, while the participants were working on the distractor, they were thinking about the decision unconsciously. According to Unconscious Thought Theory (Dijksterhuis & Meurs, 2006), the unconscious has greater processing capacity than conscious thought, which is why the group given the distractor, who were forced to use unconscious processes, performed best.

This view was extended to the realm of creativity, especially to the study of incubation. A study by Dijksterhuis and Meurs (2006) used an *immediate-incubation* design to examine unconscious processing during incubation (Table 8.4A). In this design, the control group starts to respond immediately to the target problem. The target was the unusual uses test (for details, see Table 8.3B). The immediate-incubation group is introduced to the target problem but then immediately given the *distractor task* to carry out, which means that they cannot think consciously about the target. The distractor task was a tracking task, where participants had to use the mouse to follow a moving target on a monitor. The conscious-thought

Table 8.4 *Dijksterhuis and Meurs (2006) immediate incubation study*
A. *Design*

Condition	Period 1	Period 2
Control	Work on target problem (unusual uses test)	None
Incubation	Work on distractor	Work on target problem
Conscious work	Think about target problem	Work on target problem

B. *Results*

Condition	Period 1	Period 2
Control (Immediate work)		
Number of uses	4.3	–
Rated creativity	2.5	–
Immediate incubation		
Number of uses	–	5.3
Rated creativity	–	2.9
Conscious work		
Number of uses	–	4.7
Rated creativity	–	2.6

group is instructed to *think* about the target problem but not write any responses for the same amount of time.

The results from the Dijksterhuis and Meurs immediate-incubation study are shown in Table 8.4B. The immediate-incubation group performed better than the control group: they produced more uses, and those uses were rated by independent raters as more creative. Perhaps more impressive, the immediate-incubation group performed better than the group who had a chance to think consciously about the target problem before responding. This study moved beyond subjective reports in providing evidence for unconscious processes in incubation. Several other studies have also provided support for the idea that unconscious thought can facilitate creative performance (for reviews, see Dijksterhuis and Strick (2016) and Ritter and Dijksterhuis (2014)).

Sleep and Incubation

Creative products – for example, Paul McCartney's "Yesterday" – have been reported as having come about in dreams. Cai et al. (2009) carried out a laboratory study that tried to provide evidence for the role of sleep in incubation. They brought people into the laboratory in the morning and had them try to solve CRA problems (see Table 8.3B), which, as we saw in Chapter 7, have been used as measures of creative thinking. Here is one CRA problem.

> What word can be combined with each of these three words, to form a meaningful compound word or phrase? tooth, potato, heart
> answer: sweet (sweet tooth; sweet potato; sweet heart)

After the CRA items, the people were given a verbal analogies test:

> cracker : salty :: candy : ?? answer: sweet

Some of the answers to the analogies were also answers to the CRA items, as seen in this example, although the participants were not told that. After the analogies test, the participants were given a break. Some people simply had a quiet rest period. Other participants were asked to try to sleep, and spent up to two hours in bed. Their sleep was monitored physiologically, so the researchers could determine if it was rapid-eye-movement (REM) sleep or non-rapid-eye-movement (non-REM) sleep. REM sleep is related to dreaming; NREM sleep is not. The three conditions were, therefore, quiet rest, REM sleep, and NREM sleep. The REM–NREM difference was not under the researchers' control; it depended on what happened when each participant was sleeping. After the rest/sleep interval, the participants returned to the lab and were given the CRA problems again.

For the CRA items that had solutions presented during the analogies task, solution was facilitated by sleep, but only for the people who had undergone REM sleep during the break. The researchers proposed that, during REM sleep, there is continuing activity in previously active areas in memory, which can result in solution of the problem. That activity does not occur during NREM sleep or during quiet rest. Those results pointed to a role of sleep in problem-solving, at least through activity during incubation.

While it is fascinating to contemplate the role of sleep in creativity, we must be cautious in drawing conclusions from this research. Landmann and colleagues (2016) found that a period of overnight sleep did not facilitate solution of problems left unsolved before sleep. Similarly, Schönauer and colleagues (2018) reported that an incubation period of sleep did not facilitate problem-solving performance. Although the idea that sleep can facilitate creative thinking through the operation of unconscious processes may be attractive, support for it is not as yet very strong.

Mind-Wandering and Incubation

A different process that has been linked to unconscious processing is *mind-wandering* (Smallwood & Schooler, 2015), also called *daydreaming* or *task-irrelevant thought*. One's mind "wanders" from the task at hand, intentionally or not; one thinks of other things. It has been found that 25–50 percent of the time people are thinking about things not related to the task at hand. Furthermore, if one is engaged in a not-very-demanding task, the amount of mind-wandering increases. Baird and colleagues (2012) used the delayed-incubation design (see Table 8.3), to examine the possible role of mind-wandering in incubation. The target task was the unusual uses test, and there were four conditions in the experiment. The control group worked continuously on the task, for a total of four minutes. Three incubation conditions were employed, in which the work on the target task was divided into two two-minute periods, separated by a twelve-minute incubation period. During incubation, one group had an unfilled rest interval, another group had an undemanding distractor task, and the third group had a demanding distractor.

The results indicated that, with an undemanding task during the incubation period, performance improved in the second two-minute period. There was no incubation effect found in the other conditions. After the study was completed, the participants were questioned about their mind-wandering during the incubation period. The people given the undemanding task during incubation reported more mind-wandering during incubation than did people in the rest condition or the demanding-task condition. The participants in the undemanding-task condition also reported that, when mind-wandering, their thoughts *did not* center on the target task. Therefore, the incubation effect was not due to conscious thought about the target problem during the incubation interval.

Additional evidence to support the role of mind-wandering in incubation, in a real-world context, was reported by Gable, Hopper, and Schooler (2019). Professional writers (screenwriters for film and television, novelists, and non-fiction writers) and physicists (physics researchers and PhD students) were asked, at the end of each day, to report on their most creative idea of the day. They were also asked what they were thinking about and doing when that idea occurred, as well as whether the idea came in an "*Aha!*" moment. Participants reported that one-fifth of their most creative ideas occurred during mind-wandering: they were engaged in an activity other than working, and they were thinking about something unrelated to the idea. Furthermore, the ideas that occurred during mind-wandering were more likely to be experienced as "*Aha!*" moments, and to be associated with overcoming an impasse on a problem, compared with ideas generated while specifically working on a task. Those results provide further evidence, beyond the laboratory, of the influence of mind-wandering on creative thinking. However, it should be noted that the support for unconscious processing from the mind-wandering studies is very indirect. The only evidence to support unconscious processing is the report of the participants that, during mind-wandering, they did not think about the target task.

In conclusion, we have seen indirect evidence for unconscious processing from the Dijskterhuis and Meurs (2006) immediate-incubation study, as well as research examining mind-wandering (Gable, Hopper & Schooler, 2019). However, findings are mixed from research studying the possible role of sleep in incubation. We now turn to the possibility that illuminations are the result of conscious work during the incubation period.

Continuous Conscious Work

A simple way to explain the occurrence of illumination, without assuming that unconscious processing is taking place, is to assume that people keep working *consciously* on a problem even when they "take a break" (Olton, 1979; for discussion, see Gilhooly & Webb, 2018). Perhaps Poincaré (1913) was mistaken in thinking that he had not thought about fuchsian functions when he went away to the conference. He might have thought about them very briefly, not enough to make a lasting impression, but enough to carry the process forward. One of those short episodes of conscious thinking might have been sufficient to move him to that illumination about fuchsian functions. Olton (1979) called this possibility "creative worrying." There is evidence that Poincaré was a creative worrier (Gilhooly & Webb, 2018). It was reported by people close to him that Poincaré never stopped thinking about his work, even when he was away from his desk. That continuous conscious thinking could have produced solutions to problems that he had seemingly given up on.

One way to test the conscious-work hypothesis is to give one group in an experiment the opportunity to keep thinking about the target problem during the incubation period – the Incubation Empty condition (row (2b) in Table 8.3A) – to see if that increases their performance compared to that of a group that is given a distractor task. A number of studies (see Gilhooly, 2016) have shown that an empty incubation interval produces *lower* levels of performance than an incubation condition filled with a distractor task (row (2a) in Table 8.3A). Those results raise problems for the conscious-work hypothesis. The conscious-work hypothesis also predicts that, if a participant is trying to work on the *target* problem during the incubation period, then performance on the *distractor* should suffer. That prediction also has not been supported (see Gihooly, 2016). Finally, if one asks the people in an incubation study, including the just-discussed research on mind-wandering, if they thought about the target task during the incubation period, most report that they did not. That result, too, does not support the conscious-work hypothesis.

One result that does support the conscious-work hypothesis is the finding that a medium-difficulty distractor results in greater incubation effects than a difficult distractor (Sio & Ormerod, 2009; Gilhooly, 2016). That result is consistent with the hypothesis that people are trying to work on the target task during the incubation period. A difficult distractor, which makes it harder to think about the target problem, would be expected to produce lower levels of incubation. In summary, there are several specific findings that contradict predictions from the conscious-work hypothesis, so I will not consider it further. Let us now turn to the *fresh-look* hypothesis, the idea that taking a break allows you to return to the target problem with a new perspective.

Taking a Fresh Look

The *fresh-look* viewpoint assumes that, if a person decided to stop working on a problem, it was because their approach was not succeeding (Gilhooly, 2016). Taking a break might increase the chances that the incorrect approach would be forgotten. The person might then take a *fresh look* at the problem – which might increase the chances of solution. Proposed many years ago by Woodworth (1938), this view has more recently been elaborated by Smith (1995; Beda & Smith, 2018), who suggested that initial problem-solving attempts may result in thinkers falling into *mental ruts* – that is, approaches to a problem that are unsuccessful and that interfere with thinking of new ones. According to Beda and Smith, those unsuccessful approaches – which they call "red herrings" – must be forgotten before anything new can be thought of. Time is needed for this forgetting to occur, and that time is provided by the incubation period.

One way to test the fresh-look hypothesis is to show that people do better on returning to a problem if they have forgotten the "red herrings." Smith (1995) gave people word problems to solve, some of which were presented with "red herrings" – that is, cues that made it harder to solve them. The participants were then given a break involving a distractor task. After the break, the problems were presented again but without the red herrings. Smith tested performance on the problems as well as people's ability to remember the red herrings. Solution improved only for the problems for which the red herrings had been forgotten. Beda and Smith (2018) tested the fresh look hypothesis from the opposite perspective: they reported that making it easier to *remember* the red herrings interfered with problem-solving.

Results that do not support the fresh-look hypothesis come from the immediate-incubation study of Dijksterhuis and Meurs (2006) discussed earlier (see Table 8.4). In the immediate-incubation condition, people were told about the target task but they were not given a chance to work on it before they begin the distractor. Therefore, in the immediate-incubation condition there is no need for a *fresh* look, since there was no time for red herrings to arise. The fact that immediate incubation produces positive effects cannot be explained by the fresh-look hypothesis.

Opportunistic Assimilation: Discovering the Solution

The final explanation for incubation effects is opportunistic assimilation: taking a break provides an opportunity for the person to discover some information in the environment that helps to solve the problem (Gilhooly, 2016; Kounios & Beeman, 2015). The person *assimilates* or takes in that information; and it is done *opportunistically* – that is, taking advantage of any opportunity that the environment provides. Siefert et al. (1995) designed a three-phase experiment to demonstrate opportunistic assimilation. In phase 1 (see Table 8.5A), the participants were given a set of general information questions to answer (those were the target problems to be solved). An example is: "What is a nautical instrument used to measure the position of a ship?" Answer: *sextant*. Approximately one-third of the time, the participants were not able to answer the questions. After all the questions were presented, the experiment moved to phase 2, which involved a word-recognition task. A series of verbal stimuli was presented, and, for each, the participant judged whether or not it was a word. Examples are: *mantiness* (no); *lacuna* (yes). Some phase 2 words were also the correct answers to phase 1 target questions. The next day, the participants returned

Table 8.5 *Siefert et al. (1995) study of "opportunistic assimilation"*

A. *Design*

Phase 1	Phase 2	Phase 3
Problem-solving	**Word-recognition task**	**Target problem**
Target problem	Solution word	Target problem
Target problem	No solution word	Target problem

B. *Results (% questions correct)*

Question Type	Target Solution Presented During Phase 2?	
	Yes	**No**
Old	55	38
New	48	38

for phase 3, which again involved a set of information questions, some of which were new and some of which were repeated from phase 1.

The results of the study are shown in Table 8.5B. Presentation in phase 2 of the answers to the target questions facilitated answering those questions during phase 3. Furthermore, old questions without answers during phase 2 were not answered in phase 3 more frequently than new questions, which means that "incubation" occurred only with exposure of the target word during phase 2. Siefert et al. (1995) concluded that a break may help in problem-solving because it may lead to an encounter with an external object or event that is relevant to solving the problem (p. 87).

The opportunistic assimilation view explains those results but it does not explain all the incubation results. For example, in most experiments on incubation the participants stay in the lab during the incubation period, which means that there is little in the way of new stimuli to provide the solution to the target problem. Also, if the person is working hard on the distractor task, it might not be possible for an external stimulus to have much of an effect, due to the person's attending to the distractor. The opportunistic assimilation hypothesis also cannot explain the fact that a filled incubation interval produces a stronger incubation effect than does an unfilled interval. Finally, the fact that people in an incubation study report that they did not think about the target during the incubation period contradicts the opportunistic-assimilation theory.

Explaining Illumination: There Is No Single "Correct" Theory

We have examined research support for several explanations of incubation. Much of the interest in this area has centered on the notion of unconscious processing, because it raises the most interesting implications concerning our understanding of creativity. The continuous-conscious-work, fresh-look, and opportunistic-assimilation hypotheses all assume that mechanisms of conscious thought, employed in different ways, are the explanation for incubation effects. Unconscious processing, in contrast, assumes that processes very different from our conscious experiences, and out of our awareness, play critical roles in thinking.

However, unconscious processing is very difficult to test directly, since by definition it is not visible and, if it does occur, the person is not able to report on what is happening. The best that a researcher can do at this point is to provide an *indirect* test of unconscious processing. Incubation studies typically include conditions that make it difficult for opportunistic assimilation or a fresh look to occur. If incubation effects are found in such studies, it is assumed that unconscious processing has occurred (Dijksterhuis & Meurs, 2006; Gilhooly, 2016; Ritter & Dijksterhuis, 2014). As one example, we have seen that performance is typically better after a filled versus unfilled incubation interval. Since the unfilled interval would seem to provide the best circumstances for opportunistic assimilation of environmental events, then that result provides evidence against opportunistic assimilation and therefore indirect support for the hypothesis that unconscious processing has occurred. Similarly, after going through an incubation study most people report that they did not think about the target during the distractor task in the incubation interval. Similar reports are obtained in studies that involve mind-wandering: people report that they do not "wander" to the target task. If those reports are accepted, then any positive effects of the incubation interval must have been the result of processes other than opportunistic assimilation or a fresh look. The unconscious is then brought in to provide an explanation.

However, it should also be noted the explanations that we are discussing focus on very different aspects of the incubation situation. Unconscious processing concentrates on the situation in which a person who has not been working on a problem suddenly has the solution come to mind – recall Poincaré stepping on the omnibus. The fresh-look hypothesis focuses on a different phenomenon – the possible occurrence of red herrings during

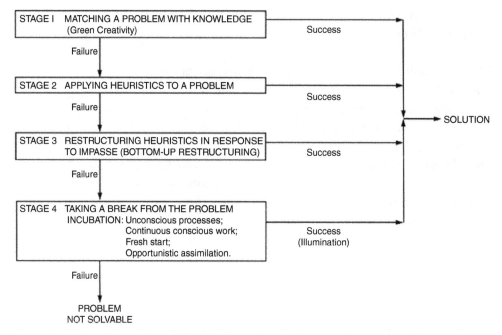

Figure 8.3 Elaborated problem-solving model: Analytic Thinking + Unconscious Incubation

problem-solving – and examines whether incubation effects might be the result of those red herrings being forgotten during the incubation period. Finally, the opportunistic-assimilation hypothesis deals with the possibility that, during the incubation interval, the person might discover something new in the environment that can be applied to the unsolved target problem (as we saw with De Mestral and Velcro). In other words, an "incubation" situation is not simple: several different processes can occur, which means that more than one of the theories proposed to explain illuminations can be correct in the sense of being able to explain some research finding(s). Each of the theories is designed to deal with a limited range of phenomena that may occur during incubation. Therefore, more than one explanation can be correct, depending on the circumstances. Rather than looking for *the* correct explanation for incubation, we should specify the circumstances in which each of those explanations is relevant to understanding how incubation works.

Figure 8.3 presents a summarized version of the model of problem-solving presented earlier that includes a place for processes occurring during incubation. If there has been no solution as a result of Stages 1–3, then, if the person takes a break from the problem, that may set the stage for other sorts of events, including unconscious thinking.

If we assume that unconscious processes may be active during creative thinking and lead to illuminations, that raises a further question: How does unconscious processing work? What are the specific mechanisms that might result in the discovery of a solution to a problem while one is thinking about something else?

How Might the Unconscious Work?

Poincaré's (1913) theory of unconscious processing, already discussed, proposed that new ideas arose out of "collisions" among "hooked atoms of thought." That view does not really add much to our understanding, as can be seen by the quotation marks in the last sentence. We know that those terms are not literal: there are no "collisions" occurring anywhere in our brains when we are thinking, nor are there hooked atoms in our heads. A different sort of proposal, one that has more recently gained support among researchers, is that, during unconscious processing, "activation" spreads in memory, from any active locations to others, along associative pathways (Gilhooly, 2016). That activation could result in links being forged between concepts that had not been linked before, producing a new idea.

As an example of how this mechanism might work, consider the memory network shown in Figure 8.4. That network represents a very small portion of a person's knowledge base. It consists of some concepts that the person is familiar with, represented by the words, and links between those concepts, represented by the lines. The length of the line between two

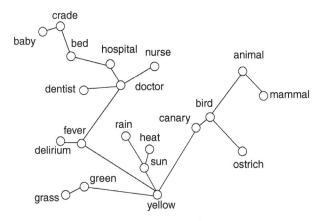

Figure 8.4 A semantic memory network

concepts represents the strength of the kink between them. So, for example, the concept "yellow" is linked strongly to "sun," and less strongly to "canary," and "fever." This theoretical analysis can be used to explain how unconscious processing might play a role in incubation in problem-solving.

When someone is looking at the words in a CRA problem, for example (see Table 8.3B), the concepts corresponding to those words would be activated, and that activation would spread along the links in the network. In order to solve the problem, activation would have to spread from the three words until it reached the solution, one word that they all were linked to. The reason that some CRA items are difficult is that the connection between one or more items and the solution word is so distant and/or so weak that the link might not be achieved. It has been proposed that during an incubation period activation can continue to spread, so that there is a chance that the required link will be achieved while the person is not attending to the problem (Gilhooly, 2016). This general conception has been applied more broadly. Consider the study of Baird et al. (2012), demonstrating that mind-wandering during an incubation period was related to increased problem-solving afterward. Baird et al. proposed that one possible explanation for their results was that mind-wandering allowed activation to spread throughout memory during the incubation period, whereas an unfilled break or a break filled with a demanding task interfered with spreading activation (see also Cai et al., 2009).

It should be noted, however, that "spreading activation" is also not very helpful in explaining what might be happening during incubation. First, no one has measured that "spread of activation" directly; researchers have simply postulated it to explain their results (see Hélie & Sun, 2010). Second, it is not clear *where* or *how* that activation would spread. Spreading activation occurs in semantic memory, which contains our knowledge of concepts. Presumably, during incubation, semantic memory is being used, as one deals with the concepts involved in the *distractor task*, for example. If so, then the "activation" from the items in the *target problem* should be wiped out by that distractor activity and there should be no support for the unconscious spreading activation that presumably occurs during incubation. That logic raises questions concerning how we might explain the operation of unconscious thinking. For now, it seems safest to say that "spreading activation" provides a suggestion of a theory of how unconscious processes might function in creative thinking but it needs to be much more fleshed out before it can be said to provide an explanation for incubation specifically and unconscious processing more generally.

Unconscious Processing in Incubation – Conclusions

Obviously, many questions remain here. One question, just discussed, focuses on exactly how unconscious thinking works. A second concerns precisely how unconscious processes might work with conscious analytic processes. Those questions are for the future, as, even though there has been interest in unconscious process for more than 100 years, rigorous research in this area is in relatively early stages. The future should hold some interesting developments concerning the processes – conscious and unconscious – underlying creative thinking. There are some thorny issues to be dealt with before we can say that we understand how unconscious processing might work during incubation. We now turn to another proposal concerning the processes underlying creative thinking, one that also goes beyond analytic thinking – the idea that psychopathology can facilitate creativity. That idea is called *genius and madness*.

9 | Genius and Madness

In Chapters 7 and 8, we critically examined two proposals that assumed that creative ideas were brought about through thinking outside the box: leaps of insight and unconscious thinking. In this chapter, we will focus on another long-standing hypothesis concerning the generation of new ideas: psychopathology plays a role in creativity. In ancient Greece, creative ideas were assumed to be gifts from the gods (see Chapter 2). An individual in the throes of creative activity was "out of her mind," in the sense that an outside source – the Muse – was providing the ideas. The person served as the *messenger* through which the ideas were presented. That idea was called *messengers of the gods* and the state of possession by the muses was called "divine madness." Over centuries, the notion of divine madness evolved into the view that *psychopathology* – mental illness – is the basis for creative thinking (Becker, 2014). I will call that view *genius and madness*.

Modern opinions on the relationship between creativity and psychopathology vary widely, ranging from the idea that psychopathology influences creativity to various degrees (e.g., Carson, 2018; Kyaga, 2014, 2018; Simonton, 2014) to the complete opposite – that is, that there is no relation whatsoever between genius and madness (e.g., Dietrich, 2014; Schlesinger, 2009, 2012). The fact that sophisticated researchers studying the same research question can come to opposite conclusions indicates that the question may be more complicated than it seems to be. The purpose of this chapter is to provide an overview of the complexities involved in trying to determine if there is a relationship between genius and madness, as well as to derive some conclusions concerning the specifics of that relationship.

Outline of the Chapter

We begin with a discussion of how one might try to test the hypothesis that psychopathology facilitates creativity. We will then turn to a review of the literature on genius and madness – specifically, an examination of the possible relationship between creativity and two disorders, bipolar disorder (manic-depressive disorder) and schizophrenia. Many researchers have concluded that mild forms of psychopathology, rather than full-blown disorder, may be related to creativity. We will examine the evidence for that conclusion. Finally, we will place the study of genius and madness in the broader social context to try to shed light on the wide range of factors that play a role in determining whether or not psychopathology and creativity are related.

How Might We Test the Hypothesis that Psychopathology Facilitates Creativity?

Let us begin by considering how a research psychologist would attempt to study the question of whether psychopathology *produces* or *causes* an increase in the capacity to think creatively. This can be called the *causal* question.

Hypothesis 1: Psychopathology Facilitates Creativity

How would one test Hypothesis 1? We can carry out a controlled experimental study. Take a large sample of individuals – say, a group of undergraduates – and randomly assign them to two groups. We make one group psychopathological – that is, mentally ill – and we carry out some neutral manipulation with the other group, the control group. We then test the two groups for creativity. If the psychopathological group performs better than the control group on our test, that would demonstrate that psychopathology increased creativity. However, that experiment cannot be carried out. It is unethical as well as immoral: one cannot set out to make people psychopathological. Even if we think that our research question – the possibility that psychopathology facilitates creativity – is of critical importance to the survival of the species, we still cannot carry out the study. Since we cannot approach the question of genius and madness directly through an experimental manipulation, we must approach it indirectly. We can turn first to a more basic question: Do psychopathology and creativity go together? We can study people who are creative, and measure whether they are psychopathological. We can also study people who exhibit psychopathology, and measure whether they are creative.

Historiometric Analysis of Genius and Madness

One study examining the possible relationship between genius and madness was carried out by Simonton (2014). Simonton analyzed a sample of 204 outstanding individuals, who had been studied earlier by Post (1994) and by Murray (2003). The individuals were categorized as scientists (n = 42 individuals), thinkers (e.g., philosophers; n = 23); writers (n = 49), artists (n = 40), and composers (n = 50). Information about those people's psychopathology came from Post, who studied "world-famous men" in Western civilization from the nineteenth and twentieth centuries, chosen because they had had biographies written about them. Post analyzed the biographies for the presence of psychopathology, rating each individual on a four-point scale: no psychopathology; mild; marked; and severe. Simonton used Post's scale as a measure (1–4) of the person's level of psychopathology. Murray's study was an examination of world history in which he attempted to assess the eminence, or importance, of individuals in various cultures at various periods of time. He used the amount of attention paid to a person in a large number of standard reference works as the measure of eminence, tabulating, for example, the total number of pages devoted to a person in those works. Simonton took Murray's measure of eminence to be equivalent to creativity and he then examined the relationship between level of psychopathology and level of eminence in each of Post's four groups.

The results of Simonton's (2014) analysis are shown in Figure 9.1. There were differences across groups in the curves relating psychopathology to eminence. The scientists showed a distinct inverted-U-shaped relationship between eminence and psychopathology: scientists in the mid-range of pathology attained the highest levels of eminence. For the other groups, the relationships were less strong. The artists and writers each showed linear relation, with a small slope; and the composers and thinkers showed perhaps weaker inverted-U-shaped relationships than did the scientists. Furthermore, for all of those groups except the scientists, the individuals with no psychopathology achieved the lowest levels of eminence.

Simonton (2014) also determined for each group the level of psychopathology that was related to the highest level of eminence. Simonton called that the "peak" level of psychopathology. The results, which can be determined from the curves in Figure 9.1A, are shown in Figure 9.1B. For the writers and artists, the peak was the maximum on Post's scale, which was not true for the other groups. Simonton summarized the different peaks across the groups in the following way:

> [S]cientists < composers < thinkers when it comes to predicting the optimal amount of psychopathology for the attainment of eminence.

A. Psychopathology and eminence.

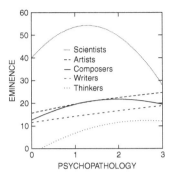

B. Peak psychopathology levels for different groups (psychopathology level associated with the highest level of eminence for the group; obtained from above curves).

Scientists – 1. 3

Composers – 2.0

Thinkers – 2.6

Writers – 3.0

Artists – 3.0

Figure 9.1 Simonton's (2014) results concerning creativity and psychopathology
A. Psychopathology and eminence graphs
B. Peak levels of psychopathology

> And all three of these field peaks fall below the "optimum" witnessed for writers and artists, namely, the most severe. (p. 57)

It is interesting that Simonton used the wording "the optimal amount of psychopathology for the attainment of eminence," which indicates that he believed that psychopathology played a *causal* role in the attainment of eminence. However, Simonton's study is a *correlational* study: all one has is a correlation between level of psychopathology and eminence. There is no basis for drawing a *causal* conclusion. It might be that achieving eminence produced the psychopathology. One reason for the ease with which causal conclusions are made in this area is that it seems very reasonable that there should be a cause–effect connection between psychopathology and creativity. It may be difficult to conceive of any other sort of relationship between those two factors. That is, how might achieving eminence cause madness? We will discuss that possibility in more detail later in the chapter.

Simonton (2014) did not examine the possible relationships between specific types of mental disorders and creativity. Let us now look at research that has investigated that question.

Bipolarity and Creativity

Much research investigating genius and madness has focused on the possible role of manic-depression, also known as *bipolar disorder*, in the creative-thinking process (for review, see Kaufmann & Kaufmann, 2014). In a pioneering analysis of bipolar disorder, Kraepelin (1921) speculated that thought processes might become quicker and more broad during mania. Such changes might promote creative thinking.

The Bipolar Spectrum

Bipolar disorder is a spectrum of conditions ranging in symptoms and severity (see Table 9.1). The critical component of all of those conditions is change in *mood* or *affect* – that is, in *emotional state*. In Bipolar Disorder I, the classic manic-depression, the individual can alternate between periods of great elation (mania) and depression (Goodwin & Jamison, 1990; Jamison, 1993). Manic episodes frequently occur following psychological or social stressors, such as conflict at work or in one's family. During the manic period, a person can work almost without sleep and may feel that he or she can do anything. Unfortunately, a person in the throes of mania also may undertake grandiose schemes without planning, such as investing savings in risky business ventures, or marrying someone they have just met. One characteristic of manic people is that they feel that ideas flow very easily and that also has led some theorists, beginning with Kraepelin (1921), to postulate that mania may facilitate creative thinking.

The other side of the mood-disorder coin is the devastating low of depression. In the typical case of Bipolar I disorder, in addition to mania, an individual suffers from major depression. The depressed individual experiences a loss of interest and/or pleasure in life; getting out of bed and washing and dressing in the morning may be too much. There may also be feelings of worthlessness and guilt, and decreased energy, as well as thoughts of death and suicide. Many depressed individuals attempt suicide, with a significant proportion (approximately 15 percent) succeeding. Bipolar disorder is more common among first-degree biological relatives of bipolar patients than among the general population, and current opinion

Table 9.1 *The bipolar spectrum*

	Positive Affect State			Negative Affect State		
Condition	Mania (severe)	Hypomania (milder)	Euthymic personality (normal)	Major depression (severe)	Dysthymia (milder)	Dysthymic personality (normal)
Bipolar I	X			X		
Bipolar II		X		X		
Cyclothymia		X			X	
Normal personalities			X			X
Cyclothymic personality			X			X

is that the bipolar spectrum of disorders has a strong genetic component (Jamison, 1993; Kaufmann & Kaufmann, 2014; Kinney & Richards, 2014).

Other conditions on the bipolar spectrum differ from Bipolar I, in the pattern of symptoms and their severity. A patient suffering from Bipolar II disorder also typically cycles through positive and negative moods, but the positive mood state is *hypomania* (literally, "below mania"), a state not as severe as full mania; the negative state is full depression, however. A still-less severe condition, *cyclothymia* ("cycling mind") is defined by the individual's cycling through hypomania and negative moods (*dysthymia*) that are less severe than major depression. At the least-severe end of the spectrum are conditions in which a person free from psychopathology has a personality marked by typical mood coloring. The *euthymic personality* is characterized by an overall positive feeling tone (someone who is always "up"); the *dysthymic personality* is marked by negative feeling tone (someone who is always gloomy). *Cyclothymic personality* is marked by changes between those moods.

Originally, it was hypothesized that there might be a link between creativity and the full-blown mania of Bipolar I (for review see Jamison, 1993), although it also has been suggested that there might be a link between depression and creativity (Kaufmann & Kaufmann, 2014). More recently, focus has shifted to the possibility that milder forms of mood disorder are related to creativity. Researchers have attempted to provide support for that hypothesis in several ways. First, researchers have attempted to show that there is a tendency for creative individuals to suffer from mood disorders. Approaching the issue from the other side, researchers have also attempted to demonstrate that individuals suffering from mood disorders are more creative than are other groups. Finally, there have been attempts to show that being in a "creative" state has the same characteristics as being in a manic state.

Mood Disorders in Creative Individuals

Mania and Creativity

Jamison (e.g., 1989, 1993) studied the lives of many world-famous creative individuals and concluded that many of them suffered from bipolar disorder. One example is the poet Lord Byron (Jamison, 1993), who led a turbulent life in which many episodes had the out-of-control up-and-down aspects of bipolar disorder. Of course, Jamison was not able to diagnose Byron's psychological state directly, since he died in 1824, but she used historical evidence, for example, reports from Byron's contemporaries about his behavior as well as medical records to support her analysis.

Other studies, examining living individuals, also reported a link between bipolar disorder and increased creative activity. Jamison (1989) interviewed a sample of forty-seven British artists and writers (poets, playwrights, novelists, and biographers) to determine their history of mental illness as well as to ascertain any pattern in their mood changes and creative productivity. More than 38 percent of the sample had been treated for some affective illness and 30 percent reported relatively severe mood swings, some of which lasted for extended periods of time. The biographers, whom we might classify as being engaged in less-creative activities than the other writers, reported fewer disorders and less severity of symptoms. Participants also reported that they experienced intense productive and creative episodes, which involved increases in enthusiasm, energy, speed and fluency of thoughts as well as elevated mood and sense of well-being. Those characteristics corresponded to the diagnostic criteria for hypomanic episodes in the *Diagnostic and Statistical Manual* of the American Psychiatric Association (the DSM), the guidebook for classifying mental disorders. Almost all the writers stated that those mood and feeling changes were very important in the development of their work. Jamison discussed the possibility that the changes in cognition found during hypomanic states – speed, fluency, and flexibility of thinking – are critical to creativity. In addition, the emotional fluctuations occurring during mood disorders might serve to provide creative writers and artists with material for their work.

However, Jamison also noted that states of creative production might be psychologically similar to hypomanic states for either of two reasons. There might be a common process underlying both or there might be just a coincidental surface similarity. In addition, the fact that artists and writers reported those changes in mood may reflect nothing more than that those people might be more sensitive to their mood changes than is the general population. If that were true, then there might be no specific causal link at all between mood change and creative production. This is an important issue that we will return to later: Should we accept at face value a creative individual's report of "symptoms"?

Depression and Creativity

If bipolar disorder is linked to creative thinking, then one might expect to find creative individuals suffering from depression. Jamison (1993) presented evidence that creative individuals, especially poets, suffer from depression to a degree much higher than one finds in the general population. In Table 9.2 are listed the eight poets born in the twentieth century whose works are included in *The Oxford Book of American Verse*, a highly regarded reference work. Of those eight, *five* committed suicide, a rate much higher than in the general population, which provides evidence for the prevalence of depression among poets. Kaufman (2001, 2003) has

Table 9.2 *Poets and suicide: partial listing of major twentieth-century American poets, born between 1895 and 1935, with documented histories of manic-depressive illness (from Goodwin & Jamison, 1990)*

Poet	Pulitzer Prize in poetry	Treated for major depressive illness	Treated for mania	Committed suicide
Hart Crane (1899–1932)		X	X	X
Theodore Roethke (1908–1963)	X	X	X	
Delmore Schwartz (1913–1966)		X	X	
John Berryman (1914–1972)	X	X	X	X
Randall Jarrell (1914–1965)		X	X	X
Robert Lowell (1917–1977)	X	X	X	
Anne Sexton (1928–1974)	X	X	X	X
Sylvia Plath[a]	X	X		X

[a] Plath, although not treated for mania, was probably Bipolar II.

provided additional evidence concerning suicide and early death among poets, which he has called the "Sylvia Plath Effect," referring to a young poet who committed suicide.

Creativity in Mood-Disordered Individuals

The possibility that mood disorder affects creativity has also been addressed by asking if being mood-disordered raises the likelihood that one will be creative. This question has been addressed by studying whether normal individuals who might carry the genes for mood disorder are more creative than people who do not carry those genes.

Andreasen (1987) gave structured diagnostic interviews to thirty creative writers who were faculty members at the prestigious University of Iowa Writers' Workshop and to thirty control participants matched to the writers for age, sex, and educational status. The writers showed more affective disorder and more bipolar disorder than the controls. These results are comparable to those of Jamison (1993) already discussed. Andreasen also examined the frequency of mental illness and the prevalence of creative achievement in the first-degree relatives of the writers and of the controls. Andreasen asked the interviewees about the lives of their relatives. The relatives of the writers showed significantly more mood disorder than the relatives of the controls and they also showed higher levels of creative accomplishment, such as having had a solo show of paintings. Andreasen concluded that a tendency toward mood disorder and a tendency toward creativity might be traits that run together in families and both might be genetically based. She also noted that the findings indicated that there might be an advantage for society – increased creative accomplishment – brought about by the prevalence of the genes for psychopathology in the human gene pool. This creative advantage compensates at the societal level for the negative aspects of psychopathology on the lives of the affected individuals.

A study by Richards et al. (1988; see also Kinney & Richards, 2014) further investigated the possibility that there is a compensatory advantage to bipolar illness in the form of increased creativity. The study examined the prevalence of creative accomplishment in bipolar individuals (individuals suffering from Bipolar I or cyclothymia), their normal relatives, and a control group of individuals who had no personal or familial link to bipolar disorder. Creativity was measured using the Lifetime Creativity Scales, which ask the person about creative accomplishments throughout life in professional activities as well as in other aspects of life, such as hobbies. Individuals suffering from cyclothymia and the normal relatives of the Bipolar I individuals had achieved the highest levels of creative accomplishment. The individuals diagnosed as suffering from Bipolar I were no more creative than were the normal controls. Richards and colleagues (Kinney & Richards, 2014) proposed that the relatives of bipolar individuals carried some of the genes underlying the disorder and those genes facilitated creative accomplishment.

The Inverted-U Hypothesis

Kinney and Richards (2014; Richards et al., 1988) proposed that the relation between bipolar spectrum and creativity is an inverted-U, as shown in Figure 9.2. Creativity is related to possession of some but not all of the genes that underlie bipolar disorder. Starting with no inherited tendency toward bipolarity, increasing levels of susceptibility to the disorder are, up to some midpoint, positively related to creativity. Beyond that point, the presence of full-blown psychopathology produces psychological and behavioral changes that interfere with creative functioning.

Mood Disorders and Creativity: Critical Analysis

The results just discussed, while impressive in showing that bipolarity and creativity may be connected, are subject to two sets of criticisms, one methodological and one logical.

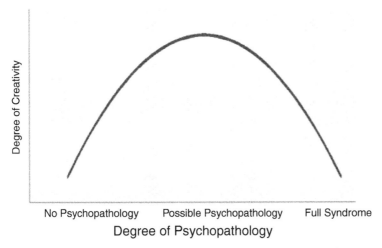

Figure 9.2 Relation between psychopathology and creativity: inverted-U curve

Studies of Bipolarity and Creativity: Methodological Issues

Several researchers have asked questions about the design of the studies that we have just reviewed. Schlesinger (2009, 2012) has raised a number of objections concerning the research of Andreasen (1987; see also Rothenberg, 1990). Andreasen did all the interviewing of the participants in her study, which means that she knew the status of each person – famous writer or control – whom she interviewed. Second, she designed the interview and did not make it public, so we cannot determine if what she asked was biased in any way. Third, we have no idea how reliable the results of her interviews were. We do not know if others would agree with her conclusions and we do not know if she would have produced the same results if she did the assessment a second time. There should have been an independent interviewer blind to the goals of the study. Schlesinger (2012) raised similar objections to Jamison's (1989, 1993) research linking bipolarity and creativity (see also Rothenberg, 1990). In addition, some of the groups studied by Jamison were very small, which raises questions about whether we can generalize from them.

The studies of Kinney and Richards (2014; Richards et al., 1988) and their associates are less subject to those criticisms. First, diagnoses were carried out by clinicians not familiar with the study and who did not know the status of the people they were interviewing. However, the studies of Kinney and Richards did have a problem with relatively small numbers of participants in the various conditions. Those problems were remedied in two studies by Kyaga et al. (2011, 2013) who used Swedish census registers to examine the relation between psychopathology and creativity for essentially the entire population of Sweden from 1973 to 2003. The Swedish authorities provided anonymous sets of data to the researchers. Health records were used to determine diagnoses of psychopathology for individuals, and the records included links to family members, which allowed the researchers to group patients and their families together for analysis. In addition, information about occupations allowed the researchers to examine the relation between psychopathology and "creativity" of occupation. For example, being a university professor carrying out scientific research was classified as a creative occupation, as were careers in the arts. There was also a comparison group made up of accountants and auditors, who were deemed noncreative, and a control group made up of randomly selected individuals who had no relatives who had been diagnosed with psychopathology.

People with bipolar disorder (30,000 individuals) were overrepresented in the creative occupations, mainly in the arts. The patients' close relatives, who had not been diagnosed as suffering from bipolar disorder, were also represented more frequently in the creative professions, although in this case it was more in science. Patients diagnosed with depression showed a different pattern: they and their relatives were *less* likely to appear in creative professions. No relations were found between the relatives of the accountants and auditors and the creative professions. The large-scale studies of Kyaga et al. (2011, 2013) provide support for the inverted-U hypothesis of the relation between bipolarity and creativity.

Studies of Bipolarity and Creativity: Logical Issues

A problem with all the studies reviewed in the last section, one that has already been raised, is that they are *correlational* studies and therefore cannot demonstrate a *causal* link between psychopathology and creativity. Furthermore, there are other possible links between bipolarity and creativity. For example, it might be that the relationship between creativity and bipolarity is the result of *creativity causing bipolarity*. There is evidence, which will be discussed later, that supports that possibility.

Beyond Correlations: Does Mania Increase Creativity of Thought?

In order to try to go beyond correlational analyses and test the hypothesis that being in a manic state increases the creativity of the thought processes, I carried out an analysis of the creative productivity of classical composer Robert Schumann (Weisberg, 1994), who is generally believed to have suffered from bipolar disorder (Slater & Mayer, 1959). Schumann experienced periods of manic elation, followed by bleak periods of depression in which he tried more than once to kill himself. He spent time in asylums, as did other members of his immediate family, and he died in an asylum of what may have been self-induced starvation. Slater and Meyer carried out a retrospective psychiatric diagnosis of Schumann's mental condition, based on doctors' records and other historical documents such as letters of Schumann and his acquaintances, and they concluded that he probably suffered from bipolar disorder. Slater and Meyer presented evidence that Schumann's disorder affected his work, as shown in Figure 9.3A, which shows the number of compositions Schumann completed in each year of

A. Productivity

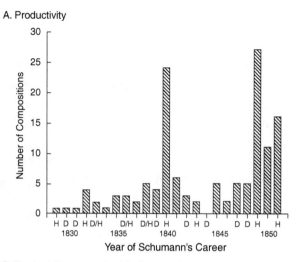

B. Productivity summarized for hypomanic versus depressed years.

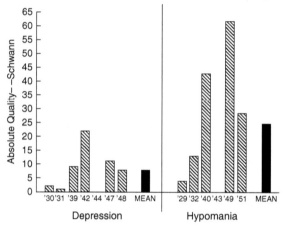

C. Quality summarized for hypomanic versus depressed years.

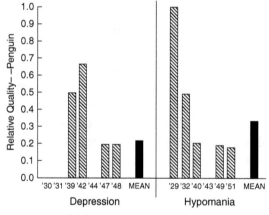

Figure 9.3 Schumann's productivity and quality as a function of his mood. Weisberg, R. W. (1994). Genius and madness? A quasi-experimental test of the hypothesis that manic-depression increases creativity. Psychological Science, 5: 361–367. Copyright © 1994 (Sage Publications Inc.).

A. Schumann's productivity over his career

B. Quantity summarized for manic versus depressive years

C. Quality summarized for manic versus depressive years

his career and the diagnosis of his prevailing mood state for that year. As is summarized in Figure 9.3B, Schumann was approximately five times more productive during his manic years. (Slater and Meyer used the term "hypomanic.") There thus seems to be no doubt that Schumann's energy and motivation to work increased greatly during the years when he was emotionally "high."

However, the results in Figure 9.3B do not say anything about whether Schumann was producing *more creative* compositions during his manic years; they only show that he was producing *more* of them. In order to go that next step, I examined whether Schumann's changing mood states might have affected his compositional process (Weisberg, 1994). In order to carry out such an analysis, one first needs a measure of the "quality" of a composition, and a number of such measures have been used by past researchers. One can, for example, ask experts, such as professional musicians and critics, to judge how good each composition is. I took a simpler measure, one that had been used by Hayes (1989) in his study on the Ten-Year Rule in creative development, discussed in Chapter 6. I counted the number of recordings available for each composition; more recordings indicated a better work. That measure is based on the opinions of critics, musicians, and the music-buying public. It should also be noted that that measure of quality correlates highly with other measures, such as how often a composition is discussed in critical analyses of music. Thus, the number of recordings is more than simply a measure of "popularity" of compositions.

If Schumann's periods of mania improved his creative thought processes, then compositions produced during his manic years should be recorded more frequently on average than compositions produced during the depressive years. The results of this analysis are shown in Figure 9.3C, and they do not support that hypothesis: compositions from manic years were *not*, on average, recorded more frequently than those from depressive years. In Schumann's case, the creative thought process was not changed by bipolar disorder, although his motivation to compose, as measured by the number of compositions produced in a given year, certainly seems to have increased.

Ramey and Weisberg (2004) carried out a similar analysis of the career of the poet Emily Dickinson, who also has been diagnosed retrospectively as having suffered from bipolar disorder (McDermott, 2000, 2001). As with Schumann, the results did not provide support for the hypothesis that mania increases the creativity of the thought processes. Poems produced during Dickinson's manic years did not appear more frequently in several poetry collections, which was our measure of the quality of a poem. There was some evidence that Dickinson's thought processes might have been changed by depression, however. In conclusion, two studies that have tried to more directly test the notion that mania increases creativity have not provided strong support for that idea.

Obviously, two small-scale studies, each examining one individual, cannot settle an issue as complicated as this, but these results, if valid, tell us something about the creative process. Contrary to much popular belief, madness, at least in the form of mania, may not have a positive effect on creative thought. That conclusion is consistent with the inverted-U hypothesis of Kinney and Richards (2014). Perhaps more importantly, the results in Figure 9.3C may be useful to creative individuals who suffer from bipolar disorder. Bipolar disorder can often be brought under control using the drug lithium carbonate. However, many individuals in creative professions who have been diagnosed with bipolar disorder do not take their medication, because they are concerned that their creativity will be wiped out (Jamison, 1993; Kinney & Richards, 2014). If it is true that mania only increases *output* without affecting *quality* of creative work then taking lithium will not wipe out the person's capacity to produce high-quality works. One might produce fewer works, but one could still produce good ones. In addition, taking lithium might save an individual from depression and what it can bring. Schou (1979) found that mania may not increase creativity and that taking lithium may not wipe it out, but more than one study is obviously needed here (see also Shaw, Mann, Stokes & Manevitz, 1986).

Might Creativity Cause Mania?

Let us assume for the sake of discussion that the correlation between bipolarity and creativity is real – that is, there is a tendency for creative individuals either to suffer from or be related to individuals who suffer from some form of bipolar disorder. The next step is to establish a causal link between them. It has usually been assumed, as we have seen, that any causal link between psychopathology and creativity must involve the psychopathological state affecting the creative process (e.g., Jamison, 1993). However, it is possible that the causal link might be in the opposite direction (Depue & Ianoco, 1989; Johnson et al., 2000; Alloy & Nusslock, 2019). It has been suggested that hard work and success in an area that results in creative output might stimulate the development of bipolar disorder.

As we have seen, there is evidence that there is a genetic basis underlying the tendency to develop bipolar disorder (Jamison, 1993; Kinney & Richards, 2014), and Depue and Ianoco (1989) have proposed that that inherited tendency may involve an overly sensitive *behavioral activation system*, which responds in a hyperactive manner to certain sorts of life events, producing full-blown mania. The behavioral activation system can be triggered by such events as goal striving and attainment (Johnson et al., 2000; Alloy & Nusslock, 2019). For example, completion of creative work might play a role in the development of bipolar disorder, rather than the converse. Many other aspects of the creative life also are stressful, such as a writer's having to submit works to editors for critical comment or an artist's having to display works to perhaps critical reviewers and audiences. Those factors might also trigger episodes in people with a hypersensitive behavioral activation system.

There is also evidence that attaining broader success in a creative field can lead to psychopathology. Schaller (1997) studied the effects of fame on three individuals: the popular songwriter Cole Porter, the rock musician Kurt Cobain, and the writer John Cheever. Schaller analyzed the effects of achieving fame on their creative output and, in Cheever's case, on alcoholism. All three became more "self-conscious" after they achieved fame, as seen in their writings. The songs of Porter and Cobain contained more first-person pronouns and Cheever's stories were more likely to be written in the first-person. More relevant to the present concerns, Cheever, who was alcoholic, kept a diary, which allowed Schaller to examine the relationship between his alcohol use and the changing level of his fame. Increasing fame and alcohol use were correlated in Cheever's life, which is consistent with the idea that fame stimulated his drinking. Although that result is correlational, it is interesting in the context of the finding, just discussed, that achievement of goals can result in development of mania (Johnson et al., 2000; Alloy & Nusslock, 2019). If there is a causal link in Schaller's correlation, it provides further evidence that another psychopathological state – alcohol addiction – can be triggered by environmental events. That would be a further caution regarding the tendency to assume that psychopathology is the causal agent when developing explanations for any relations observed between psychopathology and creativity. It should be noted, however, that there were only three individuals investigated by Schaller and there was no control group in the study, comprised of noncreative individuals.

Possible Links between Bipolarity and Creativity: Conclusions

As far as an understanding of the creative thinking process is concerned, we can say that the evidence for a relationship between genius and madness, in the form of bipolarity, is only correlational and claims for a cause-and-effect relationship have had weak support in two studies that attempted to go beyond correlation (Weisberg, 1994; Ramey & Weisberg, 2004). There seems to be no doubt that the extreme mood changes experienced by bipolar individuals affect their motivation to work and hence their output. However, the creative thought processes might not be changed by mental illness, at least not by full bipolarity. There has been support for the inverted-U hypothesis, which proposes that possession of some of the genes for bipolar disorder is related to creativity. We can extend this examination further by examining the role in people who are nonpathological of affect in creativity.

The Role of Affect in Creativity

The critical characteristic of the bipolar spectrum is *extreme change in mood*. Therefore, when one is examining the possible influence of bipolarity on creativity, one could say that one is examining the possible influence of strong mood states on creativity. There is some evidence from the laboratory that changes in affect, especially increases in positive affect, among nonpathological people can play a positive role in creative thinking. Pioneering research by Isen and colleagues (see Isen, 2008, for review) examined the influence of *induced mood* – changes in research participants' moods created by researchers' activities – on creative thinking. In these studies, undergraduates were exposed to a procedure designed to change their mood (usually, to increase positive affect); for example, people might watch a comedy film or they might be given an unexpected prize on arriving at the laboratory. Isen and colleagues have shown that a number of different behaviors, some of which are related to creativity, are affected by such manipulations.

In one study (Isen & Daubman, 1984), induced positive affect resulted in participants providing more varied word associations to stimulus words than did control participants (Isen, 2008). Those varied associations might be expected to facilitate creative thinking. Also, Isen, Daubman, and Nowicki (1987) found that induced positive affect also facilitated problem-solving. Isen and colleagues interpreted those sorts of results as indicating that positive affect serves as a retrieval cue in memory, and it cues memories with positive-feeling tone, as well as cuing a large amount of material. This cuing effect results in more varied responses, since there is more material to work with, which will facilitate creative thinking.

Lubart and Getz (e.g., 1997) have also theorized that emotional content of memories can play a role in creative thinking. They assumed that the emotional content of a situation is stored as part of one's memory for that situation. Emotional content can then serve as a retrieval cue, to assist in recalling memories, and can serve as a link between a present experience and memories that might not be related to it in terms of formal content. In Chapter 1, I discussed Goya's *Disasters of War* as a possible source for some of the characters in Picasso's *Guernica*. It was suggested that Picasso might have thought of Goya's work at that time because of the overlap in emotion between the two projects. That suggestion is consistent with these analyses.

Emotion and Creativity

Kaufmann and Kaufmann (2014) interpret the influence of affect on creative thinking, based on the "cognitive tuning" theory of Schwarz (1990; Schwarz & Clore, 2003). In this theory, emotions serve to inform a person about the current state of the environment. Positive affect indicates that things are satisfactory, while negative affect (fear, anger) indicates that something is wrong. Based on those emotional signals, the person would then process the situation in different ways. A problematic situation, which arouses negative affect, would be treated carefully and systematically ("tight" thinking), with little risk taken. The person would persist in using any familiar ways of dealing with the situation, which would seem to work against thinking in a creative or exploratory manner. A positive situation, in contrast, is "safe" and can be treated in a more relaxed manner. Therefore, situations that produce positive affect would be more likely to draw a more creative mode of processing, which the experimental and clinical research seems to indicate. However, negative mood might also have positive effects in certain situations, where it can increase a person's persistence in following a familiar path toward solution (Baas et al., 2008, 2016).

Milder Forms of Mood Disorder and Creativity: Conclusions

The research we have reviewed so far supports the conclusion that there is a positive relationship between creativity and milder forms of mood disorder (Kinney & Richards, 2014; Kyaga, 2018). Full-blown bipolar disorder may not be positively related to creative thinking (Ramey & Weisberg, 2004; Weisberg, 1994), but milder forms of the bipolar spectrum, including hypomanic states or states of positive affect, may in a variety of ways be related to creativity. We now turn to an examination of the possibility that another psychopathological state, schizophrenia, is related to creativity.

Schizophrenia and Creativity

Over the last thirty years, researchers have concentrated on the relation between bipolar disorder and creativity. More recently, however, interest has turned to the possibility that aspects of schizophrenia may be related to creativity (Kinney & Richards, 2014).

The Schizophrenia Spectrum

As with bipolar disorder, schizophrenia is looked upon as being a spectrum of disorders (Schuldberg, 2001; Kinney & Richards, 2014), ranging from full-blown psychosis, to less-severe levels of mental disorder, to personality characteristics in nonpathological individuals (see Table 9.3). Schizophrenic psychosis is characterized by a cutting-off of the individual from reality. Individuals suffering from schizophrenia are often withdrawn from the world, with *flat affect* – a lack of emotional responsiveness or inappropriate emotional responsiveness to events – and a general nonresponsiveness to external events. Schizophrenics also experience

Table 9.3 *Schizophrenia spectrum*

Increasing Severity	Disorder	Symptoms
1	Schizoid personality	Very introverted and voluntarily withdrawn from social interaction
2	Schizotypal personality	Schizoid symptoms + magical thinking and odd behavior
3	Schizophrenia	Schizotypal + psychosis (loss of touch with reality; delusions; hallucinations).
4	Schizoaffective disorder	Schizophrenia + mood disorder

hallucinations and delusions, further cutting them off from the world. Schizophrenia is characterized as a disorder of thinking. Two kinds of thought disorder can be seen in schizophrenics: disorders in *content* and in *form* of thought.

Disordered *content* of thought is seen in ideas that are false, delusional, deviant, and bizarre (Schuldberg, 2001). It should be noted that delusions are not limited to schizophrenia: some individuals suffering from bipolar disorder also suffer from delusions. The disordered *form* of schizophrenic thought is seen when one examines how thoughts flow. Schizophrenic thought shows illogical patterns in thinking. As an example, a male schizophrenic might reason as follows. You are a beautiful woman; I am beautiful as well; therefore, I am a woman. Schizophrenic thought is also characterized by loose associations, where the link from one thought to another cannot be followed by another person. Milder disorders along the schizophrenia spectrum are *schizotypal* and *schizoid* personality disorders (Sass, 2001; Kinney & Richards, 2014). Individuals suffering from these disorders show emotional coldness and difficulty in maintaining intimacy in relations, which is sometimes seen as social anxiety. They also show unconventionality or eccentricity in behavior, which can be seen as a belief in special powers, such as the ability to sense events before they occur or to read others' thoughts.

Schizophrenia and Creativity

Recent examinations of the relation between schizophrenia and creativity have followed the lead of studies of bipolarity and creativity, concentrating on milder forms of the disorder. Full-blown schizophrenia, with its delusions, hallucinations, and lack of engagement with the world, would seem to be antithetical to creative thinking. Kinney and Richards (2014) used the Lifetime Creativity Scales to examine creative accomplishment in a unique set of individuals: each was a nonschizophrenic person with one parent who suffered from schizophrenia; and each individual had been adopted and raised by nonschizophrenic individuals. It has been concluded that, like bipolarity, schizophrenia has a strong genetic component. Thus, analogous to the discussion of bipolarity, it was assumed that the set of adopted individuals with one schizophrenic parent carried some of the genes for schizophrenia but not the full complement, since they, unlike their parent, did not suffer from the disorder. The adopted individuals with one schizophrenic parent were each matched – for age, sex, age at adoption, and socioeconomic status – with an adopted individual who had no family history of schizophrenia.

Compared with the matched control group, the adopted-out offspring with one biological schizophrenic parent exhibited higher levels of peak creative accomplishment on the Lifetime Creativity Scales (Kinney & Richards, 2014). Furthermore, when the creativity levels were examined further, it was found that those individuals who exhibited more schizophrenic traits – but who, it must be emphasized, were *not* schizophrenic – exhibited the highest levels of creativity. That is, the highest levels of creative accomplishment were shown by those adoptees who exhibited the schizophrenic symptoms of magical thinking, odd thinking, and recurring illusions. Furthermore, and to the surprise of the researchers, the relationship between schizophrenic tendencies and creative accomplishment also held in the matched control group: nonschizophrenic individuals in the control group who exhibited milder symptoms of schizophrenia were more creative than control-group members who did not.

Kyaga and colleagues (2013; Kyaga, 2018) also examined the relationship between schizophrenia and creativity, as part of their large-scale study of creativity and psychopathology in Sweden. The results of the analysis of schizophrenic patients and their families provide some support for the inverted-U hypothesis. Schizophrenic patients were found in creative professions at a rate not different from baseline. Nonschizophrenic relatives of those patients, in contrast, were more frequent than baseline in creative professions.

In summary, the results of studies examining the relationship between schizophrenia and creativity support those found with the bipolar spectrum (Kinney & Richards, 2014; Kyaga, 2018). Individuals with subclinical tendencies toward psychopathology achieve more creative accomplishments than do control subjects. In addition, that link seems to be genetically based, since it is seen in adopted-out children of parents suffering from psychopathology (Kinney & Richards, 2014).

If we conclude that there is a positive relationship between milder forms of bipolarity and schizophrenia and creative accomplishment, we are led to the question of the mechanisms through which psychopathology and creativity might be related. As we have seen, many researchers take the correlational results that we have reviewed and conclude that there are causal connections between psychopathology and creativity. However, there is no justification for that causal inference. As has been mentioned, there are other possible explanations for that correlation. We should therefore consider what the possible underlying connections might be between subclinical aspects of psychopathology and creative accomplishment. We will first examine the possibility that the milder forms of psychopathology contain cognitive components that can contribute to creative thinking.

Shared Vulnerability between Creativity and Psychopathology

Carson (2014, 2018) has proposed a broad-ranging analysis of how psycho-pathology might affect creative thinking. She begins with a familiar idea: that there seems to be a creative benefit of a "little bit" of psychopathology (Carson, 2014, p. 262). Carson's model, outlined in Table 9.4, proposes that there is a set of "vulnerability factors" shared by psychopathology and creativity. Those factors serve to increase access to material normally not available to the thought processes, which can facilitate the development of ideas that otherwise could not be produced (Mednick, 1962). In addition, there is another set of factors, some of which can put a person at risk for psychopathology and others that are protective from psychopathology. Whether the person will become mentally ill or nonpathological and creative depends on the specific mix of risk versus protective factors that the person possesses. The protective factors allow the person to control the ideation process, so that he or she can keep things from getting out of hand, which the person who suffers from psychopathology cannot do.

Vulnerability Factors

The first vulnerability factor is cognitive disinhibition. (See center column in Table 9.4.) In most of our cognitive activities, is usually important to

Table 9.4 *Carson's (2014) shared vulnerability model of creativity and psychopathology*

Risk Factors	Shared Vulnerability	Protective Factors
	Cognitive Disinhibition	
	Preference for novelty	
	Hyperconnectivity	
Low IQ		High IQ
Working Memory Deficits		Working Memory Skills
Perseveration (Rigidity)		Cognitive Flexibility

Psychopathology   **Creativity**

keep unwanted material from breaking into attention and interfering with the ongoing task. An *inhibitory* process usually works to bring that about. As an example (Carson, 2014, pp. 265–266), let us say that a church clock chimes the hour, twenty-four hours a day, near your bedroom window. When you first moved into your house, the clock awakened you whenever it chimed. After living near the clock for a while, you ignore it and can sleep through the night. Now you have been hired for a job that requires that you get up early. You set your alarm clock, which chimes when it is supposed to. In the past, your alarm had been effective in waking you. However, as the result of the inhibition of the response to the *clock chime*, you now sleep through *your alarm*. A person with cognitive ***dis***inhibition would have been awakened by the alarm. Such a person would, in general, experience more stimuli entering consciousness, which in the right circumstances could play a role in producing novel ideas.

The second vulnerability factor is preference for novelty (Carson, 2014, 2018). Novelty-seeking, searching for new things in the world, is associated with alcohol addiction. However, novelty-seeking can also result in a person being motivated to carry out work, especially creative work, where the product can be novel. Creative individuals generally prefer novel stimuli and will seek out the new rather than the old. The final factor, hyper-connectivity – increased connectivity – refers to connections among brain areas that are not usually linked. There is evidence that bipolar patients are characterized by hyper-connectivity between brain areas, which might also provide ideas – remote associations – that the typically connected brain would not be able to produce, which would support creativity.

Risk/Protective Factors

As shown in the left-hand column of Table 9.4, there are three risk factors for psychopathology and, in the right-hand column, correspond-ing protective factors that support creativity. The first risk factor is low IQ; individuals suffering from mental illness typically test lower in IQ than control individuals. As seen in the right-hand column of Table 9.4, high IQ is a protective factor. The second factor centers on working memory: a person exhibiting psychopathology tends to be lower in working-memory and executive-functioning skills than a person free from psychopathology. High working-memory skills are protective from psychopathology. Finally, a person suffering from psychopathology will tend to exhibit rigidity in behavior, tending to persevere on paths once they begin. The non-mentally ill creative person, in contrast, will show flexibility in strategies for approaching tasks and will be able to switch attention from one stimulus to another.

The Shared-Vulnerability Model: Summary and Questions

Carson's (2014, 2018) model provides an explanation for how creative people are able to produce novel ideas and how that ability is related to psychopathology. Novel ideas come about because the vulnerabilities allow more information to be available for processing, which raises the probability that new ideas will arise. In the creative person, access to that additional information is under the control of protective factors – high IQ, working-memory skills, and cognitive flexibility – which enable the person to avoid being overwhelmed by the rush of information. The person who suffers from psychopathology, in contrast, cannot control the flow of information, which leads to the person being overwhelmed by what can be seen as a flood of information.

Carson's (2014, 2018) model presents an explanation for how creative ideas come about and for why creativity and psychopathology might be related. The model assumes that creative thinking requires access to ideas that are not available in normal circumstances, a version of the idea that creativity depends on thinking outside of the box, building on Mednick (1962). However, if the analysis of creative thinking presented so far in this book is on the right track – that is, if creativity is based on analytic thinking – then we do not need to explain how the creative person can have access to ideas that other people cannot have access to. If analytic thinking serves as the basis for creativity, then there is no such "privileged" access. That does not mean that we should reject Carson's model. Before we accept it, however, we should look carefully at the assumptions that it is based on, most importantly assumptions concerning how creative thinking works. Given the questions just raised about the cognitive aspects of Carson's model, it becomes interesting to examine other possible linkages between psychopathology and creativity.

How Is Psychopathology Related to Creativity? Another Look at Schizophrenia

Several researchers (Becker, 1978, 2001, 2014; Sass, 2001; see also Weisberg, 2006) have proposed that there are links between psychopathology and creativity that go beyond aspects of creative thinking and are based on very different factors, such as the reasons for a person's choice of career path. Furthermore, questions have been raised about whether the link between genius and madness is based on a set of false assumptions (Becker, 2014). These discussions take us far beyond the questions we have examined so far and are worth investigating.

Psychological Factors and Creative Achievement

Sass (2001) has examined factors that might play a role in determining why psychopathological symptoms are related to creative achievement. He has proposed that there are certain characteristics of the *postmodern* and *post-postmodern* movements in the arts that might increase the likelihood that individuals who exhibit some schizophrenic symptoms would participate in them. Those movements, which developed during the second half of the twentieth century, are noted for a "coolness" and an "ironic" posture, as the artist maintains an attitude of remove from the world so as to comment on it as an outsider. A clear example of an individual taking such a position would be Andy Warhol. Those characteristics – coolness, irony, and remove – also describe the individual who has the schizotypal personality, so such individuals might find the postmodern art world a comfortable environment. Perhaps the reason more people with schizoid-type personalities are in art is because they feel comfortable with the idea of being an artist.

Sass (2001) also noted that the artists whom Jamison (e.g., 1993) discussed as probably suffering from bipolar disorder were typically members of the Romantic movement, in which a passionate involvement in one's art was an expected characteristic of the artist. People with the high degrees of energy, emotional outflow, and flamboyant personalities that are characteristic of the bipolar spectrum might have been attracted to the artistic environment of that time. Following Sass's reasoning further, the personality characteristics found in creative individuals might change, depending on the prevailing philosophy of the arts, which might emphasize different personal aspects of the artist. This point will be discussed further in Chapter 11.

A study by Ludwig (1998) provides some fascinating data that can be taken as support for Sass's (2001) hypothesis concerning the relationship between psychopathology and the content of a creative domain. Ludwig studied biographies of eminent individuals in a broad range of creative fields to determine if the individual had suffered from some form of mental disorder. Ludwig concluded that if one separated fields into "logical, objective, and formal" versus "intuitive, subjective, and emotional" (e.g., science versus art), there were clear differences in the frequencies of psychopathology: scientists were much less likely to suffer from psychopathology than were artists. Furthermore, the same pattern held *within* the sciences and arts themselves: if one compared the "harder" or more objective sciences with the "softer" social sciences, for example, one saw higher rates of psychopathology in the latter. Similarly, if one analyzed more- versus less-formal domains within the arts (e.g., architecture versus performing arts, such as music and dance), one found less lifetime psychopathology in architecture. And if one goes still deeper, one saw the same pattern within painting, say, as those painters involved in more "emotional" styles showed more psychopathology than painters working in more formal styles.

Ludwig (1998) concluded that the more a profession relies on emotion, subjectivity, and personal expression, the greater the chances that members of that profession will exhibit psychopathology. Ludwig believed that his results show that people who are less emotionally stable may be drawn to certain professions (or to sub-domains within a given profession). This conclusion is consistent with Sass's (2001) view, although Ludwig's analysis did not focus on schizophrenia.

Schizophrenia and Choice of Career: Conclusions

Sass's (2001) analysis of the possible relation between schizophrenia and creativity has approached the question from a perspective different than that behind research examining the possible commonalities in cognitive processes. Instead of building on the assumption that creative thought processes might be facilitated by schizophrenic tendencies, Sass examined the possibility that personality characteristics might play a role in an individual's choice of an artistic career. The postulated connection between schizophrenia and creativity has changed significantly in this analysis. Let us now move even further from the idea that psychopathology affects the creative process to examine social factors that might influence the relationship between genius and madness.

Social Factors and Genius and Madness

Sass (2001) has argued that the current emphasis on the possible positive role of madness, and especially bipolar illness, in creativity can be traced to the Romantic movement of the late eighteenth and the nineteenth centuries (see also Becker, 2014; see also Chapter 2). In the Romantics' view, creativity was dependent upon the "creative imagination," which in turn was related to the spontaneous outflow of feelings unencumbered by rational and critical self-consciousness. Thus, the truly creative poet or painter, for example, was assumed to be able to tap into the emotions directly, without any interference from society's rules and restrictions. This upwelling of feeling was assumed to have been within the grasp of all of us as young children, but lost by most as we became socialized adults. The creative artist retains the ability to allow this emotional spring to flow and to channel the output into works of art. Sass quotes Koestler (1964, p. 169), who describes the

> temporary relinquishing of conscious controls [that] liberates the mind from certain constraints which are necessary to maintain the disciplined routines of thoughts but may become an impediment to the creative leap; at the same time other types of ideation on more primitive levels of mental organization are brought into activity.

Many others who have studied creativity have arrived at similar views concerning the need for a "primitive" mode of cognition in order to produce novel ideas (Kris, 1964; Eysenck, 1993; Martindale, 1989). The reason artistic symbols have emotional force for the audience, in this view, is because the artist is able to "regress" – move backward in development – to tap into primitive thinking processes and in this way create works able to arouse strong feelings in others.

This set of assumptions is one reason, in Sass's (2001) view, for the attractiveness of the idea that bipolarity is linked to creativity: the emotional upheavals that accompany that condition might serve as the basis for tapping into basic emotional activities. As Sass notes, however, this "regression" view of creativity is not universal, which raises some interesting questions concerning causal links between psychopathology and creativity.

Psychopathology and Creativity: Cultural Relativism

Other cultures have views of creativity very different from the regression view, which as just discussed proposes that creative inspiration depends on some sort of primitive thought process. Even in Western culture, the regression view of creativity has not been in favor throughout history (Sass, 2001). Both before and after Romanticism, the Western conception of creative process was very different and in some ways much more "rational." During the twentieth century, for example, the Modernist and Postmodernist views looked negatively on Romanticism and the notion that emotional irrationality is at the core of creativity. As a prime example, Warhol produced works that were essentially devoid of emotion and which functioned to draw the audience into a feeling of alienation from the world rather than passionate involvement in it. In Sass's view, it is not inevitable that high degrees of emotionality are necessary for creative inspiration.

Schuldberg (2001) and Sass (2001) also discussed the relationship between psychopathology and the kinds of creative work in science discussed by Kuhn (1962). In Kuhn's view, progress in science comes about in two ways. During *normal* science, investigation in a discipline is carried out within a *paradigm*, a set of shared beliefs concerning how science is carried out, the basic questions that are to be addressed, and the methods used to address them. An example of a paradigm in science is American Behaviorism in psychology, which flourished during the first two-thirds of the twentieth century. This paradigm focused on mapping out S–R (stimulus–response) relationships underlying all behaviors; behaviorists studied learning in simple organisms as the basis for understanding more complex phenomena in more complex organisms. During a "normal" period, when there is a dominant paradigm in a science, scientists working within that paradigm carry out *puzzle-solving* activities. These activities involve creative thinking, as new experiments are designed and carried out, but the basic assumptions underlying the paradigm are not questioned.

In contrast to normal science are periods of *revolution* in science, where the basic assumptions of a paradigm are brought into question and a new paradigm is brought forth to replace it. An example of such a revolution can be seen in the changes that occurred in American psychology in the last third of the twentieth century. Behaviorism was replaced by the "cognitive" perspective, with an emphasis on analysis of internal cognitive processes and the direct study of complex phenomena such as human problem-solving and reasoning.

Schuldberg (2001) notes that individuals with schizophrenic characteristics, with their antisocial features, a tendency to go in their own direction, and occasional eccentricities, might play a large role in revolutionary creative developments. Sass (2001) discusses evidence that individuals who suffer from disorders in the bipolar spectrum tend toward conformity and are concerned about social norms (p. 70). Such individuals might be expected to work more within existing paradigms rather than demolishing them in revolutionary creative activity.

These analyses have provided alternatives to the notion that psycho-pathological tendencies and creativity are related in a simple way (i.e., psychopathology causes creativity or creativity causes psychopathology). Sass and Schuldberg raise the possibility that psychopathological tenden-cies and creativity may be related in very indirect ways, as the personality characteristics of the individual influence whether or not he or she will attempt to participate in a given creative domain. If it were discovered, for example, that a person with schizophrenic characteristics participated in a scientific revolution, it might not have anything to do with the person's creative capacities per se. The schizophrenic characteristics might simply have led the person to become involved in a certain kind of scientific activity in which a more social individual might not have invested time and effort.

Becker (2001, 2014) has provided more richness to the discussion of the relation between psychopathology and creativity by placing it in a still-broader sociohistorical context. At the end of the eighteenth century, the development of the Romantic movement brought with it a change in the conception of genius that was related to the status at that time of creative thinkers – artists, scientists, philosophers. The reactionary political climate arising from Napoleon's defeat meant that creative endeavors, especially in the arts, and those who participated in them were not afforded the respect and freedom that they had received earlier. In order to establish themselves as individuals to be reckoned with by the establishment, Romantic thinkers proposed that the unbridled expression of imagination in creativity was the most important criterion in determining the value of a person. This led to an emphasis on those people who were capable of feeling things more deeply and directly, which in turn paved the way for a return of interest in the notion of genius and madness but with a new component. This was no longer the "divine madness" of the Greeks. It was now assumed that madness *in the sense of insanity* might be a component of the creative individual, due to his or her sensitivity to the emotional turbulence going on below the surface of life. In the view of the Romantics, any rationality or deliberation would only hinder the functioning of the imagination. As the poet Schiller said (quoted by Becker, 2001, p. 49):

> It is not well in the works of creation that reason should too closely challenge the ideas that come thronging to the doors. Taken by itself, an idea may be highly unsuitable, even venturesome, and yet in conjunction with others, themselves equally absurd alone, it may furnish a suitable link in the chain of thought. Reason cannot see this. . . . In a creative brain

reason has withdrawn her watch at the doors, and ideas crowd in pell-mell.

The Romantics, in removing the role of rationality from the creative process and giving the imagination free rein, set the stage for the serious reconsideration of the relationship between creative accomplishment and madness.

In Becker's (2014) view, this set of circumstances led to the Romantic thinkers to contemplate the possibility that they themselves might show evidence of madness. The poets Coleridge and Byron, for example, expressed fear of insanity in others and in themselves. The concern about insanity in individuals of creative accomplishment led to the study of such individuals by those with medical training. However, one problem with those early analyses was that much of the evidence in support of madness in people of genius was based on the reports of the geniuses themselves concerning their own "illnesses." Several questions can be raised about such reports. First, reporting symptoms pointing to one's own madness may be self-serving, since, in the Romantic view, the criterion for being considered a genius was that one must show such symptoms. Second, one cannot know with certainty that a description of a person's own psychological state, written by a Romantic poet, say, more than two centuries ago, uses terms in the same way that they are used today. We should therefore be cautious in concluding that self-reports of "madness" in Romantic poets are equivalent as evidence of insanity to a diagnosis drawn today by a professional on the basis of an in-depth interview with an individual.

Furthermore, creative thinkers of the Romantic era might actually *look for* and *welcome* any of their own behaviors that might be interpretable as symptomatic of insanity, assuming that the symptom was not so severe as to be threatening. Therefore, they would probably be much more likely to report evidence of such behaviors to a researcher than would people in a "normal" or control group since, among people not in the creative professions, insanity or tendencies toward insanity are usually not something to be prized. Becker (2014) presented the view of the philosopher Jaspers, who concluded that the greater frequency of mental illness in creative geniuses was the result of the way society applies judgments of "creative" to people who produce novel works. In this view, the term *genius* was reserved by society for those individuals who demonstrate high levels of talent *as well as evidence of mental illness*. In order to call someone a genius, it has become necessary that he or she be at least a bit eccentric or abnormal. Thus, in a closing of the circle, the Romantic notion of genius has changed the way in which the term was and is now applied to people, which means that there will be a correspondence between the Romantic view and "reality," if only because that "reality" – creative geniuses will indeed be at least a little "mad" – now depends on judgments that themselves are based on the premises of the Romantic view.

A Reconsideration of Some Basic Data

The discussion in the last few sections of the development and cultural relativism of the notion of genius and madness raises several interesting questions, one of which concerns some of the basic data underlying the idea that genius and madness are related. The notion that there is a relationship between genius and madness is based on a seemingly simple fact: psychopathology is present more frequently among those of genius than among the ordinary population. This seems like a straightforward finding: count the frequencies and see for yourself. However, consider how we determine that someone suffers from psychopathology. At least in part, such a diagnosis depends on what the person tells a therapist: I am hearing voices; I am afraid that the government is controlling my thoughts; I am afraid that I will kill myself.

If an individual in a creative occupation – a poet, painter, or musician – reports symptoms of madness, he or she might be misreporting things, for any of a number of reasons. The artist might *overinterpret* a passing thought or fleeting action as indicating more than it does and therefore might overreport the frequency and/or severity of that symptom. Thus, the reported frequency of symptoms in a creative group versus a noncreative control group might not reflect the "true" frequencies of those symptoms in the individuals. The artist might also be more likely to seek help for a "symptom" that we ordinary folk might not even notice, much less get worried about. Seeking treatment is another index of psychopathology. In addition, the artist, believing that "madness" is related to genius, might lie about the frequency of psychopathological symptoms that he or she suffers to enhance his or her stature as a possible "genius." Thus, "count the frequencies and see for yourself" turns out to be more complicated than it seemed.

On the other side, to the degree that observers of the art scene are aware of the possible connection between genius and madness, they might be more likely to see psychopathology in artists than in their "ordinary" friends and acquaintances. The same harmless eccentric behavior seen in, say, ourselves and an artist might be given more weight as a symptom of psychopathology in the latter. Finally, the biographical scrutiny that geniuses come under, which never happens to ordinary folks, surely makes it more likely that "madness" will be found in the lives of the greats.

In sum, an individual's deciding to become an artist might make it more likely that he or she will find psychopathology in himself or herself and/or that the audience at large will also find it. Thus, the simple "fact" that creative geniuses are subject to psychopathology with greater frequency than the general population turns out to be a fact of a different sort than determining whether creative geniuses are taller than the general population. The basic "finding" on which the whole genius and madness enterprise rests – creative geniuses are mad, count them and see for yourself – may be more apparent than real.

Genius and Madness: Conclusions

This discussion has made it clear that the relationship between genius and madness is very complicated. The concepts of genius and of madness are both highly complex, and the simple idea with which we began the discussion – psychopathology affects creativity – has become much more nuanced as we have examined a broader range of opinions on the matter. At present, the following conclusions seem to follow from the available results. There may be a relation between psychopathology and creativity – creative individuals may show more characteristics that will be labeled as psychopathology than do noncreative individuals. However, it is not clear how that increased frequency of psychopathology among creative geniuses is to be interpreted. The diagnosis of psychopathology in geniuses may be the result of factors – expectations on our part and that of the geniuses – that might result in differential criteria for such a diagnosis in the genius versus ordinary individuals. That might mean that the increased frequency of psychopathology in geniuses might not be real.

Even if there is a higher frequency of psychopathology among persons of genius, untangling the causal links in that relationship is a difficult task, since there are several causal scenarios that can explain a link between creativity and psychopathology. Most important, perhaps, is the recently emphasized possibility that creative striving and accomplishment might bring about the development of psychopathology among individuals who have inherited such tendencies (Johnson et al., 2000; Alloy & Nuslock, 2019). This finding means two things in the present context. First, at least in some cases, the causal link may be opposite from what is typically assumed to be true. Second, the frequency of psychopathology in geniuses is thus exaggerated in another way, because at least part of the high frequency of psychopathology in geniuses might be the result of their creative work.

In conclusion, the data that are presently available do not strongly support a causal link between madness and genius. Also, there are a number of factors, beyond changes in creative thinking, that can play a role in establishing a relationship between genius and madness. Those factors indicate that genius and madness may not be directly linked in a causal manner.

PART IV

The Psychometrics of Creativity

Can We Identify Creative People?

10 | Testing for Creativity

Divergent Thinking, Executive Functioning, and Creative Thinking

Measuring People's Creativity

Let's say you are a basketball coach and you are trying to build the best team for the upcoming season. There is a pool of new players available but you know very little about them. How would you go about deciding whom to choose for your team? One way would be to give each player a tryout: have her perform for you in conditions similar to game conditions. Depending on how well a player did, you would decide whether or not to put her on the team. Similarly, if you were a teacher trying to get the best math students for the math team, you could give all the students a math test and choose for the team those who performed best.

Now assume that you are a corporate recruiter, and a business organization comes to you with the request that you find a creative person who could serve as their CEO. How would you go about doing that? You might talk to everyone you can in your client's field, asking them to name the two or three most creative executives in the field, in the hope that you will find a consensus that will allow you to concentrate on one person. But how much can you trust people's opinions? Assuming for the sake of discussion that you can trust opinions, what happens if those opinions are divided among several possible candidates? You could bring in the candidates for interviews, but what could you or your client ask them to determine how creative each one is? You might ask that they recount their career achievements, but that might not give you more information than you obtained when you asked those folks in the field for their opinions, because those opinions were probably based on those same achievements. You need to be able to measure a person's creativity skills, analogous to the basketball coach's tryout and the math teacher's math test. You need a creativity test. This chapter presents an examination of creativity tests. Before reading further, please carry out the exercises in Table 10.1.

Table 10.1 *Testing cognitive skills*

You will need something to write with, a piece of paper, and a watch or other device that you can use to time yourself. Please follow the instructions for each item.

A. *Creative-Thinking Exercises*

General instructions. For each of the items below, please try to produce answers that no one else will be able to think of but which also meet the stated criteria. That is, for these items you should try to be creative.

1. List all the problems or difficulties you can think of with the present-day toaster (5 min.).
2. Suppose you could be invisible for a day. What problems might that create? What would the benefits of being invisible be? (5 min.)
3. List all the uses you can think of for a brick (3 min.).
4. List all the white edible things that you can (3 min.).
5. List all the words you can think of in response to the word *Mother* (3 min.). Bottom of Form
6. Here are some squares with little figures drawn inside of them. Try to make each little figure into something else. You can do whatever you want with these. You can make them funny or beautiful. You can add words. You can use more than one at a time – whatever you want. There is no right or wrong here.

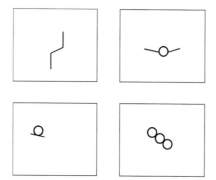

7. Read this nursery rhyme.
Old Mother Hubbard
Went to the cupboard
To get her poor doggie a bone,
When she got there
The cupboard was bare
So the poor little doggie had none.
How would you solve Mother Hubbard's problem?

B. *IQ test items*

For each item below, circle the correct answer.
1. Which number should come next in the pattern? 37, 34, 31, 28
    Answer: 25 – the numbers are decreasing by 3.
2. Find the answer that best completes the analogy:
    Book is to Reading as Fork is to:
    a. drawing   b. writing   c. stirring   d. eating
    Answer: d.
3. Which of the following can be arranged into a five-letter English word?
    a. H R G S T   b. R I L S A   c. T O O M T   d. W Q R G S
    Answer: b. (*rails*) and c. (*motto*)

Outline of the Chapter

The idea that one can use a test to measure people's creative potential has been around since the turn of the twentieth century (Runco, 2011). Modern interest in testing for creativity began around 1950 and evolved out of the mental-testing or *psychometric* movement in the United States that had developed around attempts to measure intelligence. In Chapter 2, we discussed Guilford's pioneering work in defining creativity and in proposing a psychometric perspective for creativity research. This chapter begins by examining in more detail Guilford's work (e.g., 1950, 1967), which has been of seminal influence in setting the agenda in this area. Guilford proposed that the thought processes underlying creativity are different than those measured by IQ tests and he developed a set of tests to measure them. We shall review Guilford's research and that of those who followed him, paying particular attention to the tests that have been developed to measure the capacity to think creatively. One important question in this context is whether Guilford was correct in proposing that IQ and creativity involved different sets of thinking skills. We shall review recent research addressing that issue.

Guilford and the Modern Psychometric Perspective on Creativity

Guilford (1950) used his presidential address to the American Psychological Association (APA) to propose that psychology take up the study of creativity, an area which, he felt, had been greatly neglected. He began by noting that the term *genius* had come to be used – incorrectly, in his view – to describe a person of high intelligence. The original referent of that term was someone who made outstanding creative contributions, as we already know from discussion in Chapter 2 and elsewhere. Guilford proposed that psychology return to that use. In other words, the capacity to think creatively was something different from high IQ. If so, one could *not* use IQ tests to measure people's ability to think creatively. Each item on an IQ test has one correct answer (see items in Table 10.1B), but situations that demand creative thinking do not necessarily have only one correct answer (see Table 10.1A). Indeed, some situations that demand creative thinking may not have a correct answer: is there a *correct* way for a painter to paint a landscape? A new set of tests was needed to capture creative-thinking skills.

Guilford (1950) approached the study of creativity based on his extensive experience in psychometrics (in other words, Guilford's groundbreaking discussion of creativity – his own creative advance – was another example of *green creativity*). Just as psychologists had had success in developing tests to measure intelligence and to predict performance in school, so Guilford wanted to develop tests to measure creativity and predict creative performance later in life. At the time of Guilford's address, there was great concern in the United States that dictatorial Communism was on the way to overwhelming the democratic west, and Guilford believed that identifying and nurturing creative talent would be our best chance of winning the war for people's hearts and minds.

In a further connection to the psychometric tradition, Guilford (1950) proposed that the entire person was involved in creativity, which meant that creativity was part of the *personality* of the person. Simply possessing creative-thinking ability was not enough to guarantee creative productivity in life. It was also necessary that the individual possess certain critical personality characteristics, as well as motivation, before that ability would bear fruit. As will be discussed in the next chapter, psychologists have spent much time trying to specify the personality characteristics of creative individuals. Guilford's influence is also seen in numerous *confluence* theories of creativity that have been developed over the years since his address. Those theories assume that the *confluence* or *coming together* of multiple factors is necessary to produce creativity. Several confluence theories will be reviewed later in the book.

We now turn to an examination of some of the ideas that Guilford proposed as the basis for studying creativity. Guilford (1950) assumed that creativity came about as the result of the coming together of several *traits*, or psychological characteristics. The first characteristic involved in

Table 10.2 *Guilford's components of the creative process (with some questions raised in the discussion)*

A. General component: sensitivity to problems
   (Plus curiosity; and motivation to be first to do something never done before)

B. Specific components
   1. Fluency of thought: producing many ideas
   2. Flexibility of thought: producing different types of ideas
   3. Originality of thinking: producing ideas not produced by other people
      (Originality versus *rarity*? One must be careful in measuring originality.)
   4. Elaboration: building on a simple answer

C. Divergent thinking: Made up of components B1–B4

D. Creative thinking
   1. Divergent thinking
   2. Convergent thinking

---

creativity, sensitivity to problems, was a very general one, involving what was essentially an orientation to life (see Table 10.2).

Sensitivity to Problems

In order to get the creative process started, an individual must see deficiencies in some aspect of the world. Only then, according to Guilford (1950), will one spend time contemplating what might be done to correct those problems, which is the first step in producing a creative outcome. As an example, a potential inventor might discover a problem with her new car. One very hot summer's day, when driving home from work, she finds that the car's cupholder is too small to hold the large bottle of water she just bought. That discovery could stimulate the search for a way to overcome that problem. Another person might simply put the bottle on the seat and not think further about it. Only the first person would have the chance to produce a creative idea in that situation. Similarly, two scientists might read a research paper in which some result did not come out as predicted. The first scientist might conclude that that unexpected result was due to random error in the experiment and ignore it. The second scientist, in contrast, might conclude that that unexpected result needs to be explained, which might lead her to design a new experiment in order to explore that finding further. That new experiment might lead to a creative advance.

Thus, *sensitivity to problems* is the first step toward creative thinking. Exercises 1 and 2 in Table 10.1A measure a person's sensitivity to problems; in each exercise, the person must be able to analyze a situation to determine what follows from it. One can test a large number of people – college students, say, or corporate executives – on exercises such as those, and one can determine if a person finds more or fewer problems than average, comparing students to students and executives to executives. This would allow one to rank people on their sensitivity to problems.

Is Necessity the Mother of Creativity?

The notion that sensitivity to problems is important for creativity is a variation on the old idea that necessity is the mother of invention. However, there is evidence that the creative process can sometimes be set in motion without necessity, even in the domain of invention (Weisberg, 2006). As one example, at the end of the nineteenth century there were a number of research projects underway the purpose of which was the invention of a flying machine (an airplane). At that time, there was no need for such a machine; only gradually, *after* the Wright brothers were successful in inventing the airplane, did the possible functions of their invention become apparent. The driving force behind the invention of the airplane was not necessity. There was no *need* to fly; people simply *wanted to*. Individuals sometimes think creatively because they want to be the first to accomplish something that has never been done before; or because they are curious as to what might happen when certain actions are carried out. In Table 10.2A, I have added *curiosity* and *motivation to be first to do something* as additional reasons for the creative process being set into motion.

Sensitivity to problems is a very general trait, more related to an orientation toward life than specifically to thinking. (The same is true for *curiosity* and *motivation to be first to do something*.) Guilford also discussed the specific thought processes that he assumed were involved in creative thinking, and he constructed tests to measure them. Let us now review those skills.

Guilford: The Skills that Comprise Creative Thinking

Fluency of Thought

To Guilford (1950), it was obvious that a person who produced *more* ideas – who is a *fluent* thinker – would have a greater chance of producing a creative idea. Fluency of thought – the ease with which one thinks of ideas – should therefore contribute to creative thinking. One measures fluency by counting, for a given test item, the number of acceptable responses a person produced. We can then compare that person's performance with the average for his or her peer group. Items 1–6 in Table 10.1A can be used to measure fluency of thought.

Flexibility of Thought

Guilford (1950) assumed that creativity entailed thinking outside of the box. In order to think outside the box, one must think *flexibly*, producing different *types* of ideas, rather than staying with one type. Flexible thinking makes it more likely that new perspectives will be brought to the situation. Flexibility is scored by determining how often a person changes categories on a test item while still producing acceptable responses. As an example, let us say that two people are asked to list as many foods as they can. One person says: milk, yogurt, grapes, apples, steak, lamb. The second says: milk, grapes, steak, apples, yogurt, lamb. Both people have produced six items, so their fluency scores would be the same, but they produced those items differently. The first person produced two dairy foods, two fruits, and two meats. That person switched categories only twice: yogurt (dairy) $\Rightarrow$ grapes (fruit), and apples (fruit) $\Rightarrow$ steak (meat). The second person produced five changes of category, switching categories with each item. The second person can, therefore, be looked upon as a more flexible thinker, which may indicate that he or she would be less likely to get stuck in a rut when producing ideas. Items 3 and 4 in Table 10.1A can be used to measure flexibility of thought.

Originality

The creative thinker produces original ideas, defined by Guilford (1950) as ideas that were not produced by others. Let's say that 100 people are tested, and 50 of them produce "yogurt" as one of their responses on the *white edible things* task (item 3 in Table 10.1A). In contrast, the response "carob-covered raisins" would be much less frequent, so that would get a higher score for originality. Items 1–7 can be scored for originality.

Originality versus Rarity?

Since Guilford's (1950) discussion, originality has been defined as responses that are *infrequent* (see also Wallach & Kogan, 1965; Kim,

2016; Silvia, 2015). However, in the dictionary definition, if an idea is original, it means that it was not thought of before – nothing is said about the idea's being infrequent. Assume that, on a creativity test, I produce an idea that no one else produces. Based on the usual scoring of originality, I would get credit for a very original idea. It turns out, however, that I got that idea through observing my father, so *it is not original for me.* Thus, researchers from Guilford to the present day have been giving people credit for "original" ideas without determining whether those ideas were, in fact, original. Until relatively recently, researchers never asked participants whether a given idea that they produced on the test was original *to them*.

The only exception to this mismeasurement of originality of which I am aware is a study by Gilhooly et al. (2007) in which participants were asked to provide unusual uses for a shoe and several other objects (see Table 10.1A – exercise 3). After the participants produced a response they were asked to state whether they had thought of that use (i.e., whether it was original for them) or whether it came from somewhere else. Gilhooly and colleagues found that people were able to tell you whether an idea was original. Therefore, we should be careful when trying to interpret results from tests that are presented as measuring "originality," because those tests have been scored for the *rarity of a response* rather than originality (see discussion in Silvia, 2015). Originality on creativity tests might not be related to originality in real-world creative thinking, where people do produce ideas that are novel for them.

Elaboration

Elaboration of ideas, another component of creative thinking (Guilford, 1950), is seen when a person takes a simple answer and builds on it. In elaborating an answer, one makes use of information that might not be directly related to the answer: rather than producing a simple response, one tells a story. Item 2 in Table 10.1A can be scored for elaboration. The nonverbal items in Table 10.1A #4 can also be scored for elaboration.

Divergent Thinking: A Core Component of Creative Thinking

The thinking capacities that we have just reviewed are summarized in Table 10.2B, under the heading *divergent thinking*. Divergent thinking is, in Guilford's (1967) view, the first step in production of novel ideas. One's thinking *diverges* from the known. Guilford's perspective on how creative thinking works can be seen to be a version of the outside-the-box view. In order to think creatively, you have to be able to produce many ideas, in a flexible manner. Fluency and flexibility will allow the thinker to move away from where he or she started – that is, to move outside of the box.

Divergent Thinking Is Not Creative Thinking

In Guilford's (1950, 1967) analysis of creative thinking, divergent thinking was only one component. Other skills also played a role, including "convergent thinking," the ability to evaluate and decide among ideas after they were produced (see Acar & Runco, 2014). Convergent thinking is carried out to determine which idea(s) might actually be useful. One selects among the ideas that have been produced, *converging* on the final solution. Convergent thinking is typically assessed on IQ tests (see Table 10.1B). For each item on an IQ test, one must determine a single correct answer, which is very different from the situation concerning the D-T items (Table 10.1A).

Sometimes, researchers have taken divergent thinking, by itself, to be equivalent to creative thinking (Acar & Runco, 2014). Those researchers have – mistakenly – labeled *divergent-thinking* (D-T) tests as "creativity tests." If a person scores poorly on a test made up of items like those in Table 10.1A, he or she may be described as "less creative." That description, strictly speaking, is incorrect: the person did more poorly on a D-T test; "creativity" was not measured. Similarly, sometimes creativity-training programs have used increases in D-T performance as evidence that the program has been successful in increasing creativity. Once again, however, increasing performance on D-T tests is not the same as increasing creativity. Henceforth, I will refer to tests that measure such skills as fluency, flexibility, and originality as *divergent-thinking* (D-T) tests rather than *creativity* tests.

Guilford's Analysis of Creative Thinking: Conclusions

Guilford (1950, 1967) set the agenda that many psychologists have followed for almost seventy years. Given Guilford's hypothesized set of creative-thinking skills, the next step was to develop tests to measure each of them. The final step was to demonstrate that those skills were actually related to creativity; for example, one might expect to find increased creative accomplishment among individuals who test higher for the proposed thinking skills. Many researchers followed Guilford's lead and also designed D-T tests. Tests have been designed to assess divergent-thinking (D-T) skills in children of various ages, including the very young (e.g., Hoicka et al., 2016), as well as in adults. I will now examine one set of tests, the Torrance Tests of Creative Thinking (TTCT), to explore how they are designed and what they have told us about creativity. The Torrance Tests have been used most widely in the study of creativity and many of the important issues concerning testing creativity have arisen in the context of the TTCT (Kim, 2017).

The Torrance Tests of Creative Thinking

Millions of people around the world have been tested in different contexts using the TTCT, from schools, where the tests are used as selection criteria for gifted programs, to industry, where they are used in personnel decisions (Kim, 2017; Runco & Acar, 2012). Returning to the question raised at the beginning of the chapter concerning how to select a new CEO with high creative potential, many HR departments would ask candidates to take the TTCT.

The TTCT has two forms, or *scales* – verbal (TTCT-V) and figural (non-verbal; TTCT-F) – to tap into different domains of creativity. The verbal scale requires verbal responses to both verbal and nonverbal stimuli. The figurative scale requires nonverbal responses. Torrance's (1962) tests were designed to be useful in testing a wide range of participants. Some examples of members of each of those scales are given in the next section. We are already familiar with several of the sub-tests from Table 10.1A.

Verbal Scale: Verbal Tasks Using Verbal Stimuli

Unusual Uses

Torrance adapted those tests directly from Guilford (see item 3 in Table 10.1A). After doing some preliminary testing, Torrance (1962) decided to substitute tin cans and books for bricks. It was thought that those items would be easier for children to deal with.

Consequences

This task (see items 5 and 6 in Table 10.1A) was also adapted from Guilford. Torrance chose three different improbable situations.

Just Suppose

This was an adaptation of the *consequences* type of test, designed more for children. The participant is asked to predict possible outcomes arising from some twist on an ordinary situation. As an example, just suppose we could travel wherever we wanted to, in the blink of an eye. What would be the results?

Improvement

The participants are given a list of common objects and are asked to suggest as many ways as they can to improve each object. Item 1 in Table 10.1A is an example.

Mother-Hubbard

This task (item 7 in Table 10.1A) was designed as a way to assess sensitivity to problems, in the primary grades but also for older groups.

Imaginative Stories

In this task, the child is asked to write the most interesting and exciting story she can think of. Topics are suggested to the participant (e.g., "the dog that did not bark"); or participants may use their own ideas.

Verbal Scale: Verbal Tasks Using Nonverbal Stimuli

Ask and Guess

This requires the individual first to consider questions about a picture that cannot be answered by just looking at the picture. In one picture, a car is shown, crushed by a fallen tree. The participant is then asked to formulate hypotheses about the possible causes of the event in the picture, and then the consequences of that event, both immediate and remote consequences.

Product Improvement

In this task, common toys are presented, and children are asked to think of as many improvements as they can which would make the toy "more fun to play with." Item 1 in Table 10.1A provides an example directed toward adults.

Unusual Uses (Toy)

In this task, used in conjunction with the *Product Improvement Task*, the child is asked to think of the cleverest, most interesting, and most unusual uses of a toy other than as a plaything. This test is different than the unusual uses tests (e.g., item 2 in Table 10.1A), because the item to be dealt with is a physical item that the participant can interact with.

Figurative Scale: Non-Verbal Tasks

Incomplete Figures

Item 6 in Table 10.1A provides examples of this type of test. The participant is asked to produce novel objects or designs by adding as many lines as they can to each of the figures. Examples of different solutions to this task are shown in Figure 10.1.

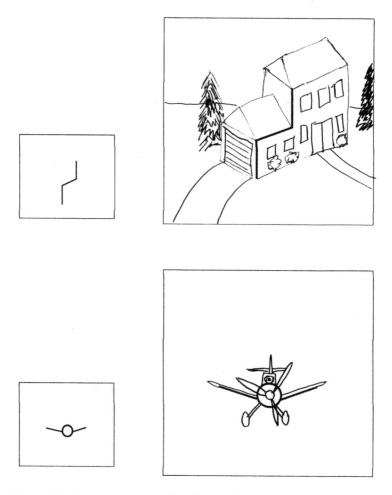

Figure 10.1 Responses to Incomplete-Figures Test

Picture Construction or Shapes

The participant is given piece of colored paper cut into a shape – a triangle or a jelly bean – and a larger sheet of white paper. The task is to create a picture in which that shape is an important part. The participant can paste the shape anywhere on the white sheet, and add lines. They also have to think of a name for the picture.

Creative Strengths

Several of the individual scores from the TTCT-F are combined in various ways to provide scores of thirteen *creative strengths*. Examples include the *colorfulness* and *richness* of the imagery produced by a person; the *humor* in a person's responses; the amount of *movement* or *action*; and the level of *fantasy*.

Verbal versus Figurative Forms of the TTCT

There have been some questions raised concerning the relationship between the verbal and figurative forms of the TTCT (Kim, 2017). Early studies indicated that the figural and verbal scores on the test were not strongly related, which was taken as indicating that they measured two separate facets of creativity or perhaps that one or both was not measuring creativity (Baer, 2015; Kim, 2017). A recent large-scale analysis by Kim (2017) indicated that the two scores are related significantly, although they do not overlap completely, which indicates that both scores can provide useful information about a person. Kim suggested that the figurative form of the test be used, because it measures a wider range of behaviors and attitudes and also because it is not biased by gender, which the verbal form may be.

D-T Tests: Are They Useful?

Now that we have examined the structure and purpose of the TTCT and other D-T tests, we can consider the question of whether the tests do what they were designed to do. If we give a D-T test to a group of children, will we be able to use the results to predict which of them will grow up to be creative adults? In other words, are D-T tests *valid* as measures and predictors of creative achievement? There are several different aspects of validity that can be determined for a test. I will review them briefly before discussing the question of the validity of D-T tests.

Predictive Validity

Guilford (1950, 1967) designed creativity tests in order to determine who among us would produce innovations. If, for example, one wants to use children's D-T scores to *predict* later creative accomplishments, the D-T tests must possess *predictive validity*. The same is true if one wants to use D-T scores as the basis for hiring a creative CEO. The question of predictive validity has been a critically important aspect of D-T testing.

Face Validity

Consider a test designed to measure a person's knowledge of professional basketball, with some of the items asking the names of the teams, players, and recent championship teams. Everyone would agree that the test measures basketball knowledge. Such a test is *valid on its face*; it possesses *face validity*. Concerning D-T tests, the question of face validity would center on whether divergent thinking as postulated by Guilford (1950) and measured by D-T tests is itself a central component of creative thinking outside of the laboratory.

Discriminant Validity

As we know, Guilford (1950) emphasized the fact that creativity was different than IQ. If so, a creativity test should be *discriminating* in what it measures. Tests of creative-thinking capacity should measure something unique, especially something different than IQ tests measure. If a D-T test measures a capacity that other tests do not measure, then the test is said to have *discriminant* validity. Much recent research has been aimed at ascertaining if D-T tests measure something different than IQ tests do. One way to determine discriminant validity is to measure if IQ and D-T scores are highly correlated within a group of people. If so, it may indicate that they are measuring the same thing. Recent advances in the study of IQ have raised questions about the sharp distinction that Guilford and other early researchers made between creativity and intelligence.

Predictive Validity of the D-T Tests

Predictive validity has been an important goal of researchers who have developed D-T test. Overall, however, support for the predictive validity of D-T tests has been mixed. Recent studies, which have used sophisticated methods of analysis, have produced mostly positive findings. In an early study, Baer (1993) reviewed the literature on the predictive validity of D-T tests, including the TTCT, and concluded that validity was poor. Predictions of creative achievement based on D-T scores were not accurate.

Torrance carried out multiple studies examining whether the TTCT were useful in predicting creative accomplishment. In one study (Torrance, 1981), all the children in two elementary schools in Minnesota were given the TTCT multiple times, over the years 1958–1965. Other measures, including IQ scores, were also obtained. Torrance focused on 400 children who had been given the D-T tests for three consecutive years over grades 5–8. Testing each child three times provided a stronger measure of D-T performance. In 1980, twenty-two years after the study was begun, the students, now more than thirty years of age, were contacted, and more than 200 participated in a follow-up, in which they were asked about creative achievements such as inventions, published scientific articles, and awards for creative work. Each participant also listed his or her most creative achievements, which were rated on overall creativity by three judges. In a reexamination of Torrance's results, Plucker (1999) used the method of structural equation modeling to examine the predictive power of the TTCT over those twenty-two years. The verbal TTCT score predicted creative achievement and did so more strongly than intelligence did. The figurative component of the TTCT did *not* successfully predict later creative achievement, however. Plucker concluded that the Torrance tests did possess predictive validity. That conclusion should be tempered, however, by the fact that only the verbal component predicted creative achievement.

Two further follow-up studies have been carried out on those individuals originally tested by Torrance. The first follow-up was based on information about creative achievements collected in 1998, thirty-five years after the TTCT scores were obtained (Cramond, Matthews-Morgan & Bandalos, 2005). Cramond, Matthews-Morgan, and Bandalos found that the figural TTCT scores predicted creative achievements, but so did IQ scores. (Because of problems carrying out detailed statistical analyses with relatively small groups of participants, Crammond, Matthews-Morgan, and Bandalos were not able to examine verbal TTCT scores.) In the most recent study, Runco et al. (2010) found that, after fifty years, the figural TTCT scores predicted creative achievement. (Runco et al. also did not examine verbal TTCT scores.) This study found no significant relationship between IQ and creative achievement. It is not clear why those various studies produced different results concerning D-T scores, IQ, and creative achievement, since the same participants were involved.

Predictive Validity of D-T Tests: Conclusions and Further Questions

The results just reviewed support the conclusion that the TTCT have some long-term predictive validity (Plucker, 1999; Cramond et al., 2005; Runco et al., 2010). The fact that any significant predictions came from fifty-year-old D-T scores is impressive. However, one must be cautious about drawing strong conclusions concerning the predictive validity of the TTCT. The results of the various studies were not always consistent, even though in some analyses the same participants were studied each time. Sometimes verbal scores predicted creative achievement, sometimes figural scores did, and sometimes IQ scores also did. Returning again to the hiring of a creative CEO, you could test the candidates using the TTCT and the results would be helpful, but you should not rely only on those results.

Let us now turn to the face validity of D-T tests. A test does not have to be valid on its face to be useful: it can still possess predictive validity. However, as discussed earlier, the design of the TTCT and other D-T tests was based on assumptions made by Guilford (1950, 1967) and others concerning how creative thinking operated. The components of divergent thinking – fluent thought, flexible thought, and original thinking – were postulated as critical to the generation of creative ideas. We should see evidence of divergent thinking if we examine the cognitive processes underlying creative advances. It is important to consider whether those assumptions are confirmed. We can answer that question based on what we know already about how the creative process works from the discussions earlier in this book. Analyzing the face validity of D-T tests will have implications for our broader understanding of creativity.

Face Validity of D-T Tests as Measures of Creativity

We have concluded that D-T tests are valid as predictors of creative achievement – not perfect but strong enough to be useful. However, that still leaves us with a question: *Why* do D-T scores predict creative achievements later in life? D-T scores might be correlated with later creative achievements for several reasons. First, divergent thinking – fluent thought, flexible thought, and original thinking – might be an essential part of the creative thought process, as just discussed (Guilford, 1950, 1967). Evidence of D-T skills should be seen in real-life situations. If such evidence were found, then D-T tests would possess face validity. On the other hand, the processes underlying D-T performance might not be the same as those underlying creative accomplishments in real-life contexts. If so, one would not find direct evidence for D-T skills in creative thinking outside the laboratory. There might be some other factor that is related to both divergent thinking and creative accomplishment, which would mean that D-T ability is not related causally to creative accomplishment.

Guildford (1950, 1967) assumed that the components of divergent thinking were critical in creativity. However, neither he nor any creativity researchers that followed his lead (e.g., Torrance, 1981; Wallach & Kogan, 1965) ever tested that assumption directly by actually *studying how creativity worked*. Guilford never carried out case studies examining creative advances, like those in Chapters 1 and 4; and he did not carry out analyses of problem-solving like those in Chapters 3 and 7. In my view, such research would have been a critical step in testing hypotheses about the components of creative thinking. Because of his background in mental testing, Guilford took a different tack. He *assumed* that certain skills were important in creative thinking and then he set out to develop tests to measure them.

Guilford's (1950, 1967) basic assumption was that the creative process works in two stages: first by producing many ideas (through divergent thinking) and then by keeping the good ones (through convergent thinking). Many other researchers have adopted this position (see, for example, Campbell, 1960; Jung et al., 2013; Kaufman & Gregoire, 2015; Simonton, 2016). Producing many and varied ideas is postulated as the critical first step in producing creative ones. We can call this the *D-T theory* of creative thinking. From the discussions in earlier chapters, we have evidence that Guilford's analysis – the D-T theory – is not correct. None of the numerous creative products that we have examined was produced by such a two-phase process. Consider Picasso's creation of *Guernica*. In the first sketches, which would presumably provide the strongest evidence for divergent thinking, we did not see many possible structures being produced, with one then being selected. The structure that is present in the final version of the painting can already be seen in the first sketch. Picasso knew from the beginning the important aspects of the painting.

The discovery of DNA followed a similar path. Watson and Crick from the beginning decided that they would pursue a helical structure, using the method of molecular modeling. There was no divergent production of multiple possible paths that were then narrowed down through convergent thinking. Fallingwater, Wright's house cantilevered over the stream, was created in a similar way. We saw that Wright reported that, after visiting the site, "a domicile has taken vague shape in my mind to the music of the stream" (Toker, 2003, pp. 139–140). Again, one idea was present from the beginning. There was not, in any of those cases, an initial "divergent-thinking" period, during which numerous ideas were produced in the hope that something relevant might be chosen at a later stage. In each case, the creative process was focused from the beginning, so that specific directions were taken from the start.

Laboratory studies of problem-solving, including studies of solution of insight problems, have produced similar conclusions (see Chapters 3 and 7). Problems are not approached in two stages, the first of which involves producing many varied ideas. Solutions are based on the match between the problem and one's knowledge, rather than on some D-T process. At each step, the process is constrained and directed, rather than "divergent."

Face Validity of D-T Tests: Conclusions and Implications

Based on this brief review of several familiar examples of creative thinking, it seems reasonable to conclude that D-T tests do not possess face validity as measures of the creative process. That conclusion leads us to the question of why D-T tests are able to predict creative achievements. One possibility is that there is some other factor linking D-T performance and creative achievement, and several researchers have raised the possibility that IQ might be important in D-T performance and in creative accomplishment more generally. We have seen that IQ scores sometimes predict later creative achievement (Kim, 2017; Runco et al., 2010). That finding has raised a further set of questions among some researchers. Are IQ and creativity really independent, as Guilford (1950) originally proposed? That question is closely related to the question of discriminant validity: Do D-T tests measure something different than IQ tests do? Recent advances in the study of IQ have resulted in new analyses of the possible role of intelligence in creativity and have raised important issues concerning how we should think about creative thinking.

Discriminant Validity of the TTCT: D-T Tests versus IQ Tests in Predicting Creativity

Guilford's (1950, 1967; see Table 10.2) distinction between divergent and convergent thinking provided a useful focus for researchers concerning the possible relationship between creativity and intelligence (Silvia, 2015). Divergent thinking, with its emphasis on production of many new ideas, was seen as the core of creativity. Convergent thinking, with its focus on choosing the best one from those produced divergently, was seen as being based on the abilities associated with intelligence. Based on that perspective, people's D-T scores might be independent of their scores on IQ tests. That general distinction played a role in early analyses of the discriminant validity of D-T tests.

Discriminant Validity of D-T Tests

An early large-scale examination of the discriminant validity of D-T tests was carried out by Wallach and Kogan (1965). They developed a D-T test battery along the lines suggested by Guilford (1950), but the items were designed so that they could be given to children of various ages. Wallach and Kogan gave their D-T battery and an IQ test to a large sample of children. They found a correlation of +.09 between D-T scores and overall IQ, which indicated that there was no relation between them. They concluded, in support of Guilford, that D-T tests measured cognitive capacities different than those measured by IQ tests. In a more recent analysis, Kim (2008) reviewed the results from a large number of studies from 1964 to 2003. She concluded that there was a "negligible" relationship between D-T scores and IQ, with a mean correlation of +.17. That result also indicated that the two types of tests measured different capacities or abilities, meaning that D-T tests possessed discriminant validity.

Threshold Theory

Kim (2008) took the negative results from her analysis as indicating that you do not need a high IQ to be creative. In contrast, it has been proposed by other researchers that IQ and creativity are related but in a complex way. There might be a *minimum threshold* for IQ, about 120, that must be met in order for a person to function fully in a situation demanding creativity (Jauk et al., 2013). Above that threshold, IQ does not matter, but below it,

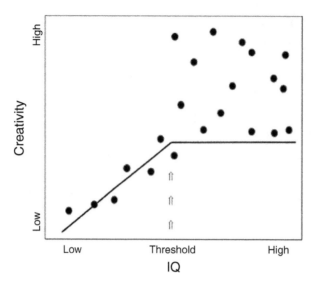

Figure 10.2 Threshold Theory of the relationship between IQ and creativity

creativity increases as IQ increases. The threshold hypothesis is outlined in Figure 10.2.

It has been difficult to test the threshold hypothesis, because no one knows exactly what the IQ threshold is. Researchers tried to test the threshold hypothesis by measuring the IQs and D-T performances of a group of people, dividing them into high versus low IQ groups and examining whether the relationship between IQ and D-T scores was different for the two groups. The results of those studies typically did not support the threshold hypothesis (Kim, 2005, 2008), but a possible problem is that the analyses might not have split the two groups at the right place (Jauk et al., 2013).

Jauk et al. (2013) carried out a study that provided a stronger test of the threshold hypothesis. They scored general intelligence using four measures, including reasoning, word meaning, and short-term memory. The researchers also measured performance on a set of D-T tasks, including unusual-uses tests. They also employed a questionnaire to determine creative achievements, from everyday to high-level achievements. Participants were asked, for example, if they had any involvement with music, ranging from playing an instrument, an everyday achievement, up to composing music that had been played in public by others, a high-level achievement. Assessment of achievement was carried out across a wide range of areas, including literature and science.

The possibility of an IQ threshold was determined using a statistical algorithm (Jauk et al., 2013). Rather than the researchers setting a possible threshold, based essentially on guesswork, the algorithm was designed to find any point, across the entire range of IQ scores, at which there was a break in the relationship between IQ and D-T or between IQ and creative accomplishment. The results indicated that there was an IQ threshold for D-T performance: D-T performance increased as IQ increased, up to around 120. Above that, there was no relationship between D-T and IQ. The results looked like Figure 10.2. For creative *achievement*, in contrast, there was no threshold: creative achievement increased with IQ across the entire range of IQs in the sample. Similar results were reported by Jauk, Benedek, and Neubauer (2014). Those results indicated that there might be different relationships between IQ and different aspects of creativity.

One way to understand the results of Jauk et al. (2013) is to assume that creative achievement is more complex intellectually than is D-T performance. If so, higher levels of IQ might be needed to excel in a creative field. Additional evidence to support that conclusion comes from the Study of Mathematically Precocious Youth (SMPY; see Park, Lubinski & Benbow, 2008; Kell, Lubinski & Benbow, 2013). This research has traced the accomplishments of several thousand young people, who earned very high SAT math ($\geq$ 700) and/or verbal ($\geq$ 630) scores before age thirteen. Studies have examined the accomplishments of those individuals as adults, including creative accomplishments such as obtaining patents, writing poems and novels, and creating artworks.

Overall, the participants in the SMPY were very successful (Kell, Lubinski & Benbow, 2013), which supports the analysis of Jauk et al. Furthermore, if one looks at the lower- versus higher-scoring individuals within this outstanding group (the "super smart" versus the "scary smart"), there were differences in accomplishments, creative and noncreative. The highest-ability individuals – the scary smart – earned more PhD degrees, for example, and those degrees came from more prestigious universities. They also produced more in the way of creative accomplishments, such as patents and artistic achievements. Even though the SMPY includes the most intellectually able people, differences in intellectual ability within that elite group were related to their ultimate levels of accomplishment. Those results provide strong support for the idea that intelligence is related to creative accomplishment throughout the entire range of intelligence.

Intelligence and IQ: Preliminary Conclusions

The skills measured by IQ tests seem to play a larger role in creative thinking than Guilford (1950) and other early researchers believed (Sternberg, 2018). Recent analysis has indicated that there may be an IQ threshold for D-T performance. In contrast, broader creative accomplishment seems to be related to IQ throughout the IQ range, even at the very highest level, as demonstrated by the SMPY results. The research examining divergent thinking and IQ that we have just reviewed looked at relationships among general measures of IQ as well as their relationship to different aspects of creative performance. Over the past twenty-five years, however, advances in the analysis of IQ have resulted in new conceptions of how the human intellect is structured. That new perspective has been brought to the study of IQ and creativity, and it has changed the way researchers think about creativity and IQ.

Cattell-Horn-Carroll Theory, IQ, and Creativity

Carroll (1993) is generally credited with being the force behind the development of modern conceptions of IQ (Carroll, 1993; Flanagan & Dixon, 2013; Schneider & McGrew, 2012). Carroll, in turn, built upon ideas developed by Horn and Cattell (1960), so the modern conceptualization of IQ is generally labeled the Cattell-Horn-Carroll (CHC) theory. CHC theory proposes that there several levels of IQ, with multiple components at each level (see Table 10.3). At the highest level – level I – is general intelligence, or *G*, which is a summary of an individual's intellectual capacity and performance across a wide range of domains. Sometimes a single score – *G* – is derived from an IQ test; sometimes, two scores, verbal and figural (or visual), are calculated. Researchers analyze IQ into several factors at the level below *G* (see "level II" in Table 10.3; Flanagan & Dixon, 2013; Schneider & McGrew, 2012). In modern research, it is more usual to examine the relationship between creative thinking and those more-specific components of IQ. For our discussion, four level II factors are most important: fluid intelligence (*Gf*); short-term memory (*Gsm*); long-term retrieval (*Glr*); and crystallized knowledge (*Gc*). At level III are specific tests for each of those level II factors.

Fluid intelligence – *Gf* – represents the individual's ability to reason in novel situations. This intelligence is "fluid" because it can be adapted to new situations, indicating that *Gf* has a creative component. *Gf* is

Table 10.3 *Levels and components of IQ in CHC theory*

	Level of Component	
I	**II Component**	**III Specific skills tested**
G General intelligence	*Gf* Fluid intelligence	**Numerical reasoning**: Given the following series of numbers, which number comes next? 6, 11, 15, 18, 20 (answer: 21; the differences are decreasing by 1) **Problem-solving**
	Gsm Short-term memory	**1) Memory span**: recall the following items, in order – *man, car, pencil, orange.* **2) Working-Memory Capacity** (WMC; executive functioning) **Backward memory span**: recall the following items, in reverse order – *paper, window, watch, cup*
	Glr Long-term retrieval	**Learning efficiency; retrieval fluency** Sensitivity to problems/alternative solution fluency Associational fluency – Unusual Uses Test: quality of ideas Ideational fluency – objects that are red, round, and solid Originality/creativity
	Gc Crystalized knowledge	**Depth and breadth of acquired knowledge** Learned reasoning skills; general verbal information; vocabulary; communication skill

demonstrated through items testing various forms of reasoning, including inductive and deductive reasoning; drawing inferences from relationships; and solving problems. Table 10.3 presents an example of a number-series reasoning test, not directly related to creativity, that has been used to measure *Gf*. That sort of a test can be used to assess *Gf* independently of creative thinking.

The second factor, *short-term memory – Gsm* – centers on understanding and use of information over a short period of time. It involves two subfactors. First is *memory span*, the ability to store some information briefly and reproduce it in the same order as it was just presented, which is familiar from the discussion in Chapter 6 of S. F.'s extraordinary memory. The second subfactor of *Gsm* is efficiency of manipulation of information within short-term memory. Another label for this subfactor is working-memory capacity (WMC). That capacity involves attentional focus – the ability to focus attention in order to manipulate, combine, and transform information while avoiding distracting stimuli. Attentional focus in working memory also entails the ability to engage in strategic and controlled searches for information in long-term memory. The *Gsm* factor, especially the working-memory component, is similar to what we have discussed in earlier chapters as *executive functioning*. It has been argued by some researchers that WMC and *Gf* might be related, with WMC actually being the foundation of *Gf*. Current opinion is that WMC and *Gf* are closely related, but that other factors, beyond WMC, contribute to *Gf* (Engle, 2018; Kyllonen & Kell, 2017).

The third factor, long-term retrieval – *Glr* – includes storing information and retrieving it later. The difference between *Glr* and *Gsm* is that, in the latter, you are dealing with information that is the focus of consciousness. In *Glr* tests, information is retrieved from long-term memory. Many of the components of *Glr* are also seen in D-T tests (Flanagan & Dixon, 2013). One example is Sensitivity to Problems/Alternative Solution Fluency, discussed earlier in this chapter, the ability to rapidly think of a number of solutions to particular practical problem. That is one component of *Glr*. Another, Associational Fluency, is the ability to rapidly produce a series of original or useful ideas related to a particular concept, such as synonyms for a word. Another measure of Associational Fluency is the number of responses rated as highly creative on an unusual uses test. Ideational Fluency, still another component of *Glr*, is the ability to rapidly produce a series of ideas, words, or phrases related to a specific condition or object. An example is listing objects that are red, round, and solid. Quantity, not quality, is emphasized. Finally, Originality/Creativity (*FO*) is the ability to rapidly produce original, clever, and insightful responses (expressions, interpretations) to a given topic, situation, or task. In developing the *Glr* factor, CHC theory incorporated creativity directly into IQ (Flanagan & Dixon, 2013).

Crystallized knowledge – *Gc* – is also called comprehension-knowledge, or crystallized intelligence, and it represents the breadth and depth of a person's knowledge, based on previously learned procedures. The results of previous fluid reasoning incidents become part of one's crystallized knowledge. The term "crystallized" indicates that the knowledge is not readily adapted to new situations, as fluid skills are.

CHC Factors and Creativity

Researchers have examined the relationships between several level II factors and creativity, most particularly fluid intelligence (*Gf*). As mentioned, *Gf* can be measured using several tests that are not directly related to creativity or divergent thinking, such as letter-series tasks, number-series tasks, and figural reasoning tasks. A number of studies using such measures have demonstrated that *Gf* is related to creativity. Silvia (2008) found that higher *Gf* was related to better performance on the unusual uses test. Benedek and colleagues (2012) measured *Gf* through a random-sequence-generation test, in which participants had to generate random series of keyboard presses. They reported that *Gf* was related to judges' ratings of originality of ideas on an unusual uses test.

Additional evidence for the positive role of *Gf* in creativity comes from a study by Nusbaum, Silvia, and Beaty (2014) that examined the effects of instructions to be creative on performance of individuals differing in fluid intelligence. Instructing people to be creative increases performance on D-T tests. Nusbaum, Silvia, and Beaty tested people on two unusual-uses tests: unusual uses for a rope or for a box. One test was given under instructions to be creative; the other under instructions to produce many responses ("fluency" instructions). Under "be creative" instructions, people high in fluid intelligence produced uses that were rated more creative than were uses produced by people low in *Gf*. In other words, with "be creative" instructions, there was a positive relationship between *Gf* and creativity. Under fluency instructions, all the participants produced more uses than under the instructions to be creative, but those uses were rated as less creative. Also, there was no difference between the high- versus low-*Gf* groups in numbers of uses produced or in the rated creativity of the responses.

In sum, within one study, Nusbaum, Silvia, and Beaty (2014) showed that sometimes fluid intelligence is relatively strongly related to creativity – with "be creative" instructions – and sometimes it is weakly related to creativity – with fluency instructions. An explanation for that pattern of results may be that "be creative" instructions make higher cognitive demands on the individual than fluency instructions do (try to produce a lot of responses). The greater difficulty of the be-creative condition may demand higher *Gf* skills. This explanation assumes that trying to produce creative responses is a difficult problem-solving task that may demand complex strategies. The ability to produce and use such strategies may demand fluid intelligence. This finding may tell us much about how the creative process works in D-T tasks and will be discussed in more detail shortly.

Several other studies have shown that long-term retrieval (*Glr*) and crystallized knowledge (*Gc*) are related to several aspects of creative production. One creative ability that has been studied is the creation of metaphors, a skill that plays a role in poetry and fiction writing. Silvia and Beaty (2012) had individuals generate metaphors to describe a familiar situation, such as sitting through a boring class ("sitting in a boring lecture is like: _____"). The rated creativity of the metaphors was related to *Gf*. In addition, high *Grl* and *Gc* were also related to creativity of metaphors. Similarly, the ability to produce humorous captions for cartoons, or to complete jokes with funny endings, is related to *Gf* and *Gc*.

CHC Factors and Creativity: Conclusions

It seems that several aspects of CHC IQ are related to D-T performance and to other creative abilities. That finding leads us to a further question, of broad importance, concerning what the CHC results tell us about the mechanisms underlying creative thinking. What cognitive processes are being tapped by asking a person to produce creative uses for a shoe, to list all the white edible things they can think of, or to provide a funny caption for a cartoon? Carrying this line of inquiry further, why it is that some people, when asked to produce unusual uses for a brick, produce responses that are judged as creative? What is the process – or processes – underlying creative thinking in general and divergent thinking specifically? And what role do *Gf* and related processes play? Researchers have proposed two types of answers to the "process" question.

Possible Mechanisms Underlying Creative Thinking: Associative Processes versus Executive Functioning

Associative Processes in D-T Performance

One long-standing answer to the question concerning the processes underlying D-T performance is that the process is *associative*, involving links

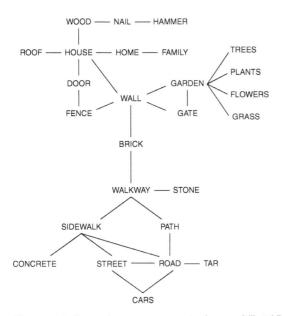

Figure 10.3 Semantic memory organized around "brick"

among items in semantic memory (see Figure 10.3, which presents a representation of a person's semantic memory). We have already discussed this idea in Chapter 8, when we considered the "spreading activation" explanation for unconscious processing. Consider a person who has been asked to produce an unusual use for a brick. Upon presentation of that D-T test item, associations "run off" in memory, starting from *brick* and going in all directions, until a connection is made that results in an idea that can lead to an unusual use. Let us say that a person produces the following string of associations when *brick* is presented: *brick, wall, house, wood, nail, hammer.* *Hammer* leads to the possibility that a brick could be used as a hammer.

As was discussed earlier, Mednick's (1962) theory proposes the mechanism of flat associative hierarchies to explain the ability to think divergently. Flat hierarchies, made up of responses of near-equal strength, allow some people – people who can think creatively – to produce "remote" or infrequent associations when presented with a stimulus item such as producing "hammer" in response to "brick" during an unusual-uses test (Nusbaum & Silvia, 2011). That associative process is assumed to work automatically and unconsciously, without "executive" control. The stimulus word is presented and activation simply spreads through memory until a possible new use surfaces in consciousness. We can call this the *associative* theory of divergent thinking.

Testing Mednick's Associative Hierarchies

Mednick's (1962) theory was tested by Benedek and Neubauer (2013), who compared the associative hierarchies of high- versus low-creative individuals. Creativity was defined by the combination of several measures, including two unusual-uses tests as well as two measures of self-rated creativity. High- versus low-creative groups were formed by taking people scoring in the top third versus the bottom third of a large sample group. Associative hierarchies were determined by having participants produce all the words they could in response to a stimulus word, such as "street," in sixty seconds. A total of ten stimulus words was presented. The researchers measured how common, on average, a given person's responses were, based on all the responses produced by the participants. Mednick's theory predicts that more-creative individuals would produce less-common words (a "flatter" associative hierarchy). In contrast, less-creative people should produce more-common responses. That prediction was not upheld: the associative hierarchies were identical for the two groups.

One difference in responding between high- versus low-creative individuals was that on average the high creatives produced more of the uncommon responses; they also produced more responses overall. Thus, creative individuals' ability to produce *uncommon* responses might be related to their ability to produce *more* responses. As we will see, that latter ability might be related to executive functioning, but Benedek and Neubauer (2013) did not measure executive functioning in this study.

Executive Functioning in Divergent Thinking

The associative explanation of divergent thinking assumes that the structure of a person's knowledge determines their ability to produce novel ideas. Several recent studies have examined divergent thinking from a different perspective, assuming that people working on unusual-uses tests are *actively trying to solve a problem*. From this perspective, an important factor in the production of novel ideas is what one can do with one's knowledge based on the strategies that one can develop and utilize in a given situation (Silvia, 2015). This view is similar to the analysis in Chapters 3 and 7 of the development and use of heuristics during problem-solving. From this perspective, executive functioning is assumed to be crucial in generating new ideas. Executive functioning includes executive abilities (e.g., working-memory capacity (WMC), inhibition, and fluid intelligence) and executive processes (e.g., interference management and strategy use). A growing number of studies have presented evidence for the role of executive functioning in divergent thinking.

In groundbreaking research, Gilhooly et al. (2007) asked people to carry out an unusual-uses test while thinking aloud and discovered several strategies that were used on the task. *Memory Use Production* involved retrieving already-known uses from memory, which resulted in non-novel uses. Other strategies were used in producing novel uses. In the *Disassembly* strategy, the person took apart the object to see if the parts could provide a novel use. So, if you were asked to produce unusual uses for a shoe, you might think about taking the laces out and using them, which could result in an unusual use for a shoe. One could tie one's hair in a ponytail using a shoelace. In the *Property Use* strategy, the person retrieved a property of the object and then used that property as a cue to produce possible uses, for example, "A pencil is sharp, so can be used to poke holes in paper." In the *Broad Use First* strategy, the person considered the target object against an initially broad use category, for example, "Could a barrel be used as a kind of weapon? A means of transport? Yes, you could float things in it down a river." People who more frequently used the *Disassembly*, *Property*, and *Broad Use First* strategies produced novel uses that were rated more creative than those produced by people who used the *Memory Use Production* strategy.

In a second study, briefly discussed earlier, Gilhooly et al. (2007) examined the relationship between executive functioning and strategy use. They gave people an usual-uses test and then asked them to specify which of their responses were new – just created – and which uses had been familiar – not just created. The participants were also given two other tasks after the unusual-uses test. First was *letter fluency*: naming words beginning with a specific letter, such as *f*. That task measures executive functioning, because the person has to develop a strategy to search memory, since our knowledge about words is not organized by letter. The second task was *category fluency*: generating members of a given category, such as *dogs*. Category fluency does not involve executive functioning to the same degree, since our knowledge is already organized into categories. The person can simply use that organization. Gilhooly et al. made several predictions. First of all, *new* uses would be rated as more creative than the *old* ones. Also, the number of *new* uses produced would be related to high performance on the letter-frequency task – that is, to higher *Gf*. In contrast, *old* uses would be related to performance on the category-fluency task. Those predictions were all upheld, which supported the idea that executive functioning plays a role in generation of new ideas.

Beaty and Silvia (2012) examined the relationship between several measures of *Gf*, which they equated with executive functioning, and performance on the unusual-uses test. The measures of executive functioning included WMC; a spatial reasoning task; and letter-series and number-series tasks. One interesting aspect of performance on the unusual-uses test is that later uses are judged more creative than earlier ones. Based on Mednick's (1962) associative perspective, later uses are more creative because the associations for noncreative uses must first be worked through before unusual uses can be discovered. (See the associative chain for *brick* ⇒ *hammer* discussed earlier; Figure 10.3.) Based on the executive-functioning view, Beaty and Silvia took a different perspective. They hypothesized that the increasing creativity of later uses occurred because people had to consider and *eliminate* the familiar and not-creative uses before they could get to thinking about novel uses. If so, then an important skill in carrying out the unusual-uses task is the ability to *inhibit* the uninteresting familiar uses, which would allow the person to focus on creating new ones. The researchers found that people with higher levels of executive function were able to more quickly produce novel responses. They interpreted that result as indicating that the ability to inhibit ordinary uses, which is an executive-function skill, was playing a significant role in D-T. Nusbaum and Silvia (2011) reported similar results.

Further evidence for the role of executive functioning in creative thinking comes from a study by Smith, Huber, and Vul (2013) that examined performance on compound remote associates (CRA) problems, which are already familiar. Here is an example problem:

> What word can be combined with the following three words, to produce a compound word (or phrase)?
> age mile sand
> The solution word is *stone*: stone age; milestone; sandstone.

Smith, Huber, and Vul asked people to guess possible solution words as they worked toward solution of each of a set of CRA problems. An explanation of performance on CRA problems based on associations and spreading activation would propose that activation from the three stimulus words would combine to influence the words that are produced as possible solutions. However, when the researchers examined the possible solution words that people produced, they found that the incorrect guesses were not related to all three words. Rather, the guesses seemed to arise from two strategies. First, the individual chose one word from the problem and used that word as the basis for generating possible solutions. Second, when a proposed solution was incorrect, the individual would use that word as the basis for the next guess. The use of such strategies points to the role of executive functioning in solution of CRA problems, although it should be noted that Smith, Huber, and Vul did not test directly the possible role of executive functioning in their participants' performance.

Associative Processes versus Executive Functioning in Divergent Thinking: A Role for Each?

The results from the studies just reviewed indicate that executive functioning is important in D-T performance. That conclusion – along with the Benedek and Neubauer (2013) study just reviewed that did not find evidence for flat versus steep associative hierarchies in high- versus low-creative individuals – raises questions about the role of associative processes in creativity. However, a number of recent studies have provided evidence that both executive functioning *and* the structure of people's knowledge – another way of saying flat versus steep associative hierarchies – play roles in creative thinking.

In one investigation, Beaty et al. (2014) examined the relationship among associative processes, executive functioning, and divergent thinking. Participants completed several Gf tasks as measures of executive functioning. Participants were also given two associative fluency tasks, involving listing synonyms to a stimulus word (e.g., synonyms to *hot*). The researchers determined the "semantic distance" between each participant's associative responses and the stimulus word. That distance provided a measure of the structure of each participant's knowledge base. Some people produced synonyms that were closely related to the stimulus: for example, *blazing, boiling, heated* as synonyms to *hot*. They were classified as having had a tightly structured knowledge base, which would correspond to Mednick's steep associative hierarchy. In contrast, some people produced a wider range of words as synonyms for *hot* – *blistering, smoky, sexy* – which was taken as evidence for a "loose" knowledge base. All participants also completed two unusual-uses tests. Results indicated that both associative structure and executive functioning were independently related to D-T performance. People with looser knowledge bases produced more-creative responses on the unusual-uses test, as did people high in Gf (see also Kenett et al. (2016); Benedek and colleagues (2013); and Lee and Therriault (2013)). It therefore seems that both associative and executive processes are important in creative thinking.

A Remaining Question: What Is the Basis for "Loose Associations"?

If we conclude that both associative and executive processes are important in creative thinking, however, we are left with at least one critical question. Concerning "associative" processes, what is the basis for "tight" versus "loose" knowledge bases or, in different words, the basis for "steep" versus "flat" associative hierarchies? Why does one person say *blazing, boiling, heated* as synonyms of *hot*, while another says *blistering, smoky, sexy*? Are those differences based on their experiences? Do people with a broader range of experiences to draw on have "looser" knowledge bases? On the other hand, people's experiences might be essentially the same, but the way those experiences are stored in memory might be different. Perhaps some people's brains are "more loosely wired," so that, when some stimulus is presented, a broader range of responses is available to them. Finally, perhaps people's knowledge bases are the same, but people search memory differently. That possibility leads to a possible link among knowledge structure and executive functioning and fluid intelligence. That is, differences in "associative structures" might be the result of differences in strategies used to search memory. At present, those questions await answers.

The Generality versus Domain-Specificity of Creative-Thinking Skills

One critical assumption underlying the development of tests to measure creative potential is that creativity is a general trait of people. That is why researchers assumed that responses on an unusual-uses-for-a-brick test would predict creative production in areas such as literature, poetry, and painting. However, research results are contradictory concerning whether or not creativity is a general trait. First of all, recall the finding that creative achievement depends on domain-specific expertise that takes years to acquire (the Ten-Year Rule; see Chapter 6). That result, by itself, raises questions for any theory that assumes that creative achievement depends on general creative-thinking skills. The Ten-Year Rule indicates that highly specific skills – not general skills – are crucial in creative achievement.

Baer (see Baer (2015) for review) has taken a different approach to assessing the possible generality of creativity. He has asked ordinary people, ranging from schoolchildren to adults, to produce creative products in a variety of domains, such as poems, short stories, collages, and mathematical puzzles. The products in each domain were then rated for creativity by judges. Results from several studies indicated that performance across domains was not related; that is, the person who wrote the best poem did not necessarily construct the best collage. Baer concluded that creative ability is specific in nature. Indeed, creative production in Baer's studies was highly domain-specific: even the domains of poetry and story-writing, which one might think would be related, were not. The best poets did not produce the best stories.

Baer (2012, 2015) also used training in D-T skills in an attempt to examine the general versus specific nature of creative-thinking skills. In one study, seventh-grade students were given practice using D-T skills that were related to poetry (e.g., the students practiced producing words that rhymed with a given stimulus word). The trained students and a non-trained control group then wrote poems and short stories, which were evaluated by judges. The training had a very specific effect: the poetry-writing skills increased for the trained group compared with the control group, but the story-writing skills did not. This is evidence that training in skills potentially relevant to creative thinking has effects only within the domain to which the training is directed. One does not seem to get general increases in creative thinking from such training.

Testing Creativity: Summary and Conclusions

Guilford (1950, 1967) was successful in urging that psychologists study creativity, and that they should do so through the development of tests, to assess the components of creative thinking and to enable us to predict who among us was creative. Guilford proposed that there was a set of skills – D-T skills – that were different than those measured by IQ tests and were the foundation of the capacity to think creatively. Divergent thinking involved *fluency*, the ability to produce many ideas in response to a situation demanding creativity; *flexibility*, the ability to produce many different sorts of ideas; and *originality*, the ability to produce ideas not produced by others. Many researchers followed Guilford's lead, and "creativity tests" have become part of the landscape in education and psychometrics. Those tests have demonstrated predictive validity – they are useful in predicting who will grow up to be creative. Furthermore, the set of skills that those tests were designed to measure have become part of the psychologist's tool kit in analyzing creative thinking.

However, there are a number of areas in which Guilford's analysis can be questioned. First, although D-T performance predicts later creativity, it seems that divergent thinking may not be the core component of creative thinking. Case studies of creative thinking, discussed elsewhere in this book (see also Weisberg, 2006, ch. 5), have provided evidence that the creative process does not begin by producing numerous and varied ideas. Rather, the creative process is, from the beginning, directed by the match between one's knowledge and the problem one is facing. In other words, divergent thinking does not possess face validity as a measure of creative thinking. The fact that D-T tests can possess predictive validity – can predict later creative achievement – while, at the same time, divergent thinking is not part of the process of creative thinking is puzzling. That question will be addressed in Chapter 11.

Also, there is evidence that creative thinking may not be independent of IQ, contrary to Guilford's (1950) proposal. Recent theoretical and statistical advances concerning the measurement and interpretation of IQ have indicated that components of IQ, most particularly components of fluid intelligence and executive functioning, play important roles in creative production. Those results provide support for the analytic-thinking framework that underlies the viewpoint presented in this book.

11 | The Search for the "Creative Personality"

In Chapter 10, we explored Guilford's (1950, 1967) proposal that psychologists should study creativity by developing tests to measure creative thinking and to enable us to predict who would develop into creative individuals. Guilford was successful in stimulating many researchers to design tests to analyze cognitive components of creative thinking. However, the development of creativity tests was one only part of Guilford's (1950) proposed program for the study of creativity. In Guilford's view, creative achievement was an expression of an individual's *personality*. In this chapter, we will examine the role of personality in creativity.

Outline of the Chapter

Researchers have examined two general questions concerning the relationship between personality and creativity. The first is whether there are any components of personality that distinguish creative individuals from noncreative. Those components would comprise the "creative personality." The chapter begins with a review of research that has tried to specify the creative personality. Psychologists measure personality as a set of *traits*: relatively permanent aspects of our thinking and behavior (Feist, 2018; Guilford, 1950). We will first examine current theorizing concerning the measurement of personality in general. That will lead to a discussion of the traits that are related to creative achievement in the arts versus science. There are difficulties that arise when one tries to specify the personality traits that are related to creativity and we will address those issues. The second question addressed by researchers is how personality plays a role in real-world creative activities. We will review research examining how personality traits might support creativity. Here, too, researchers face many thorny issues in trying to specify the mechanisms that might connect personality traits to creative achievement.

As one can see from this brief outline, there are questions that researchers have to deal with when they try to specify the personality characteristics of creative individuals and how those characteristics contribute to creative achievement. Those questions mean that there will be criticisms raised at various points in this chapter concerning the conclusions drawn by researchers. However, it must be kept in mind that this critical analysis is indicative of the difficulties that researchers are trying to deal with. To provide a framework for the discussion in the chapter, please carry out the exercise in Table 11.1.

Table 11.1 *A personality inventory: The Big-5 Inventory – 2 Extra-Short Form (BFI-2-XS)*

Here are a number of characteristics that may or may not apply **to you**. For example, do you agree that you are someone who *likes to spend time with others*? Please write a number next to each statement to indicate the extent to which you agree or disagree with that statement.

1 Disagree strongly	2 Disagree a little	3 Neutral; no opinion	4 Agree a little	5 Agree strongly

I am someone who. . .

1.	Tends to be quiet.	9.	Tends to feel depressed, blue.	
2.	Is compassionate, has a soft heart.	10.	Has little interest in abstract ideas.	
3.	Tends to be disorganized.	11.	Is full of energy.	
4.	Worries a lot.	12.	Assumes the best about people.	
5.	Is fascinated by art, music, or literature.	13.	Is reliable, can always be counted on.	
6.	Is dominant, acts as a leader.	14.	Is emotionally stable, not easily upset.	
7.	Is sometimes rude to others.	15.	Is original, comes up with new ideas.	
8.	Has difficulty getting started on tasks.			

Please check: Did you write a number in front of each statement?
BFI-2 items copyright 2015 by Oliver P. John and Christopher J. Soto. Reproduced by permission.

Measuring Personality

The Big-5

You filled out a brief personality inventory (or personality test) in Table 11.1 (Soto & John, 2017a, 2017b). That inventory provided measures of five traits that have become central in modern theorizing about personality. Those traits, called the Big-5 (Soto & John, 2017a), are Open-mindedness; Conscientiousness; Extraversion; Agreeableness; and Negative Emotionality. Over the last thirty years, research on personality has been dominated by the Big-5, also called the Five-Factor conception of personality. The 5-Factor perspective proposed, not surprisingly, that personality was comprised of five factors, or *domains* (Feist, 2017; Fürst & Lubart, 2017), as outlined in Table 11.2, which also presents some additional specific questionnaire items – the *facets* – that contribute to each domain (DeYoung, Quilty & Peterson, 2007). The five domains that comprise the Big-5 are the following.

(1) Open-mindedness: A tendency to be curious and open to new ideas; and to be flexible in behavior and thought. This domain is sometimes referred to as Openness, or Openness/Intellect. Items 5, 10, and 15 in the inventory in Table 11.1 measure Open-mindedness (Item 10 is "reversed-scored": people who disagree with this item are scored positively).

(2) Conscientiousness: A tendency to control one's impulses; to be detail-oriented and careful; and to prefer order to disorder. Items 3 (reverse-scored), 8 (reverse-scored), and 13 in the inventory in Table 11.1 measure Conscientiousness.

(3) Extraversion: A tendency to be social; to enjoy social activities; to seek out stimulating experiences; to be confident and to take on leadership roles in groups. Items 1 (reverse-scored), 6, and 11 in the inventory in Table 11.1 measure Extraversion.

(4) Agreeableness: A tendency to be caring of others, warm, and empathetic in social relationships. Items 2, 7 (reverse-scored) (reverse-scored), and 11 in the inventory in Table 11.1 measure Agreeableness.

(5) Negative Emotionality: A tendency toward negative affect, such as anxiety, depression, stress, and guilt. Sometimes called Neuroticism. Items 4, 9, and 14 (reverse-scored) in the inventory in Table 11.1 measure Negative Emotionality.

Table 11.2 *Big-5: five-factor personality dimensions and facets*

Dimensions	Facets – Items on Personality Scale
1. Open-mindedness	
Openness	Get deeply immersed in music.
	See beauty in things others might not notice.
	Need a creative outlet.
	Often get lost in thought.
	Often notice the emotional aspects of art
Intellect	Am quick to understand things.
	Like to solve complex problems.
	Formulate ideas clearly.
	Join philosophical discussions.
	Enjoy difficult reading material.
2. Extraversion	
	Have a strong personality.
	Am the first to act.
	Warm up quickly to others.
	Show my feelings when I'm happy.
3. Conscientiousness	
	Finish what I start.
	Get things done quickly.
	Follow a schedule.
	Want everything to be "just right."
4. Agreeableness	
	Feel others' emotions.
	Take an interest in other people's lives.
	Respect authority.
	Hate to seem pushy.
5. Negative Emotionality	
	Feel threatened easily
	Worry about things.
	Get angry easily.
	Change my mood a lot.

The Big-2

It was thought originally that the Big-5 domains were independent of each other and therefore they were the highest levels of personality. In addition, it was assumed that each domain was unified and comprised a core component of personality. Both of those assumptions have been questioned (Digman, 1997; Feist, 2018; Fürst & Lubart, 2017; Peterson & Carson, 2000;

Table 11.3 *The Big-2 or Huge-2 model of personality*

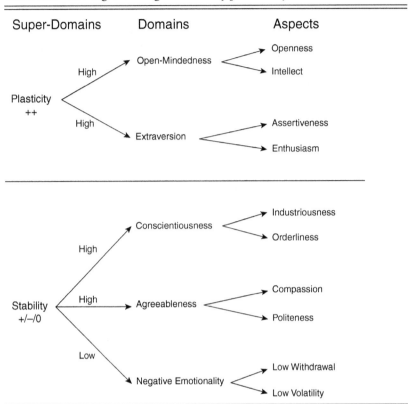

Note: "High" and "Low" labels indicate that high versus low scores in domains contribute to super-domain (e.g., *high* Open-mindedness = *high* Plasticity; *low* Negative Emotionality = *high* Stability); and so forth for domains and aspects

Soto & John, 2017). First, research has indicated that the Big-5 domains are not the highest levels of personality. The Big-5 can be grouped into two higher-order domains – "super-domains" – *plasticity* and *stability* (see the left of Table 11.3). This analysis has been called the Big-2 or Huge-2 (Feist, 2018; Fürst & Lubart, 2017; Karwowski & Lebuda, 2016). Furthermore, it has been shown that each of the Big-5 domains can be divided into *aspects*, as shown in the far right in Table 11.3.

The super-domain of Plasticity combines the domains of Open-mindedness and Extraversion, which have been found to be positively related; in other words, people scoring high on one tend to score high on the other. High Plasticity includes tendencies toward exploration of the environment and of ideas; flexibility in thought; adapting to novel situations; questioning social norms; seeking out stimulating experiences; and having a tendency toward positive emotions. Stability is very different and centers on coping with stress and negative emotions; conforming to social norms; being warm and friendly in one's social relationships; and being careful and controlling of one's impulses. It is made up of *high* Conscientiousness, *high* Agreeableness, and **low** Negative Emotionality (i.e., a tendency away from negative emotions).

Personality and Creativity: An Overview

Figure 11.1 presents a general model of personality developed by Feist (2017, 2018; Grosul & Feist, 2014), who has been a leader in the study of the creative personality. The model outlines the various types of personality traits that play roles in a person's producing some outcome, in this case creative achievement. Biological factors – genetic and other influences – are primary since they influence brain development. Brain structures, in turn, affect the development of traits of personality that affect creativity. Those traits include cognitive traits, or skills, such as divergent-thinking (D-T) ability; as well as social traits such as extraversion; and motivational traits such as conscientiousness. We will not examine D-T abilities further in this chapter since they were the focus of Chapter 10. The model also includes clinical traits associated with psychopathology. Those traits are included because of the possible connection between genius and madness, discussed in Chapter 9. The various psychological traits can affect each other, as indicated by the arrows between them. Feist assumed that personality traits indicate a lowered tendency to behave and think in specific ways.

> The fundamental assumption . . . is that the "who" in creative thought and behavior is not equally distributed in the population and that certain people are more likely than others to have truly creative ideas. And one of the mechanisms that make these ideas more likely in some than in others is certain traits and qualities of personality. (Feist, 2017, p. 64)

In Feist's view, certain personality traits function to "lower the threshold" for creative thought and behavior – that is, to make creative activities more likely. This model can serve as an overarching framework that can guide the discussion in this chapter.

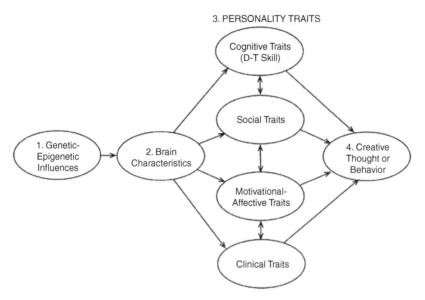

3. PERSONALITY TRAITS

Cognitive Traits
(D-T Skill)

Social Traits

1. Genetic-
Epigenetic
Influences

2. Brain
Characteristics

4. Creative
Thought or
Behavior

Motivational-
Affective Traits

Clinical Traits

Figure 11.1 Grosul and Feist's general model of personality and creativity, elaborating on Guilford (Feist, 2010, 2017; Grosul & Feist, 2014)

The relationships among the various components of the Big-2 and creativity are summarized in Table 11.4. The super-domain Plasticity is consistently found to be related to creativity. Its components are not equally strongly related to creativity, however. Open-mindedness is related to creative outcomes of all sorts, from divergent-thinking scores to creative achievements, as are its aspects. Extraversion, on the other hand, is sometimes associated with creativity, depending on which aspect is examined. The Assertiveness aspect – taking leadership – is related to creativity, but Enthusiasm is not. As far as the super-domain Stability is concerned, its overall relationship to creativity is not consistent. Conscientiousness has mixed relationships with creativity, with Industriousness positively related to creativity but Orderliness not related. Agreeableness, overall, has a negative relationship with creativity, as do both its aspects. Finally, scoring low on Negative Emotionality is also not simply associated with creativity; low volatility is associated with creativity, while low withdrawal is not (Kaufman et al., 2015).

In sum, research has shown that some personality characteristics are related to creativity. However, the discussion so far has been at a very general level. Let us now look at how psychologists have attempted to determine in more detail the traits that characterize creative people in different domains. More specifically, we will examine what research has

Table 11.4 *Big-2 model and creativity*

Super-Domains	Domains	Aspects
Plasticity ++	Open-mindedness +++	Openness +++
		Intellect +++
	Extraversion +/0	Assertiveness +
		Enthusiasm 0
Stability +/−/0	Conscientiousness +/0	Industrialness +
		Orderliness 0
	Agreeableness −/−	Compassion −
		Politeness −
	Negative Emotionality 0/+	Low Withdrawal 0
		Low Volatility + (art); − (science)

told us about the relationship between personality traits and creativity in the arts versus science.

Examining the Personalities of Creative Artists versus Creative Scientists

Feist (1998, p. 294) reviewed research examining the personality characteristics of artists and scientists. He included studies in which *artists* had been defined by the researchers as students majoring in or studying art or as anyone earning an income in an "artistic" domain, such as writing, painting, music, or poetry. *Scientists* were defined as any sample, from junior high school through adulthood, that showed special talent in science, majored in science, or worked professionally in academic or commercial science. *Science* ranged from the natural and biological sciences to the social sciences and also to invention, engineering, and mathematics.

A critical question in such research is what group should be used as a comparison for determining the "creative personality" in artists and scientists. In his analysis of studies of artists, Feist (1998) included only studies that examined a comparison or control group of *nonartists*. For the studies of scientists, the comparison groups were either noncreative scientists or nonscientists. Thus, there were different control or comparison groups in the studies of artists versus scientists. The motivation for choosing studies with different control groups in the two areas was based on differences in the arts versus sciences as professions. People working as research scientists can carry out their work with differing degrees of creativity but can still maintain careers as scientists. For example, people can be employed as research scientists at a university with very different levels of contributions to the advancement of the field – that is, with different degrees of creative achievement. If one then compares more-versus less-creative scientists, one would have real differences in creativity between the groups and so one could make meaningful comparisons of their personalities.

For artists, in contrast, one could argue that all practicing artists are creative, although some might not be recognized by the outside world. In most of the studies of artists that Feist (1998) reviewed, the creative group was comprised of people who were earning income as artists. Choosing as a comparison group artists who were not well known would result in groups that were both creative. Therefore, there might be no important differences between them in personality. That reasoning led to the concentration on studies of the artistic personality in which the control group was composed of "nonartist ordinary people." This is an important issue, and we will return to it later in the chapter.

The Creative Personality

Researchers have found similarities but also differences in the personality profiles for artists versus scientists (Feist, 1998, 2017; see Table 11.5).

The Artistic Personality

Artists rated themselves as being more open-minded and open to fantasy and imagination than did nonartists. Artists also are less conforming to society's norms and expectations; they are impulsive; not conscientious; nonconforming; and independent. This set of characteristics fits the "job description" of an artist in our culture, which is questioning and rebelling

Table 11.5 *Summary of personality characteristics of the creative personality of artists and scientists (from Feist, 1998)*

Trait Category	Trait	
	Artists	Scientists
Nonsocial	Open-mindedness	Open-mindedness
	Fantasy-oriented	Flexibility of thought
	Imagination	
	Impulsivity	
	Lack of conscientiousness	
	Anxiety	
	Affective illness	
	Emotional sensitivity	
	Drive	Drive
	Ambition	Ambition
		Achievement
Social	Norm doubting	Autonomy
	Nonconformity	Introversion
	Independence	Independence
	Hostility	Hostility
	Aloofness	Arrogance
	Unfriendliness	Self-confidence
	Lack of warmth	

against society's norms. Artists are also driven and ambitious and are not particularly friendly people. Related to their lack of sociability, they are also introverted. In addition, there is evidence that artists have tendencies toward anxiety and affective illness. As we saw in Chapter 9, Ludwig (1998) reported that individuals in artistic fields that rely more on emotional or subjective modes of expression show greater rates of psychopathology. The personality profile of the artist that emerges from these studies is an individual who is imaginative and open to new ideas; driven and anxious; and not social.

The Personality of the Creative Scientist

Creative scientists, like artists, rate themselves as open-minded. Scientists, again like artists, are ambitious and driven, and they want to achieve more than their noncreative peers do. The creative scientists were also arrogant, hostile, dominant, and, perhaps not surprisingly, self-confident. They, like the artists, were not social; they were autonomous, aloof, and independent. One sees overall similarities to the artists in the scientists' drive and ambition as well as in their open-mindedness and lack of sociability. Scientists are also flexible in their thinking, which fits the idea that creative individuals in the sciences have to go beyond what they know. One interesting finding noted by Feist (1998) but not summarized in Table 11.5 is that outstanding science *students* seem to be *not* flexible in their thinking. That finding raises important questions about cause-and-effect relationships between personality and creative achievement, which will be discussed shortly.

Open-mindedness and Creativity: A Closer Look

We have seen that both creative scientists and artists rate themselves as more open-minded than the respective control groups do (Feist, 1998). Grosul and Feist (2014) recently carried out a further examination of personality factors related to scientific creativity, using the overall Big-5 as their measure of personality. A random sample of 3,100 scientists, from a wide range of disciplines, anthropology to physics, was contacted by email and asked to participate in the study. Approximately 10 percent agreed to do so, and, of those, a total of 145 were included. The participants completed personality inventories and supplied information about their scientific achievements. The researchers obtained measures of the total number of publications and the number of times the person's research had been cited by others, which was taken as evidence that the work was seen as valuable. In addition, Grosul and Feist calculated a *creativity index* (Soler, 2007), which used a formula to determine how groundbreaking a person's work has been.

The results of the study are shown in Table 11.6. As can be seen, the only significant relationships between personality and creativity were seen for Open-mindedness. None of the other factors was significantly related to creativity, and many of those other correlations were negative. As noted, this study did not analyze the personality measures more deeply than the Big-5. However, as we know, Open-mindedness is composed of two aspects: Openness and Intellect. If one looks at those aspects in detail (see Table 11.7A), one sees clear differences between the personality-inventory items – the facets – that contribute to Openness versus Intellect. The Openness items point to artistic or aesthetic interests – for example, enjoying the beauty of nature, or needing a creative outlet. In contrast, Intellect contains items that seem related to science – for example, being quick to understand, liking complex problems, and liking difficult reading

Table 11.6 *Grosul and Feist (2014) results concerning 5-Factor model and scientific creativity*

Personality Factor	Creativity Measure	
	Creativity Index	Overall Creativity Score
Open-mindedness	.22	.21
Conscientiousness	−.02	−.03
Extraversion	−.14	.01
Agreeableness	−.08	−.08
Negative Emotionality	−.02	−.03

Table 11.7 *Open-mindedness and creativity*

A. *Open-Mindedness Facets*

Openness	Get deeply immersed in music.
	See beauty in things others might not notice.
	Need a creative outlet.
	Often get lost in thought.
	Often notice the emotional aspects of art
Intellect	Am quick to understand things.
	Like to solve complex problems.
	Formulate ideas clearly.
	Join philosophical discussions.
	Enjoy difficult reading material.

B. *Results from study of Kaufman et al. (2015)*

Personality Measure	Creativity Measure			
	Total Creativity (CAQ)	Artistic Creativity	Scientific Creativity	Divergent Thinking (DT)
Openness	.38	.39	.10	.18
Intellect	.22	.16	.27	.27
Intelligence (g)	.11	.06	.24	.37

material. Thus, it seems reasonable that Openness might be related to creativity in art and Intellect might be related to creativity in science.

Kaufman et al. (2015) tested that prediction. They tested four groups of people, including students in the upper level of a selective high school in England; more than 300 undergraduates at a university in Canada; and a 305-person Internet sample from Minneapolis–St. Paul, Minnesota. There was no attempt made specifically to sample groups of creative scientists or artists. Each participant-group provided information about their creative achievements, using the Creative Achievements Questionnaire (CAQ; Carson, 2018), which asks about achievements in a wide range of domains, including poetry, dance, and music in the arts; and invention and scientific discovery in the sciences. Participants also completed a Big-5 inventory, and people in some of the groups completed IQ measures and divergent-thinking (D-T) tests.

The results of the study are shown in Table 11.7B. In the second column, one sees that, overall, Openness and Intellect were both related to total creativity (the sum of the CAQ scores for artistic and scientific creativity), with Openness more strongly related. Looking at the third and fourth columns, however, one sees that the specific predictions made by Kaufman et al. (2015) were supported. Openness was more strongly related to artistic than scientific creativity, and the reverse held for Intellect. Looking at IQ and creativity, intelligence was significantly correlated only with scientific creativity. Intelligence was also correlated with divergent thinking, which is consistent with the results discussed in the last chapter (Gilhooly et al., 2007; Beatty & Silvia, 2012).

Open-mindedness and Creativity: Summary

Open-mindedness is the personality factor most consistently related to creative thinking and creative achievement. However, Open-mindedness is composed of two separable aspects, one of which – Openness – is related to artistic creativity, and the other of which – Intellect – is related to scientific creativity. As mentioned, that result is not surprising if one looks at the items that comprise those two separate aspects of the combined factor (see Table 11.7A).

Studies of the Creative Personality: The Question of the Control Group

As noted earlier, many of the studies that have investigated the artistic personality have used a comparison group of ordinary individuals – that is, people who are not engaged in art in any way. If one compares the personality characteristics of artists, at least some of whom have achieved success in their field, with those of a control group of ordinary people (i.e., nonartists), the two groups differ in *two* ways: artistic success versus lack of it; and artists versus nonartists. Therefore, any differences between the groups in discovered personality characteristics could be the result of either difference in their backgrounds. One cannot confidently conclude that one has isolated the personality characteristics of successful (creative) artists using such a design. As noted, Feist (1998) included only results from comparisons with a nonartist control group, so one can raise questions about any conclusions that are drawn from those studies. There can be differences in the level of creativity that artists demonstrate – people who change their field versus people who do not (Sternberg, Kaufman & Pretz, 2002). Therefore, if one hopes to isolate the personality characteristics that might contribute to innovation in the arts, one needs to compare an innovative artistic group to a group of noninnovative artists.

One can also raise similar questions about more recent studies not covered in Feist's (1998) review. Consider again the study by Kaufman et al. (2015) that examined the relationships among Openness and Intellect, as well as creativity in the arts versus science. Participants in that study were groups of individuals ranging from upper-level students at a select high school to an Internet sample. Kaufman and colleagues found that there was a correlation between artistic creative achievement and Openness but not Intellect; and vice versa for science. When one studies personality characteristics and creative accomplishments of groups of random people, one surely is including, by chance, a wide range of people, ranging from professional artists and scientists (with, presumably, varying degrees of success in their fields); to people who were *interested* in those areas but not working professionally in them; to people who had no interests in either art or science. If so, it becomes very difficult to specify exactly what the results mean. People high in artistic accomplishment, for example, are being compared with people who differ from them in accomplishment, as well as in multiple other ways. Perhaps those other differences, beyond creative accomplishment, played a role in the results. The researchers measured and controlled for IQ, for example, as well as some demographic measures, but there might still be some factor, not measured in the study, that played an important role in the lives of some people, pushing them toward a creative career in art or science. To simply assume that everything that was not measured is simply randomized across participants, and therefore cannot affect the outcomes of the study, might be a mistake.

There were at least two early studies that attempted to include "non-innovative" artistic comparison groups, and the results raise important questions concerning the creative personality in art. Mackinnon (1962) examined the personality characteristics of eminent architects (Architects I), as nominated by professors in schools of architecture. There were two comparison groups, each of which was matched with the Architects I group for age, sex, education, and location of practice: a group of noncreative architects (Architects II), each of whom, at some point, worked for at least two years as an assistant for a member of the eminent group; and a second group of noncreative architects (Architects III), obtained from a directory of architects. Comparing the personalities of the Architects I group those of the Architects II group turned out to be especially illuminating.

MacKinnon (1962) measured the eminence of the architects by determining how many articles had been published by or about each of them. The Architects I were much higher than the other two groups, who were closer to each other. All the architects were also rated for creativity by members of the profession, and again clear differences were found. In examining the results concerning personality, the Architects I differed from the Architects III group in ways consistent with the results reported by Feist (1998). However, when the eminent architects were compared with their former assistants (Architects II), the differences in personality were much less. For example, on the California Personality Inventory, a 16-scale personality measure, the Architects I and II groups differed on only one scale. That finding raises questions about differences in personality between more- versus less-creative individuals as well as about the role of personality characteristics in creative accomplishment.

A study of creativity in fine-art students by Getzels and Csikszentmihalyi (1976) is also relevant to the question of the role of personality factors in creative achievement. Getzels and Csikszentmihalyi measured the personality characteristics of their participants in art school and then examined the relationship between those characteristics and early career success. The students were followed over the first seven years of their careers, and there were already some clear differences in accomplishment. Some had dropped out of the art world, while at least one artist had had a solo show, and one of his paintings had been purchased by a museum. Concerning the role of personality in creative achievement, Getzels and Csikszentmihalyi found that *none* of the personality characteristics measured in art school predicted early career success, which raises questions about the causal role of the "creative personality" in creative achievement.

In sum, questions of several sorts can be raised about the methods used in the study of the creative personality. We should, therefore, be cautious in accepting many of the conclusions from those studies. However, for the present, let us put those questions aside and look further at research that has attempted to specify the relation between creativity and personality.

The Role of Creative Personality in Creative Achievement in Science

As we have seen, Feist (2017, 2018; Grosul & Feist, 2014) has developed a model that outlines a possible set of relations between personality character-istics and creativity (see Figure 11.1). Feist (1993) carried out an early study of the creative personality based on those same assumptions. He contacted 205 male scientific researchers – physicists, chemists, and biologists – at first-rank universities, asking them to participate in an examination of the relationship between personality characteristics and creative achievement in science. Of the 205, approximately half agreed to participate, which is a high number for studies of this sort. The participants were interviewed and also asked to fill out personality questionnaires. Based on the interviews, research assistants rated the personalities of the scientists on a standard personality measure.

Several measures of creativity were also obtained. Each scientist rated the work of each of the other scientists in his or her discipline based on its historical significance and its creativity, assuming that the work was famil-iar. In addition, two objective measures of creative productivity were used: how many publications the person had produced; and how many times the person's work had been cited by others. Presumably, if other people cite a person's work, that work is seen as creative. This study does not have the possible problems discussed earlier concerning the comparison group. Because there was a wide range of eminence achieved by the scientists in the sample, there was no need to obtain a separate comparison group.

The findings are summarized in Figure 11.2. The ratings of historical significance and creativity were very similar for each scientist, so they were combined into a single score of the person's *eminence*, or importance in the field. Being rated high in eminence was related to several factors, including high productivity (see the arrow from productivity to eminence in Figure 11.2). Productivity, in turn, was related to two aspects of the scientists' personalities. First, the most productive scientists had what Feist called an *arrogant working style*: they were vain and competitive, and they did not want to have others set

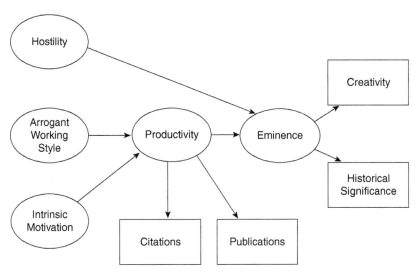

Figure 11.2 Feist's model of scientific eminence (simplified) (2006, p. 176)

goals for them. Productivity was also related to the scientists' being *intrinsically motivated* in their work: the more productive scientists reported that they worked not because of external rewards (fame, money, prizes, etc.), but because they gained pleasure from work (see Amabile, 1996). The eminent scientists were also rated as being more hostile. To summarize, Feist's model links the following factors to eminence in science: (1) being productive; (2) being intrinsically motivated; (3) being competitive; (4) setting one's own goals.

The Question of Personality as a Cause of Creativity

One of the reasons for researchers' interest in specifying the personality characteristics of creative individuals is because it is assumed that those characteristics played a causal role in making those individuals creative. Interpreting Feist's (1993) model from this perspective, we should advise young people to become arrogant – if they are not arrogant already – if they hope to become great scientists.

Correlation versus Causation in the Study of the Creative Personality

However, based on the design of Feist's study, and also the designs of the other studies already discussed, one cannot assume a causal connection between personality and creative achievement (see Figures 11.1 and 11.2). All those studies are *correlational* studies – that is, they have not manipulated any variables, as they only measured relationships among variables. Correlational studies do not allow one to make inferences about cause-and-effect relationships. They tell us only that higher levels of creative achievement are associated with – go with – certain personality characteristics. Although it might seem reasonable to assume that the personality characteristics brought about the differing levels of creative achievement, it is equally possible, from a logical point of view, that the opposite relationship holds. Perhaps the eminent scientists in Feist's (1993) study developed an arrogant working style *because they were creative.* In other words, they were creative to begin with, which led to success in their fields, and *that success made them arrogant.* Perhaps the differences in creative achievement were the cause of the differences in personality.

Furthermore, it is also possible that both the scientists' eminence *and* their personality characteristics were the result of some third variable, meaning that eminence and personality were not related directly. Perhaps certain childhood experiences affect one's personality *and* one's creative capacity, with no direct connection between personality and eminence. In conclusion, a correlation between personality characteristics and creative achievement could mean one of three things, as outlined in Table 11.8. We ran across a similar issue in Chapter 9, in examining the relationship between genius and madness.

Feist (1998; see also Feist 2017, 2018) has discussed the problem of making inferences about causality from studies of personality. In order to

Table 11.8 *Possible relations between personality and creativity*

A) Personality influences creativity:
  arrogant working style ⇒ creativity and eminence
B) Being creative influences personality
  Creativity and eminence ⇒ arrogant working style
C) Some other factor influences both creativity and personality, which are not directly related

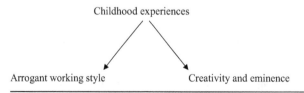

establish a causal link between two variables, one must demonstrate the following (Rosenthal & Rosnow, 1991). First, the two variables must *go together*; they must be correlated. Second is the *time order of cause versus effect*; the proposed cause must come before the effect. Third, in order to conclude that A causes B, we must be able to *rule out all other possible causes* of B. Let us examine how well studies of the creative personality meet those criteria.

The Logic of Cause and Effect

Correlation of Personality Characteristics and Creative Achievement

Let us say that I want to test the hypothesis that eating tuna fish increases creative achievement. I measure the food intake of a large group of people who are rated as highly creative and also that of a comparison group of less-creative individuals. I find that the creative group does not eat more tuna fish than the comparison group does. Since the hypothesized cause (eating tuna fish) and the hypothesized effect (increased creativity) have not been found to go together (I have not found them to be correlated), eating tuna fish cannot be the cause of the increased creativity in the people I tested. The requirement that cause and effect go together is met by the studies in Feist's review (Feist, 1999; see also Barron & Harrington, 1981). We have seen that certain personality characteristics are associated consistently with artistic success and a partially overlapping set of personality characteristics is associated with scientific success.

Time Order of Cause versus Effect

If A is the cause of B, in addition to being correlated with B, A must occur *before* B. In order to establish that one of two variables was present before the other, one must carry out a *prospective* or *longitudinal* study, in which one examines relationships among variables over time. One begins with young people, before they have a chance to become creative achievers (Feist, 1999). One measures their personality characteristics and then follows them *over their lives* to see who produces outstanding creative work. Assume that one found consistent differences in early personality characteristics between the people who turned out to be creative versus noncreative. That result would support the idea that those early characteristics in the future-creative group played a role in causing them to develop into creative individuals. As Feist (1993) has noted, since his study was not longitudinal, the results do not allow us to draw any conclusions concerning the causal role of personality in creativity. The requirement that the proposed cause must precede the effect also is not met by the studies analyzed by Feist (1998, 1999). None of those studies was longitudinal, so we cannot determine if the personality characteristics were present before the creative individuals achieved their success.

As an example of the implications of this issue, consider again Feist's (1993) study of the personality characteristics of eminent scientists (see Figure 11.2). Feist concluded that an arrogant working style *contributed to* achieving eminence. However, the personality measurements were obtained from already-mature scientists – that is, after they had achieved eminence. We do not know if their arrogant working style was the cause or effect of their eminence, or whether the arrogant working style and eminence might be results of some other cause. In addition, those few studies that have looked over time at the relationship between personality characteristics and creativity have typically not begun with very young people and followed them over their development into possibly creative adults (e.g., Feist & Barron, 2003; Helson, 1999). In those studies, the data collection usually began when the participants were in college or even later. By that time, most people are already set on the creative/noncreative path, so it is too late to determine the personality characteristics that preceded creativity. The study of art students by Getzels and Csikszentmihalyi (1976), which has already been discussed, did measure personality characteristics and did follow individuals longitudinally. One might argue that testing art students is already too late: they have already chosen their career path. Nonetheless, as we saw, Geztels and Csikszentmihalyi found no personality characteristics measured early in art school that predicted later creative success.

A second piece of evidence, mentioned earlier, that raises questions about causal relations between personality and creative achievement is the finding noted by Feist (1999) that successful science *students* are less flexible than are successful scientists. If one can assume that those students will become successful scientists, that finding indicates that the flexibility of the successful scientists might be a *result* of the process of becoming successful, rather than the cause of that success. A similar finding was reported by Dunbar (1995), who carried out an investigation of the creative process in scientific research by studying the activities in several world-class microbiology laboratories. When scientists were faced with experimental results that did not fit their hypotheses, older scientists were more likely than younger scientists to accept the negative results as valid and, in response, modify or discard their hypotheses. The younger scientists tended to dismiss negative results as being the result of error and, therefore, not important. The more-experienced scientists explained their tendency to take seriously negative data as being the result of having been wrong many times before. The senior scientists *learned* to be flexible through being *wrong*. This finding is further evidence that young scientists' personalities may change significantly as they progress through their careers, and the traits of the mature scientist might not be the same as those that he or she possessed as a beginner in the enterprise.

In conclusion, one cannot assume that the personality characteristics of the mature individual have always been that way and therefore must have preceded and contributed to creative achievement. Given the lack of prospective studies in Feist's (1999) analysis, one can raise questions about any cause-and-effect conclusions drawn concerning personality characteristics and creative accomplishment. Let us now examine the third component in establishing cause and effect. If we are to conclude that A is the cause of B, we must be able to rule out all other possible causes for B.

Eliminating Other Possible Causes

Even if it were found that creative adults, when they were children, possessed some unique set of personality characteristics, one still cannot conclude that those characteristics played a part in *causing* the adult creativity. In order to establish Factor A as the cause of Behavior B, *all other possible causes must be eliminated*. If creative adults were hostile as children, that does not guarantee that the early hostility was the cause of adult creativity. Perhaps early-childhood trauma made the individuals both hostile in childhood and creative as adults. One way to eliminate other possible causes is to carry out an experimental study, with large groups of participants randomly assigned to experimental and control conditions. One can then be confident that, at the beginning of the study, the two groups were identical on all variables except the variable that you were hoping to establish as the cause of some behavior.

Experimental manipulation was not carried out in the studies reviewed by Feist (1999), because carrying out an experimental manipulation is very difficult in this context. We cannot randomly *assign* personality characteristics to people; people bring personality characteristics with them into the laboratory. Also, for ethical as well as practical reasons, an experimenter cannot randomly select a group of young people and turn them into hostile individuals, say, to see if they become creative as adults. On the other hand, it might be possible to make people more open-minded through some sort of intervention, which might lead to increases in creative achievement. However, at present there are, to my knowledge, no studies available that meet this criterion (Batey & Furnham, 2006). In sum, the causal conclusions that can be drawn from studies of the creative personality are very limited. This is one example of the difficulties that can arise when one tries to study the role of personality characteristics in creativity.

Personality, Cognition, and Creativity Reconsidered: A Causal Model Linking Open-mindedness and Creativity

The results discussed so far are at best weak support for the view that there is a causal relation between personality and creativity. However, there is a stream of research that presents a different picture of the relationship between personality and the creative process. This view was discussed briefly in Chapter 9 in the context of how mild forms of psychopathology might foster creative thinking. The analysis centers on the cognitive implications of Open-mindedness (e.g., Kaufman et al., 2015; see also Carson, 2018; Vartanian, 2018). As we know, it has been proposed by numerous researchers, beginning with Poincaré (1913) and continuing into the present, that creative individuals produce novel ideas because they are able to make connections among ideas that are not made by noncreative individuals (e.g., Batey & Furnham, 2006; Carson, 2018; Feist, 2018; Fürst, Ghisletta & Lubart, 2014; Glosur and Feist, 2014; Koestler, 1964; Kounios & Beeman, 2014; Martindale, 1989; Mednick, 1962; Simonton, 1988, 1999, 2014; Vartanian, 2018). It is proposed that "open-mindedness" allows the person to make those connections. The basic idea underlying this theorizing is the notion that "open-mindedness" includes openness to a wider range of stimuli, internal and external.

It has been hypothesized that the creative individual is able to spread attention internally, over ideas, so that more ideas in memory can be activated at the same time (Carson, 2018; Fürst, Ghisletta & Lubart, 2014; Martindale, 1989; Vartanian, 2018). This spread of attention would make it more likely that two previously unrelated ideas would "come into contact" – through being activated at the same time (Mednick, 1962) – which might result in a new synthesis. It has also been hypothesized that creative individuals might be able to spread their attention more widely when dealing with *external* stimuli and therefore would be sensitive to a wider range of stimuli (Carson, 2018; Fürst, Ghisletta & Lubart, 2014; Martindale, 1989; Vartanian,

2018). That sensitivity might allow a wider range of external stimuli to come into contact with whatever the person is thinking about, which also might increase the chances of a novel combination of ideas being developed. The noncreative thinker, with a narrow focus of attention, might not even become aware of the potentially relevant external event.

The mechanism through which this openness comes about is a reduction in *cognitive inhibition*. As discussed in Chapter 9, in most of our cognitive activities it is important to keep irrelevant material from breaking into attention and interfering with the task. An *inhibitory* process usually works to bring that about. As an example, presented in Chapter 9 (Carson, 2014, pp. 265–266), let us say that a church clock chimes the hour, twenty-four hours a day, near your bedroom window. When you first moved into your house, the clock awakened you whenever it chimed. After living near the clock for a while, you ignore it and can sleep through the night. Now you have been hired for a job that requires that you get up early. You set your alarm clock, which chimes when it is supposed to. In the past, your alarm had been effective in waking you. However, as the result of the inhibition of the response to the *clock chime*, you now sleep through *your alarm*. A person with a **lack** of cognitive inhibition – that is, a person with **dis**inhibition – would have been awakened by the alarm. Such a person would, in general, experience more stimuli entering consciousness, which in the right circumstances might play a role in producing novel ideas. Thus, the creative person would be assumed to be low in cognitive inhibition or high in **dis**inhibition.

Those ideas have been tested in several ways. One series of studies, by Carson and colleagues (for review, see Carson, 2018), has focused on the phenomenon of *latent inhibition*, or *hidden inhibition*, which is outlined in Table 11.9. The task (Table 11.9A) consists of two phases, analogous to the experience with the clock chime just discussed. In phase 1, the person responds to a set of stimuli. Irrelevant stimuli are presented "in the background" and play no part in the task. In phase 2, unknown to the participant, those previously irrelevant stimuli become relevant. People who went through phase 1 take longer to realize that the previously irrelevant stimuli are now relevant than do people who are seeing the situation for the first time in phase 2 (see Table 11.9B). Ignoring the stimuli in phase 1 made it harder to attend to them in phase 2. Thus, "ignoring" a stimulus involves active inhibition – cognitive inhibition – of the responses to that stimulus. Processing of the irrelevant stimuli was inhibited, or blocked, during the initial phase of the experiment. The inhibition is *latent*, or *hidden*, because it is not seen until the situation is changed, so that the previously ignored stimuli now become relevant.

Table 11.9 *Latent inhibition task and sample results*

A. *Outline of latent inhibition task*

Phase 1: Person hears a long list of nonsense syllables (thirty syllables repeated five times) and is told to keep track of how many times one of those syllables (e.g., BIM) appears. At the same time, occasional bursts of white noise are heard in the background. Nothing is said about the white noise. White noise occurs approximately 20 percent of the time.

Syllables (Person's Count)	White Noise
WUG	
DIF	XXX
BIM (1)	
FIP	
JUR	
GUJ	XXX
BIM (2)	
KIP	
PUZ	
RUW	
QOB	XXX
LUR	
WAZ	
BIM (3)	
	XXX
MUR	

B. *Example results*

Phase 2: Nonsense syllable/noise tape played again. This time there are yellow disks presented on a screen. Appearance of the disks coincides with the white noise. Person's task is to determine which auditory stimulus signaled the appearance of the disks. The dependent measure is how long it takes the person to determine that the white noise signals the appearance of the disks.

Experimental Condition	Number of Syllables to Solution
Control (only goes through Phase 2)	10
Latent inhibition (Phase 1 followed by Phase 2)	30

The relation between cognitive inhibition and creativity comes from the hypothesis, just discussed, that creative individuals are more open to external stimuli (Carson, 2018; Vartanian, 2018). If creation of new ideas involves connecting ideas that were far apart psychologically, as Poincaré (1913), Mednick (1962), and many others have proposed, then *focusing* attention might interfere with creative thinking. Focusing might limit the range of stimuli that are potentially available for combination. Based on that reasoning, more-creative individuals, who make those connections between far-apart ideas, should be less likely to inhibit stimuli irrelevant to the task they are carrying out. Therefore, more-creative individuals might be less likely to show latent inhibition than would less-creative people. More-creative individuals, when placed in the situation outlined in Table 11.9A, should learn to respond to the previously-irrelevant-but-now-relevant stimulus more quickly than do noncreatives. Predictions of this sort have been upheld: more-creative undergraduates, based on creative achievements, demonstrated less latent inhibition in situations like that in Table 11.9A. In addition, people who are designated as high in Open-mindedness also show less latent inhibition, and, as we know, people high in Open-mindedness are also more creative (Carson, 2018; Fürst, Ghisletta & Lubart, 2014; Vartanian, 2018).

Eysenck's Theory: Psychoticism and Creativity

Eysenck (e.g., 1993, 1995; Fürst, Ghisletta & Lubart, 2014; Vartanian, 2018) has proposed a theory of creativity closely related to the ideas just outlined, based on the idea that creative persons are more likely to possess a specific cluster of personality characteristics, which fall under the general trait of *psychoticism*. Psychoticism is an inherited tendency to *develop* psychopathology, in response to, among other things, situations of high stress. The person who is high in psychoticism is not suffering from psychopathology; he or she is within the normal range of behavior. People high in psychoticism are aggressive, emotionally cold, egocentric, impersonal, impulsive, antisocial, and without empathy. Such a person may impress an observer as odd or eccentric. Some investigators have described psychoticism as *mild psychopathology*.

Psychoticism provides a basis for creativity, because the person high in psychoticism has a "wide horizon" of responding to situations, much like Carson's (2018) cognitive disinhibition, which results in the production of unusual responses. That unusual production, in Eysenck's view, provides the foundation for creative ideas. Eysenck discussed overinclusive or "allusive" thinking, one of the characteristics of thinking in psychopathology and in people high in psychoticism, as the basis for creative thinking. In allusive thinking, one *alludes* to something – that is, one talks about it by suggestion rather than by explicitly referring to it. For example, if you owe me money, I might say something about being short of money to buy something, which I hope will cause you to remember your debt to me. Eysenck also discussed attentional deficits and a lack of latent inhibition as characteristics of thinking in psychopathology as well as in creativity.

Studies have indicated that people who score high on psychoticism also produce unusual responses on a word-association test (Eysenck, 1993). That result supports Eysenck's notion that psychoticism is related to a wide horizon of responding and to breaking away from usual responses, which is assumed by Eysenck (1993, 1995; see also Batey & Furnham, 2006; Fürst, Ghisletta & Lubart, 2014; Vartanian, 2018) to be critical in production of creative ideas. Eysenck's theory is another variant on the view just outlined, which assumes that the "openness" of the thought processes in some people supports creative thinking.

Openness, Lack of Inhibition, and Creativity: Summary and Critique

This stream of research is built on what one could call a "remote-association" or "openness" view of creativity (Carson, 2018; Eysenck, 1993, 1995; Fürst, Ghisletta & Lubart, 2014; Kaufman et al., 2015; Vartanian, 2018). A core component of this view is the idea that creative thinking depends on breaking away from the past, since it assumes that producing creative ideas comes about through "linking" ideas that previously had been "remote" or far from each other in one's conceptual space. This is still another variant of the view that creativity depends on thinking outside of the box.

It should be noted, however, that questions can be raised about this viewpoint, similar to those that were raised in Chapter 9 concerning the idea that psychopathology might facilitate creative thinking and in Chapter 10 concerning the proposal that divergent thinking is the basis for creativity. We have, in earlier chapters, seen much evidence that the creative process does not work by associating remote ideas. In examining IDEO's production of a new shopping cart, Picasso's creation of *Guernica*, Watson and Crick's discovery of the double helix of DNA, Edison's invention of the electric light, and Frank Lloyd Wright's creation of *Fallingwater*, among other major creative advances, as well as undergraduates' solutions to problems of several sorts, including "insight" problems, we have found no evidence that the thinker worked by formulating new ideas based on remote associative connections. The novel components of IDEO's shopping cart were based on near analogies. The structure of *Guernica* was based on *Minotauromachy*, another near analogy. Watson and Crick based their analysis of DNA on Pauling's alpha-helix, another near analogy; and *Fallingwater* was a *Prairie House* cantilevered over a stream, still another near analogy.

In all those cases, the process worked in a structured, top-down manner, in which knowledge served to direct the thinker to potentially relevant ideas, based on what the person knew about the situation he or she was facing. The individual did not have to make a "leap" to a remote idea; in all those cases – and others not discussed in this book because of lack of space (see Weisberg, 2006, ch. 5) – the person's knowledge could be applied more or less directly to the world. This is a restatement of Gentner's "kind world" hypothesis (Gentner & Maravilla, 2018), discussed earlier. If those conclusions concerning the operation of the creative process are valid, they raise the question of how we are to interpret the results demonstrating a relationship between creativity and disinhibition. Assuming that the latent-inhibition and creativity results just presented are also valid, then we are left with a set of results without an explanation. In other words, we are left facing a dilemma.

One resolution to that dilemma is to assume that the conclusions concerning the creative process drawn from the case studies are incorrect. One possible objection to presenting case studies as "data" relevant to the creative process is that the kinds of information they are based on – that is, artists' early sketches and sketchbooks, and scientists' and inventors' laboratory notebooks – might be produced relatively far into the creative process and so tell us little about how the process actually begins. When an artist fills a sketchbook with sketches, for example, it might be that he or she has already made most of the decisions concerning the work to which the sketches are related. Perhaps the more "remote-associative" components of the creative process have already taken place before an artist or scientist sets anything down on paper (perhaps before he or she even experiences any ideas at all, at a conscious level). However, in all of the cases just mentioned and in many other cases not discussed here the final outcome was *not* remotely related to the situation where the creative process began. Therefore, there is no evidence that a remote-associative process was working at any time in the process. That conclusion would mean that the results from the studies demonstrating a relationship between openness, creativity, and latent inhibition should not be taken as supporting a wide-ranging theory linking the creative personality and creative thinking.

Another possible way out of this dilemma is to assume that the "openness" results should not be taken as demonstrating a causal connection. Those results are correlational: people high in "openness" are also low in cognitive inhibition and high in creativity. Perhaps some other variable – such as fluid intelligence, for example – links all of those variables. At present, there is no direct evidence concerning such a possibility, so we must await more research.

Personality and Creativity: Conclusions

Specifying the "creative personality," and its role in creative achievement, is a difficult enterprise. At this time, as Feist (1999) noted (see also Grosul & Feist, 2014), we can do little more than speculate about the personal characteristics that might contribute to a person's becoming successful in a creative field. On a positive note, numerous studies have found that Open-mindedness is related to creative achievement in the arts and sciences. However, interpreting that relationship is difficult. First of all, there are weaknesses in method in some of those studies. Second, there have been very few studies that have examined prospectively the relationship between personality and creative achievement, and the limited results available indicate that personality may change as an individual develops in a creative career, which raises questions about the causal role of adult personality characteristics.

Finally, there is the difficulty of carrying out experimental manipulations of personality variables, which limits the causal conclusions that one can draw from studies of the creative personality. That limitation concerning causal conclusions has left unanswered the question of why it is that there is a correlation between some personality traits and creative achievement of various sorts. One possibility that we have not considered in detail is that specific personality characteristics *and* creative achievement are the products of a common cause. Recent work in personality theory by Joy (2004, 2017; Joy & Hicks, 2004) may provide that cause. Joy has proposed that people differ in the *need to be different*. This very general personality characteristic affects their behavior in all situations, including those in which creativity is possible.

The Need to Be Different and Creativity

Joy (2017) proposed that the need to be different arises from a person's experience receiving rewards for producing novel behavior and ideas versus doing what others have done. If a person has had a wide range of experiences in which he or she has been rewarded for not conforming to what others have done, there will be a tendency for that person to approach new situations with novel behaviors. This tendency might be seen in an overall "bohemian," or nonconforming, approach to life, as well as in specific responses to situations in which varying degrees of novelty are possible, as when someone is faced with a problem to solve, a D-T test, or an artistic task to carry out. People may produce novel outcomes in creative-thinking situations because of their need to be different. Joy developed a scale to measure this hypothesized need, consisting of pairs of adjectives, some of which are shown in Table 11.10.

Joy (2017) has examined correlates of the need to be different. In one study, it was shown that need-to-be-different scores correlate with peer ratings of a person's creativity. People were given two descriptions of people, one of whom was middle-of-the-road in opinions, appearance, relationships, and so forth, and the other of whom was described as different than others in dress, in musical and artistic tastes, in suggesting new and unexpected ideas, etc. Individuals who rated themselves as high on

Table 11.10 *Items from the Need-to-be-Different Scale (Joy, 2004)*
Please choose from each pair below the item that you value more highly. In evaluating each pair, ask yourself: "Which of these would I rather be, if I had to choose one over the other?" Some words appear more than once, but no pair is repeated.

1.	productive	6.	congenial
	creative		*independent*
2.	*radical*	7.	prudent
	conforming		*unconventional*
3.	*individualistic*	8.	*ingenious*
	respectable		sensible
4.	*eccentric*	9.	cooperative
	conventional		*individualistic*
5.	ambitious	10.	moderate
	original		*unconventional*

Italicized words are scored as indicating the need to be different.

the need to be different were more frequently chosen by their peers as fitting the "nonconforming" description. Need to be different was also found to be positively correlated with the personality characteristic of openness to experience. The need to be different is also correlated with rated creativity of drawings and stories produced by people, as well as with divergent-thinking scores (Joy, 2017).

Those results can lead to a deeper understanding of the relation between personality traits and creativity. Perhaps creative achievement and certain personality traits – for example artistic achievement and "Open-mindedness" – are correlated because both are related to the need to be different. A person high in the need to be different might adopt a nonconforming lifestyle, and that lifestyle will lead to creative accomplishments. Similarly, creative achievement might be related to divergent thinking because each is an independent result of the need to be different. In sum, contrary to the assumptions of Guilford (1950, 1967) and those who followed his theorizing, divergent thinking and creative accomplishment might not be related in a cause–effect manner.

In conclusion, a person's need to be different shapes how he or she approaches a creative-thinking task as well as how he or she approaches "life tasks" more generally. Therefore, personality traits are not to be looked upon as some basic components that underlie creative thinking. General "creative lifestyles," specific personality traits, and specific creative accomplishments might all be the result of a person's need to be different. We now conclude this discussion with an examination of several remaining broad questions, of potential importance concerning the creative personality.

Personality and Creativity: Some Remaining Questions

Is It a Waste of Time and Effort to Search for "the" Creative Personality?

A basic assumption underlying much of the research reviewed in this chapter is that there is a set of psychological characteristics that we could call "the creative personality" (or perhaps two creative personalities, one in the arts and one in science). However, several researchers have raised questions concerning whether such a simple outcome should be expected (Abuhamdeh & Csikszentmihalyi, 2004; Helson, 1999; Ludwig, 1998; Sass, 2001). When one examines the diverse environments in which artistic or scientific creativity can be expressed, it seems unlikely that a single set of personality characteristics or even two overlapping sets of characteristics will be relevant to all of them. Consider an architect, who must exhibit creativity within constraints set by a client, restrictions set by construction materials, and regulations set by governments. Surely the personality characteristics needed to succeed in such an environment are different from those that would be important in a painter's spending time in isolation trying to bring to realization a new work which may have nothing to do with the representation of external reality. In both those hypothetical cases, artistic creativity may be expressed, but the people involved might be very different psychologically.

One might also expect that even within the domain of painting different personality characteristics are involved in the creation of, for instance, Piet Mondrian's precise, nonrepresentational, geometrically based abstractions versus Pollock's poured paintings, also nonrepresentational but built out of swirling streams of paint. As discussed in Chapter 9, Ludwig (1998) found that aspects of psychopathology differed within sub-domains of the sciences and the arts, related to the "rationality" involved in the domain. It seems reasonable that Ludwig's conclusions would be broadly relevant and would lead to the expectation that nonpathological personality characteristics would also vary across sub-domains in the arts and in the sciences. Further support for this view was seen in Sass's (2001) analysis presented in Chapter 9 concerning the schizotypal personality and artistic creativity. Sass proposed that people with that personality – aloof, nonsocial, slightly eccentric, and unemotional – will be drawn to postmodern art with its ironic slant on modern society. In this view, the "artistic personality" will change as the dominant artistic style changes, because the stylistic changes may result in different types of people being drawn to an area of creative activity. From this perspective, the conclusions from one time period concerning the artistic personality will not necessarily transfer to another period; and conclusions within one period might not generalize across all artistic domains or all scientific domains.

A similar conclusion can be drawn from a historical study of changes in the status and societal position of artists in Western culture (Becker, 2001). Until the Renaissance, the artist was looked upon more or less as a skilled craftsperson and was not expected to produce works of originality or to question society's values. That Renaissance "job description" of an artist would probably draw a different type of person than those who are attracted to the arts today, where the artist is expected to produce original works and to be an outsider and a critic of society. In sum, there is reason to believe that there are numerous "creative personalities" and that people working within even the same subfield of the arts or the sciences can approach their work from very different perspectives, meaning that their personalities would probably be different. Therefore, looking for simple relations between personality characteristics and creative achievement may be a fruitless task.

Should "Open-mindedness" Be Relabeled "Creative"?

We know that Open-mindedness is the personality scale most consistently and strongly related to creative achievement. Those results are typically interpreted in causal terms: Open-mindedness is assumed to play a role in causing a person to be creative. It is possible, however, to interpret the Open-mindedness–creativity correlation in a different way. As noted, many of the items on the Open-mindedness scales seem to be asking about creative experiences and accomplishments (Feist, 2018) Martindale, 1989; see Table 11.7). It may not be surprising – or particularly informative – to find that a person who checks the item "is original, comes up with new ideas" and does not check "has few artistic interests" also reports having produced more than average in the way of creative accomplishments. A number of years ago, Martindale (1989) noted that the items on the Open-mindedness scale were, at that time, almost synonymous with creativity, so it was not surprising that openness correlated with creative production. The same reservations can be raised about the items on the newer Open-mindedness scales: they also seem to be asking about aspects of creativity. In other words, one can raise the question of whether postulating Open-mindedness as an *explanation* of creativity adds anything to our understanding of creativity. Is Open-mindedness simply *another name* for creativity?

In response to such challenges to the usefulness of the Open-Mindedness scale as an independent assessment of creativity, researchers who supported the 5-Factor model attempted to show that Open-mindedness was more than simply another way of saying "I am creative" (King, Walker & Broyles, 1996). The scale was modified, so some of the adjectives on the openness scale were more removed from creativity per se. However, as just noted, examination of the items on the updated Open-mindedness scales still indicates, to me at least, that many if not all are asking about creativity or closely related areas. Second, King, Walker, and Broyles (1996) concluded that Open-mindedness and creativity are not identical because when one examines the relationship between them, it is not uniform, which implies that the two are not the same. King, Walker, and Broyles found that creative achievement is seen in people high in Open-mindedness only when they are also high in creative-thinking potential, as measured by divergent-thinking tests. Since people high in Open-mindedness but low in divergent thinking are not high in creative achievement, it seems that Open-mindedness and creativity are not identical, although they may overlap. However, it is not clear whether this argument is relevant to the newer version of Open-mindedness. In conclusion, one can raise questions as to whether Open-mindedness, the most heavily researched component of the "creative personality," is anything more than a slight rephrasing of the definition of creativity.

Can We Identify Creative People?

Measuring Divergent Thinking and the Creative Personality

The psychometric stream of research on creativity – examining divergent thinking and assessing the creative personality – has produced thousands of studies over the past fifty years (for reviews, see chapters in Feist, Reiter-Palmon & Kaufman, 2017; Jung & Vartanian, 2018; Kaufman & Sternberg, 2010). The psychometric viewpoint has undoubtedly been valuable in stimulating much research, which we have reviewed in the last two chapters. In addition, Guilford's (1950, 1956, 1967) assumption that the capacity for creative thinking was present in all of us to at least some degree helped tie the study of creativity to other areas of mainstream psychology, such as the study of cognition and of personality. However, Guilford's basic idea, that creative thinking is based on divergent thinking, has not received strong support from studies of "real-world" creative thinking. Studies of the creative personality likewise have not provided strong evidence for causal effects of personality variables on creativity. Based on these negative results, one can draw the conclusions that creativity might not be based on some special sort of thinking, and creative people might not possess some special set of personality characteristics. On the other hand, some researchers (Carson, 2018; Kaufman et al., 2015; Vartanian, 2018) have recently carried out research linking together (1) the personality characteristic of Open-mindedness, (2) creative accomplishment, and (3) cognitive disinhibition. At present we are not able to resolve the apparent conflict between those perspectives, so we will have to wait for advances in research and theory to clarify the relation between personality, divergent thinking, and creativity.

12 | Two Confluence Theories of Creativity

In the last two chapters, we broadened our focus to the psychometric perspective on creativity, examining research concentrating on testing for creative capacity and on models relating personality characteristics to creative achievement. In this chapter, we will go further, examining *confluence* theories of creativity, which assume that the *confluence*, or *coming together*, of many factors is critical for creative achievement (Sternberg & Lubart, 1995; Sternberg, 2018). Confluence theories have gone beyond the individual person, examining social and environmental factors that might influence the creative process.

Outline of the Chapter

This chapter will examine Sternberg's (2018) Triangle theory of creativity, which concentrates more on the individual, and Amabile's componential theory of creativity, which places more emphasis on factors outside the individual (Amabile, 1996; Amabile & Pratt, 2016). Amabile has examined creativity and innovation in organizations, including business organizations. I will present the general aspects of each theory as well as research relevant to it. Points of commonality and difference between the two theories will be noted, and a critique of each theory will be presented. The basic question being asked in this research is: How far beyond the individual do we have to go to obtain a full understanding of creativity?

Sternberg's Triangle Theory of Creativity

Sternberg's (2018) "Triangle" theory of creativity is the most recent development in a series of proposals that he and his colleagues have presented over the last thirty years (see also Lubart & Sternberg, 1995; Sternberg & Lubart, 1995, 1996; Zhang & Sternberg, 2011). In examining this body of research, we will begin with Sternberg and Lubart's "investment theory" of creativity, since the Triangle theory builds on many of its components.

The Investment Theory of Creativity: Buy Low, Sell High

Sternberg and Lubart (1995, 1996; Lubart & Sternberg, 1995; Zhang & Sternberg, 2011) used an economic metaphor, based on investment in the stock market, to analyze creativity (see also Rubenson & Runco, 1992). Success in investing in the stock market depends on *buying low* and *selling high*. The smart investor buys good stocks that are low in price; when they go up, they can be sold for a profit. Similar concepts can be used to describe the activity of a person engaged in a creative enterprise. A new idea or product generated by a creative thinker is usually not valued highly by others. The person who produced the new idea, however, has "invested" in it: the creator has "bought low." The creator/investor's task becomes one of convincing others of the value of the idea, be it a scientific theory, a style of painting, or an invention. In "selling" a new theory, for example, a scientist can present it to other scientists, which increases the likelihood that they will come to accept it.

In carrying out research on creative individuals, Sternberg and Lubart found that they were willing to go against the grain (1996, p. 683). Investment in a not-yet-popular idea requires, in Sternberg and Lubart's (1995, p. viii) words, the "guts to defy the crowd." Professionals interviewed in various fields, such as artists, scientists, and businesspeople, emphasized that the creative individual went against conventional thinking, took risks, and followed through on the consequences of taking those risks.

Heuristics for Buying Low

Sternberg and Lubart (1995, pp. 80–87) provided heuristics, rules of thumb, for determining whether to "invest" in some idea. First, be wary of a popular idea. If "everyone is doing it," you would be buying high rather than low. A piece of information that can tell you that you are buying low is that people think you are at least slightly crazy when you present your idea and you, too, may also feel a bit uncomfortable with it. Because many unpopular ideas are unpopular because they are *bad* ideas, Sternberg and Lubart provided several questions that one can ask in choosing good ideas. First, is there any evidence to support your idea? Even though others may not accept your idea, there may still be evidence that supports it. Also, since your new idea will overthrow conventional wisdom, is there evidence that current beliefs are incorrect? Finding such evidence would raise one's confidence in the new idea.

Resources Needed for Creativity

The investment theory proposed that creativity requires the confluence of six distinct *resources*: intellectual abilities (i.e., intelligence, broadly conceived); knowledge; styles of thinking; personality characteristics; motivation; and the environment (Sternberg & Lubart, 1995, especially their table 2.3).

Intellectual Skills

Sternberg and Lubart (1995, ch. 5) analyzed intelligence into several sets of skills – creative intelligence, analytic intelligence, and practical intelligence – each of which plays a different role in creativity. *Creative intelligence*, concerned with generating novel ideas, is obviously critical in creativity. Creative intelligence underlies a person's ability to formulate a problem in a new way that will allow the thinker to go beyond convention. Sternberg and Lubart cited a number of important creative thinkers, including Einstein, who emphasized the importance of formulation of problems.

Sternberg and Lubart (1995, pp. 100–108) presented examples of tests that they developed to assess people's abilities to redefine problems. In one type of exercise, the person is given analogies to solve, but each problem is preceded by a presupposition, which requires that the person accept as true something that in reality is not true and reason from there. Here is an example (Sternberg & Lubart, 1995, p. 105).

> *Assume that goats are robots.* Given that assumption, complete this analogy:
>   CHICKEN is to HATCHED as GOAT is to:
>   BORN FARM BUILT FACTORY

Given the information that is assumed, the answer is "built"; ignoring that information, the answer is "born." The critical question is whether the person will be able to accept the new information and reason using it.

An especially important set of skills in problem reformulation are three *insight* skills – selective *encoding*, selective *comparison*, and selective *combination* – which were proposed initially by Sternberg and Davidson (1982; Davidson, 1995) in the narrower context of the analysis of insight problems. Those same processes can lead to buying low in the market of ideas. *Selective encoding* occurs when a person trying to solve a problem recognizes the potential importance of a piece of information that is not immediately obvious. An example of a selective-encoding insight is Alexander Fleming's discovery of penicillin (Sternberg & Lubart, 1995). Fleming had been growing bacteria in the lab when he noticed that some of the bacteria had been killed by mold that had developed as the result of airborne spores being deposited in the dish. Rather than disposing of the "contaminated" colonies and starting again, as most other scientists would have done, Fleming concentrated on the organisms that had destroyed the bacteria. As the result of that selective-encoding insight, he began the work that resulted in the discovery of penicillin.

Selective comparison insights occur when an individual brings information from the past to bear in the current situation. Such insights usually involve analogical transfer. Sternberg and Lubart (1995, p. 115) discussed Kekulé's "snake dream" – of the discovery of the circular structure of benzene, also discussed in Chapter 9 – as an example of a selective-comparison insight. Kekulé brought together two realms – chemistry and snakes – which would not usually be connected, and that juxtaposition resulted in a creative advance. The final type of insight, *selective combination*, occurs when an individual, examining readily available information, finds an organization that no one else saw. An example is Darwin's development of the theory of evolution. According to Sternberg (1988), the information available to Darwin was available to anyone else who was knowledgeable in the area. Darwin succeeded in developing a comprehensive theory because he was able to see how to fit the pieces of the puzzle together.

The second class of intellectual skills, *analytic intelligence*, plays an important evaluative role in creative thinking: the thinker must be on the lookout for errors and also must be ready to revise creative products to deal with inadequacies that might be found in them. The third type of intelligence, *practical intelligence*, is needed in the choice of a problem to work on; one must pick a problem that others will find of interest. One component of practical intelligence is the ability to communicate to others the value of what one has done. In addition, the ability to deal effectively with the inevitable criticisms that any new idea will receive is a facet of practical intelligence.

Thinking Style

Sternberg and Lubart (1995, ch. 7; Sternberg, 2018) also assumed that general styles of thinking play a role in determining whether a person will be creative. Creativity is fostered by a *legislative* style of thinking, which centers on a preference for thinking in novel ways of one's own choosing rather than following rules set by others (that would be an *executive* style) or taking a judgmental attitude toward situations (that would be a *judicial* style). A person with a legislative style, when working on a writing project, will concentrate on presenting new ideas. Someone with an executive style might also take up a writing project but would be most comfortable providing an exposition of others' ideas. A person with a judicial style might in a piece of writing critique someone else's ideas. In addition, a *global* style, in which one is more interested in larger issues rather than details plays a role in creativity, since it affects the person's determination of which questions are important and worth working on.

Creative Personality

Sternberg and Lubart (1995, ch. 8) noted that, to produce creative work one needs to possess personality characteristics that maximize the likelihood that one will utilize one's potential. One critical characteristic is a willingness to persevere in the face of obstacles. Problems which demand creativity may be difficult, so producing the solution may require a long period of commitment. Similarly, anyone who hopes to succeed in the creative arena must be willing to take a risk. A number of studies have demonstrated that people's willingness to take risks (e.g., their willingness to take a gamble on a highly valued outcome) is correlated with performance on divergent-thinking tests as well as with responses to creative-attitude scales.

The creative person must also be willing to tolerate ambiguity – that is, be willing to deal with situations in which it appears that no closure may be forthcoming in the near future. Sternberg and Lubart (1995, ch. 8) also emphasize open-mindedness (see Chapter 11) as critical in some people's being able to consistently come up with new ideas. People who are open to experience will constantly seek out information from the world and thereby will maximize the chances that they will have available information that might be relevant to their problem. Finally, in order to produce creative work one must also have confidence in oneself and one's ideas, so that one can stand up to the establishment.

Motivation

In order for the characteristics outlined so far to be effective, the individual must be motivated to do creative work. Sternberg and Lubart (1995, ch. 9) discuss the possible roles of intrinsic and extrinsic motivation in creativity. Intrinsic motivation involves a commitment to an activity for its own sake, rather than to earn some reward. Extrinsic motivation involves working for an external outcome. Sternberg and Lubart put emphasis on intrinsic motivation, but they also concluded that extrinsic motivators can play positive roles in creative endeavors. Ochse (1990) reviewed the literature on motivation in creativity and summarized a wide range of motivating factors reported by creative people.

1. To obtain mastery or to overcome ignorance
2. To achieve immortality through one's work
3. To make money
4. To prove oneself, to oneself and to others
5. To attain recognition
6. To attain self-esteem
7. To create a thing of beauty
8. To discover an underlying order to things

Of those factors, 1, 7, and 8 are intrinsic; 2, 3, and 5 are extrinsic; and 4 and 6 might be intrinsic or extrinsic. Thus, it seems that both intrinsic and extrinsic factors can be important in motivating creative accomplishment. The question of motivation for creativity will be discussed later in this chapter (see also Amabile & Pratt, 2016).

The Environment

The environment can play a critical role in creativity, because it can stimulate and reward innovative thinking, which will increase the chances that an individual will engage in such activities. However, the environment can also be a source of obstacles that the creative person must overcome (Sternberg & Lubart, 1995, ch. 10). Environmental factors will also be discussed in detail later in this chapter.

The Triangle Theory

In the investment theory, the ability to defy the crowd was seen as crucial in creative achievement. The Triangle theory (Sternberg, 2018), an extension of the investment theory, discusses three types of defiance that a person can carry out in producing something novel (see Table 12.1).

Table 12.1 *Three types of defiance in the Triangle theory of creativity (Sternberg, 2018)*

Type of Defiance	Definition
Defying the crowd	Defying the beliefs, values, and practices of one's field.
Defying oneself	Defying (moving beyond) one's earlier values, practices, and beliefs.
Defying the zeitgeist	Defying the often unconsciously accepted presuppositions and paradigms in one's field.

Three Types of Defiance in Creative Production

Defying the Crowd

Defying the crowd pits the creative thinker against others in the field, many of whom have already produced ideas that have shaped the field. We just discussed the possible role of ambition and related factors in the motivation for creativity (Ochse, 1990; Sternberg & Lubart, 1995, ch. 9). A new idea can pose a threat to the reputations of already-established investigators. Sometimes, it is easier to get one's ideas accepted if one develops ideas that build on those of others rather than challenging those ideas.

Defying Oneself

The second type of defiance – defying oneself – may be a greater challenge than defying the crowd (Sternberg, 2018). One can become *entrenched* in one way of thinking, or stuck on one early idea that one produced, and never go beyond it. Support for the idea of entrenchment came from a study by Frensch and Sternberg (1989), in which bridge players of different levels of expertise were asked to play versions of bridge in which the rules were changed in various ways. *Surface* changes involved things like changing the relative importance of the various suits; *conceptual* changes centered on the basic structure of the game, such as making the person who *lost* the last trick lead on the next one. The more-expert players had more difficulty in adapting to the conceptual changes. Sternberg (2018) explained this difficulty as being the result of having memorized patterns from the game, through many of hours of practice and play. (See the discussion of expertise in Chapter 6.) The novices, in contrast, had no investment in the game. Therefore, it was, in Sternberg's terms "far more costly for the experts than for the novices to endure a major change in the rules of the game" (p. 54).

Sternberg and Lubart (1995, p. 161) noted that it is not always the world-class expert who has the best ideas; sometimes a person who is a newcomer to a field will think in new ways because he or she has not yet become entrenched in the standard ways of looking at things (thinking "outside the box"; see also Simonton, 1984, ch. 4). Sternberg and Lubart (1995, ch. 6) emphasized that the expert is not the only one who can be caught in the web of "stale knowledge" when a fresh viewpoint is demanded. We are all experts in various ways, so we all are subject to entrapment by our knowledge. Therefore, we must be ready to deal with the entrenchment problem when it arises, as it inevitably will. One can fight entrenchment in a number of ways. First, one can vary one's usual routines. Second, one can invite feedback from others concerning how one could do things differently. Finally, one can defy oneself by starting over, in a new field, which would force one out of one's habits. However, in order to contribute to the new field, you would have to learn it well enough so that you do not make basic errors due to ignorance. The history of science is full of examples of researchers renowned for their contributions to one field who switched fields and made fools of themselves.

Defying the Zeitgeist

The third type of defiance is the most difficult to carry out, because it involves overcoming a set of presuppositions that we may not know we adhere to: the presuppositions on which one's field is built (Sternberg, 2018). The term *zeitgeist* refers to the "spirit" of the time, the set of beliefs and attitudes that characterize a particular era. In biology, for example, before Darwin developed the theory of evolution through natural selection, there was a set of beliefs – concerning how organisms were created and species developed, based on religious doctrine – that was accepted by scientists and nonscientists. Darwin's theory challenged that set of beliefs, which most people did not even realize could be challenged. Thus, the zeitgeist can be difficult for a researcher to challenge, because one may not be aware of the deep assumptions that provide the foundation for one's orientation to one's research area.

An individual may defy the zeitgeist in several ways (Sternberg, 2018). Sternberg, Kaufman, and Pretz (2002) analyzed the different effects that creative contributions can have on a field. Several of those effects depend on defying the zeitgeist. A *reinitiation* occurs when a researcher begins a field anew. An example is the influence Chomsky (1957) had on the field of psycholinguistics, the psychology of language. Although Chomsky was not a psychologist, his ideas had relevance to the way psychologists thought about language, and the field was entirely different after his ideas became well known. A *synthesis* involves bringing together ideas from two different disciplines – two different zeitgeists. Simon's ideas, which brought together economics, business, psychology, and computer science, were critical in the development of modern cognitive science (Newell & Simon, 1972).

Three Types of Defiance: Summary

New ideas can break from the old in several ways, depending on what aspects of the current situation the creative person defies. One can defy the crowd, proposing a new idea that goes against current beliefs but which stays within the overall stream of research that one is engaged in. One may also have to defy oneself – to break away from one's old ideas or ways of looking at things – in order to produce something that goes beyond what one has produced before. Finally, the hardest advances to make are those that go against the unstated beliefs that we hold about how our disciplines are structured – the zeitgeist. Most of the time, we are not aware of those beliefs, which makes their hold on our thinking particularly strong.

Types of Creativity

Sternberg (2018) used the three types of defiance as the basis for categorizing seven different types of creativity, outlined in Table 12.2. At one extreme is lack of creativity, which occurs when an idea is not new – it represents no defiance. At the other extreme is consummate creativity ("big-c" creativity; Kaufman & Beghetto, 2009), which involves all three types of defiance. In the middle are situations in which one defies only the crowd (sparse creativity), in which case one will produce something new but it will not change the world. "Quiet creativity" occurs when the individual produces a new idea that goes beyond the way that he or she had been looking at the world and that challenges the zeitgeist. However, sometimes a person is not interested in publicizing the work or the person may be prohibited from doing so because of a business agreement. In those cases, the advance will not have the world-changing effect that it might

Table 12.2 *Sternberg's (2018) types of creativity, according to the Triangle theory*

Type of Creativity	Kind of Defiance		
	Crowd	Individual	Zeitgeist
None			
Sparse	x		
Minor		x	
Isolated			x
Major	x	x	x
Sparse major	x		x
Quiet		x	x
Consummate	x	x	x

have were it known widely. The various other combinations of defiance produce other types of creativity.

Testing the Triangle Theory

Since the Triangle theory is new, there have not as yet been direct tests of it. However, the Triangle theory builds on Sternberg and Lubart's (1995) investment theory and there has been research that has tested aspects of the latter theory. Also, Sternberg (2018) proposed a number of different ways in which the Triangle theory might be tested.

An Empirical Examination of the Investment Theory

A study by Lubart and Sternberg (1995) examined the relationships among creativity and the resources postulated by the investment theory, which are also incorporated in the Triangle theory. Adult participants were given several creativity tasks as well as tests to measure the intellectual processes postulated to be relevant to creativity. The participants also filled out self-report measures designed to obtain information concerning their knowledge, intellectual styles, personality traits, and motivation. There were four types of creativity tasks.

1. Writing short stories in response to a list of topics provided by the researchers. The participant chose the one he or she wished to write on.

Examples of topics are "Beyond the Edge" and "The Octopus's Sneakers."
2. Drawing a picture in response to topics chosen from a list. Examples are "hope" and "rage."
3. Creating a television commercial. Example topics are "the IRS" and "bowties."
4. Solving a scientific problem. An example is "How could we detect the presence of aliens among us?"

Participants were encouraged to "be imaginative" and "have fun." The products were rated for creativity.

Intellectual tasks were chosen to measure general intelligence as well as the three insight processes – selective encoding, selective comparison, and selective combination – assumed to be crucial in redefinition of problems and therefore in production of new ideas. Knowledge was assessed with a questionnaire in which participants were asked how often they engaged in activities related to the creativity tasks, as well as others (e.g., working on social problems, writing poetry). Questionnaires were also used to assess thinking styles, and personality characteristics were also measured. Finally, the person's motivation for creative work was measured with a scale that asked such things as how well the person felt that he or she was described by such statements as "I would like to write a short story to challenge myself." The statements assessed motivation across a range of areas, including those involved in the creativity tests, and also examined intrinsic and extrinsic motivation.

The results of the study indicated, first, that there was only a weak positive relationship among the creativity ratings of the products across the various domains (see Table 12.3A). This meant that each domain had its own specific factors. Lubart and Sternberg (1995) attributed the positive relations across domains to the possibility that the intellectual processes (the insight processes, for example) were generally relevant, which would produce overall positive relationships. Interestingly, Lubart and Sternberg concluded that personality characteristics were probably domain-specific. So, for example, one might be a risk-taker when creating an advertisement but not when attempting to solve a scientific problem. In addition, there was not a very strong correlation among the creativity scores *within* each domain. The two stories produced by a given person were positively correlated, but the correlations were only moderate in strength: if one story by a person was highly rated, the second one might not be.

Table 12.3 *Sternberg and Lubart (1995) results*

A) *Correlations across creative performance domains*

	CREATIVE PERFORMANCE DOMAIN			
	Drawing	Writing	Advertising	Science
Drawing	–	.32*	.31*	.23
Writing		–	.41**	.62***
Advertising			–	.44**
Science				–

* $p < .05$; ** $p < .01$; *** $p < .001$

B) *Correlations of resources with rated creative performance (N = 48)*

	CREATIVE PERFORMANCE DOMAIN				
RESOURCE	Drawing	Writing	Advertising	Science	Overall
Intellectual processes	.51***	.59***	.50***	.61***	.75***
Knowledge	.35	.37**	.33*	.41**	.49***
Intellectual styles	-.08	-.28	.51***	-.28	-.39**
Personality	.25	.25	.26	.32*	.36*
Motivation	.28	.31*	.61***	.34*	.53***
Combined resources	.61**	.63***	.73***	.66***	.83***

* $p < .05$; ** $p < .01$; *** $p < .001$

Table 12.3B presents the correlations among the summary scores for each of the postulated resources and creative performance in the various domains. The theory predicted that each of the resources should be significantly related to creative performance, but those relationships varied across domains. Some of the correlations were not significant, and some were negative. Summarizing across all the creativity domains, as shown in the last column of the table, intellectual processes and knowledge were significant, but intellectual styles were significant in the opposite direction than predicted. In conclusion, there was some support for the specific predictions of the investment theory, although not all the resources followed the predictions. However, this study does demonstrate how one can examine the possible roles of different resources in creative accomplishment. Zhang and Sternberg (2011) also carried out research testing aspects of the investment theory.

Proposed Tests of the Triangle Theory

Sternberg (2018) made several suggestions concerning how the new theory might be tested, similar to the research just discussed. One possibility is to take descriptions of creative advances and have experts in the field rate them for the three postulated types of defiance. The experts should agree on the different types of defiance. One could also ask experts to rate historically important members of their fields as to the different types of creativity that they exhibited.

Critique of the Triangle Theory

The Triangle theory of creativity incorporates a wide range of processes and factors (Sternberg, 2018; Sternberg & Lubart, 1995). I will first examine two general aspects of the theory and then will turn to more specific issues.

Defiance and Creativity

One can raise questions about the importance of *defiance* in creative advances. Sternberg (2018) discussed Picasso and Braque's creation of Cubism, in the years around 1912, as a case of defying the crowd. In addition, after Cubism became common, Picasso then moved on to other styles, so he "sold high." That phase of Picasso's career fits the Triangle theory. The creation of *Guernica*, however, does not. As discussed in Chapter 1, *Guernica* was not in defiance of the crowd, and it did not break with Picasso's earlier style, so it was not the result of Picasso's defying himself. It also did not defy the zeitgeist. However, *Guernica* was a work that was accepted as a masterpiece immediately upon its completion. The Triangle theory cannot explain why *Guernica* was acclaimed a masterpiece.

One can raise similar questions about Watson and Crick (see Chapter 5). When they started their research, they adopted Pauling's orientation toward model building and his helical idea, which could be described as buying *high*, since those ideas had already been successful. Also, once they had produced the double helix, there was little in the way of a struggle to have it accepted (see Olby, 1994). In addition, several groups of researchers were working toward determining the structure of DNA. Thus, Watson and Crick did not defy the zeitgeist. Similarly, Wright's *Fallingwater* was acclaimed as a masterpiece immediately (see Chapter 4). Wright adapted the *Prairie House* design to the Bear Run location. He did not defy the crowd, since the *Prairie Houses* had been acclaimed years before. He did not defy himself, since he recycled that idea, and he did not defy the zeitgeist. And yet the house was a masterpiece. It is also notable that case studies are what Sternberg (2018) suggested could be used to test the Triangle theory. The case studies just presented indicate that the Triangle theory may be facing problems.

Negative Consequences of Expertise

The Triangle theory (Sternberg, 2018; Sternberg & Lubart, 1995) places emphasis on the negative consequences of knowledge on creative thinking, focusing on the negative role of entrenchment on creativity. That view is contradicted by the numerous case studies, discussed in earlier chapters, demonstrating the critical role of expertise in creative advances. Furthermore, other researchers have raised questions concerning the assumption that expertise causes inflexibility in thinking (Bilalic, McLoed & Gobet, 2008). Therefore, the notion that knowledge can be a barrier to creative adaptation to a changed environment may not be correct.

The Triangle Theory: Summary

The Triangle theory represents the latest advance in a long arc of research and theorizing by Sternberg concerning the creative process and the creative person (1988; 2018; Sternberg & Lubart, 1995, 1996). The important components of the theory are, first, the types of defiance that play roles in the creative process; and, second, the various resources contributing to creative production. The three types of defiance differ in several ways. Defying the crowd assumes that a creative idea has already been produced. It focuses on what has to happen afterward – on what the person must do to have the idea accepted. Defying oneself and defying the zeitgeist both involve factors that can interfere with the production of a new idea. Defying oneself requires that you go beyond what you have done before. Defying the zeitgeist requires that you think about the basic assumptions that underlie your field, which is not something we typically do. The resources postulated by the theory range from intellectual resources to personality characteristics to resources from the environment. Although questions can be raised about aspects of the theory, there are components of the theory that are useful in advancing our understanding of creative production in its broadest aspects. A critical issue that remains is how widely the theory is applicable and in what ways it might have to be revised in the face of research results.

We now turn to a second confluence theory, that of Amabile (1983, 1996). Amabile places special emphasis on the role of factors outside the individual – social-environmental factors – in the creative process. In discussing Amabile's theory, we will place the individual in the context of an organization, and we will examine how creativity plays out in the workplace.

The Social Psychology of Creativity

Amabile (1983, 1996) was the first researcher to emphasize the importance of social factors – factors originating outside the person – in the creative process, and she has continued to play a dominant role in this area. When we consider the organizational context in which creativity can come about, new factors play critical roles in the process, because the individual's job may be part of the creative component of the organization. In addition, there is typically a two-way process involved: the individual's creative output can affect the organization and the structure and functioning of the organization can affect the individual and the creative process. In Sternberg and Lubart's (1995) terms, Amabile (1983) defied the crowd, suggesting that the study of creativity had to move beyond the individual and include the influence of social-environmental factors on creativity. One reason for that suggestion was that there was evidence that those factors could affect creativity. It was known, for example, that features of the environment could affect performance on "tests" of creativity and personality. People perform differently when an unusual-uses test is labeled as a *creativity test* versus a *word exercise*. Similarly, when people are filling out personality measures in studies designed to determine the "creative personality," their responses change if they are told to fill it out as a creative person would. Those sorts of influences required that one go beyond the individual in order to understand creativity.

Amabile (1983) also discussed reports by creative individuals of negative influences on creativity brought about by social-environmental variables. As one example, winning prizes for literary accomplishment could result in a person's ceasing to work; also, critics' responses to one's work – negative as well as positive responses – could greatly affect creative productivity. Amabile (1983, 1996) interpreted such results as evidence that a complete understanding of creative production required that we deal with social factors and their influences.

Creativity and Innovation

Amabile (1983, ch. 2) defined creativity as production of some out-come that is novel and judged to be of value by some reference group of individuals. That is, artists can judge the creativity of a work of art, physicists can judge the creativity of a theory in physics, and so forth. However, Amabile added that the product must have come about through the use of *heuristic*, rather than *algorithmic*, methods. If one uses specific, well-defined procedures, such as the rules of addition, to carry out some task, the outcome is not creative. If a child solves an addition problem correctly using the rules of addition, then, even if the child has not solved that specific problem before, in Amabile's view, no creativity is involved.

Amabile (1983, ch. 2) also assumed that there is a continuum of crea-tivity. It begins with the artistic projects – collages, drawings, stories, or poems – produced by schoolchildren in the classroom; continues through products produced by college students during classroom or laboratory exercises or as leisure activities; goes on to the products of people who work as artists, musicians, writers, and poets; and ends with the master-pieces that have changed our lives. All those products are, in Amabile's view, brought about by the same processes.

Creativity versus Innovation

The creative process results in new ideas. In the corporate world, however, ideas are not enough. Corporations rely on *innovations*, which involve the utilization of a new idea as the basis for a new product or service. In order to innovate, the corporation must be able to make use of creative ideas from its employees. Also, as noted, the innovative success of a corporation can foster the development of creative ideas within the corporation, so we have a cyclic set of processes interacting.

Measuring Creativity

Amabile (1983) used her definition of creativity, with its emphasis on the judgment of some reference group, as the basis for development of the *consensual assessment technique* (CAT) as a measure of creativity. Judges who are expert in the domain, relying solely on their expertise, rate the creativity of products that the participants create. If one uses tasks like constructing collages out of materials provided by the researcher or writing very simple poems, there are no complex skills involved, so essentially everyone can produce something to be rated. In addition, those sorts of tasks are ones in which creativity is found in the real world, so the tasks have face validity. The consensual assessment technique has been used in a large number of studies in Amabile's laboratory (Amabile, 1996) and elsewhere. Baer and McKool (2014) called the CAT the "gold standard" of creativity measurement.

Amabile's Componential Theory: Individual Creativity

Amabile's theory is presented in Table 12.4. There are two levels of components, that interact in order to result in production of an innovation by an organization (Amabile & Pratt, 2016). The upper level (Table 12.4A), involving creativity by the individual or small group, can result in a new idea. That idea provides the input to the organization (see down arrow in the center of Table 12.4), where the innovation process operates (Table 12.4B). The innovation process can result in a new product built on that idea. We will begin our examination at the level of individual creativity (Table 12.4A), which Amabile analyzed as a five-stage process.

Stages of the Creative Process

The creative process is initiated (Stage 1) when a task is set. Either a person identifies a problem to work on (a poet decides to compose a poem about a recent experience – an *internal* task) or a problem is presented from outside (an artist is given a commission to paint a portrait – an *external* task). In the first case, it is assumed that the poet is *intrinsically* motivated to carry out the task. The poet is interested in creating the poem for its own sake and not for any external reason or reward. In the second case, the motivation is *extrinsic*; it comes from the commission. The second stage, *preparation*, entails gathering information and resources potentially relevant to the problem. In the third stage, information from memory as well as from the environment is used as the basis for generation of ideas that might serve as a solution to the problem. Any generated ideas are evaluated at stage 4, which can, at stage 5, result in solution of the problem or a recycling through the earlier stages in order to deal with inadequacies of the proposed idea. If no candidate responses have been generated, the person might give up.

Table 12.4 *Amabile's analysis of creativity*

A. *At the level of the individual*

Individual Component	Stage of Individual Creative Process					Progress?	
	1. Task setting: external/internal source	2. Preparation: gather info and resources	3. Generate idea: produce idea or product	4. Validation: check against criteria	5. Outcome assessment:	Yes	No
A. Motivation: intrinsic & synergistic external	√		√	√	Solution	Return to 1?	End
B. Skills in domain		√		√	Failure	Return to 1	End
C. Creativity-relevant processes		√	√	√	Progress	Return to 1	End

⇓ ⇑

B. *At the level of the individual*

	Stage of Organizational Creative Process					Progress?	
Organizational Component (Work Environment)	1. Agenda setting: statements and actions	2. Stage setting: goals, resources, work context	3. Produce ideas: individuals or teams produce idea or product	4. Testing and implementing ideas	5. Outcome assessment:	Yes	No
A. Motivation to innovate	√				Success	Return to 2?	End
B. Resources in domain		√		√	Failure	Return to 2	End
C. Skills in innovation management		√		√	Progress	Return to 2	End

The Progress Loop

An important component of the theory, shown in the two right-hand columns of Table 12.4, is the *progress loop*: if the person has been making progress on the task, he or she will continue to cycle through it even though solution has not yet been obtained. That persistence raises the chances that solution might occur. The progress loop is affected by the *meaningfulness* of the work being carried out. In research by Amabile and her colleagues (Amabile & Pratt, 2016), people were asked to keep electronic diaries of their work experiences and their responses to each day's activities. The most positive days were those in which people reported progress in what they considered meaningful work. Meaningful work was seen as important for the individual or the organization. When progress was seen, it influenced the person's emotional response, which colored the person's feelings about the day's activities.

Components of Individual Creativity

There are three components playing a role in the individual's creative process (see left-hand column of Table 12.4A). Individual creativity is the outcome of the combination of motivation (Individual Component A); skills in the domain of the task (the raw materials; Individual Component B); and more general skills relevant to creativity itself (skills to produce new ideas; Individual Component C). For creativity to occur, all those components must be present.

Component A: Intrinsic versus Extrinsic Motivation and Creativity

As noted, the aspect of Amabile's (1996) theory that distinguished it from other work in creativity was an emphasis on the effects of the social environment on creativity. The social environment affects the motivation of the individual to carry out the task, as represented by *Individual Component A*. Motivation affects the first four stages of the creative process, but its most important influence is at stage 3, during which the person is generating a possible response. In Amabile's original theory (1983), it was emphasized that creative outcomes were most likely to occur when the person was *intrinsically motivated* to carry out some task – that is, when he or she carried out a task for its own sake. Amabile (1996; Ruscio, Whitney & Amabile, 1998) used the concept of a person working through a maze to illustrate how motivation affects the creative process. Using an algorithmic approach to solving a problem is equivalent to taking a straight-line path in a maze, directly from the entrance to the exit. However, in this hypothetical maze there are other exits from the maze that are possible but can be reached only through the use of heuristic methods that allow deviation from the straight path and entail taking some risk, because the path to the exit is not apparent. The motivation of the individual is critical in determining which sort of method they choose.

> We propose that extrinsically motivated individuals, because they are motivated primarily by some task-extrinsic factors, will be more likely to rely on common, well-worked algorithms they have learned for doing a particular task. ... By contrast, intrinsically motivated individuals, because they enjoy the task itself and the process of searching for a new solution, will be more likely to explore the maze, attempting to find their way to one of the more novel exits. (Amabile, 1996, p. 122)

This passage makes clear the importance that Amabile placed on intrinsic motivation in setting in motion the processes that are critical in producing a creative outcome.

How Might External Factors Affect Creativity?

Amabile (1983, p. 100) described extrinsic factors such as rewards or the expectation of one's work being evaluated as *constraints* on the creative process. Amabile considered two different sorts of explanations concerning how constraints might negatively affect the creative process. First, an external factor operating during a task – such as the expectation or hope of getting a reward or having others evaluate one's work – might occupy some of the person's working-memory capacity so that he or she cannot deal fully with the demands of the task. The second explanation is that concern with external factors such as reward or evaluation might change the way in which the individual approaches the task (Amabile, 1996). Most particularly, the presence of a possible reward might make the person less likely to take risks, because risks might be perceived as lowering the chances to receive the reward. If creativity depends on taking risks, that strategy will result in lowered creativity. These two explanations are not mutually exclusive: the presence of an external reward, for example, could be a distraction *and* could result in the person's changing the strategy for approaching the task.

Evidence for Negative Effects of Extrinsic Factors on Creativity

Much research evidence demonstrated negative effects of extrinsic factors on creativity. Several early studies demonstrated that expectation of evaluation had negative effects on creativity (Amabile, 1979; Amabile, Goldfarb & Brackfield, 1990). In an examination of artistic creativity, undergraduates were asked to create collages using a set of standardized materials, including more than 100 pieces of paper of different sizes, shapes, and colors (all of which were presented in the same arrangement for each participant), glue, and a 15- by 20-inch piece of white cardboard, on which the collage was to be constructed. In order to study verbal creativity, undergraduates were asked to create simple haiku-like five-line poems.

The students in the expectation-of-evaluation conditions were told that their work would be judged by experts in the area and that the judges would report their evaluations to the experimenters, who would also send them to the participant. Thus, not only was there the possibility of evaluation, but the outcome would be known to someone beside the evaluator and the participant. The results from those studies were clear: creativity scores in both artistic and verbal domains were lower in the groups expecting evaluation. More recent research (summarized in Amabile, 1996, ch. 5) has made things a bit more complicated, as Amabile and others have gone on to examine more subtle aspects of the relationship between creativity and expectations of evaluation. However, the general conclusion, that expectation of evaluation will lower creativity, has held up.

A second set of studies examined the influence of reward on creativity. Working for a reward lowers intrinsic motivation, which should result in lowered levels of creativity. In one early study (Amabile, Hennessy & Grossman, 1986), children were asked to construct collages. One group was told that, if they agreed to carry out the collage task, they could have the opportunity of playing with a Polaroid camera (which was a strong reward at that time). All the children agreed to make the collage for the chance to use the camera. After agreeing, the children first played with the camera and then constructed the collage. This reversal in what might be the expected order of the tasks has interesting implications for our understanding of how reward might affect creativity, which will be discussed shortly. A control group also played with the camera before constructing the collage, but nothing was said about the use of the camera depending on an agreement to make the collage. This group simply was exposed to two activities in succession.

The children who received the reward produced collages that were rated less creative by judges. In addition, the fact that the reward activity – playing with the camera – was carried out *before* the creative activity means that the reward could not have been a distractor. The reward might have changed how the children approached the task, as Amabile (1983) proposed in her analogy of creativity as working through a maze. A number of other studies have supported the finding that reward can interfere with the creativity with which a task is carried out (for review see Eisenberger & Byron, 2011). However, as with the question of evaluation, the pattern of results has become more complicated, as researchers have examined more subtle aspects of the possible influence of reward on creativity. We will examine those studies shortly, when a critique of the theory is presented.

"Immunization" against the Negative Effects of Reward

Amabile (1996, p. 173) reported a study in which an attempt was made to "immunize" children against the negative effects of reward. The participants were first given exposure to a video in which children talked about their schoolwork in terms that emphasized its intrinsic-motivational aspects. For example, they said that they worked hard, not for grades (i.e., not for an extrinsic reward) but because they liked to learn new things. A control group saw a video in which children talked about food preferences, which was not relevant to intrinsic versus extrinsic motivation. The videos were then discussed by the participants in order to enable them to "internalize" the intrinsic-motivational message.

The two groups of children were then given two tasks to carry out, the first of which was presented as a reward. The second task was a creative task. In this experiment, the children in the immunization group actually exhibited an increased level of creativity in the reward condition, while the control group's creativity decreased under reward. In addition, the immunized group reported more intrinsic motivation in their response to the creative task. Thus, it is possible to counteract the negative effects of reward on creativity through training and practice. Amabile (1996, p. 174) reported a tactic used by the poet Anne Sexton to deal with monetary details in negotiation of a book contract: she had her agent do it. Sexton said that she was interested in money, but first she wanted to write good poems, and she wanted to maximize the chances of that happening by not dealing with reward.

Negative Effects of Rewards in Organizations

Amabile and her colleagues have also carried out nonexperimental investigations of the effects of reward on creativity, mainly in organizations (summarized in Amabile, 1996, pp. 174–175). Interview studies indicated that rewards have a negative effect when people feel that they are being rewarded as an inducement to carry out some work. On the other hand, when people feel that the organization rewards creative work, the reward will have a positive effect on creativity. One example of rewarding people for producing a creative solution on some project is to allow them to choose the next project they will work on and/or the team with which they will work.

Constraining versus Enabling Effects of Rewards

A particularly interesting study examined the effects of external *constraint*, rather than reward, on creativity (summarized in Amabile, 1996, pp. 174–175). Professional artists were asked to submit randomly chosen works that they had done over the past seven years, ten of which had been commissioned and ten of which were noncommissioned. The artists also filled out a questionnaire that asked about the conditions under which each work had been produced as well as the artist's feelings about the work, including its creativity. The works were then rated by artist judges who were unaware of the conditions under which each painting had been created. The works produced on commission were rated as less creative than the noncommissioned works. In addition, among the commissioned works there was a negative correlation between the ratings of creativity and the artist's report of being constrained by the commission. On the other hand, the commission had a positive effect on creativity (as rated by the artists producing the work) if the artist perceived the commission as *enabling* – that is, as providing the opportunity for the artist to carry out interesting work.

Positive Effects of External Motivation: The Synergy Effect

As we have just seen, research has indicated that extrinsic motivation does not necessarily interfere with creativity. Based on such results, there have been changes to the roles that different sorts of motivation are assumed to play in the creative process, as can be seen in the *Individual Component A* cell in Table 12.4A (Amabile & Pratt, 2016). It is now believed that there is more than one type of extrinsic motivation. *Controlling* extrinsic motivation leads people to feel that they are being controlled by external circumstances, as when they are working to earn a reward and for no other reason. That motivation has negative effects on creative production. In contrast, *informational* extrinsic motivators provide information about one's competence in carrying out the task or about the value of one's work. Informational extrinsic motivation can work *synergistically – in coordination –* with intrinsic motivation to play a positive role in the creative process (Amabile, 1996, p. 118; Amabile & Pratt, 2016, p. 176). That possible positive influence of synergistic external motivation has been added to independent component A in Table 12.4.

Increasing Creativity

Based on her theory, Amabile (1996, ch. 9) discussed ways of increasing creativity. First of all, because her research has demonstrated that extrinsic constraints can have a negative impact on creativity, those factors should be minimized. Teachers, for example, should talk less about grades in the classroom; and, when they do talk about grades, grades can be described as providing information that can lead to higher levels of skills. One can also increase the synergistic influences of external factors by ensuring that reward and recognition serve to inform individuals about their competence and how to improve it rather than simply serving in evaluation of performance.

Component B: Skills in the Domain

The second component of Amabile's theory is skills in the domain (Individual Component B in Table 12.4A). In order to produce a creative outcome, a person must possess the skills required to understand the domain and function in it. Those skills are the foundation on which any creative response must be built. For the analysis of creativity, domain-specific skills are taken for granted and will not be discussed further here in any detail.

Component C: General Aspects of Creativity – The Creativity-Relevant Processes

The third component of the theory at the individual level is the *creativity-relevant processes* (see Individual Component C in Table 12.4A), which are general processes that can enhance a person's creativity (Amabile, 1983, pp. 72–73; Amabile & Pratt, 2016). In Amabile's view, the difference between a good or acceptable outcome versus a creative outcome depends on the utilization of creativity-relevant processes. Amabile (1983, pp. 72–73) listed many examples of such processes, which can be grouped into three areas: cognitive style; knowledge of heuristics for generating new ideas; and personality characteristics.

Cognitive Style

The cognitive style supporting creativity is characterized by an ability to deal with complexity and to *break set* during problem-solving. Breaking set refers to the ability to change one's approach to a situation (one's *set*). Specific examples of this cognitive style include the ability to break *perceptual set*, to perceive things differently than others do. This ability can play a role in the use of accidental events in the external environment in one's creative endeavors. Similar to breaking perceptual set is the ability to break *cognitive set*, which involves abandoning unsuccessful strategies and searching in a new direction. A related process is keeping one's options open as long as possible and suspending judgment concerning the value of one's ideas until one has gathered multiple ideas, some of which might seem useless at first glance. This strategy echoes Osborne's (1963) brainstorming method, discussed in Chapter 1 as a component of IDEO's innovation strategy. Creativity is also fostered by the ability to break out of *performance scripts* – that is, well-used algorithms – and to produce the changes in one's routine actions that will result in novel – that is, creative – outcomes. Many if not all of those components of the creative cognitive style are variations on one basic process: breaking away from the constraints of past experience. That is, of course, a variation on the outside-of-the-box view.

Heuristics for Generating New Ideas

The second component of the creativity-relevant skills involves knowledge of heuristics for generating new ideas. Examples are taking a different perspective on a problem or adopting an open or playful attitude to the problem. Such an approach may also encourage risk-taking, which may increase the creativity of the outcome.

Creative Working Style

The third component of the creativity-relevant skills is a working style conducive to creative production. Components of this working style include an ability to concentrate effort as well as the ability to abandon unproductive strategies and to put aside problems on which one is making no progress. Also relevant to the creative work style are persistence and a high overall level of productivity. Amabile (1996, ch. 9) also proposed that creativity-relevant skills can be improved if parents and teachers can model independent and intrinsically motivated activity. Creative and playful exploration of activities should also be encouraged.

Personality

Personality factors are also cited by Amabile (1983, p. 74) as playing an important role in creative production, also through their influence on the creativity-relevant skills. Some of those personality factors are a high degree of self-discipline, the ability to delay gratification, a tolerance for ambiguity, and perseverance in the face of lack of success and frustration. Other relevant personality factors are independence of judgment, a high degree of autonomy, an internal locus of control (i.e., the person works under his or her own direction), a high level of self-initiated striving for excellence, and, perhaps most importantly, independence in thinking and an absence of dependence on social approval. Finally, as noted already, there is a willingness to take risks. Those components are related to the components of the creative personality discussed in Chapter 11.

Individual Creativity: Summary

Amabile's theory of creativity as applied to the individual (Amabile, 1983, 1996; Amabile & Pratt, 2016) involves components of several different sorts: task motivation, domain-specific processes, and more general creativity-relevant processes. Those components influence a five-stage process. An important component is motivation, which affects the creative process in multiple ways. In addition, progress in working on a meaningful problem plays an important role in creative production. We now turn to Amabile's analysis of creativity at the level of organizational innovation. Factors analogous to those at the level of the individual affect organizational innovation.

Amabile's Componential Theory: Organizational Innovation

The Five-Stage Organizational Innovation Process

There are five stages in the innovation process, analogous to the five stages at the individual level (Table 12.4B; Amabile & Pratt, 2016, p. 162). Stage 1 is the setting of the overall agenda for the organization. That agenda typically is seen in the statements and behaviors of the leaders. An agenda can also be set by something outside the usual organizational channels, such as the discovery of a potentially useful innovation by someone inside the organization. Sometimes a customer can bring a new idea to the corporation involving a change or improvement to a product. Stage 2, *Stage Setting*, involves preparation for the project. It begins with setting the goals for the project within the organization; gathering resources, including people and information; and carrying out market research. Stage 3 (*Individuals or Teams Produce Ideas or Trial Projects*) is a summary of the individual-level processes, outlined in Table 12.4A, that we have already discussed. Stage 4, *Testing and Implementing Ideas*, entails the organization as a whole considering the potential value of any ideas that have been produced by an individual at Stage 3 in Table 12.4A. Stage 4 is of critical importance, because it is there that a distinction is made between potentially valuable ideas, which should be supported and developed further, and less-valuable or useless ideas, which should either be put aside or sent back for more work.

The final stage of the innovation process – *Stage 5: Outcome Assessment* – is the result of the processes taking place at the first four stages. When a possible innovation has been developed and tested in Stage 4, the possible outcomes are success, failure, or progress. In the cases of clear success or clear failure, the process can stop, but there is also the possibility of returning to Stage 2, where a successful project can be refined further or a failure can be looked at again to see if anything can be salvaged from it. If there has been progress made, then the process cycles to Stage 2, where more work can be carried out.

Organizational Components in Innovation

Comparable to the three components that play roles in the individual's creative process, there are also three organizational components that work together to produce innovation (see the left-hand column of Table 12.4B). First, the organization must be motivated to innovate (Organizational

Component A). Second, there must be resources available in the domain in which innovation is sought (Organizational Component B). Third, there must be skills in managing innovation (Organizational Component C). The organizational components comprise the *work environment*. Like the individual components in Table 12.4A, all the organizational components have to be present if corporate innovation is to occur.

Organizational Component A: Motivation to Innovate

Organizational motivation to innovate is seen in the statements and actions of the leaders of the organization. Without evidence of organizational interest in and support of innovation, employees will be reluctant to engage in such activities. The organization must accept some degree of risk-taking on the part of the employees; also, the organization must be open to new ideas and be willing to foster the development of new products, which may disrupt the current activities of the organization. There must also be a system in place for developing new ideas. The motivation to innovate has its main effects in Stage 1.

Organizational Component B: Resources in the Domain

The second organizational component involves resources in the task domain. Organizational resources include people who have the skills, interest, and motivation needed to carry out creative work in the area; financing and other material support for the work; and access to necessary information. Perhaps the most important organizational resource is *time*, which is needed to explore and implement creative ideas. The resource component affects mainly Stages 2 and 4 of the innovation process in Table 12.4B, which occur before and after the ideas are produced. The effectiveness of Stage 2 depends on the organizational resources available and the organizational skills in managing innovation, to which we now turn.

Organizational Component C: Innovation Management

The factors involved in managing innovation include setting clear goals that allow individuals to explore possible new ideas on their own. Providing meaningful work – that is, work that matches employee interests and skills – is also important. Positive feedback should be given in response to creative efforts, whether or not they are successful, including generous rewards. There should also be open communication within the organization, so that employees can exchange ideas easily. Those factors play roles at Stages 2 and 4 of the innovation process.

The ⇓ arrow between the two levels of the theory is presented because the output of the individual process feeds into Stage 3 of the innovation process. However, the connection between the organization and the individual (the ⇑ from the organization level to the individual) emphasizes the idea that forces outside the individual play roles in affecting whether creative work will be carried out in the first place, as well as in determining the fate of any ideas that are produced. The interaction between the individual and the organization is a two-way path.

The Componential Theory: Critique

In critiquing Amabile's theory, one can raise questions about several points: the definition of creativity; the issue of creativity as a general skill; and the question of creativity-relevant processes versus domain-relevant skills. Finally, questions can be raised about the role of rewards in creativity.

Defining Creativity

Amabile (1983, 1996; Amabile & Pratt, 2016) defined creativity as the production of a novel product that is of value to some group and that was produced through the use of heuristic, rather than algorithmic, methods. I have already discussed in Chapter 2 what I see as problems with using value as a criterion for calling something creative; that point does not need to be revisited. Considering the issue of the heuristic versus algorithmic basis of the creative product, I believe, contrary to Amabile, that one should consider a child's response to an addition problem, discussed earlier, to be creative, although perhaps minimally so. The novelty of the situation requires *some* adjustment by the child, and that entails creativity. The crucial aspect in calling some product creative is that in producing that object the individual has had to adjust his or her behavior in some way. The important point for the researcher is to determine the details of that process. From this perspective, applying an algorithm to a new situation involves creativity.

Is Creativity a General or Domain-Specific Process?

Amabile (1996; Amabile & Pratt, 2016) proposed that creative production depends on a number of general heuristic processes directed at breaking away from the past. One can raise questions concerning the generality of creative skills. As documented in Chapter 6, evidence concerning the Ten-Year Rule and the importance of expertise in creative achievement raises questions for the notion that creativity involves general skills. In addition, a number of studies, some of which were reviewed in Chapter 10, raise problems for the notion of general creative skills. Baer (2015) has shown that there are only weak correlations among creative performances across different domains, which he took as evidence for domain-specific skills in creativity. As we saw earlier, similar results were reported by Sternberg and Lubart (see Table 12.3A). In addition, Baer (2015) exposed schoolchildren to creativity training and found that the skills developed are relevant to very narrow domains.

Amabile and colleagues (Conti, Coon, & Amabile, 1996) reviewed the results of several studies carried out in Amabile's laboratory, in which individuals were given several different creativity tasks to carry out. In the domain of creative writing, the participants were asked to write three short stories, each one in response to a different picture. In a separate activity, the participants were also asked to write a short story about two characters they had previously read about in a learning exercise. Participants also engaged in three art activities: making a collage out of paper shapes; making a drawing using only straight lines; and using sponges of different shapes to paint a picture. Table 12.5 presents the correlations among performances within the various domains. There are relatively large correlations within each of the domains (i.e., within writing or art; see correlations presented in bold font in the upper left for writing and the lower right for art). The correlations across domains (across writing and art), presented in normal font in the upper right of the table, are smaller; none are significant, and several are negative. Amabile (1996) interpreted those results as providing evidence for the general nature of creative performance. I would conclude, in contrast, that there are not creativity skills that strongly bridge those domains.

Breaking Away from Experience as a Creativity-Relevant Skill

Many of the creativity-relevant skills proposed by Amabile (1983, 1996) center on methods of breaking out of constraints arising from experience.

Table 12.5 *Results of study of Conti, Coon, and Amabile (1996) examining generality of creative accomplishment*

	1) Story 1	2) Story 2	3) Story 3	4) Story Mean	5) Reading Story	6) Collage	7) Drawing	8) Painting	9) Art Mean
1	X	.64**	.43**	.86**	.47*	.36	.33	−.07	.27
2		X	.50**	.87**	.46*	.19	.31	−.22	.12
3			X	.75**	.21	.35	.31	−.13	.23
4				X	.43*	.35	.36	−.16	.25
5					X	.12	−.22	.09	.00
6						X	.43**	.27*	.77**
7							X	.15	.73**
8								X	.66**
9									X

* p < .05; **p < .0

Based on the case studies discussed in several places in this book, one can raise the question of whether such skills are relevant to most situations that require creativity. If Picasso *had* broken with the past, there would be no *Guernica*. A similar claim can be made about Frank Lloyd Wright's creation of *Fallingwater*, IDEO's shopping cart, Watson and Crick and the double helix, Leonardo's aerial screw, and Edison's light bulb. Interested readers can consider each of the other case studies as well to see if it came about as the result of a strategy of abandoning the past.

The Role of Reward in Creativity

In response to Amabile's (1996) conclusion that creative outcomes were most likely to occur when the person was *intrinsically motivated* to carry out a task, several researchers presented evidence that reward or reinforcement could have a positive effect on creative production.

Divergent Thinking

One set of studies (Eisenberger & Byron, 2011) examined the effect of reward on performance on divergent-thinking tasks. People were given reinforcement for some aspect of divergent production: for example, for fluency – number of responses; for flexibility – number of different categories of responses; or for originality – rarity of responses. Results indicate that each of those aspects could be influenced separately through reinforcement. Those results seemed to raise problems for Amabile's theory, but she proposed that divergent-thinking tasks were *algorithmic* tasks, not heuristic-based creativity tasks. The reason Amabile (1996) assumed that divergent-thinking tasks do not involve creativity is that those tasks are highly structured and the participant essentially knows how to do well on them. There is no heuristic component, where the individual must construct the solution strategy. One can question that algorithmic interpretation of divergent-thinking tasks. In Chapter 10, we reviewed research that examined the role of executive functioning in divergent thinking (Beatty & Silvia, 2012; Gilhooly et al., 2007; Nusbaum & Silvia, 2011). That research indicated that divergent thinking is a task that is dealt with through the development of strategies and that executive functioning plays a critical role. If that conclusion is correct, then divergent-thinking tasks are not algorithmic, and the finding that reward increases divergent thinking raises problems for Amabile's theory.

Reward and Creativity: Additional Results

Eisenberger and Byron (2011) proposed that one reason some studies have not found positive effects of reinforcement on creativity is that they have had design problems which resulted in negative effects. If those design problems are corrected, then reinforcement can be shown to positively influence creativity. As one example, consider again at the study of Amabile, Hennessey, and Grossman (1986) in which participants were told to create collages. A reward – playing with a Polaroid camera – resulted in lower creativity. However, in the instructions to the participants nothing was said about producing a *creative* collage. Therefore, according to Eisenberger and Byron, one cannot expect the reward to have a positive effect on creativity. In studies that have made it clear that reward depended on the creativity of the response, reward has been found to have a positive effect on creativity (Eisenberger & Byron, 2011; Byron & Khazanchi, 2012), and the greater the magnitude of the reward, the greater the effect. In conclusion, questions can be raised about one core assumption of the componential theory, the idea that reward is detrimental to creativity.

Amabile's Confluence Theory: Conclusions

Amabile's theory (1983, 1996; Amabile & Pratt, 2016) attempts to deal with a wide range of phenomena concerned with creative production and creative people. She began with a unique emphasis on the possible role of social-environmental factors in creativity. Her theory and research have stimulated others to investigate factors beyond the creative thought process, and the results have pointed to the importance of motivational and environmental factors in creativity. Amabile's influence can be seen in the theorizing of Sternberg and Lubart (1995), discussed earlier in the chapter. Sternberg and Lubart placed emphasis on internal motivation and the environment as resources, and that emphasis can be traced to Amabile's earlier theorizing in those areas. Amabile's theorizing has brought together two levels at which creativity unfolds – the individual and the organization – and she has tried to draw parallels between the factors that are important at each level. In addition, her development of the CAT changed how researchers measure the creativity of products of different sorts.

Confluence Theories of Creativity: Summary

The two confluence theories discussed in this chapter have several commonalities. First, and perhaps most important, both assume that a complete understanding of the creative process requires that we consider many factors beyond the cognitive processes that were the focus of the first half of this book. Confluence theories assume that the creative process is embedded in a large matrix of factors, some within the individual – motivation and personality characteristics – and some outside – socio-environmental factors. The two theories reviewed here are different in details but similar in overall structure and the kinds of components they include in their analysis of creativity.

Given the analysis of creative thinking presented in the earlier chapters, with its emphasis on green creativity and the recycling of ideas, it is interesting to note that both theories emphasize the need for creative thinking to break away from the past, although the mechanisms postulated to bring about this break are different between theories. Sternberg (2018) assumed that creative intelligence, including the insight processes of selective encoding, selective combination, and selective comparison (Davidson, 1995; Sternberg & Davidson, 1982), played a critical role in the reformulation of problems. Amabile (1996) emphasized general creative-thinking skills, such as set-breaking. Both theories also emphasized the role of personality factors in creativity. As noted in the previous chapter, there are questions that can be raised about the direction of causality in the study of the creative personality, and the researchers who developed the models discussed here have not presented any direct evidence that personality factors play a causal role in creative production. They simply assume, based on the correlations typically found between creative achievement and personality factors (Feist, 2017, 2018), that the latter play a causal role in the former.

In conclusion, confluence theories of the sort reviewed here provide the general shape of the ultimate theory of creativity that will be developed in psychology. However, at this point, questions can be raised about specifics of two of the important theories of today, as outlined in this chapter. There remains some work to be done before we can specify with confidence the range of factors beyond the individual that play a role in creative production.

PART V

The Neuroscience of Creativity

13 | The Neuroscience of Creativity

Neuroscience has witnessed an explosion of growth, and the study of creativity has become a focal point in discussions of the role of brain structures and processes in psychological functioning (Abraham, 2018; Jung & Vartanian, 2018). Many neuroscience writings on creativity begin by noting the critical importance of creativity in our lives, which makes it a prime candidate for analysis. Several neuroscience methods have been employed to try to specify the role of the brain in creativity. The method most frequently used is recording brain activity while people are carrying out tasks involving creative thinking (Kounios & Beeman, 2015). When neuroscience researchers began to study creative thinking seriously, about twenty years ago, the focus was on the role of specific brain areas in creativity. More recently, interest has shifted to the study of brain networks – groups of brain areas that work together – in creativity (Fox & Beaty, 2019). Researchers have also studied creative functioning in individuals who have suffered brain injuries by measuring the areas that have been damaged and also measuring any changes – positive or negative – that have occurred in creative functioning. A third method, also of increasing interest (Chrysikou et al., 2017), involves stimulating specific brain areas in various ways and measuring the effects of that stimulation on cognitive functioning, in this case on creativity.

Outline of the Chapter

The first part of the chapter will examine studies that have tried to isolate brain areas involved in creative thinking, specifically areas involved in bringing about insight in problem-solving. The second section of the chapter will review research that has looked at the link between brain structures involved in memory and those underlying imagination and other creative activities. Some aspects of creative thinking may build on processes involved in memory, so this work provides an important link between components of creative thinking and one everyday cognitive process, recalling information from memory. The third section of the chapter examines changes in brain structure that come about as the result of the acquisition of expertise, which will link cognitive research on expertise discussed in Chapter 6 with findings from neuroscience. The fact that changes in brain structure can be brought about as a result of deep immersion in a domain provides support for the idea that acquisition of expertise – rather than innate brain structures – may serve as the basis for world-class performance, including creative performance.

The fourth section of the chapter changes the focus a bit and reviews research that has demonstrated that creative performance can be affected through brain stimulation. Brain-stimulation methods are particularly important, because they enable researchers to carry out controlled experimental studies in which brain activity is manipulated by the researchers. That sort of design supports stronger inferences concerning causal links between brain activity and behavior. The effects of brain stimulation on creative performance can be positive or negative, depending on the task being carried out and the specific brain areas being stimulated.

The final section of the chapter reviews research that goes beyond the study of isolated brain areas and focuses on the role of brain networks in creative thinking. We shall also consider some new issues arising from the study of the neuroscience of creativity, which will demonstrate that findings from neuroscience can sometimes move us beyond what we have learned from the cognitive-experimental study of creativity.

The chapter will conclude by bringing the discussion full circle and examining the influence of the genius view on the neuroscience of creativity. In many places throughout the book, beginning in Chapter 1, we have examined the various ways in which the genius view is seen in modern theorizing. It is especially interesting to see how the genius view has shaped the most cutting-edge research, the neuroscience of creativity.

As we review neuroscience research on creativity, it is important to remember that this topic has only recently become an area of concentrated study and, therefore, the findings and conclusions that we discuss here are tentative. Because of the expanding importance of neuroscience in modern psychological science, the research examined in this chapter can be looked upon as a preview of how the study of creativity will develop in the near future. Thus, the examination of the neuroscience of creativity is a fitting way to end this book.

Measuring Brain Activity during Creative Thinking: Searching for the Location of Creativity in the Brain

One of the initial goals of modern research in neuroscience was to specify the brain areas that are active when a specific psychological process is carried out. Assume that you are a creativity researcher looking to examine which brain region – or regions – are active when someone produces a new idea. You might be interested, for example, in determining what happens in the brain when a person has a moment of insight, an *Aha!* experience. When researchers design a brain-imaging study to analyze the role of specific brain regions in carrying out a task, they cannot simply present the task, measure brain activity, and draw conclusions. If you are trying to determine the brain areas involved in insight, you first need a situation in which insight regularly occurs, so you have a chance to measure activity in the brain during the phenomenon in which you are interested. In Chapter 7, we examined several "insight problems" that researchers have used to investigate insight in the laboratory. However, even if you can "capture" insight in the laboratory, determining the exact brain areas underlying any specific psychological process is a difficult task. Those difficulties will become clear if we consider a simpler situation, adding two digits.

Measuring Brain Activity Underlying Simple Arithmetic

Let us say you were interested in determining the brain activity that occurs when someone carries out addition. You present a simple arithmetic problem to a participant in the MRI apparatus, so you can measure brain activity as the task is carried out. The person has been told that she will see two numbers. She is to add them silently, press a button when she has the answer, and then say the answer aloud. The person sees "7, 4" on the screen, presses the button, and says "11." It would seem that you would then have a record of brain activity during addition. However, that conclusion is not correct, because the task included processes other than addition. The individual had to understand the instructions, read the numbers, carry out the addition, press the button, and say the answer. All those components are included in the brain recording that you just obtained. If you want to determine the specific brain activity underlying addition – let us call that the *target task* – you first have to "subtract," or remove, that other unwanted activity. Researchers carry out such a subtraction by utilizing a control or baseline condition in their studies.

Pure Insertion

In a well-designed brain imaging study, the baseline differs from the target condition by only the process in which you are interested. Such a research design is called "pure insertion," because in the target task you "insert" only

Table 13.1 *Subtraction method to determine brain activity underlying addition Read the information below as if it were a subtraction problem, comparable to:* $\frac{X}{Z}$

(a) Brain activity: Target – Add #s	(a) Activity A + B + C + D
– (b) Brain activity: Baseline – Read #s	(b) Activity – A – B – 0 – D
(c) Result: "Addition" area in the brain (difference between (a) and (b))	(c) Result 0 + 0 + C + 0

Components of the tasks:

  A. Remember instructions

  B. Read numbers

  C. Carry out addition

  D. Press button

one additional process beyond the baseline. It can then be assumed that any differences between the target and baseline brain recordings are due to the process that you are interested in, because everything else has been "subtracted out." The diagram in Table 13.1 demonstrates how pure insertion works. In the arithmetic example just discussed, a baseline condition might involve presenting the same written materials to the participant (7, 4) but with the instruction that she just *read* them silently, press the button when she has done so, and then say the numbers aloud (without adding them). Subtracting the brain activity during baseline from that during the target addition condition would allow you to draw conclusions about the brain areas involved in addition. We now turn to an examination of recent research that has used the subtraction method in an attempt to isolate the brain areas underlying insight.

The Neuroscience of Insight

As discussed in Chapter 7, the study of insight is an area in which there has been more than 100 years of discussion and debate concerning whether there are two basically different ways of solving problems: analysis versus insight. The Gestalt psychologists and their modern followers dismissed analytic thinking as "reproductive thinking" and concluded that such analysis, since it depended on the past, could not be the basis for true creative advances. The Gestalt view equates *creative* thinking with thinking with *insight*. A research program by Kounios and Beeman (2014, 2015) and their colleagues briefly discussed in Chapter 7 has tried to use the methods of neuroscience to provide evidence for the occurrence of insight in problem-solving.

Kounios and Beeman define insight as "any sudden comprehension, realization, or problem solution that involves a reorganization of the elements of a person's mental representation of a stimulus, situation, or event to yield a nonobvious or nondominant interpretation" (2014, p. 74). The researchers have used compound remote associates (CRA) problems – discussed in Chapter 7 – as their laboratory model of situations that can result in problem-solving through insight. Three example CRA problems are presented in Table 13.2. Please take a moment to try to solve those problems.

Table 13.2 *CRA problems*

For each problem, your task is to find one word that, when combined with each of the problem words, will produce a common phrase or compound word. Here is an example problem: age, mile, sand. Answer: *stone* **(stone age; milestone; sandstone)**

Problems	Solution?
1) Fox, Man, Peep	
2) Sleeping, Bean, Trash	
3) Dust, Cereal, Fish	

Note: Solutions are in text.

The solutions to the problems in Table 13.2 are: 1. *hole* (foxhole, manhole, peephole); 2. *bag* (sleeping bag, bean bag, trash bag); 3. *bowl* (dust bowl, cereal bowl, fish bowl). A CRA problem is designed in a specific way. The solution word is one that forms a familiar compound word when it is combined with each problem word. However, ideally the solution word is not *strongly* related to any of those words. For most of those compound words, the connection to the solution word is not one that comes to mind when the words in the problem are presented individually. For example, a typical response to "man" is "woman," not "hole" (problem 1). Similarly, "dust" elicits "dirt" or "sweep," not "bowl" (problem 3).

CRA problems have been of particular interest to researchers studying insight in problem-solving, because people report that they solve them in two ways: through analysis or through insight. In an analytic solution, the person works through the problem words one by one, producing a possible solution word and checking to see if it fits with the other two problem words. The individual works through various possible solutions in this way until one is found or time runs out. In an insight solution, the solution word comes suddenly to mind without the person having first slowly worked through possible solutions. Also, the person feels confident that the solution is correct without having to check it carefully with all the words, which does not happen with analytic solutions (Kounios & Beeman, 2014).

When a person participates in a study examining the possible role of insight in solving CRA problems, he or she is first given a description of the differences between solutions through analysis versus insight. Here are examples of those instructions (in the instructions below, solution though analysis is called solution by using a strategy; from Chein and Weisberg (2013)).

> We are also interested in finding out how you solved each problem. Problems can be solved in two general ways: as the result of a STRATEGY or as the result of a sudden INSIGHT.
>
> Solving the problem by a STRATEGY means that when you first thought of the word, you did not know whether it was the answer, but after thinking about it strategically (for example, trying to combine the single word with each of the three problem words), you figured out that it was the answer.
>
> Solving the problem by a sudden INSIGHT means that as soon as you thought of the word, you knew that it was the answer. The solution word came with a feeling that it was correct ("It popped into my head"; "Of course!"; "I had an *Aha!*").

The participant is then given a series of problems to work on, perhaps thirty or more. After each problem that the person solves, he or she reports whether it was solved through insight or analysis.

Assume that the participant is able to solve a significant number of problems and reports that some are solved through each method. The researcher then has a set of problems solved by the same person, some through insight and some through analysis. Since all the problems are identical in structure, the only difference between the two sets of results should be the difference between analysis versus insight. If one has measured brain activity during the solution of those problems, one could compare the two sets of results and find the differences, if any, between brain activity during insight versus analysis. This design would seem to be a perfect example of "pure insertion." The researcher has "inserted" a single component – solution through insight – beyond the baseline. As Kounios and Beeman (2014, p. 75) noted, "[I]nsight solutions can be directly compared to analytic solutions for the same type of problem because this comparison controls for all factors except for the cognitive solving strategy – insight versus analytic processing – that is the factor of primary interest." That research design, outlined in Table 13.3, serves as the basis for much research that has tried to isolate the brain processes underlying insight.

A number of significant results have been discovered using the subtraction method to study insight. Compared with solution of CRA problems through analysis, solution through insight involves activity in certain areas of the right hemisphere, shown in Figure 13.1. Although there was several years ago interest in the right hemisphere as "the seat of creativity," the current understanding of hemispheric differences is more subtle. There is evidence that the right hemisphere processes the meanings of words in a manner "more coarse" than the left hemisphere does (Kounios & Beeman, 2014). When a word is presented to the left hemisphere, it activates words and concepts that are relatively closely related to it; in other words, the meaning of the word is processed relatively precisely. When a word is presented to the right hemisphere, in contrast, it activates a wider network of associated words and concepts; that is, the meaning of the word is processed "coarsely." That coarse processing may result in greater activation of information that is less directly related to the word itself, which is what seems to be necessary for solution of CRA problems.

Kounios and Beeman (2014) explained those processing differences as being the result of the ways in which language-related information is dealt

Table 13.3 *Subtraction method: outline of design to isolate brain processes underlying insight*

A basic design of subtraction method, based on Kounios and Beeman's analysis. Insight solution differs from analytic solution in the addition of only one process – insight.

(a) Brain activity: "Insight" solution:	Activity	A + B + C + D
– (b) Brain activity: Analytic solution:	Activity –	A + B + C + 0
(c) "Location of insight" in the brain:	Result	0 + 0 + 0 + D

Components of the tasks:
  A. Understanding instructions and problem
  B, C. Various processes involved in problem-solving
  D. "Insight" process

A. Right anterior superior temporal gyrus (dark gray)

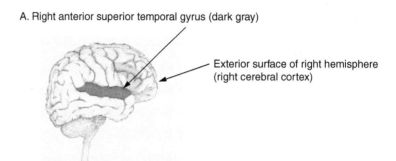

Exterior surface of right hemisphere
(right cerebral cortex)

B. Parahippocampal gyrus and anterior and posterior cingulate gyri.

Interior of right hemisphere (right
cerebral cortex)

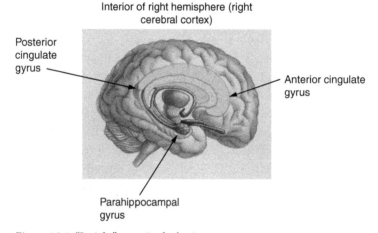

Posterior
cingulate
gyrus

Anterior cingulate
gyrus

Parahippocampal
gyrus

Figure 13.1 "Insight" areas in the brain.
A. Digital illustration of right superior temporal sulcas, and anterior cingulate cortex
highlighted in red and grey in human brain, Dorling Kindersley, Getty Images.
B. Cross section illustration of human brain showing limbic system and primitive
forebrain, Dorling Kindersley, Getty Images.

with in the two hemispheres. In the language areas of the right hemisphere,
neurons are connected to a wider range of inputs than in the comparable
areas of the left hemisphere. That difference in connectivity is taken to be
the basis for the differences in solution types. The wider range of inputs to
right-hemisphere neurons means that more distant connections between
words and concepts can be made in the right hemisphere, which would
facilitate solution of CRA problems with insight.

Recordings of brain activity, of several sorts, support this analysis.
Using electroencephalogram (EEG) recordings, one finds that, when
problems are solved with insight, there is activity in the right temporal
lobe (see Figure 13.2A and B). That activity begins approximately
300 ms (1/3 sec) before the person presses the key to signal that

a. fMRI recording during solution of CRA problems with insight. Activity in right temporal lobe. (See also Figure 13.1A.) b. EEG recordings, also showing activity in the right temporal region. c. Time course of EEG recording leading to solution by insight versus analysis. Approximately 300 ms before solution, insight solutions diverge from analytic solutions. See text for additional discussion. (Adapted from Kounios & Beeman, 2014)

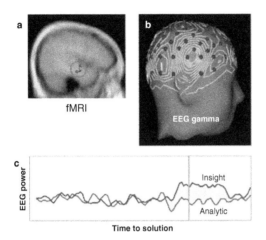

Figure 13.2 Neuroscience of insight: further results of studies using subtraction method. Jung-Beeman M, Bowden EM, Haberman J, Frymiare JL, Arambel-Liu S, Greenblatt R, et al. (2004) Neural Activity When People Solve Verbal Problems with insight. PLoS Biol 2(4): e97 https://doi.org/10.1371/journal .pbio.0020097

a solution has been found (see Figure 13.2C). It takes approximately 300 ms for an individual to make a key press in response to a signal, so that separation of the insight versus analysis records, approximately 300 ms before the key press, may indicate that the EEG activity is from an area controlling the pressing response. Thus, that right-temporal-lobe activity may be from the area in which insight comes about.

Another finding of interest is an increase, in the right occipital cortex, in EEG activity in what is called the *alpha* range, which is a frequency of about 10 Hz (10 cycles per second). That is, electrical activity in the occipital cortex (see Figure 13.3) goes from positive to negative 10 times/sec. Alpha activity is taken to indicate that a brain area has been *inhibited* – that is, reduced in activity. The occipital cortex is involved in processing of sensory input, most importantly visual information. In the context of insight, it is proposed that, when the insight process is being carried out, there is an inhibition of responding to visual input (Kounios & Beeman, 2014). There is what is called "sensory gating" occurring, so there is no distraction from external stimuli. In sum, activity in several areas in the right hemisphere has been found to be related to solution of problems through insight.

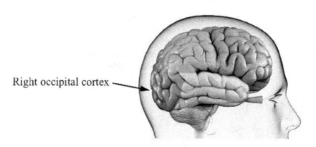

Right occipital cortex

Figure 13.3 Right occipital cortex

Preparation for Insight

One fascinating finding from the research by Kounios and Beeman (2014, 2015) is what they call "preparation for insight." Brain activity recorded *prior to presentation of the problem* predicts whether the person will solve the problem through analysis or in an *Aha!* of insight. Problems solved through analysis are preceded by activity in the occipital or visual cortex (see Figure 13.3), which is assumed to indicate that the person's attention is focused outward, in preparation of processing the problem information. Solution through insight, in contrast, is preceded by activity in the anterior cingulate, a region inside the brain; and in both temporal lobes (see Figure 13.1). The temporal lobe activity is presumed to involve a readiness for processing the words in the problem. The anterior cingulate is assumed to be involved in detecting and processing conflicting solution possibilities. Kounios and Beeman (2014) proposed that, when attention is directed outward and cingulate activity is low, the person is more ready to respond to the dominant features of a problem. In contrast, when attention is directed internally and cingulate activity is high, it becomes more likely that that the individual would be able to detect the weak activation from the solution word and be able to ignore the stronger associations activated by the words in the problem. That sensitivity would enable the person to break away from the dominant responses in the problem and produce the solution. It is notable that Kounios and Beeman reason analogically when discussing people's "sensitivity" to "weak" activation. It is as if the person is searching an internal environment, comparable to trying to find your ringing cell phone in a noisy room. The internal "activation" from the solution word is analogous to a weak stimulus in the external world.

Resting-State Brain Activity: "Analytics" versus "Insightfuls"

Kounios and Beeman (2014) have taken the distinction between analysis versus insight one step further back. We have just seen that a researcher can, before a problem is presented, measure brain changes that will allow one to predict whether the person will solve the to-be-presented problem through analysis or in an *Aha!* experience. That result leads to the possibility that there might be consistent differences between people concerning whether they will in general be more likely to solve problems through analysis or through insight. Kounios and Beeman classified people as analytic versus insightful problem-solvers, based on their performance on a series of CRA problems. "Insightful" people reported solving most problems with insight; "analytic" people reported solving most CRA problems through analysis.

The researchers then measured *resting-state* brain activity – that is, brain activity when the person was "at rest" and not engaged in any specific task imposed by the researcher. The "insightfuls" showed more right-hemisphere activity than the "analytics." This finding may be related to the right-hemisphere dominance during insightful problem solution, discussed earlier. It can be taken to indicate that the differences in brain activity between insight and analysis during problem-solving might be traceable to more or less permanent differences beyond the problem-solving situation. In addition, the insightful participants had more-diffuse activation in the visual cortex; that is, activity in the visual cortex was spread more widely. That difference in activity occurred even though the brain activity was measured with eyes closed, so that no processing of external visual stimuli was occurring. The difference in activity in the right-hemisphere visual cortex might be related to the "coarser" processing of language information in the right hemisphere, also discussed earlier.

Analysis-Insight Differences in Brain Processes: Summary

Kounios and Beeman (2014, 2015) have reported a consistent pattern of results pointing to differences between analysis and insight at the level of brain processes. First, there are differences at the moment of insight, with insight solutions accompanied by right-hemisphere activity. There are also differences in the moments before the solution occurs, with right-hemisphere EEG activity increasing before insight solutions. Kounios and Beeman also reported differences in brain activity before the problem was presented which predicted how it would be solved. Finally, there are long-term differences in people's resting-state brain activity which are related to their tendencies to solve problems through insight versus analysis. Those results together are taken by Kounios and Beeman as strong support for the difference between analysis and insight as separate modes of thinking.

The Neuroscience of Insight – Critique

Kounios and Beeman's (2014, 2015) research program is impressive in a number of ways, including the range of results they present, as well as their attempt to integrate those results into a coherent picture of how brain processes might be related to insight and, therefore, to creativity. There are a number of questions that can be raised about aspects of this work, however.

Has "Insight" Occurred? The Question of Reorganization in Solving CRA Problems

The theoretical analysis proposed by Kounios and Beeman (2015) is built on the distinction between problem solutions based on insight versus analysis, which comes from people's reports concerning how they solved the problems. Kounios and Beeman (2014) defined "insight" as "reorganization of the elements of a person's mental representation" of a problem (p. 74). Therefore, in order for CRA problems to be useful in the study of insight, we need evidence that a reorganization occurs when people report an insight solution. However, Kounios and Beeman have not provided independent evidence that reorganization has taken place. Furthermore, as we know from earlier discussion, there is evidence that subjective reports concerning solution processes might not be trustworthy. Specifically, as mentioned in Chapter 7, Cranford and Moss (2012) obtained verbal protocols while people solved CRA problems and they found that participants sometimes reported an *Aha!* experience when the solution came quickly, even though there was no evidence of a reorganization in the people's thinking about the problem. That result from Cranford and Moss means that the brain-imaging information is difficult to interpret, because we do not know if reorganization actually occurred when the participant reported that a solution occurred through insight. Until we know the details of the *cognitive processes* that underlie solution to CRA problems, we will not be able to say anything about what brain recordings tell us about insight and creativity.

Problems with the Subtraction Design Used to Isolate Insight

Even if we were able to obtain independent evidence that reorganization had occurred when a CRA problem was solved with insight, there is another issue that arises, concerning the subtraction design used to collect the data (Table 13.3). In order to draw conclusions about the specific brain regions involved in carrying out some task, it is critically important that the "pure insertion" method be adhered to. The target condition and the baseline must differ by only one process. However, that requirement may not be met by the studies conducted by Kounios and Beeman (2014, 2015) and their colleagues. The two conditions in those studies may have differed by more than one process (Weisberg, 2013). Based on Kounios and Beeman's analysis of what occurs during insight, it seems that solution through insight is not just solution through analysis plus one other thing – that is, plus insight.

Solution through analysis involves strategic search of memory for possible solution words, using one problem-word as the stimulus. If a possible solution word is found, the individual then tries to combine that word with all the other words in the problem, to see if it is indeed the solution. If the tentative solution turns out not to be correct, the process begins again. In addition, the determination that the solution has been found is based on a process of judgment. Consider now the solutions through insight. There is, according to Kounios and Beeman (2014), no use of strategies. The sudden intrusion of the solution into consciousness is the antithesis of strategic processing. Therefore, solution through insight is *not* solution through analysis plus one additional process, as the pure insertion design requires. Rather, based on Kounios and Berman's interpretation, analysis involves one set of processes, and insight involves a *different* set of processes. The situation as just described is outlined in Table 13.4, which makes clear the problems that arise when one uses the subtraction design with CRA problems solved through insight versus analysis as the experimental versus baseline conditions. Contrary to the claims of Kounios and Beeman (2014, 2015), we do not know what the brain recordings tell us concerning the brain areas involved in insight.

Given those questions, it becomes interesting to try to design a study using the subtraction method to determine the brain areas involved in insight. That design must contain two conditions that differ in only one element – the occurrence of insight. In one possible design, the experimental condition consists of brain recordings obtained when people solve a problem through insight (see Table 13.5A). (I will assume, for the sake of discussion, that people's reports are useful here.) The components that we have discussed are included. That experimental condition can be called "discovered

Table 13.4 *An alternative interpretation of subtraction design applied to the study of insight*

Insight and analysis may differ in multiple ways.

(a) Brain activity: "Insight" solution:	Activity	A + B + C + D
− (b) Brain activity: Analytic solution:	Activity	− A + 0 + 0 + 0 + E + F
(c) "Location of insight" in the brain:	Result	0 + B + C + D+ E + F

Activities
  A, B, C. Various processes involved in insight problem-solving.
  D. "Insight" process.
  E, F. Various processes involved in analytical problem-solving.

insight," since the participants discover the insight on their own. The brain areas underlying the process of discovering insight are what we are interested in. The baseline condition therefore must *also include insight* but not the *discovered* type. That is, we must *produce* insight in the participant. The two conditions will then differ only in the process involved in discovered insight and the subtraction method will produce what we need.

So, how do we produce insight in an individual? One way might be to present a difficult CRA problem, followed after a short interval by *the solution word*. If the problem is difficult, the person should not solve it on seeing the problem words. Therefore, presenting the solution might induce or "trigger" an insight and an *Aha!* (see Table 13.5A). That would be the baseline we are looking for, except for one complication. We now have the person *reading* the solution word, which adds another process to the activity (see Table 13.5B). Therefore, we need a *second* baseline, where the person reads a clue word but the clue does not solve the problem (see Table 13.5B). That condition would allow us to subtract the activity involved in reading the solution word. Those two baselines combined might bring us to the point of isolating the area in the brain in which the "insight process" is carried out.

The Neuroscience of Insight: Conclusions

The findings from the research of Kounios and Beeman (2014, 2015) and their colleagues are intriguing, and there is no doubt that the methods of neuroscience will play a large role in future research on insight. However, at

Table 13.5 *Redone subtraction method for insight*

A. *One possible baseline: "Discovered" versus "Triggered" Insight*

"Discovered" Insight:	A + B + C
A = Problem presented & interpreted	
B = "Insight" process	
C = Solution (+*Aha!*)	
"Triggered" Insight:	A + B' + C
B' = Cue to Insight	
Subtraction:	
Discovered Insight:	A + Discovered Insight + C
– Triggered Insight:	– A + Triggered Insight + C
Result:	0 + Insight Process + 0

B. *Another baseline, with additional component to "triggered" insight*

"Discovered" Insight:	A + B + C
A = Problem presented & interpreted	
B = "Insight" process	
C = Solution (+*Aha!*)	
"Triggered" Insight:	A + B' + C
B' = Cue to Insight	
B" = Read cue to insight	
"Discovered" Insight:	A + Discovered Insight + C
"Triggered" Insight (Solution):	– A + Triggered Insight + C
"False" Insight (Nonsolution):	– A + Read Clue + C
Result	0 + Insight Process + C

present it may be premature to make strong claims about having determined the "location of insight in the brain." There are several questions that can be raised about the studies used to investigate the neuroscience of insight and at present those design problems seem to stand in the way of definitive conclusions about the brain regions underlying insight (Weisberg, 2013).

Remembering the Past and Imagining the Future: A Link between Memory and Creativity

We have seen in many places in the earlier chapters the important role played by memory in problem-solving specifically and in creative thinking more generally. Memory is important, first, in the transfer of old ideas to new situations. Memory also plays a critical role in evaluation of new ideas

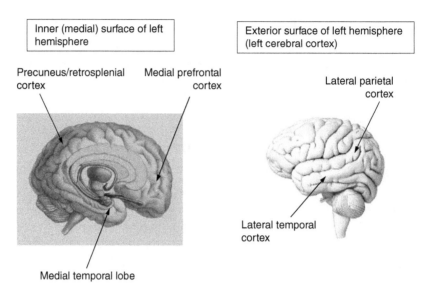

Figure 13.4 Core memory network Left. Digital illustration of right superior temporal sulcas, and anterior cingulate cortex highlighted in red and grey in human brain, Dorling Kindersley, Getty Images. Right. Human brain illustration, SEBASTIAN KAULITZKI, Science Photo Library, Getty Images.

through the imagination, as people use their knowledge to develop possible responses and to determine the consequences of their actions. Additional evidence concerning the importance of memory in imagination has come from a very different area of research: the study of brain damage and its effects on memory. Over the past sixty years, much information has been accumulated about the functioning of memory from studies of people who have suffered *amnesia* – the inability to remember – brought about by brain damage of various sorts. A set of brain areas (the "core memory network") has been found to be important in memory of various sorts (Mullally & Maguire, 2014; see Figure 13.4).

One of the core-network areas is the hippocampus, an area inside the temporal lobe on each side of the brain, already discussed in relation to insightful problem-solving (see also Figure 13.1). Much of the early interest in the role of the brain in memory centered on the hippocampus. Damage to the hippocampus – from, for example, encephalitis, an inflammation of the brain most commonly caused by a viral infection – can result in profound loss of memory of two sorts. First, hippocampal damage results in *retrograde* amnesia: the inability to remember events that occurred before the illness, sometimes extending back many years. The amnesia is for *episodic memories*, memories for *specific episodes* in one's life; the patients can remember general information, such as the meanings of words. Second, patients with hippocampal damage also suffer from *anterograde* amnesia: the inability to acquire new memories. Thus, a patient with hippocampal damage will not be able to remember events from his childhood, although he will not forget how to speak. He will also not be able to remember the names of the attending physicians in the hospital or how to make his way back to his hospital room from the nurses' station. In addition, even after seeing the same physicians for many years subsequent to the illness, he will not remember their names.

Studies of patients with hippocampal damage have found that the hippocampus plays a role beyond memory, as those patients are also deficient in imagining the future. (Other components of the core memory network have also been found to be related to imagining future events; see Barry et al. (2019); Campbell et al. (2018). Those areas will not be considered here.) Hassabis et al. (2007) tested patients – and control participants, matched with the patients on age, education level, and IQ – on a task in which they were asked to imagine a series of events and to describe their imagined scenes. One example was "imagine lying on a white sandy beach in a beautiful tropical bay." The instructions emphasized that the individuals should not base their descriptions on remembered events; they should create something new, giving their imaginations free rein. They were to imagine the situation "in their mind's eye," as if they were experiencing the event.

The patients were greatly deficient in carrying out the imagination task compared to the controls, as the examples in Table 13.6 make clear. The patients' difficulties seemed to center on producing an integrated *scene*, because they were able to imagine individual items. When they had to integrate information into a coherent event, they were unable to do so. Similar problems with remembering the past and imagining the future have been found in other populations in which damage to the hippocampus and other components of the core network have been found, such as the elderly, some depressed individuals, and individuals suffering from schizophrenia (Mullally & Maguire, 2014; Roberts & Addis, 2018).

Maguire and colleagues (Hassabis et al., 2007; Maguire & Mullally, 2013; Mullally & Maguire, 2014) proposed that the hippocampus plays a critical role in imagining complex scenes because it underlies *scene construction*; the hippocampus provides a framework into which the items and experiences that make up a scene – either a recalled scene or an imagined one – can be placed. For example, in imagining oneself on a beach, one uses general knowledge about beaches, accumulated through experiences at beaches, as a framework within which to place the events and experiences that comprise the imagined scene. Damage to the hippocampus means that the individual will be unable to integrate

Table 13.6 *Scene descriptions from amnesic patient (P03) and control*

Cue: "Imagine you are lying on a white sandy beach in a beautiful tropical bay"

P03: As for seeing I can't really, apart from just sky. I can hear the sound of seagulls and of the sea . . . um . . . I can feel the grains of sand between my fingers . . . um . . . I can hear one of those ship's hooters [laughter] . . . um . . . that's about it. *Are you're actually seeing this in your mind's eye?* No, the only thing I can see is blue. So *if you look around what can you see?* Really all I can see is the colour of the blue sky and the white sand, the rest of it, the sounds and things, obviously I'm just hearing. *Can you see anything else?* No, it's like I'm kind of floating . . .

Control: It's very hot and the sun is beating down on me. The sand underneath me is almost unbearably hot. I can hear the sounds of small wavelets lapping on the beach. The sea is a gorgeous aquamarine colour. Behind me is a row of palm trees and I can hear rustling every so often in the slight breeze. To my left the beach curves round and becomes a point. And on the point there are a couple of buildings, wooden buildings, maybe someone's hut or a bar of some sort. The other end of the beach, looking the other way, ends in big brown rocks. There's no one else around. Out to sea is a fishing boat. It's quite an old creaking looking boat, chugging past on its small engine. It has a cabin in the middle and pile of nets in the back of the boat. There's a guy in the front and I wave at him and he waves back . . . [continues]

into a "scene" any information that might be available. Hassabis et al. (2007) showed that even when the hippocampal patients were given cues consisting of information regarding the things that might be found on a beach they were still unable to produce a coherent imagined scene. Mullally and Maguire (2014) concluded that the hippocampus functions in more than a memory role: its functioning underlies coherent perception and memory for scenes and events.

Madore, Jing, and Schacter (2019) proposed a similar account, specifically linking memory, imagination, and divergent thinking. A process of *event construction* can be recruited for remembering a past event, imagining an event that has not occurred, and, also, for carrying out divergent thinking. In support of the event construction hypothesis, Madore, Jing, and Schacter had participants take part in *episodic-specificity induction* training. Individuals are trained in strategies for recalling details of events. Practice in recalling details facilitates memory for events and also facilitates *imagining* events that have not occurred – a creative act. In addition, Madore, Addis, and Schacter (2015) showed that the episodic-specificity induction increased performance on a divergent-thinking task, the unusual-uses test. Madore, Addis, and Schacter concluded that there are common mechanisms underlying remembering, imagining, and divergent thinking.

Roberts and Addis (2018) also discussed similarities between imagining new scenes and divergent thinking, specifically performance on the unusual uses test. Consider a person who produces a new use for a paper clip – say, as a toothpick. To produce that response, one has to focus on specific properties of the paper clip, in this case that it is thin and sharp. Those properties can be used to match it with objects in memory – in this case, toothpicks – that can serve as the basis for proposing a new use for the paper clip. (We discussed this strategy – the Property Use Strategy – in Chapter 10 when examining research by Gilhooly et al., 2007.) Addis et al. (2014) found that imagining future events was positively correlated with divergent-thinking performance. People who included more details in their imagined future events performed better on producing usual uses for common objects, such as a brick or an automobile tire. There is also evidence from research using fMRI that divergent thinking and imagining future events activate some brain areas in common (Benedek et al., 2014).

This area of research is potentially of great importance in the understanding of creative thinking, since, as we have already seen, imagination is a critical component of the creative process. Neuroscientific studies of brain function in imagination have begun to uncover how the imagination works and have also provided further evidence of the close ties between creative thinking and "ordinary" or analytic thought processes, such as retrieval of information from memory. This research also provides an interesting example of multidisciplinary streams coming together: the cognitive study of memory; the psychometric study of creativity; the study of patient populations; and neuroscientific methods. One question remaining is whether hippocampal function plays a role in the wide-ranging creative imagination of the artist, as when, for example, an author of science fiction imagines a new world. A second question centers on the causal relations among those various phenomena. For example, if D-T performance and the ability to imagine future events are correlated, what is the causal link between the two? Does D-T ability contribute to skill in imagining, or does imagination skill play a role in divergent thinking? Or might some more basic processes – for example, processes involved in retrieving information from memory – play a role in both divergent thinking and imagining the future (Hass, 2017; Hass & Beatty, 2018)?

Brain Changes in the Development of Expertise

Memory is also a critical component in the development of expertise, as we saw in Chapter 6, where it was concluded that expertise played a critical positive role in the careers of many outstanding creative thinkers. When one examines the brains of experts, one often finds changes in parts of the brain relevant to the area of expertise. As an example, violinists have enlarged brain areas representing the fingers of their *left* hands, which are used extensively in fingering the notes to be played (Woollett & Maguire, 2011). A question that arises from that finding is whether the enlarged brain areas were the *cause* or the *result* of the development of expertise. That is, are people able to achieve expertise because of the way their brains are structured? Do some people become great violinists because they are born with enlargement in the areas in their brains that support their left hands? In terms of the discussion in Chapter 6, do they possess innate *talent* for that domain? Or does the development of expertise *produce* those differences in brain structure? Does the extensive practice needed for the development of world-class performance result in those enlargements? Again, as was discussed in Chapter 6, is genius *born* or *made*?

Maguire and colleagues (Maguire, Woollett & Spiers, 2006; Woollett & Maguire, 2011) studied London taxi-cab drivers – an exceptional group of individuals – to determine if brain differences were the cause or result of the development of expertise. To become a cabbie in London, one must learn the layout of streets and landmarks in the city so that one can determine the correct route when a customer requests to be taken to any destination. Prospective cabbies must pass examinations to demonstrate their grasp of that information, which is called *the knowledge*. To acquire *the knowledge*, individuals spend about three years studying maps of London and driving throughout the city. Woollett and Maguire investigated the relationship between development of *the knowledge* and structural changes in the brain. The researchers followed a group of individuals who began training as taxi-cab drivers, some of whom continued to success while others dropped out before the end of training. A control group consisted of age-matched individuals who had no connection with taxi-cab driving. Brain scans were carried out twice: Time1, before anyone started training, and Time2, after the successful cabbies had passed their examinations. The various groups' knowledge of the layout of London was also tested.

At the Time1 scan, *all* the participants – those who ultimately were successful; those who dropped out; and the controls – were *identical* in brain structure. Those results provide a baseline. After training, at Time2, the successful cabbies, as would be expected, performed better than the drop-outs and the controls on a test for knowledge of the layout of London, including streets and landmarks. Also, the brains of the successful participants had changed at Time2: the *anterior* hippocampus (the frontal part of the hippocampus, part of the core memory network, just discussed; see Figures 13.1 and 13.4), an area that is involved in navigation through the environment, had gotten larger, on both sides of the brain. Those brain changes were brought about by the acquisition of *the knowledge*, supporting the idea that, in this case at least, genius was made.

Interestingly, there were also some *deficits* that came about as the result of the training. The successful trainees performed *worse* on some tests of memory, involving non-navigational information. For example, the cabbies were worse than the others in recalling a complex visual diagram. In addition, the *posterior* hippocampi (see Figures 13.1 and 13.4) on both sides of the brain were *smaller* for the successful cabbies than they were for the dropouts or the controls. Recall that all brain measures for the various groups of participants were equal when the study began. Thus, acquiring *the knowledge* had negative effects on some aspects of memory performance and on some components of brain structure. It may be that the increased development of the brain areas related to memory for London streets resulted in reduction in size of other areas and in decreased capacity for other sorts of information. That is, the development of one part of the hippocampus might have been at the expense of another.

The research by Maguire and colleagues (Maguire, Woollett & Spiers, 2006; Woollett & Maguire, 2011) provides additional support for the idea discussed in Chapter 6 that world-class performance can be acquired by ordinary people if they put in enough study. Concentrated study results in brain changes, positive and negative, as the person tries to deal with a large amount of new information. In addition, these results raise the possibility that creative individuals, as they work through a career in a field like musical composition, painting, literature, biology, or physics, are changing the structures of their brains. Indeed, to carry that reasoning further, as each of us becomes "expert" at various aspects of our lives, we are all changing our brains. In addition, the results from the studies of brain changes as cabbies acquire *the knowledge* indicate that, even in adulthood, the human brain is able to change and develop in response to experience. That capacity for development, called "plasticity" of the brain, indicates that our nervous systems might remain flexible long into our lives.

Going beyond Correlation: Turning the Brain On and Off

The research studies that we have reviewed so far investigating the role of the brain in various processes related to creativity present a logical problem as far as making inferences about the causal role of the brain in cognition: they were not experimental studies. That is, no *manipulation* of brain states was carried out. In the studies of insight, for example, behavior was measured at the same time as brain states were recorded. Therefore, we have no basis for concluding that the brain states played a role in producing the behavior – the brain states might simply have *accompanied* the behavior rather than *causing* it. In order to arrive at a causal conclusion, one has to in some way manipulate brain states and then measure the results. If one can *produce* some brain activity and then show that behavior changes in a specific way compared to an appropriate control condition, then one can conclude that the brain state was the cause of the behavior.

There are several techniques available that provide researchers control over brain activity. Two of the techniques involve stimulating the brain with electric current. The procedures are noninvasive and have minimal side effects. Electrodes are placed on the scalp, and weak electric current is applied, which flows from one electrode, through the scalp and skull and through the brain, to the other electrode. The participant feels nothing, but the current affects the brain areas below the electrodes. There are two types of stimulation. In transcranial direct current stimulation (tDCS) of the brain, a low level of direct current electrical stimulation is applied. It is believed that, depending on the polarity of the electrical current (anodal, or positive, versus cathodal, or negative), the activity of the stimulated brain areas is increased or inhibited. In other words, one can turn parts of the brain on and off. Cranial electrotherapy stimulation, a similar technique, uses alternating current in the same way. The brain can also be stimulated using magnetic pulses, another noninvasive technique.

The Thinking Cap – Brain Stimulation and Creative Thinking

Studies using tDCS have produced several sorts of interesting results concerning problem-solving and creative thinking. Chi and Snyder

(2011, 2012) investigated performance on several problems, including the familiar Nine-Dot problem (see Figure 7.2E). As discussed in Chapter 7, the Nine-Dot problem is extremely difficult, with average performance in groups of undergraduate participants at about 10 percent solutions or less. Chi and Snyder (2012) gave one group of participants negative stimulation of the left anterior temporal lobe and, at the same time, positive stimulation of the right anterior temporal lobe (abbreviated as -L/+R). Those areas were chosen because previous research – that of Kounios and Beeman (2014, 2015) on insight, discussed earlier in the chapter – had linked the right temporal lobe to insight in problem-solving. A control group was given *sham* stimulation: electrodes were attached to their scalp at the same locations, but no stimulation was presented.

The control participants performed very poorly on the Nine-Dot problem, as expected; none of them solved it after 10 minutes of work. The group given the tDCS, on the other hand, performed well, given the extreme difficulty of the Nine-Dot problem. Forty-four percent of the participants solved the problem at some point during or after the stimulation period (the effects of tDCS last for a few minutes after the stimulation is turned off). Chi and Snyder's (2012) interpretation of their results is centered on the idea that the left hemisphere plays an executive role in cognitive processing, including producing "top-down" interpretations of the situations in which we find ourselves. The left hemisphere analyzes the array of dots in the Nine-Dot problem and interprets it as a square. That interpretation pushes the individual to draw lines within the square, making solution impossible. Turning off the left hemisphere makes it more likely that the person will be able to go beyond the obvious interpretation of the problem and look at the problem in a new way. A second component of Chi and Snyder's explanation of the positive effects of their tDCS procedure is that, when the left hemisphere is inhibited, stimulating the right hemisphere increases the chances that a new analysis of the problem will occur. That analysis would be less subject to the constraints of the one's knowledge, since the left hemisphere has been inhibited, and so will be more likely to produce the solution. Another study by Chi and Snyder (2011) provided further evidence of the role of the temporal lobes in insight in problem-solving.

One question that can be raised about Chi and Snyder's interpretation of their results is that Weisberg and Alba (1981) explicitly told participants that, in order to solve the Nine-Dot problem, they had to draw lines outside the square formed by the dots (see Chapter 7). That instruction resulted in people going beyond the square shape, but it did not increase solution rates by a great amount. Therefore, interpreting the shape of the dots as a square might not be critical in making the Nine-Dot problem difficult (see also MacGregor, Ormerod & Chronicle, 2001; and Weisberg, 2006). Chi and Snyder (2012) seem to have facilitated performance on the Nine-Dot problem using tDCS, but exactly how that facilitation was brought about is not clear.

Other research has used brain stimulation to link memory and imagination. Thrakal, Madore, and Schacter (2017) reported a study using transcranial magnetic stimulation (TMS) to *inhibit* part of the core memory network. That inhibitory stimulation resulted in reduced production of details for remembered events and imagined events. That is, we have here further evidence that remembering and imagining are linked, and this time the design of the study allows us to conclude that interfering with the functioning of one specific area of the brain affected memory and imagination in similar ways.

The results of Chi and Snyder (2011, 2012) and Thrakal, Madore, and Schacter (2017) indicate that problem-solving and imagination can be facilitated by stimulating or inhibiting activity in specific areas of the brain, which is a step toward understanding the way in which the brain supports creative thinking. In addition, the results are interesting because they point to the possibility that sometimes turning off a brain area might result in a positive change in behavior. Evidence to support that idea also comes from studies of people who have suffered trauma that has resulted in the loss of functioning of areas of the brain. The people who are of special interest here are those who have suffered damage in the frontal lobes (see Figure 13.4), which are important in control over cognitive activities, or executive functioning. These patients provide examples of what has been called "hypofrontality" – that is, a reduction of functioning in the frontal lobes.

Hypofrontality and Problem-Solving

In an early study, Reverberi and colleagues (2005) examined performance of patients with lesions in the lateral prefrontal cortex on matchstick arithmetic problems such as those in Table 13.7. The study involved two types of problems. All the Type 1 problems were solved in the same way: one matchstick was moved, to make one number into another; an "X" into a "V," for example (see Problem Type 1 in Table 13.7). The Type 2 problems involved changing the "equation" itself in a significant way,

Table 13.7 *Reverberi et al. (2005) study of problem-solving in "hypofrontal" patients*

Matchstick-Arithmetic Problems. Each problem consists of a false arithmetic equation, written in Roman numerals formed by matchsticks. *All lines* are matchsticks. For each problem, it is possible to change it into a true equation by moving only one matchstick. Try to solve each problem before reading further. Solutions are shown at the bottom of the table.

Problem Type	False Statement
1	III = IX – I
2	VI = VI + VI

Solutions	
1	III = IV – I (Move one matchstick in the "X" to make it "V")
2	VI = VI = VI (Move one matchstick in the "+" to change it to "=")

from X = Y + Z to X = Y = Z (see Table 13.7). Type 2 problems are more difficult than Type 1 problems. Performance of the patients on both types of problems was compared to that of matched controls. There was no difference between the patient group and the controls on the Type 1 problems – the easier problems, which just involved rearranging the matchsticks in the numbers. On the Type 2 problems, however, the patient group performed *better* than the controls. Thus, hypofrontality improved performance on a difficult problem.

The next question is exactly why the patients performed better. There are at least two possibilities. One reason why Type 2 problems might ordinarily be difficult is that one has to change a mathematical *operator*, rather than a *number*. When working with an equation, one typically cannot change the operators: one changes the numbers. Due to the hypofrontality, the patients might simply have considered all the matchsticks as equivalent, ignoring their function as specific mathematical symbols. A second possibility arises from the fact that the term "equation" is not an accurate description of the Type 2 problems. An equation contains **two** mathematical expressions, separated by an equal sign. However, the solution to the Type 2 problems involves *three* expressions, separated by *two* equal signs. Perhaps the patients were able to ignore that inaccuracy in description, while the controls could not. This second possibility hinges on the patients' possible lack of sensitivity to subtleties of language. At this point it is not possible to determine which of those possibilities is correct, but the results of the study by Reverberi and colleagues (2005) are nonetheless interesting, as they present a situation in which one might be better off without frontal control.

Chrysikou et al. (2013) have also presented evidence that hypofrontality can facilitate certain sorts of creative thinking. They examined performance on the unusual-uses test while participants were undergoing inhibitory tDCS – of either the left prefrontal cortex (see Figure 13.4) or the right prefrontal cortex – or sham stimulation. The left prefrontal cortex plays a role in executive functioning, so inhibiting that area produces hypofrontality. That inhibitory stimulation facilitated production of unusual uses. Inhibition of the right prefrontal cortex did not have a comparable effect nor did sham stimulation. Chrysikou and colleagues explained their results as coming about because under normal conditions the left prefrontal cortex analyzes objects based on conceptual knowledge, which makes it difficult to analyze the object into features that might facilitate production of unusual uses (see also Gilhooly et al., 2007). When the left prefrontal cortex is inhibited, the lower-level features of the object become more salient, which can facilitate new-use production.

Supporting results were reported by Chrysikou and Thompson-Schill (2011), who used fMRI to measure brain activity while individuals produced either unusual or common uses for objects. Production of unusual uses was accompanied by activity in the occipital-temporal cortex, areas involved in processing low-level visual information, such as color and shape. The left prefrontal cortex was active during production of common uses, which are based on one's conceptual knowledge about objects. Chrysikou (2018; see also Weinberger, Green & Chrysikou, 2017) has proposed that less cognitive control – that is, hypofrontality – can be useful in dealing with problem situations in which one must break away from habitual responding and deal with the specific features of the object.

Brain Areas to Brain Networks: Brain Networks and Creativity

We have now examined a range of studies that have looked at the role of different brain areas in creative functioning. We have seen results that have been interpreted as pointing to specific brain areas being involved in insight, imagination, and one domain of expertise. In addition, we have seen that stimulating or inhibiting specific brain areas can have significant effects on creative performance. One characteristic that is common to those studies is that they focused on specific areas of the brain and examined the possible role of each of those areas in creative activity. A recent change in thinking about brain functioning has been a movement away from analysis of relatively small-scale areas to examination of brain *networks*, groups of interconnected areas that function together as a person is carrying out some task. Interest in brain networks is based on the belief that the brain is more than a group of loosely linked areas. There is an integrated aspect of the brain that plays an important role in its functioning. In order to understand the role that the brain plays in functioning of any sort, including creative functioning, one must identify the important brain networks and examine their role in that functioning.

The Default Mode Network

Several years ago, a discovery was made concerning brain activity during different kinds of tasks (Buckner, 2012). A number of brain-imaging studies had used as a baseline a "rest" condition in which the participant simply lay quietly in the MRI scanner. That condition served for comparison with any assigned task. One surprising finding from rest conditions was that overall brain metabolism did not decrease when compared with metabolism during an "active" task such as memorizing a list of words. Thus, the "rest" condition did not seem to involve a "resting" brain – the brain does not seem to rest. That result was interesting but, since it involved metabolism, it was not directly relevant to psychology. A more interesting result was found when researchers examined brain recordings obtained from those "resting" baseline conditions. When people were doing nothing, there was a set of interconnected brain areas – a network – that increased in activity. That brain network, which is shown in Figure 13.5A, was called the "default mode" network (DMN), because it was the "default" system – that is, the system that functioned when nothing of importance was happening. Discovery of the default mode network led to questions about the functions it might serve.

The DMN is active during rest, and the person in the brain-imaging apparatus, although he or she is lying quietly, is also cognitively active. People reported "self-initiated" cognition during the baseline rest task. Not surprisingly, when people are lying in the scanner, doing nothing required by the experiment, they *think* about things – they imagine future events,

A. Default Mode Network (DMN)

REGION
1. Ventral medial prefrontal cortex
2. Posterior cingulate/retrosplenial cortex
3. Inferior parietal lobe
4. Lateral temporal cortex
5. Dorsal medial prefrontal cortex
6. Hippocampal formation

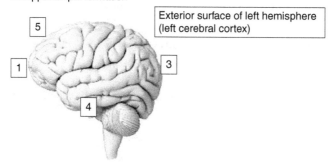

Exterior surface of left hemisphere
(left cerebral cortex)

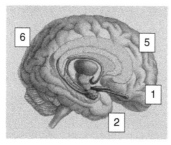

Inner (medial) surface of left
hemisphere

B. Executive-control (EC) network

REGION
1. Posterior parietal cortex
2. Anterior cingulate cortex
3. Dorsolateral prefrontal cortex
4. Ventrolateral prefrontal cortex
5. Medial temporal lobe

Inner (medial) surface of left
hemisphere

Exterior surface of left
hemisphere

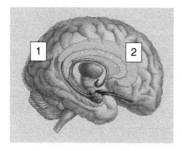
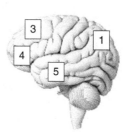

Figure 13.5 Brain networks related to creativity.
A, Top. Human brain illustration, SEBASTIAN KAULITZKI, Science Photo Library, Getty
Images.A, Bottom. Digital illustration of right superior temporal sulcas, and anterior cingulate
cortex highlighted in red and grey in human brain, Dorling Kindersley, Getty Images.
B, Left. Digital illustration of right superior temporal sulcas, and anterior cingulate cortex
highlighted in red and grey in human brain, Dorling Kindersley, Getty Images.
B, Right. Human brain illustration, SEBASTIAN KAULITZKI, Science Photo Library, Getty
Images.

they think about things they have experienced; in general, they let their *minds wander* (Smallwood & Schooler, 2015). In addition, people are always thinking during their daily activities. If the task one is working on, such as routine driving, is not totally demanding, one can spend some time thinking. Similarly, one's mind may wander during TV watching, during reading, during a conversation, when gardening, and so forth. Klinger (1999) had people report on the frequency and duration of their thoughts and found that the average "thought interval" was approximately five seconds and that there were approximately 4,000 thoughts per day. People spend about 50 percent of waking time mind-wandering – that is, in the default mode – which means that there might be 2,000 self-initiated thoughts per day.

The DMN consists of several different brain areas, as shown in Figure 13.5A. For the present discussion, the hippocampal area is of most interest, since we have already discussed its possible role in imagination. Research has indicated that lesions – damage – in the medial temporal lobe (i.e., the location of the hippocampus) do not affect the frequency of mind-wandering thoughts (Smallwood & Schooler, 2015). However, hippocampal lesions seem to affect the *kinds* of thoughts that people experience while mind-wandering. The thoughts of a person with hippocampal lesions are more centered on the present and are more general in nature, rather than focusing on specific detailed possible experiences in the future.

Further investigation revealed evidence of several different sorts indicating that the DMN played a role in tasks requiring creative thinking. Brain imaging studies have found activation of the DMN network during divergent-thinking tasks, such as the unusual-uses test (Beaty et al., 2016). In addition, studies have also found DMN activity during creative thinking in several specific areas, such as generation of poetry and creation of visual art. In sum, the relevance of the DMN goes far beyond simple seemingly random generation of thoughts during situations in which a person must lie quietly. It is now believed that the DMN plays an important role in creative thinking. However, the DMN does not, by itself, produce creative output. Another network, the executive-control network, also seems to play a role in creativity. It functions in conjunction with the DMN during the creative process.

Executive Control in the Brain

We are familiar with the notion of executive function from the discussion in earlier chapters and earlier in this chapter of the processes involved in directing the thought process. The executive-function network (ECN), shown in Figure 13.5B, consists of a set of areas that serve directive functions during behavioral activities of all sorts. Usually, the executive-control network and the DMN work in opposite directions; that is, they usually are *anticorrelated*. When a person is *engaged* in a directed activity, such as a task involving working memory, the ECN is active, and the DMN is inhibited. In contrast, when a person is *disengaged* from the present, and involved in mind-wandering, say, the DMN is engaged and the ECN is less active. However, there is at least one time at which the DMN and ECN work in coordination: during the creative process.

Network Coordination during Creativity

We have already seen that the DMN is active during various creative-thinking tasks, such as the unusual-uses test. However, there are two phases to such tasks: generation of a candidate idea; and then determination of whether that idea is useful. We discussed similar ideas in earlier chapters: *retrieving* an old idea as a possible solution to a problem; and trying to *extend* that idea to the new situation. An example would be an artist producing a sketch for a painting and then making a judgment as to whether the idea in the sketch is worth using as is or if the idea is in need of modification. There is evidence that the DMN and the ECN work in coordination during that sort of activity (Beaty et al., 2016). The DMN is active when ideas are being generated, and then the ECN plays a role during verification of the idea. Thus, the anticorrelation between the two networks breaks down when a creative task is carried out, and they work in conjunction.

Research has also demonstrated correlations between aspects of network structure and creative performance of various sorts (for review, see Beaty et al., 2016). For example, divergent-thinking ability as measured by performance on unusual-uses tests is related to higher resting-state connectivity between parts of the DN and ECN. That is, when people are at rest, not working on any specific task, those who will perform better in *later* D-T tests show more connectivity between the DN and the ECN; one can predict later D-T performance from earlier resting-state activity. That result might mean that brains of creative people, even when they are at rest, are connected in ways that facilitate creative thinking. Other research indicates that the brains of people who score high on D-T tests make more transitions between different patterns of connectivity among the brain networks involved in creativity. That result has been interpreted to mean that flexible thinking as demonstrated by high levels of performance on D-T tests may be related to a flexible brain.

Network Integration during Creative Thinking: Summary

The analysis of brain networks and their role in creative thinking is the direction in which research is moving (Beaty et al., 2016; Fox & Beaty,

2019). The discussion in this chapter has presented a brief summary of a very active research area. The relative novelty of research in the neuroscience of creativity, and the high level of activity in the area, has resulted in some disagreements concerning the specifics of how brain-network activity contributes to creative thinking. It should be noted first that the separation between the two networks is not complete – there are areas that may play a role in more than one network and not all the areas in a given network contribute to all activities that the network is involved in. However, overall, the distinction between those two networks seems reasonable. In addition, there are other networks that play roles in creative thinking, such as the "salience" network, which was not discussed here due to lack of space (Beaty, Seli & Schacter, 2019).

Dual-Process Conceptions of Creativity: The Genius View in New Clothes

The discussion in this chapter was detailed enough to present the flavor of the kinds of analyses that researchers are currently carrying out, and the general outlines of what one might call a theoretical overview can be seen. A number of neuroscience researchers have proposed that creative thinking can be separated into two processes: *generation*, the production of an idea; and *evaluation*, the assessment of the adequacy of that idea in dealing with the situation the person is facing. Those two processes are seen as corresponding to the activity in the DMN and ECN, respectively. There seems to be a parallel to the discussion in earlier chapters of *generating* a new idea, based on a partial overlap – an analogy – between a new situation and information in memory; and *extending* that idea to the new situation.

The distinction between idea generation and evaluation can be called a "dual-process" analysis of creativity, since the creative process is divided into two subprocesses: generation of an idea; and its evaluation. That distinction is one with which we are familiar. It can be seen in the separation between divergent and convergent thinking proposed by Guilford (1950; see Chapter 10). It can also be seen in the distinction made by the Gestalt psychologists, between productive and reproductive thinking (see Chapter 7). Some neuroscientists (Jung et al., 2013; Dietrich, 2018) have made a connection between the generation/evaluation processes and the blind variation/selective retention theory proposed by Campbell (1960), based on Darwin's theory and elaborated by Simonton (e.g., 2016; see Chapter 8). The DMN serves in production of new ideas and the ECN

Table 13.8 *Two-stage analyses of creative thinking*

Theoretical Perspective	Distinction between Processes
A. Remote-Associates View	
Gestalt psychologists	Productive/reproductive thinking
Guilford	Divergent/convergent thinking
Campbell	Blind variation/selective retention
Jung	Campbell: blind variation/selective retention
Dietrich	Campbell: blind variation/selective retention
Beaty	Idea generation/idea evaluation
Chrysikou	Idea generation/idea evaluation
B. Analytic View	
Idea retrieval, based on analogy/extension of old idea to new situation; creative advances are based on "near" associations	

underlies their retention. Thus, as outlined in Table 13.8A, there seems to be a coming together here of several streams of theorizing.

As just noted, we have discussed two similar processes throughout this book, specifically when analyzing the case studies of creative thinking – IDEO's shopping cart and Picasso's *Guernica*, for example. That analysis involved what seems to be a similar distinction, between generation of new ideas and their extension to a new situation, in the context of research on analogical transfer. That distinction was also discussed in the context of the model of problem-solving, presented in Chapter 3, and elaborated in Chapter 7, to deal with insight. Thus, there seems here to be a coming together of several streams of theorizing that have originated in different places.

Are All Dual-Process Theories Equivalent?

However, it is not clear that all those theoretical analyses are based on the same set of assumptions concerning how creative thinking functions. Guilford's view, the Gestalt view, and Campbell's analysis – and those that built on them, such as the work of Beaty et al. (2016), Chrysikou et al. (2013), Dietrich (2018), Jung et al. (2013), and Roberts and Addis (2018) – are, from my perspective, modern variants of the genius view.

All assume that the idea-generation stage of creative thinking involves breaking away from what one knows. The creative thinker generates new ideas by accessing "remote associations," those previously unlinked ideas that were important to Poincaré (1913) and those who followed him (e.g., Campbell, 1960; Mednick, 1962; Simonton, 1995). Neuroscience researchers, when discussing the generation of ideas, refer to "spontaneous" generation of thoughts carried out by the DMN. Those spontaneous thoughts are not based on the person's analysis of the situation; they are responses to "low-level" aspects of the environment such as colors and shapes (Chrysikou, 2018). The new ideas are not based on the individual's filtering the situation through their knowledge, as proposed in the model of problem-solving presented earlier (see Chapters 3 and 7).

Here is a clear example of this "remote association" view of creative thinking, and one can clearly see the influence of Poincaré's thoughts on it:

> The associative theory of creativity (Mednick, 1962) proposes that creative individuals have a richer and more flexible associative network than less creative individuals. According to this theory (Mednick, 1962), creative individuals are characterized by "flat" (more and broader associations to a given concept) instead of "steep" associational hierarchies (few, common associations to a given concept ...). .... Thus, when attempting to think creatively, the less creative individual is likely to become "stuck" on these dominant, common, associations whereas the more creative individual can overcome them and proceed to establishing more distant associations, via spreading activation (Kenett & Austerweil, 2016). Within this framework, semantically "close" concepts are considered less likely to be creative, whereas semantically "distant" concepts are often considered creative. (Beaty et al., unpublished, p. 4)

Analytic Thinking versus Remote Associations

The analysis presented in this book is very different than the dual-process ideas just discussed, since it assumes that idea generation comes about through the *match* between a problem and one's experience, not through *rejection* of that experience. That is, the process underlying generation of new ideas is not "freewheeling" or "spontaneous." From the beginning, the retrieval of ideas is built on the match between the situation and information in memory, as has been discussed numerous times throughout this book. Thus, one should not assume that all the views listed in Table 13.8 are based on the same set of assumptions and, therefore, that everything is falling into place as far as theorizing about creative thinking is concerned. Significant differences among theoretical views remain (compare Table 13.8A and B). On the one hand, we have the "remote-associations" version of the genius view, in its modern form as the study of brain networks. In contrast is the "analytic" view outlined in this book, which proposes that "near" associations are the basis for *all* creative advances, even the most radical. Evidence to support that claim was presented in many places, perhaps most importantly in the discussions of case studies of creative thinking. It will be interesting to see how those differences in theoretical perspectives come to be worked out in the future.

The Neuroscience of Creativity: Summary and Conclusions

We have in this chapter reviewed a set of advances linking the study of creativity to developments in neuroscience. The research reviewed has covered a range of approaches. We first considered research that has in various ways tried to pinpoint areas in the brain that play roles in carrying out various creative processes. The methods used to localize brain areas included brain imaging and recording of brain activity as an individual is carrying out a task requiring creative thinking. That method has been used by Kounios and Beeman and their colleagues (2014, 2015) in an attempt to determine the brain areas involved in insight. A related method uses stimulation of the brain in order to directly bring about changes in behavior (Chi & Snyder, 2011, 2012). A third method examines creative thinking in individuals who have suffered brain injuries (Reverberi et al., 2005). These methods have produced some fascinating findings, although questions can be raised about some of the methods (Dietrich & Kanso, 2010; Weisberg, 2013). Assuming that those methodological issues can be resolved, we can look forward to further interesting findings coming from research examining the role of specific brain areas in creativity.

However, network analysis, a new development in neuroscience research, takes a broader perspective on the relation between brain activity and cognition, including creative thinking (Beaty et al., unpublished; Fox & Beaty, 2019). In network analysis, it is assumed that areas in the brain work together to carry out tasks. Network analysis may provide new understanding of the complex relationship between the brain and the thought processes underlying creativity, as well as illuminating our understanding of the creative process itself. The critical question here concerns whether that new understanding of creativity will be based on analytic thinking – ordinary thought processes – or whether theoretical developments will move away from analytic thinking. That question seems a fitting one on which to end this exploration of creativity.

References

ABC News. (1999). The Deep Dive: One company's secret weapon for innovation. *Nightline* program transcript, February 9, 1999. ciow.org/docs1/IDEO_Nightli ne.pdf, accessed July 10, 2019.

Abraham, A. (2018). The forest versus the trees: Creativity, cognition and imagination. In R. E. Jung & O. Vartanian (eds.), *Cambridge Handbook of the Neuroscience of Creativity* (pp. 195–210). Cambridge: Cambridge University Press.

Abuhamdeh, S., & Csikszentmihalyi, M. (2004). The artistic personality: A systems perspective. In R. J. Sternberg, E. L. Grigorenko & J. L. Singer (eds.), *Creativity: From Potential to Realization* (pp. 31–42). Washington, DC: American Psychological Association.

Acar, S., & Runco, M. R. (2014). Assessing associative distance among ideas elicited by tests of divergent thinking. *Creativity Research Journal* 26(2): 229–238.

Addis, D. R., Pan, L., Musicaro, R. & Schacter, D. L. (2014). Divergent thinking and constructing episodic simulations. *Memory* 24(1): 89–97.

Alloy, L. B., & Nusslock, R. (2019). Future directions for understanding adolescent bipolar spectrum disorders: A reward hypersensitivity perspective. *Journal of Clinical Child & Adolescent Psychology* 48(4): 669–683.

Altman, L. K. (1987). *Who Goes First? The Story of Self-Experimentation in Medicine*. Berkeley: University of California Press.

Amabile, T. M. (1979). Effects of external evaluation on artistic creativity. *Journal of Personality and Social Psychology* 37(2): 221–233.

Amabile, T. M. (1983). *The Social Psychology of Creativity*. New York: Springer-Verlag.

Amabile, T. M. (1996). *Creativity in Context: Update to the Social Psychology of Creativity*. Boulder, CO: Westview.

Amabile, T. M., & Pratt, M. G. (2016). The dynamic componential model of creativity and innovation in organizations: Making progress, making meaning. *Research in Organizational Behavior* 36: 157–183.

Amabile, T. M., Goldfarb, P., & Brackfield, S. C. (1990). Social influences on creativity: Evaluation, coaction, and surveillance. *Creativity Research Journal* 3(1): 6–21.

Amabile, T. M., Hennessy, B. A., & Grossman, B. S. (1986). Social influences on creativity: The effects of contracted-for reward. *Journal of Personality and Social Psychology* 50(1): 14–23.

America's Test Kitchen (eds.). (2006). *834 Kitchen Quick Tips: Techniques and Shortcuts for the Curious Cook*. Brookline, MA: America's Test Kitchen.

Andreasen, N. C. (1987). Creativity and mental illness: Prevalence rates in writers and their first-degree relatives. *American Journal of Psychiatry* 144(10): 1288–1292.

Ash, I. K., Cushen, P. J., & Wiley, J. (2009). Obstacles in investigating the role of restructuring in insightful problem solving. *Journal of Problem Solving* 2(2): 6–41.

Baas, M., De Dreu, C. K. W., & Nijstad, B. A. (2008). A meta-analysis of 25 years of mood–creativity research: Hedonic tone, activation, or regulatory focus? *Psychological Bulletin* 134(6): 779–806. doi:10.1037/a0012815.

Baas, M., Nijstad, B. A., Boot, N. C., & De Dreu, C. K. W. (2016). Mad genius revisited: Vulnerability to psychopathology, biobehavioral approach-avoidance, and creativity. *Psychological Bulletin* 142(6): 668–692. doi:http://dx.doi.org/10.1037/bul0000049.

Baer, J. (1993). *Creativity and Divergent Thinking: A Task-Specific Approach*. Hillsdale, NJ: Erlbaum.

Baer, J. (2012). Domain specificity and the limits of creativity theory. *The Journal of Creative Behavior* 46(1): 16–29.

Baer, J. (2015). The importance of domain-specific expertise in creativity. *Roeper Review* 37(3): 165–178.

Baer, J., & McKool, S. S. (2014). The gold standard for assessing creativity. *International Journal of Quality Assurance in Engineering and Technology Education* 3(1): 81–93.

Baird, B., Smallwood, J., Mrazek, M. D., Kam, J. W. Y., Franklin, M. S., & Smallwood, J. W. (2012). Inspired by distraction: Mind wandering facilitates creative incubation. *Psychological Science* 23(10): 1117–1122.

Barron, F., & Harrington, D. M. (1981). Creativity, intelligence, and personality. *Annual Review of Psychology* 32: 439–476.

Barry, D. N., Barnes, G. R., Clark, I. A., & Maguire, E. A. (2019). The neural dynamics of novel scene imagery. *The Journal of Neuroscience* 39(22): 4375–4386.

Barzun, J. (1960). The cults of "research" and "creativity." *Harper's Magazine*, October, 69–74.

Barzun, J. (1989). The paradoxes of creativity. *The American Scholar* 58(3): 337–351.

Bassok, M., & Novick, L. R. (2012). Problem solving. In K. J. Holyoak & R. G. Morrison (eds.), *The Oxford Handbook of Thinking and Reasoning* (pp. 413–432). New York: Oxford University Press.

Batey, M., & Furnham, A. (2006). Creativity, intelligence, and personality: A critical review of the scattered literature. *Genetic, Social, and General Psychology Monographs* 132(4): 355–429.

Beaty, R. E., Benedek, M., Kaufman, S. B., & Silvia, P. J. (2015). Default and executive network coupling supports creative idea production. *Scientific Reports* 5: 10,964. doi:10.1038/srep10964.

Beaty, R. E., Benedek, M., Silvia, P. J., & Schacter, D. L. (2016). Creative cognition and brain network dynamics. *Trends in Cognitive Sciences* 20(2): 87–95. doi:10.1016/j.tics.2015.10.004.

Beaty, R. E., Kenett, Y. N., Christensen, A. P., Rosenberg, M. D., Benedek, M., Chen, Q., . . ., & Silvia, P. J. (2018). Robust prediction of individual creative ability from brain functional connectivity. *Proceedings of the National Academy of Sciences of the United States of America* 115(5): 1087–1092. doi:www.pnas.org/cgi/doi/10.1073/pnas.1713532115.

Beaty, R. E., Kenett, Y. K., Hass, R. W., & Schacter, D. L. (Unpublished). A fan effect for creative thought: Semantic richness facilitates idea quantity but constrains idea quality.

Beaty, R. E., Nusbaum, E. C., & Silvia, P. J. (2014). Does insight problem solving predict real-world creativity? *Psychology of Aesthetics, Creativity, and the Arts* 8(3): 287–292.

Beaty, R., Seli, P., & Schacter, D. L. (2019). Network neuroscience of creative cognition: Mapping cognitive mechanisms and individual differences in the creative brain. *Current Opinion in Behavioral Sciences* 27: 22–30. doi:https://doi.org/10.1016/j.cobeha.2018.08.013.

Beaty, R. E., & Silvia, P. J. (2012). Why do ideas get more creative across time? An executive interpretation of the serial order effect in divergent thinking tasks. *Psychology of Aesthetics, Creativity, and the Arts* 6(4): 309–319.

Beaty, R. E., Silvia, P. J., Nusbaum, E. C., Jauk, E., & Benedek, M. (2014). The roles of associative and executive processes in creative cognition. *Memory & Cognition* 42(7): 1186–1197. PMID 24898118; doi:10.3758/s13421-014-0428-8.

Becker, G. (1978). *The Mad Genius Controversy: A Study in the Sociology of Deviance*. Beverley Hills, CA: Sage.

Becker, G. (2001). The association of creativity and psychopathology: Its cultural-historical origins. *Creativity Research Journal* 13(1): 45–53.

Becker, G. (2014). A socio-historical overview of the creativity–pathology connection: From antiquity to contemporary times. In J. C. Kaufman (ed.), *Creativity and Mental Illness* (pp. 3–24). Cambridge: Cambridge University Press

Beda, Z., & Smith, S. M. (2018). Chasing red herrings: Memory of distractors causes fixation in creative problem solving. *Memory & Cognition* 46(5): 671–684.

Benedek, M., & Neubauer, A. C. (2013). Revisiting Mednick's model on creativity-related differences in associative hierarchies: Evidence for a common path to uncommon thought. *The Journal of Creative Behavior* 47(4): 273–289.

Benedek, M., Jauk, E., Fink, A., Koschutnig, K., Reishofer, G., Ebner, F., & Neubauer, A. (2014). To create or to recall? Neural mechanisms underlying the generation of creative new ideas. *NeuroImage* 88(100): 125–133. doi:10.1016/j.neuroimage.2013.11.021.

Best, J. B. (1987). The subgoal heuristic and its effect on internal representations. *Journal of General Psychology* 114(4): 383–391.

Bilalić, M., McLeod, P., & Gobet, F. (2008). Inflexibility of experts – reality or myth? Quantifying the Einstellung effect in chess masters. *Cognitive Psychology* 56(2): 73–102.

Bloom, B. (1985). *Developing Talent in Young People*. New York: Ballantine Books.

Bloom, H. (2002). *Genius: A Mosaic of One Hundred Exemplary Creative Minds*. New York: Warner Books.

Boden, M. A. (1990). *The Creative Mind: Myths and Mechanisms*. London: Routledge.

Bourne, L. E., Ekstrand, B. R., & Dominowski, R. L. (1971). *The Psychology of Thinking*. New York: Prentice-Hall.

Bowden, E. M., & Grunewald, K. (2018). Whose insight is it anyway? In F. Vallée-Tourangeau (ed.), *Insight: On the Origins of New Ideas* (pp. 28–50). London: Routledge.

Buckner, R. L. (2012). The serendipitous discovery of the brain's default network. *Neuroimage* 62(2): 1137–1145. doi:10.1016/j.neuroimage.2011.10.035.

Byron, K., & Khazanchi, S. (2012). Rewards and creative performance: A meta-analytic test of theoretically derived hypotheses. *Psychological Bulletin* 138(4): 809–830.

Cai, D. J., Mednick, S. A., Harrison, E. M., Kanady, J. C., & Mednick, S. C. (2009). REM, not incubation, improves creativity by priming associative networks. *Proceedings of the National Academy of Sciences of the United States of America* 106: 10,130–10,134. PMID 19506253; doi:10.1073/pnas.0900271106.

Campbell, D. T. (1960). Blind variation and selective retention in creative thought as in other knowledge processes. *Psychological Review* 67: 380–400.

Campbell, K. L., Madore, K. P., Benoit, R. G., Thakral, P. P., & Schacter D. L. (2018). Increased hippocampus to ventromedial prefrontal connectivity during the construction of episodic future events. *Hippocampus* 28(2): 76–80.

Carrroll, J. B. (1993). *Human Cognitive Abilities: A Survey of Factor-Analytic Studies*. Cambridge: Cambridge University Press.

Carson, S. H. (2014). Cognitive disinhibition, creativity, and psychopathology. In D. K. Simonton (ed.), *The Wiley Handbook of Genius* (pp. 198–221). Hoboken, NJ: John Wiley.

Carson, S. H. (2018). Creativity and psychopathology: A relationship of shared neurocognitive vulnerabilities. In O. Vartanian & R. E. Jung (eds.), *The Cambridge Handbook of the Neuroscience of Creativity* (pp. 136–159). New York: Cambridge University Press.

Catrambone, R., & Holyoak, K. J. (1989). Overcoming contextual limitations on problem-solving transfer. *Journal of Experimental Psychology: Learning, Memory, and Cognition* 15: 1147–1156.

Ceulemans, C. (2010). The reputation of Baroque composers 1790–2000. *Empirical Studies of the Arts* 28(2): 223–242. doi:https://doi.org/10.2190/EM.28.2.g.

Chan, J., & Schunn, C. D. (2015). The importance of iteration in creative conceptual combination. *Cognition* 145: 104–115.

Chan, J., Dow, S. P., & Schunn, C. D. (2015). Do the best design ideas (really) come from conceptually distant sources of inspiration? *Design Studies* 36: 31–58.

Chase, W. G., & Ericsson, K. A. (1982). Skill and working memory. In G. H. Bower (ed.), *The Psychology of Learning and Motivation* (Vol. 16, pp. 1–58). New York: Academic Press.

Chase, W. G., & Simon, H. A. (1973a). Perception in chess. *Cognitive Psychology* 4: 55–81.

Chase, W. G., & Simon, H. A. (1973b). The mind's eye in chess. In W. G. Chase (ed.), *Visual information processing* (pp. 215–281). New York: Academic Press.

Chein, J. M., & Weisberg, R. W. (2014). Working memory and insight in verbal problems: Analysis of compound remote associates. *Memory and Cognition* 42: 67–83.

Chein, J. M., Weisberg, R. W., Streeter, N. L., & Kwok, S. (2010). Working memory and insight in the 9-Dot Problem. *Memory and Cognition* 38(7): 883–892.

Chi, R. P., & Snyder, A. W. (2011). Facilitate insight by non-invasive brain stimulation. *PLoS ONE* 6(2): e16655. doi:10.1371/journal.pone.0016655.

Chi, R. P., & Snyder, A. W. (2012). Brain stimulation enables the solution of an inherently difficult problem. *Neuroscience Letters* 515(2012): 121–124. doi:10.1016/j.neulet.2012.03.012.

Chipp, H. B. (1988). *Picasso's "Guernica": History, Transformations, Meanings.* Berkeley: University of California Press.

Chomsky, N. (1957). *Syntactic Structures.* The Hague: Mouton.

Christensen, B. T., & Schunn, C. D. (2007). The relationship of analogical distance to analogical function and pre-inventive structure: The case of engineering design. *Memory & Cognition* 35(1): 29–38.

Chrysikou, E. G. (2018). The costs and benefits of cognitive control for creativity. In O. Vartanian & R. E. Jung (eds.), *The Cambridge Handbook of the Neuroscience of Creativity* (pp. 299–317). New York: Cambridge University Press.

Chrysikou, E. G. (2019). Creativity in and out of (cognitive) control. *Current Opinion in Behavioral Sciences* 27: 94–99.

Chrysikou, E. G., Berryhill, M. E., Bikson, M., & Coslett, H. B. (2017). Revisiting the effectiveness of transcranial direct current brain stimulation for cognition: Evidence, challenges, and open questions (Editorial). *Frontiers in Human Neuroscience* 11: 448.

Chrysikou, E. G., Hamilton, R. H., Coslett, H. B., Datta, A., Bikson, M., & Thompson-Schill, S. L. (2013). Non-invasive transcranial direct current stimulation over the left prefrontal cortex facilitates cognitive flexibility in tool use. *Cognitive Neuroscience* 4: 81–89.

Chrysikou, E. G., & Thompson-Schill, S. L. (2011). Dissociable brains states linked to common and creative object use. *Human Brain Mapping* 32: 665–675.

Chuderski, A., & Jastrzębski, J. (2018). Much ado about aha!: Insight problem solving is strongly related to working memory capacity and reasoning ability.

Journal of Experimental Psychology: General 147(2): 257–281. doi:http://dx
.doi.org/10.1037/xge0000378.

Cinan, S., Özen, G., & Hampshire, A. (2013). Confirmatory factor analysis on
separability of planning and insight constructs. *Journal of Cognitive Psychology*
25(1): 7–23. doi:https://doi.org/10.1080/20445911.2012.729035.

Coleman, R. (1995). *McCartney. Yesterday & Today*. Los Angeles, CA: Dove Books.

Conti, R., Coon, H., & Amabile, T. M. (1996). Evidence to support the componential model of creativity: Secondary analyses of three studies. *Creativity Research
Journal* 9: 385–389.

Cope, D. (2014). *Experiments in Musical Intelligence*. Middleton, WI:
A-R Editions, Inc.

Cramond, B., Matthews-Morgan, J., Bandalos, D., & Zuo, L. (2005). A report on the
40-year follow-up of the Torrance Tests of Creative Thinking: Alive and well in
the new millennium. *Gifted Child Quarterly* 49: 283–291.

Cranford, E. A., & Moss, J. (2012). Is insight always the same? A protocol analysis of
insight in compound remote associate problems. *The Journal of Problem Solving*
4: 128–153.

Csikszentmihalyi, M. (1988). Society, culture, and person: A systems view of creativity. In R. J. Sternberg (ed.), *The Nature of Creativity: Current Psychological
Perspectives* (pp. 325–339). Cambridge: Cambridge University Press.

Csikszentmihalyi, M. (1996). *Creativity: Flow and the Psychology of Discovery and
Invention*. New York: Harper Collins.

Csikszentmihalyi, M. (2014). The systems model of creativity and its applications.
In D. K. Simonton (ed.), *The Wiley Handbook of Genius* (pp. 533–545).
Hoboken, NJ: John Wiley.

Csikszentmihalyi, M., & Sawyer, K. (1995). Creative insight: The social dimension
of a solitary moment. In R. J. Steinberg & J. E. Davidson (eds.) *The Nature of
Insight* (pp. 329–361). Cambridge, MA: MIT Press.

Cushen, P.J., & Wiley, J. (2018). Both attentional control and the ability to make
remote associations aid spontaneous analogical transfer. *Memory & Cognition*
46(8): 1398–1412. doi:https://doi.org/10.3758/s13421-018-0845-1.

Danek, A. H. (2018). Magic tricks, sudden restructuring and the Aha! experience:
A new model of non-monotonic problem solving. In F. Vallée-Tourangeau
(ed.), *Insight: On the Origins of New Ideas* (pp. 51–78). London: Routledge.

Danek, A. H., & Salvi, C. (2018). Moment of truth: Why Aha! experiences are
correct. *The Journal of Creative Behavior*.

Danek, A. H., Williams, J., & Wiley, J. (2018). Closing the gap: Connecting sudden
representational change to the subjective Aha! experience in insightful problem
solving. *Psychological Research* 84(1): 1–9. doi:https://doi.org/10.3758/s13421-
018-0845-1.

Davidson, J. E. (1995). The suddenness of insight. In R. J. Sternberg, &
J. E. Davidson (eds.). *The Nature of Insight* (pp. 125–155). Cambridge, MA:
MIT Press.

DeCaro, M. S. (2018). When does higher working memory capacity help or hinder insight problem solving? In F. Vallée-Tourangeau (ed.), *Insight: On the Origins of New Ideas* (pp. 51–78). New York: Routledge.

De Groot, A. (1965). *Thought and Choice in Chess.* The Hague: Mouton.

Depue, R. A., & Iacono, W. G. (1989). Neurobehavioral aspects of affective disorders. *Annual Review of Psychology* 40: 457–492.

DeYoung, C. G., Quilty, L. C., & Peterson, J. B. (2007). Between facets and domains: 10 aspects of the Big Five. *Journal of Personality and Social Psychology* 93: 880–896.

Dietrich, A. (2004). The cognitive neuroscience of creativity. *Psychonomic Bulletin & Review* 11(6): 1011–1026.

Dietrich, A. (2014). The mythconception of the mad genius. *Frontiers of Psychology* 5, Article 79. doi:10.3389/fpsyg.2014.00079.

Dietrich, A. (2018). Types of creativity. *Psychonomic Bulletin & Review* 11(6): 1011–1026. doi:https://doi.org/10.3758/s13423-018-1517-7.

Dietrich, A., & Kanso, R. (2010). A review of EEG, ERP, and neuroimaging studies of creativity and insight. *Psychological Bulletin* 136(5): 822–848. doi:10.1037/a0019749.

Digman, J. M. (1997). Higher-order factors of the Big-5. *Journal of Personality and Social Psychology* 73: 1246–1256.

Dijksterhuis, A., & Meurs, T. (2006). Where creativity resides: The generative power of unconscious thought. *Consciousness and Cognition* 15: 135–146.

Dijksterhuis, A., & Strick, M. (2016). A case for thinking without consciousness. *Perspectives on Psychological Science* 11(1): 117–132. doi:10.1177/1745691615615317.

Dodds, R. A., Ward, T. B., & Smith, S. M. (2012). Incubation in problem solving and creativity. In M. A. Runco (ed.), *The Creativity Research Handbook, Volume 3* (pp. 251–284). New York: Hampton Press.

Dunbar, K. (1995). How scientists really reason: Scientific reasoning in real-world laboratories. In R. J. Sternberg & J. E. Davidson (eds.), *The Nature of Insight* (pp. 365–395). Cambridge, MA: MIT Press.

Dunbar, K. (2001). The analogical paradox: Why analogy is so easy in naturalistic settings, yet so difficult in the psychological laboratory. In D. Gentner, K. J. Holyoak, & B. Kokinov (eds.), *Analogy: Perspectives from Cognitive Science* (pp. 313–334). Cambridge, MA: MIT Press.

Dunbar, K., & Blanchette, I. (2001). The in vivo/in vitro approach to cognition: The case of analogy. *Trends in Cognitive Sciences* 5(8): 334–339.

Duncker, K. (1945). On problem-solving. *Psychological Monographs* 68(5): whole no. 270.

Edwards, B. J., Williams, J. J., Gentner, D., & Lombrozo, T. (2014). Effects of comparison and explanation on analogical transfer. In P. Bello, M. Guarini, M. McShane, & B. Scassellati (eds.), *Proceedings of the 36th Annual Conference of the Cognitive Science Society.* Red Hook, NY: Curran.

Eisenberger R. & Byron K. (2011). Rewards and creativity. In M. A. Runco & S. R. Pritzker (eds.), *Encyclopedia of Creativity, 2nd ed., Vol. 2* (pp. 313–318). San Diego, CA: Academic Press.

Elgammal, A., & Saleh, B. (2015). Quantifying creativity in art networks. In H. Toivonen, S. Colton, M. Cook, & D. Ventura (eds.), *Proceedings of the Sixth International Conference on Computational Creativity*, pp. 39–46. Provo, UT: Brigham Young University.

Engle, R. (2018). Working memory and executive attention: A revisit. *Perspectives on Psychological Science* 13(2): 190–193. doi:10.1177/1745691617720478.

Ericsson, K. A. (1999). Creative expertise as superior reproducible performance: Innovative and flexible aspects of expert performance. *Psychological Inquiry* 10: 329–333.

Ericsson, K. A. (2006). The influence of experience and deliberate practice on the development of superior expert performance. In K. A. Ericsson, N. Charness, P. Feltovich, & R. R. Hoffman (eds.), *Cambridge Handbook of Expertise and Expert Performance* (pp. 683–704). Cambridge: Cambridge University Press.

Ericsson, K. A., Chase, W. G., & Falloon, S. (1980). Acquisition of a memory skill. *Science* 208: 1181–1182.

Ericsson, K. A., Hoffman, R. R., Kozbelt, A., & Williams, A. M. (eds.) (2018). *Cambridge Handbook of Expertise and Expert Performance*. 2nd ed. Cambridge: Cambridge University Press.

Ericsson, K. A., Krampe, R. T., & Tesch-Römer, C. (1993). The role of deliberate practice in the acquisition of expert performance. *Psychological Review* 100: 363–406.

Ericsson, K. A., & Pool, R. (2016). *Peak: Secrets from the New Science of Expertise*. New York: Eamon Dolan Books/Houghton Mifflin & Harcourt.

Ericsson, K. A., & Simon, H. A. (1996). *Protocol Analysis: Verbal Reports as Data*. Cambridge, MA: MIT Press

Erlin, M. & Tatlock, L. (2014). *Distant Readings: Topologies of German Culture in the Long Nineteenth Century*. Rochester, NY: Camden House.

Everett, W. (2001). *The Beatles as Musicians. The Quarry Men through Rubber Soul*. New York: Oxford.

Eysenck, H. J. (1993). Creativity and personality: Suggestions for a theory. *Psychological Inquiry* 4: 147–178.

Eysenck, H. J. (1995). *Genius: The Natural History of Creativity*. New York: Cambridge University Press.

Fatović-Ferenčić, S., & Banić, M. (2011). No acid, no ulcer: Dragutin (Carl) Schwarz (1868–1917), the man ahead of his time. *Digestive Diseases* 29(5): 507–510. doi:10.1159/000334384.

Feist, G. J. (1993). A structural model of scientific eminence. *Psychological Science* 4: 366–371.

Feist, G. J. (1998). A meta-analysis of personality in scientific and artistic creativity. *Personality and Social Psychology Review* 2(4): 290–309.

Feist, G. J. (1999). The influence of personality on artistic and scientific creativity. In R. J. Sternberg (ed.), *Handbook of Creativity* (pp. 273–296). Cambridge: Cambridge University Press.

Feist, G. J. (2017). Personality, behavioral thresholds, and the creative scientist. In G. J. Feist, R. Reiter-Palmon, & J. C. Kaufman (eds.), *The Cambridge Handbook of Creativity and Personality Research* (pp. 64–83). Cambridge: Cambridge University Press.

Feist, G. J. (2018). Creativity and the Big Two model of personality: plasticity and stability. *Current Opinion in Behavioral Sciences* 27: 31–35.

Feist, G. J. & Barron, F. (2003). Predicting creativity from early to late adulthood: Intellect, potential, and personality. *Journal of Research in Personality 37*: 62–88.

Feist, G. J., Reiter-Palmon, R., & Kaufman, J. C. (2017). *The Cambridge Handbook of Creativity and Personality Research*. Cambridge: Cambridge University Press.

Flanagan, D., & Dixon, S. (2013). The Cattell-Horn-Carroll theory of cognitive abilities. In C. R. Reynolds, K. J. Vannest, & E. Fletcher-Janzen (eds.), *Encyclopedia of Special Education*. Hoboken, NJ: Wiley.

Fleck, J. I., & Weisberg, R. W. (2004). The use of verbal protocols as data: An analysis of insight in the candle problem. *Memory & Cognition* 32: 990–1006.

Fleck, J. S., & Weisberg, R. W. (2013). Insight versus analysis: Evidence for diverse methods in problem solving. *Journal of Cognitive Psychology* 25: 436–463.

Foer, J. (2011). Moonwalking with Einstein: The Art and Science of Remembering Everything. New York: Penguin.

Forbus, K. D., Ferguson, R. W., Lovett, A., & Gentner, D. (2017). Extending SME to handle large-scale cognitive modeling. *Cognitive Science* 41: 1152–1201. doi:10.1111/cogs.12377.

Fox, K. C. R., & Beaty, R. E. (2019). Mind-wandering as creative thinking: neural, psychological, and theoretical considerations. *Current Opinion in Behavioral Sciences* 27: 123–130.

Friedel, R., & Israel, P. (1986). *Edison's Electric Light: Biography of an Invention*. New Brunswick, NJ: Rutgers University Press.

Frensch, P. A., & Sternberg, R. J. (1989). Expertise and intelligent thinking: When is it worse to know better? In R. J. Sternberg (ed.), *Advances in the Psychology of Human Intelligence*, Vol. 5 (pp. 157–188). Hillside, NJ: Erlbaum.

Fürst, G., & Lubart, T. (2017). An integrative approach to the creative personality: Beyond the Big Five paradigm. In G. J. Feist, R. Reiter-Palmon, & J. C. Kaufman (eds.), *The Cambridge Handbook of Creativity and Personality Research* (pp. 140–164). New York: Cambridge University Press.

Fürst, G., Ghisletta, P., & Lubart, T. (2014). Toward an integrative model of creativity and personality: Theoretical suggestions and preliminary empirical testing. *The Journal of Creative Behavior* 50(2): 87–108. doi:10.1002/jocb.71.

Gable, S. L., Hopper, E. A., & Schooler, J. W. (2019). When the Muses strike: Creative ideas of physicists and writers routinely occur during mind wandering. *Psychological Science* 30(3): 396–404. doi:10.1177/0956797618820626.

Gagné, F. (2009). Debating Giftedness: Pronat vs. Antinat. In L. V. Shavinina (ed.), *International Handbook on Giftedness* (pp. 155–204). New York: Springer.

Gagné, F. (2015). From genes to talent: The DMGT/CMTD perspective. *Revista de Educación* 368: 12–37.

Galton, F. (1979 [1869]). *Hereditary Genius: An Inquiry into Its Laws and Consequences*. London: Friedmann.

Gardner, H. (1993). *Creating Minds: An Anatomy of Creativity Seen through the Lives of Freud, Einstein, Picasso, Stravinsky, Eliot, Graham, and Gandhi*. New York: Basic.

Gentner, D., & Maravilla, F. (2018). Analogical reasoning. In L. J. Ball & V. A. Thompson (eds.), *International Handbook of Thinking & Reasoning* (pp. 186–203). New York: Psychology Press.

Gentner, D., Loewenstein, J., Thompson, L., & Forbus, K. D. (2009). Reviving inert knowledge: Analogical abstraction supports relational retrieval of past events. *Cognitive Science* 33: 1343–1382. doi:10.1111/j.1551-6709.2009.01070.x.

George T., & Wiley, J. (2018). Breaking past the surface: Analogical transfer as creative insight. In F. Vallée-Tourangeau (ed.), *Insight: On the Origin of New Ideas* (pp. 143–168). New York: Routledge.

Gerard, A. (1774). *An Essay on Genius*. London: Stranahan Caddell.

Getzels, J., & Csikszentmihalyi, M. (1976). *The Creative Vision: A Longitudinal Study of Problem Finding in Art*. New York: Wiley.

Ghiselin, B. (1996 [1952]). *The Creative Process: A symposium*. New York: Mentor.

Gick, M. L., & Holyoak, K. J. (1980). Analogical problem solving. *Cognitive Psychology* 12: 306–355.

Gick, M. L., & Holyoak, K. J. (1983). Schema induction and analogical transfer. *Cognitive Psychology* 15: 1–38.

Gilhooly, K. J. (2016). Incubation and intuition in creative problem solving. *Frontiers in Psychology* 7. doi:10.3389/fpsyg.2016.01076.

Gilhooly, K. J., & Fioratou, E. (2009). Executive functions in insight versus non-insight problem solving: An individual differences approach. *Thinking & Reasoning* 15(4): 355–376

Gilhooly, K., Fioratou, E., Anthony, S., & Wynn, V. (2007). Divergent thinking: Strategies and executive involvement in generating novel uses for familiar objects. *British Journal of Psychology* 98(4): 611–625.

Gilhooly, K., & Murphy, P. (2005). Differentiating insight from non-insight problems. *Thinking and Reasoning* 11: 279–302.

Gilhooly, K. J., & Webb, M. E. (2018). Working memory in insight problem solving. In F. Vallée-Tourangeau (ed.), *Insight: On the Origins of New Ideas* (pp. 105–119). London: Routledge.

Ginsburgh, V., & Weyers, S. (2006). Persistence and fashion in art Italian Renaissance from Vasari to Berenson and beyond. *Poetics* 34: 24–44.

Ginsburgh, V., & Weyers, S. (2010). On the formation of canons: The dynamics of art history. *Empirical Studies of the Arts* 28(1): 37–72.

Ginsburgh, V., & Weyers, S. (2014). Evaluating excellence in the arts. In D. K. Simonton (ed.), *The Wiley Handbook of Genius* (pp. 509–532). Hoboken, NJ: Wiley.

Glucksberg, S., & Weisberg, R. (1966). Verbal behavior and problem solving: Some effects of labeling in a functional fixedness task. *Journal of Experimental Psychology* 71: 659–664.

Gobet, F., & Ereku, M. H. (2014). Checkmate to deliberate practice: The case of Magnus Carlsen. *Frontiers in Psychology 5*, Article 878.

Goodwin, F. K., & Jamison, K. R. (1990). *Manic-Depressive Illness*. New York, Oxford University Press.

Grosul, M., & Feist, G. J. (2014). The creative person in science. *Psychology of Aesthetics, Creativity, and the Arts* 8(1): 30–43. doi:10.1037/a0034828.

Guilford, J. P. (1950). Creativity. *American Psychologist* 5: 444–454.

Guilford, J. P. (1956). The structure of intellect. *Psychological Bulletin* 53: 267–293. doi:http://dx.doi.org/10.1037/h0040755.

Guilford, J. P. (1967). *The Nature of Human Intelligence*. New York: McGraw-Hill.

Hadamard, J. (1945). *The Psychology of Invention in the Mathematical Field*. New York: Dover.

Hambrick, D. Z., Macnamara, B. N., Campitelli, G., Ullén, F., & Mosing, M. A. (2016). Beyond born versus made: A new look at expertise. In B. H. Ross (ed.), *The Psychology of Learning and Motivation: Vol. 64* (pp. 1–55). London: Elsevier Academic Press.

Hass, R. (2017). Semantic search during divergent thinking. *Cognition* 166: 344–357. doi:http://dx.doi.org/10.1016/j.cognition.2017.05.039.

Hass, R. W., & Beaty, R. E. (2018). Use or consequences: Probing the cognitive difference between two measures of divergent thinking. *Frontiers in Psychology* 9. doi:https://doi.org/10.3389/fpsyg.2018.02327.

Hass, R. W., & Weisberg, R. W. (2009). Career development in two seminal American songwriters: A test of the equal-odds rule. *Creativity Research Journal* 21: 183–190.

Hass, R. W., Weisberg, R. W., & Choi, J. (2010). Quantitative case-studies in musical composition: The development of creativity in popular-songwriting teams. *Psychology of Music* 38(4): 463–480.

Hassabis, D., Kumaran, D., Vann, S. D., & Maguire, E. A. (2007). Patients with hippocampal amnesia cannot imagine new experiences. *Proceedings of the National Academy of Sciences of the U.S.A.* 104(5): 1726–1731.

Hayes, J. R. (1989). Cognitive processes in creativity. In J. A. Glover, R. R. Ronning, & C. R. Reynolds (eds.). *Handbook of Creativity* (pp. 135–145). New York: Plenum.

Hedne, M. R., Norman, E., & Metcalfe, J. (2016). Intuitive feelings of warmth and confidence in insight and noninsight problem solving of magic tricks. *Frontiers in Psychology* 7, Article 1314. doi:10.3389/fpsyg.2016.01314.

Hélie, S., & Sun, R. (2010). Incubation, insight, and creative problem solving: A unified theory and a connectionist model. *Psychological Review* 117(3): 994–1024. doi:10.1037/a0019532.

Helson, R. (1999). A longitudinal study of creative personality in women. *Creativity Research Journal* 12: 89–101.

Hofstadter, D., & Sander, E. (2013). *Surfaces and Essences: Analogy as the Fuel and Fire of Thinking*. New York: Basic Books.

Hoicka, E., Mowat, R., Kirkwood, J., Kerr, T., & Carberry, M. (2016). One-year-olds think creatively, just like their parents. *Child Development* 87(4): 1099–1105. doi:10.1111/cdev.12531.

Holyoak, K. J. (2012). Analogy and relational reasoning. In K. J. Holyoak & R. G. Morrison (eds.), *The Oxford Handbook of Thinking and Reasoning* (pp. 234–259). New York: Oxford University Press

Horn, A. (1966). Jackson Pollock: The hollow and the bump. *Carleton Miscellany* 7: 80–87.

Horn, J. L., & Cattell, R. B. (1966). Refinement and test of the theory of fluid and crystallized intelligence. *Journal of Educational Psychology* 57: 253–270.

Howe, M. J. A., Davidson, J. W., & Sloboda, J. A. (1998). Innate talents: Reality or myth? *Behavioral and Brain Sciences* 21: 399–442.

Hsu, N. S., Novick, J. M., & Jaeggi, S. M. (2014). The development and malleability of executive control abilities. *Frontiers in Behavioral Neuroscience* 8: 221. doi:10.3389/fnbeh.2014.00221.

Isen, A. M. (2008). Some ways in which positive affect influences decision making and problem solving. In M. Lewis, J. M. Haviland-Jones, & L. F. Barrett (eds.), *Handbook of Emotions* (pp. 548–573). New York: Guilford Press.

Isen, A.M., & Daubman, K.A. (1984). The influence of affect on categorization. *Journal of Personality and Social Psychology* 47: 1206–1217.

Isen, A. M., Daubman, K. A., & Nowicki, G. P. (1987). Positive affect facilitates creative problem solving. *Journal of Personality and Social Psychology* 52: 1122–1131.

Jamison, K. R. (1989). Mood disorders and patterns of creativity in British writers and artists. *Psychiatry 52*: 125–134.

Jamison, K. (1993). *Touched with Fire: Manic-Depressive Illness and the Artistic Temperament*. New York: Free Press/Macmillan.

Jarosz, A. F., Colflesh, G. J. H., & Wiley, J. (2012). Uncorking the muse: Alcohol intoxication facilitates creative problem solving. *Consciousness & Cognition* 21: 487–493. doi:http://dx.doi.org/10.1016/j.concog.2012.01.002.

Jauk, E., Benedek, M., & Neubauer, A. C. (2014). The road to creative achievement: A latent variable model of ability and personality predictors. *European Journal of Personality* 28(1): 95–105. doi:10.1002/per.1941.

Jauk, E., Benedek, M., Dunst, B., & Neubauer, A. C. (2013). The relationship between intelligence and creativity: New support for the threshold hypothesis by means of empirical breakpoint detection. *Intelligence* 41(4): 212–221.

Johnson, S. L., Sandrow, D., Meyer, B., Winters, R., Miller, I., Keitner, G., & Solomon, D. (2000). Increases in manic symptoms following life events involving goal-attainment. *Journal of Abnormal Psychology* 109: 721–727.

Joy, S. (2004). Innovation motivation: The need to be different. *Creativity Research Journal* 16(2–3): 313–329.

Joy, S. (2017). Innovation motivation: A social learning model of originality. In G. J. Feist, R. Reiter-Palmon, & J. C. Kaufman (eds.), *Cambridge Handbook of Creativity and Personality Research* (pp. 214–234). New York: Cambridge University Press.

Joy, S., & Hicks, S. (2004). The need to be different: Primary trait structure and impact on projective drawings. *Creativity Research Journal* 16(2–3): 330–339.

Jung, R. E., Mead, B. S., Carrasco, J., & Flores, R. A. (2013). The structure of creative cognition in the human brain. *Frontiers in Human Neuroscience* 7, Article 330. doi:10.3389/fnhum.2013.00330.

Jung, R. E., & Vartanian, O. (eds.). (2018). *Cambridge Handbook of the Neuroscience of Creativity*. Cambridge: Cambridge University Press.

Kaiser, D. (2005). *Drawing Theories Apart: The Dispersion of Feynman Diagrams in Postwar Physics*. Chicago, IL: University of Chicago Press.

Kant, I. (1951 [1892]). *Critique of Judgment*, trans. J. H. Bernard. New York: Hafner Publishing.

Kaplan, C. A., & Simon, H. A. (1990). In search of insight. *Cognitive Psychology* 22: 374–419.

Karwowski, M., & Lebuda, I. (2016). The big five, the huge two, and creative self-beliefs: Ameta-analysis. *Psychology of Aesthetics, Creativity, and the Arts* 10(2): 214–232. doi:http://dx.doi.org/10.1037/aca0000035.

Kaufman, J. C. (2001). The Sylvia Plath effect: Mental illness in eminent creative writers. *Journal of Creative Behavior* 35: 37–50.

Kaufman, J. C. (2003). The cost of the muse: Poets die young. *Death Studies* 27: 813–822.

Kaufman, J. C., & Beghetto, R. A. (2009). Beyond big and little: The Four C model of creativity. *Review of General Psychology* 13: 1–12.

Kaufman, J. C., & Sternberg, R. J. (eds.). (2010). *Cambridge Handbook of Creativity*. New York: Cambridge University Press.

Kaufman, S. B., & Gregoire, C. (2015). *Wired to Create: Unraveling the Mysteries of the Creative Mind*. New York: Perigee.

Kaufman, S. B., Quilty, L. C., Grazioplene, R. G., Hirsh, J. B., Gray, J. R., Peterson, J. B., & DeYoung, C. G. (2015). Openness to experience and intellect differentially predict creative achievement in the arts and sciences. *Journal of Personality* 84: 248–258.

Kaufmann, G., & Kaufmann, A. (2014). When good is bad and bad is good: Mood, bipolarity, and creativity. In J. Kaufman (ed.), *Creativity and Mental Illness* (pp. 205–235). Cambridge: Cambridge University Press. doi:10.1017/CBO9781139128902.014.

Keane, M. (1987). On retrieving analogues when solving problems. *The Quarterly Journal of Experimental Psychology Section A* 39(1): 29–41.

Kell, H. J., Lubinski, D., & Benbow, C. P. (2013). Who rises to the top? Early indicators. *Psychological Science* 24(5): 648–659.

Kenett, Y. N., & Austerweil, J. L. (2016). Examining search processes in low and high creative individuals with random walks. In A. Papafragou, D. Grodner, D. Mirman, & J. C. Trueswell (eds.), *Proceedings of the 38th Annual Meeting of the Cognitive Science Society* (pp. 313–318). Austin, TX: Cognitive Science Society.

Kenett, Y. N., Beaty, R. E., Silvia, P. J., Anaki, D., & Faust, M. (2016). Structure and flexibility: Investigating the relation between the structure of the mental lexicon, fluid intelligence, and creative achievement. *Psychology of Aesthetics, Creativity, and the Arts* 10: 377–388.

Kershaw, T. C., & Ohlsson, S. (2004). Multiple causes of difficulty in insight: The case of the nine-dot problem. *Journal of Experimental Psychology: Learning Memory and Cognition* 30: 3–13.

Kershaw, T. C., Flynn, C. K., & Gordon, L. T. (2013). Multiple paths to transfer and constraint relaxation in insight problem solving. *Thinking & Reasoning* 19(1): 96–136.

Ketner, J. D. (2013). *Andy Warhol*. London: Phaidon.

Kim, K. H. (2005). Can only intelligent people be creative? A meta-analysis. *Journal of Secondary Gifted Education* 16: 57–66.

Kim, K. H. (2008). Meta-analyses of the relationship of creative achievement to both IQ and divergent thinking test scores. *Journal of Creative Behavior* 42: 106–130.

Kim, K. H. (2016). *The Creativity Challenge: How We Can Recapture American Innovation*. New York: Prometheus Books.

Kim, K. H. (2017). The Torrance Tests of creative thinking – figural or verbal: which one should we use? *Creativity: Theories-Research-Applications* 4(2): 302–321.

King, L. A., Walker, L. M., & Broyles, S. J. (1996). Creativity and the five-factor model. *Journal of Research in Personality* 30: 189–203.

King, R. (2006). *The Judgment of Paris: The Revolutionary Decade That Gave the World Impressionism*. New York: Walker Publishing Co.

Kinney, D. K., & Richards, R. (2014). Creativity as "compensatory advantage": Bipolar and schizophrenic liability, the inverted-U hypothesis, and practical implications. In J. C. Kaufman (ed.), *Creativity and Mental Illness* (pp. 295–317). New York: Cambridge University Press.

Klahr, D., & Simon, H. A. (1999). Studies of scientific discovery: Complementary approaches and convergent findings. *Psychological Bulletin* 125: 524–543.

Klinger, E. (1999). Thought flow: Properties and mechanisms underlying shifts in content. In J. A. Singer & P. Salovey (eds.), *At Play in the Fields of Consciousness: Essays in Honor of Jerome L. Singer* (pp. 29–50). Mahwah, NJ: Erlbaum.

Knoblich, G., Ohlsson, S., Haider, H., & Rhenius, D. (1999). Constraint relaxation and chunk decomposition in insight problem solving. *Journal of Experimental Psychology: Learning, Memory, and Cognition* 25: 1534–1556.

Knoblich, G., Ohlsson, S., & Raney, G. (2001). An eye movement study of insight problem solving. *Memory & Cognition* 29: 1000–1009.

Koestler, A. (1964). *The Act of Creation*. New York: Macmillan.

Köhler, W. (1925). *The Mentality of Apes*. New York: Harcourt, Brace and Co.

Kounios, J., & Beeman, M. (2014). The cognitive neuroscience of insight. *Annual Review of Psychology* 65: 71–93.

Kounios, J., & Beeman, M. (2015). *The Eureka Factor: Aha Moments, Creative Insight, and the Brain*. New York: Random House.

Kozbelt, A. (2004). Reexamining the equal-odds rule in classical composers. In J. P. Frois, P. Andrade, & J. F. Marques (eds.), *Art and Science: Proceedings of the XVIII Congress of the International Association of Empirical Aesthetics* (pp. 540–543). Lisbon, Portugal: IAEA.

Kozbelt, A. (2005). Factors affecting aesthetic success and improvement in creativity: A case study of the musical genres of Mozart. *Psychology of Music* 33: 235–255.

Kozbelt, A. (2008). A quantitative analysis of Beethoven as self-critic: Implications for psychological theories of musical creativity. *Psychology of Music* 35: 147–172.

Kraepelin, E. (1921). *Manic-Depressive Insanity and Paranoia*. London: Churchill Livingstone.

Kretz, D. R., & Krawczyk, D. C. (2014). Expert analogy use in a naturalistic setting. *Frontiers in Psychology* 5: 1333. doi:10.3389/fpsyg.2014.01333.

Kris, E. (1952). *Psychoanalytic Explorations in Art*. New York: International Universities Press.

Kuhn, T. (1962). *The Structure of Scientific Revolutions*. Chicago, IL: University of Chicago Press.

Kurtz, K. J., & Loewenstein, J. (2007). Converging on a new role for analogy in problem solving and retrieval: When two problems are better than one. *Memory & Cognition* 35(2): 334–341.

Kyaga, S. (2014). *Creativity and Mental Illness: The Mad Genius in Question*. London: Palgrave Macmillan.

Kyaga, S. (2018). A heated debate: Time to address the underpinnings of the association between creativity and psychopathology? In R. E. Jung & O. Vartanian (eds.), *The Cambridge Handbook of the Neuroscience of Creativity* (pp. 114–135). Cambridge: Cambridge University Press. doi:https://doi.org/10.1017/9781316556238.008.

Kyaga, S., Landen, M., Boman, M., Hultman, C. M., Langstrom, N., & Lichtenstein, P. (2013). Mental illness, suicide and creativity: 40-year prospective total population study. *Journal of Psychiatric Research* 47: 83–90.

Kyaga, S., Lichtenstein, P., Boman, M., Hultman, C., Langstrom, N., & Landen, M. (2011). Creativity and mental disorder: Family study of 300,000 people with severe mental disorder. *British Journal of Psychiatry* 199: 373–379.

Kyllonen, P., & Kell, H. (2017). What is fluid intelligence? Can it be improved? In M. Rosén, K. Yang Hansen, & U. Wolff (eds.), *Methodology of Educational Measurement and Assessment: Cognitive Abilities and Educational Outcomes: A Festschrift in Honour of Jan-Eric Gustafsson* (pp. 15–37). Cham, Switzerland: Springer International Publishing. doi:10.1007/978-3-319-43473-5_2.

Landau, E. (1989). *Jackson Pollock*. New York: Abrams.

Landmann N., Kuhn M., Maier J. G., Feige B., Spiegelhalder K., Riemann D., & Niussen, C. (2016). Sleep strengthens but does not reorganize memory traces in a verbal creativity task. *Sleep* 39(3): 705–713. doi:10.5665/sleep.5556.

Laramée, F. D. (2018). Introduction to stylometry with Python. *The Programming Historian* 7. https://programminghistorian.org/en/lessons/introduction-to-stylometry-with-python, accessed August 3, 2018.

Lee, C. S., & Therriault, D. J. (2013). The cognitive underpinnings of creative thought: A latent variable analysis exploring the roles of intelligence and working memory in three creative thinking processes. *Intelligence* 41: 306–320.

LePort, A. K., Mattfeld, A.T., Dickinson-Anson, H., Fallon, J. H., Stark, C. E., Kruggel, F., Cahill, L., & McGaugh, J. L. (2012). Behavioral and neuroanatomical investigation of highly superior autobiographical memory (HSAM). *Neurobiology of Learning and Memory* 98(1): 78–92. doi:10.1016/j.nlm.2012.05.002.

Lewisohn, M. (1992). *The Complete Beatles Chronicle*. New York: Harmony.

Lewisohn, M. (2013). *The Beatles – All These Years: Volume 1: Tune In*. New York: Crown Archetype.

Li, J., Yao, L., Hendriks, E., & Wang, J. Z. (2012). Rhythmic brushstrokes distinguish van Gogh from his contemporaries: Findings via automated brushstroke extraction. *IEEE Transactions on Pattern Analysis and Machine Intelligence* 34(6): 1159–1176.

Llano, M. T., Colton, S., Hepworth, R., & Gow, J. (2016). Automated fictional ideation via knowledge base manipulation. *Cognitive Computation* 8: 153–174.

Loewenstein, J. (2010). How one's hook is baited matters for catching an analogy. In B. Ross (ed.), *Psychology of Learning and Motivation*, Volume 53 (pp. 149–182). Amsterdam: Elsevier.

Lord, W. (1983). *The Miracle of Dunkirk*. New York: The Viking Press.

Lowenstein, J., Thompson, L., & Gentner, D. (2003). Analogical learning in negotiation teams: Comparing cases promotes learning and transfer. *Academy of Management Learning and Education* 2: 119–128.

Lubart, T. I., & Getz, I. (1997). Emotion, metaphor, and the creative process. *Creativity Research Journal* 10: 285–301.

Lubart, T. I., & Sternberg, R. J. (1995). An investment approach to creativity: Theory and data. In S. M. Smith, T. B. Ward, & R. A. Finke (eds.), *The Creative Cognition Approach* (pp. 269–302). Cambridge, MA: MIT Press.

Ludwig, A. M. (1998). Method and madness in the arts and sciences. *Creativity Research Journal* 11: 93–101.

Lung, C.-T., & Dominowski, R. L. (1985). Effects of strategy instructions and practice on nine-dot problem solving. *Journal of Experimental Psychology: Learning, Memory, and Cognition* 11(4): 804–811. doi:https://doi.org/10.1037/0278-7393.11.1-4.804.

Luria, A. R. (1968). *The Mind of a Mnemonist: A Little Book about a Vast Memory.* New York: Basic Books.

MacGregor, J. N., Ormerod, T. C., & Chronicle, E. P. (2001). Information processing and insight: A process model of performance on the nine-dot and related problems. *Journal of Experimental Psychology: Learning, Memory, and Cognition* 27: 176–201.

Mackinnon, D. W. (1962). The personality correlates of creativity: A study of American architects. In G. S. Nielsen (ed.), *Proceedings of the 14th International Congress of Applied Psychology* (pp. 11–39). Copenhagen, Denmark: Munksgaard.

Maclean, N. (1972). *Young Men and Fire.* Chicago, IL: University of Chicago Press.

Macnamara, B. N., Hambrick, D. Z., & Oswald, F. L. (2014). Deliberate practice and performance in music, games, sports, education, and professions: A meta-analysis. *Psychological Science* 25(8): 1608–1618. doi:10.1177/0956797614535810.

Madore, K. P., Addis, D. R., & Schacter, D. L. (2015). Creativity and memory: Effects of an episodic-specificity induction on divergent thinking. *Psychological Science* 26(9): 1461–1468.

Madore, K. P., Jing, H. G., & Schacter, D. L. (2019). Selective effects of specificity inductions on episodic details: evidence for an event construction account. *Memory* 27(2): 250–260.

Maguire, E. A., & Mullally, S. L. (2013). The hippocampus: A manifesto for change. *Journal of Experimental Psychology: General* 142(4): 1180–1189

Maguire, E. A., Woollett, K., & Spiers, H. J. (2006). London taxi drivers and bus drivers: A structural MRI and neuropsychological analysis. *Hippocampus* 16: 1091–1101.

Mandler, J. M., & Mandler, G. (eds.) (1964). *Thinking: From Association to Gestalt.* New York: Wiley.

Marshall, B. J. (2002). The discovery that *helicobacter pylori*, a spiral bacterium, caused peptic ulcer disease. In B. Marshall (ed.), *Helicobacter Pioneers* (pp. 165–202). Singapore: Blackwell Science Asia.

Marshall, B. J., & Warren, J. R. (1984). Unidentified curved bacilli in the stomach of patients with gastric and peptic ulceration. *The Lancet* 323(8390): 1311–1315.

Martindale, C. (1989). Personality, situation, and creativity. In J. A. Glover, R. R. Ronning, & C. R. Reynolds (eds.), *Handbook of Creativity* (pp. 211–228). New York: Plenum.

McCarter, R. (1997). *Fallingwater: Frank Lloyd Wright*. New York: Barnes & Noble.

McDermott, J. F. (2000). Emily Dickinson's "nervous prostration" and its possible relationship to her work. *The Emily Dickinson Journal* 9: 71–86.

McDermott, J. F. (2001). Emily Dickinson revisited: A study of periodicity in her work. *American Journal of Psychiatry* 158: 686–690.

McMahon, D. M. (2013). *Divine Fury: A History of Genius*. New York: Basic Books

Mednick, S. A. (1962). The associative basis of the creative process. *Psychological Review* 69: 220–232.

Metcalfe, J. (1986). Premonitions of insight predict impending error. *Journal of Experimental Psychology: Learning, Memory, and Cognition* 12: 623–634.

Metcalfe, J., & Wiebe, D. (1987). Intuition in insight and non-insight problem solving. *Memory & Cognition* 15: 238–246.

Miles, B. (1997). *Paul McCartney: Many Years from Now*. New York: Henry Holt.

Miller, A. I. (1996). *Insights of Genius: Imagery and Creativity in Science and Art*. New York: Copernicus, an Imprint of Springer-Verlag.

Mullally, S. L., & Maguire, E. A. (2014). Memory, imagination, and predicting the future: A common brain mechanism? *The Neuroscientist* 20(3): 220–234.

Murray, P. (1989a). Poetic genius and its classical origins. In P. Murray (ed.), *Genius: The History of an Idea* (pp. 9–31). Oxford: Blackwell.

Murray, P. (1989b). *Genius: The History of an Idea*. Oxford: Blackwell.

Murray, C. (2003). *Human Accomplishment: The Pursuit of Excellence in the Arts and Sciences, 800 B.C. to 1950*. New York: Harper Collins.

Newell, A., Shaw, C., & Simon, H. A. (1962). The processes of creative thinking. In H. E. Gruber, G. Terrell, & M. Wertheimer (eds.), *Contemporary Approaches to Creative Thinking* (pp. 153–189). New York: Pergamon.

Newell, A., & Simon, H. A. (1972). *Human Problem Solving*. Englewood Cliffs, NJ: Prentice-Hall.

Nordau, M. (1900). *Degeneration*. New York: D. Appleton & Co.

Nusbaum, E. C., & Silvia, P. J. (2011). Are intelligence and creativity really so different? Fluid intelligence, executive processes, and strategy use in divergent thinking. *Intelligence* 39: 36–45.

Nusbaum, E. C., Silvia, P. J., & Beaty, R. E. (2014). Ready, set, create: What instructing people to "be creative" reveals about the meaning and mechanisms of divergent thinking. *Psychology of Aesthetics, Creativity, and the Arts* 8(4): 423–432.

Ochse, R. (1990). *Before the Gates of Excellence: The Determinants of Creative Genius*. Cambridge: Cambridge University Press.

Ohlsson, S. (1992). Information-processing explanations of insight and related phenomena. In M. T. Keane & K. J. Gilhooly (eds.), *Advances in the Psychology of Thinking*, Vol. 1 (pp. 1–44). New York: Harvester Wheatsheaf.

Ohlsson, S. (2011). *Deep Learning: How the Mind Overrides Experience.* Cambridge: Cambridge University Press.

Ohlsson, S. (2018). The dialectic between routine and creative cognition. In F. Vallée-Tourangeau (ed.), *Insight: On the Origins of New Ideas* (pp. 8–27). London: Routledge.

Olby, R. (1994). *The Path to the Double Helix. The Discovery of DNA.* New York: Dover.

Öllinger, M., Jones, G., & Knoblich, G. (2014). The dynamics of search, impasse, and representational change provide a coherent explanation of difficulty in the nine-dot problem. *Psychological Research* 78: 266–275.

Olton, R. M. (1979). Experimental studies of incubation: Searching for the elusive. *Journal of Creative Behavior* 13: 9–22.

Osborn, A. F. (1963). *Applied Imagination: Principles and Procedures of Creative Problem Solving,* 3rd rev. ed. New York: Charles Scribner's Sons.

Palmer, E. D. (1954). Investigation of the gastric mucosa spirochetes of the human. *Gastroenterology* 27(2): 218–220.

Pariser, D. (1987). The juvenile drawings of Klee, Toulouse-Lautrec, and Picasso. *Visual Arts Research* 13: 53–67.

Park, G., Lubinski, D., & Benbow, C. P. (2008). Ability differences among people who have commensurate degrees matter for scientific creativity. *Psychological Science* 19(10): 957–961.

Perkins, D. N. (1981). *The Mind's Best Work.* Cambridge, MA: Harvard University Press.

Perkins, D. N. (2000). *The Eureka Effect: The Art and Logic of Breakthrough Thinking.* New York: Norton.

Peterson, J. B., & Carson, S. (2000). Latent inhibition and openness to experience in a high-achieving student population. *Personality and Individual Differences* 28: 323–332.

Petroski, H. (1998). *Invention by Design: How Engineers Get from Thought to Thing.* Cambridge, MA: Harvard University Press.

Plucker, J. (1999). Is the proof in the pudding? Reanalyses of Torrance's (1958 to present) longitudinal study data. *Creativity Research Journal* 12: 103–114.

Poincaré, H. (1913). *The Foundations of Science.* Lancaster, PA: Science Press.

Post, F. (1994). Creativity and psychopathology: A study of 291 world-famous men. *The British Journal of Psychiatry* 165: 22–34. doi:10.1192/bjp.165.1.22.

Ramey, C. H., & Weisberg, R. W. (2004). The "poetical activity" of Emily Dickinson: A further test of the hypothesis that affective disorders foster creativity. *Creativity Research Journal* 16: 173–185.

Reeves, L. M., & Weisberg, R. W. (1994). Models of analogical transfer in problem solving. *Psychological Bulletin* 116: 381–400.

Reverberi, C., Toraldo, A., D'Agostini, S., & Skrap, M. (2005). Better without (lateral) frontal cortex? Insight problems solved by frontal patients. *Brain* 128: 2882–2890.

Richards, R., Kinney, D. K., Benet, M., & Marzel, A. P. C. (1988). Assessing everyday creativity: Characteristics of the Lifetime Creativity Scales and validation with three large samples. *Journal of Personality and Social Psychology* 54: 476–485.

Richardson, J. (with M. McCully) (1991). *A Life of Picasso. Vol. 1: 1881–1906.* New York: Random House.

Richland, L. E., Holyoak, K. J., & Stigler, J. W. (2004). Analogy generation in eighth grade mathematics classrooms. *Cognition and Instruction* 22: 37–60.

Richter, I. (ed.). (1952). *The Notebooks of Leonardo da Vinci.* Oxford: Oxford University Press.

Ritter, S. M., & Dijksterhuis, A. (2014). Creativity – the unconscious foundations of the incubation period. *Frontiers in Human Neuroscience* 8: 215. doi:10.3389/fnhum.2014.00215.

Roberts, R. P., & Addis, D. R. (2018). A common mode of processing governing divergent thinking and future imagination. In O. Vartanian & R. E. Jung (eds.), *The Cambridge Handbook of the Neuroscience of Creativity* (pp. 211–230). Cambridge: Cambridge University Press.

Robinson, A. G., & Stern, S. (1997). *Corporate Creativity: How Innovation and Improvement Actually Happen.* San Francisco, CA: Berrett-Koehler Publishers.

Rocke, A. J. (2010). *Image and Reality: Kekulé, Kopp, and the Scientific Imagination.* Chicago, IL: University of Chicago Press.

Rosenthal, R., & Rosnow, R. L. (1991). *Essentials of Behavioral Research: Methods and Data Analysis*, 2nd ed. New York: McGraw-Hill.

Rothenberg, A. (1989). *The Emerging Goddess: The Creative Process in Art, Science, and Other Fields.* Chicago, IL: University of Chicago Press.

Rothenberg, A. (1990). *Creativity and Madness: New Findings and Old Stereotypes.* Baltimore, MD: Johns Hopkins University Press.

Rubenson, D. L., & Runco, M. A. (1992). The psychoeconomic approach to creativity. *New Ideas in Psychology* 10: 131–147.

Runco, M. A. (2011). Tests of creativity. In M. A. Runco & S. Pritzker (eds.), *Encyclopedia of Creativity*, 2nd ed. (pp. 423–426). San Diego, CA: Elsevier.

Runco, M. A., & Acar, S. (2012). Divergent thinking as an indicator of creative potential. *Creativity Research Journal* 24(1): 66–75.

Runco, M. A., & Jaeger, G. J. (2012). The standard definition of creativity. *Creativity Research Journal* 21: 92–96.

Runco, M. A., Millar, G., Acar, S., & Cramond, B. (2010). Torrance tests of creative thinking as predictors of personal and public achievement: A fifty-year follow-up. *Creativity Research Journal* 22(4): 361–368.

Ruscio, J., Whitney, D., & Amabile, T. M. (1998). Looking inside the fishbowl of creativity: verbal and behavioral predictors of creative performance. *Creativity Research Journal* 11: 243–263.

Sadler-Smith, E. (2015). Wallas' four-stage model of the creative process: More than meets the eye? *Creativity Research Journal* 27(4): 342–352.

Sass, L. A. (2001). Schizophrenia, modernism, and the "creative imagination": On creativity and psychopathology. *Creativity Research Journal* 13: 55–74.

Schaller, M. (1997). The psychological consequences of fame: Three tests of the self-consciousness hypothesis. *Journal of Personality* 65(2): 291–309.

Scheerer, M. (1963). On problem-solving. *Scientific American* 208: 118–128.

Schlesinger, J. (2009). Creative mythconceptions: A closer look at the evidence for the "mad genius" hypothesis. *Psychology of Aesthetics, Creativity, and the Arts* 3(2): 62–72.

Schlesinger, J. (2012). *The Insanity Hoax: Exposing the Myth of the Mad Genius.* Ardsley-on-Hudson, NY: Shrinktunes Media.

Schneider, W. J., & McGrew, K. (2012). The Cattell-Horn-Carroll model of intelligence. In D. Flanagan & P. Harrison (eds.), *Contemporary Intellectual Assessment: Theories, Tests, and Issues*, 3rd ed. (pp. 99–144). New York: Guilford.

Schönauer, M., Brodt, S., Pöhlchen, D., Breßmer, A., Danek, A. H., & Gais, S. (2018). Sleep does not promote solving classical insight problems and magic tricks. *Frontiers in Human Neuroscience* 12, Article ID 72.

Schou, M. (1979). Artistic productivity and lithium prophylaxis in manic-depressive illness. *The British Journal of Psychiatry* 135: 97–103.

Schuldberg, D. (2001). Six subclinical "spectrum" traits in "normal creativity." *Creativity Research Journal* 13: 5–16.

Schwarz, N. (1990). Feelings as information: Informational and motivational functions of affective states. In E. T. Higgins & R. M. Sorrentino (eds.), *Handbook of Motivation and Cognition: Foundations of Social Behavior*, Vol. 2 (pp. 527–561). New York: The Guilford Press.

Schwarz, N., & Clore, G. L. (2003). Mood as information: 20 years later. *Psychological Inquiry* 14: 296–303.

Seifert, C. M., Meyer, D. E., Davidson, N., Patalano, A. L., & Yaniv, I. (1995). Demystification of cognitive insight: Opportunistic assimilation and the prepared-mind perspective. In R. J. Sternberg & J. E. Davidson (eds.), *The Nature of Insight* (pp. 65–124). Cambridge, MA: MIT Press.

Shaw, E. D., Mann, J. J., Stokes, P. E., & Manevitz, A. Z. (1986). Effects of lithium carbonate on associative productivity and idiosyncrasy in bipolar outpatients. *The American Journal of Psychiatry* 143(9): 1166–1169.

Silvia, P. J. (2008). Another look at creativity and intelligence: Exploring higher-order models and probable confounds. *Personality and Individual Differences* 44: 1012–1021.

Silvia, P. J. (2015). Intelligence and creativity are pretty similar after all. *Educational Psychology Review* 27: 599–606.

Silvia, P. J., & Beaty, R. E. (2012). Making creative metaphors: The importance of fluid intelligence for creative thought. *Intelligence* 40: 343–351.

Simon, H. A. (1986). The information-processing explanation of Gestalt phenomena. *Computers in Human Behavior* 2: 241–255.

Simonton, D. K. (1984). *Genius, Creativity, and Leadership: Historiometric Inquiries*. Cambridge, MA: Harvard University Press.

Simonton, D. K. (1988). Creativity, leadership, and chance. In R. J. Sternberg (ed.), *The Nature of Creativity: Current Psychological Perspectives* (pp. 386–426). Cambridge: Cambridge University Press.

Simonton, D. K. (1995). Foresight in insight? A Darwinian answer. In R. J. Sternberg & J. E. Davidson (eds.), *The Nature of Insight* (pp. 465–494). Cambridge, MA: MIT Press.

Simonton, D. K. (1999). *Origins of Genius: Darwinian Perspectives on Creativity*. New York: Oxford.

Simonton, D. K. (2011). Exceptional talent and genius. In T. Chamorro-Premuzic, S. Stumm & A. Furnham (eds.), *The Wiley-Blackwell Handbook of Individual Differences* (pp. 635–655). New York: Wiley-Blackwell.

Simonton D. K. (ed.) (2014). *Wiley Handbook of Genius*. Chichester: Wiley–Blackwell.

Simonton, D. K. (2016). Creativity, automaticity, irrationality, fortuity, fantasy, and other contingencies: An eightfold response typology. *Review of General Psychology* 20: 194–204.

Simonton, D. K. (2017). Creative genius and psychopathology: Creativity as positive and negative personality. In G. J. Feist, R. Reiter-Palmon & J. C. Kaufman (eds.), *Cambridge Handbook of Creativity and Personality Research* (pp. 235–250). New York: Cambridge University Press.

Simonton, D. K. (2018). Creative ideas and the creative process: Good news and bad news for the neuroscience of creativity. In R. E. Jung & O. Vartanian (eds.), *The Cambridge Handbook of the Neuroscience of Creativity* (pp. 9–18). New York: Cambridge University Press.

Sio, U. N., & Ormerod, T. C. (2009). Does incubation enhance problem solving? A meta-analytic review. *Psychological Bulletin* 135(1): 94–120.

Slater, E., & Mayer, A. (1959). Contributions to a pathography of the musicians: I. Robert Schumann. *Confinia Psychiatrica* 2: 65–94.

Sloboda, J. A., Davidson, J. W., Howe, M. J. A., & Moore, D. G. (1996). The role of practice in the development of performing musicians. *British Journal of Psychology* 87(2): 287–309.

Smallwood, J., & Schooler, J. W. (2015). The science of mind wandering: Empirically navigating the stream of consciousness. *Annual Review of Psychology* 66: 487–518.

Smith, S. M. (1995). Getting into and out of mental ruts: A theory of fixation, incubation, and insight. In R. J. Sternberg & J. E. Davidson (eds.), *The Nature of Insight* (pp. 121–149). Cambridge, MA: MIT Press.

Smith, K. A., Huber, D. E., & Vul, E. (2013). Multiply-constrained semantic search in the Remote Associates Test. *Cognition* 128(1): 64–75.

Soler, J. M. (2007). A rational indicator of scientific creativity. *Journal of Informetrics* 1(2): 123–130.

Soto, C. J., & John, O. P. (2017a). The next Big Five Inventory (BFI-2): Developing and assessing a hierarchical model with 15 facets to enhance bandwidth, fidelity, and predictive power. *Journal of Personality and Social Psychology* 113: 117–143.

Soto, C. J., & John, O. P. (2017b). Short and extra-short forms of the Big Five Inventory-2: The BFI-2-S and BFI- 2-XS. *Journal of Research in Personality* 68: 69–81.

Speck, R. M, Weisberg, R. W., & Fleisher, L. A. (2015). Varying goals and approaches of innovation centers in academic health systems: a semistructured qualitative study. *Academic Medicine* 90(8): 1132–1136.

Sternberg, R. J. (1996). Costs of expertise. In K. A. Ericsson (ed.), *The Road to Excellence: The Acquisition of Expert Performance in the Arts and Sciences, Sports, and Games* (pp. 347–354). Mahwah, NJ: Erlbaum.

Sternberg, R. J. (1998). Darwinian creativity as a conventional religious faith. *Psychological Inquiry* 10(4): 357–359.

Sternberg, R. J. (2018). A triangular theory of creativity. *Psychology of Aesthetics, Creativity, and the Arts* 12(1): 50–67.

Sternberg, R. J., & Davidson, J. E. (1982). The mind of the puzzler. *Psychology Today* 16 (June): 37–44.

Sternberg, R. J., & Bridges, S. L. (2014). Varieties of genius. In D. K. Simonton (ed.), *Handbook of Genius* (pp. 185–197). Chichester: Wiley–Blackwell.

Sternberg, R. J., & Davidson, J. E. (eds.). (1995). *The Nature of Insight*. Cambridge, MA: MIT Press.

Sternberg, R. J., Kaufman, J. C., & Pretz, J. E. (2002). *The Creativity Conundrum: A Propulsion Model of Kinds of Creative Contributions*. New York: Psychology Press.

Sternberg, R. J., & Lubart, T. I. (1995). *Defying the Crowd*. New York: Free Press.

Sternberg, R. J., & Lubart, T. I. (1996). Investing in creativity. *American Psychologist* 51: 677–688.

Taylor, C. L. (2017). Creativity and mood disorder: A systematic review and meta-analysis. *Perspectives on Psychological Science* 12(6): 1040–1076. doi:10.1177/1745691617699653.

Thagard, P. (1999). *How Scientists Explain Disease*. Princeton, NJ: Princeton University Press.

Thrakal, P. P., Madore, K. P., & Schacter, D. L. (2017). A role for the left angular gyrus in episodic simulation and memory. *The Journal of Neuroscience* 37(34): 8142–8149. doi:10.1523/JNEUROSCI.1319-17.2017.

Toker, F. (2003). *Fallingwater Rising: Frank Lloyd Wright, E. J. Kaufmann, and America's Most Extraordinary House*. New York: Knopf.

Torrance, E. P. (1962). *Guiding Creative Talent*. Englewood Cliffs, NJ: Prentice-Hall.

Torrance, E. P. (1981). Predicting the creativity of elementary school children (1958–80) – and the teacher who "made a difference." *Gifted Child Quarterly* 25(2): 55–62. doi:https://doi.org/10.1177/001698628102500203.

Treffert, D. A. (2011). *Islands of Genius: The Bountiful Mind of the Autistic, Acquired, and Sudden Savant*. London and New York: Jessica Kingsley Publishers.

Trench, M., & Mervino, R. A. (2015). The role of surface similarity in analogical retrieval: Bridging the gap between the naturalistic and the experimental traditions. *Cognitive Science* 39: 1292–1319.

Ullén, F., Hambrick, D. Z., & Mosing, M. A. (2016). Rethinking expertise: A multifactorial gene–environment interaction model of expert performance. *Psychological Bulletin* 142(4): 427–446.

Underwood, T., Bamman, D., & Lee, S. (2018). The transformation of gender in English-language fiction. *Cultural Analytics* (February 13). doi:https://doi.org/10.22148/16.019.

Vallée-Tourangeau, F. (ed.). (2018). *Insight: On the Origins of New Ideas*. London: Routledge.

Vartanian, O. (2018). Openness to Experience: Insights from Personality Neuroscience. In O. Vartanian & R. E. Jung (eds.), *The Cambridge Handbook of the Neuroscience of Creativity* (pp. 464–475). New York: Cambridge University Press.

Vartanian, O., & R. E. Jung (eds.). (2018). *The Cambridge Handbook of the Neuroscience of Creativity*. New York: Cambridge University Press.

Vasari, G. (1991 [1550]). *The Lives of the Artists*. Oxford: Oxford University Press.

Volle, E. (2018). Associative and controlled cognition in divergent thinking: Theoretical, experimental, neuroimaging evidence, and new directions. In R. E. Jung & O. Vartanian (eds.), *The Cambridge Handbook of the Neuroscience of Creativity* (pp. 333–362). New York: Cambridge University Press.

Wallach, M., & Kogan, N. (1965). *Modes of Thinking in Young Children: A Study of the Creativity–Intelligence Distinction*. New York: Holt, Rinehart, & Winston.

Wallas, G. (1926). *The Art of Thought*. London: Cape.

Ward, T. B. (1995). What's old about new ideas? In S. M. Smith, T. B. Ward & R. A. Finke (eds.), *The Creative Cognition Approach* (pp. 157–178). Cambridge, MA: MIT Press.

Ward, T. B. (2018). Creativity as a continuum. In R. J. Sternberg & J. C. Kaufman (eds.), *The Nature of Human Creativity* (pp. 335–350). Cambridge: Cambridge University Press.

Warren, J. R., & Marshall, B. J. (1983). Unidentified curved bacilli on gastric epithelium in active gastritis. *The Lancet* 321(8336): 1273–1275.

Watson, J. B. (1930). *Behaviorism* (revised edition). Chicago, IL: University of Chicago Press.

Watson, J. D. (1968). *The Double Helix: A Personal Account of the Discovery of the Structure of DNA*. New York: New American Library.

Weinberger, A. B., Green, A., & Chrysikou, E. G. (2017). Using transcranial direct current stimulation to enhance creative cognition: Interactions between task, polarity, and stimulation site. *Frontiers in Human Neuroscience* 11: 246.

Weisberg, R. W. (1986). *Creativity: Genius and Other Myths*. New York: Freeman.

Weisberg, R. W. (1993). *Creativity: Beyond the Myth of Genius*. New York: Freeman.

Weisberg, R. W. (1994). Genius and madness? A quasi-experimental test of the hypothesis that manic-depression increases creativity. *Psychological Science* 5: 361–367.

Weisberg, R. W. (2004). On structure in the creative process: a quantitative case-study of the creation of Picasso's Guernica. *Empirical Studies in the Arts* 22: 23–54.

Weisberg, R. W. (2006). *Creativity: Understanding Innovation in Problem Solving, Science, Invention, and the Arts*. Hoboken, NJ: John Wiley.

Weisberg, R. W. (2013).On the "demystification" of insight: A critique of neuroimaging studies of insight. *Creativity Research Journal* 25: 1–14.

Weisberg, R. W. (2014). Case studies of genius: Ordinary thinking, extraordinary outcomes. In D. K. Simonton (ed.), *The Wiley Handbook of Genius* (pp. 139–165). Hoboken, NJ: John Wiley.

Weisberg, R. W. (2015). On the usefulness of *value* in the definition of creativity. *Creativity Research Journal* 27(2): 111–124.

Weisberg, R. W. (2018a). Expertise and structured imagination in creative thinking: Reconsideration of an old question. In K. A. Ericsson et al. (eds.), *The Cambridge Handbook of Expertise and Expert Performance*, 2nd ed. (pp. 812–834). Cambridge: Cambridge University Press.

Weisberg, R. W. (2018b). Insight, problem solving, and creativity: An integration of findings. In F. Vallée-Tourangeau (ed.), *Insight: On the Origins of New Ideas* (pp. 191–215). London: Routledge.

Weisberg, R. W. (2018c). Response to Harrington on the definition of creativity. *Creativity Research Journal* 30(4): 461–465.

Weisberg, R. W., & Alba, J. W. (1981). An examination of the alleged role of "fixation" in the solution of several "insight" problems. *Journal of Experimental Psychology: General* 110: 169–192.

Weisberg, R. W., & Reeves, L. M. (2013). *Cognition: From Memory to Creativity*. Hoboken, NJ: John Wiley Publishers.

Weisberg, R. W., Speck, R. M., & Fleisher, L. A. (2014). Fostering innovation in medicine: A conceptual framework for medical centers. *Healthcare* 2: 90–93. doi:http://dx.doi.org/10.1016/j.hjdsi.2013.09.007.

Weisberg, R. W., & Suls, J. M. (1973). An information-processing model of Duncker's candle problem. *Cognitive Psychology* 4: 255–276.

Wertheimer, M. (1982). *Productive Thinking* (enlarged ed.). Chicago, IL: University of Chicago Press.

Whitehead, A. N. (1929). *The Aims of Education and Other Essays*. New York: The Free Press.

Wiley, J. (1998). Expertise as mental set: the effects of domain knowledge in creative problem solving. *Memory & Cognition* 26: 716–730.

Wiley, J., & Jarosz, A. F. (2012). Working memory capacity, attentional focus, and problem solving. *Current Directions in Psychological Science* 21(4): 258–262.

Winner, E. (1996). The rage to master: The decisive role of talent in the visual arts. In K. A. Ericsson (ed.), *The Road to Excellence: The Acquisition of Expert Performance in the Arts and Sciences, Sports, and Games* (pp. 271–301). Mahwah, NJ: Erlbaum.

Winner, E. (2014). Child prodigies and adult genius: A weak link. In D. K. Simonton (ed.), *Handbook of Genius* (pp. 297–320). Chichester: Wiley-Blackwell.

Woodworth, R. (1938). *Experimental Psychology.* New York: Holt.

Woollett, K., & Maguire, E. A. (2011). Acquiring "the knowledge" of London's layout drives structural brain changes. *Current Biology* 21: 2109–2114.

Wordsworth, W. (1899 [1802]). *Lyrical Ballads with Pastoral and Other Poems,* 3rd ed. London: T. N. Longman and Rees.

Zabelina, D. (2018). Creativity and attention. In R. E. Jung & O. Vartanian (eds.), *The Cambridge Handbook of the Neuroscience of Creativity* (pp. 161–179). Cambridge: Cambridge University Press.

Zhang, L., & Sternberg, R. J. (2011). Revisiting the investment theory of creativity. *Creativity Research Journal* 23(3): 229–238.

Zimmerman, R. (2010). *The Universe in a Mirror: The Saga of the Hubble Space Telescope and the Visionaries Who Built It.* Princeton, NJ: Princeton University Press.

Index

CPSIA information can be obtained
at www.ICGtesting.com
Printed in the USA
LVHW100503180920
666363LV00016B/267